What They're Saying
Street's Guide to the Cape Verde Islands

Street's Guide to the Cape Verde Islands, will convince you to visit these often overlooked cruising grounds. Through maps, photos, and the sorts of stories only Don can tell, the Cape Verdes come alive.
Mark Pillsbury; Editor, *Cruising World* (USA)

Much more than a mere pilot book, this new guide from the venerable Don Street will enhance any visit to the Cape Verdes, tempting you to linger and explore.
Sarah Norbury; Editor, *Practical Boat Owner* (UK)

As good as having Don on board tapping you on the shoulder . . .
Tom Cunliffe (UK)

Don Street has done it again. …Sensational, comprehensive, and incredibly detailed…Lavishly illustrated with excellent charts and photographs, for its depth, insight, and pioneering spirit, *Street's Guide to the Cape Verde Islands* might just be his best cruising guide ever.
Herb McCormick (USA)

With this new guide to the Cape Verdes, Don Street has reasserted himself as the pre-eminent authority on North Atlantic cruising grounds. No one visiting the Cape Verdes should be without it.
Charles J. Doane; Executive Editor, *SAIL* (USA)

Seamanship and the cruising ethos are ingrained in Street's work. Anyone planning to sail in this fascinating Atlantic archipelago should make this pilot a constant companion.
David Glenn; Editor, *Yachting World* (UK)

The old sea dog gives us his usual experienced and offbeat take on passagemaking. To run off the beaten path it's always wise to listen to Street.
Patience Wales (USA)

Street's Guide to the Cape Verde Islands...full of useful charts, bearings, advice, and guidance...opens up an unspoiled Atlantic archipelago that has for too long been overlooked by sailors making the trade-wind passage from Europe to the Caribbean.
George Day; Publisher, *Blue Water Sailing* (USA)

Don Street, now 80, is a salty legend of the sea. His *Street's Guide to the Cape Verde Islands* is chatty, informative, and highly entertaining. As indispensable as Don's well-traveled sunhat!
Paul Gelder; Editor, *Yachting Monthly* (UK)

Street's Guide to the Cape Verde Islands

Donald M. Street Jr. at the helm of Sincerity, on which he cruised the Cape Verde Islands.

by

Donald M. Street Jr.

Cocoa Beach, Florida

Street's Guide to the Cape Verde Islands

Copyright © 2011
by
Donald M. Street Jr.
ISBN 978-1-892399-34-2

Published in the USA by:
Seaworthy Publications, Inc.
2023 N. Atlantic Ave., Unit #226
Cocoa Beach, Florida 32931
Phone 321-610-3634
Fax 321-400-1006
email orders@seaworthy.com
www.seaworthy.com - Your Bahamas and Caribbean Cruising Advisory

All rights reserved. No part of this book may be reproduced, stored in a retrieval system, or transmitted in any form, or by any means, electronic, mechanical, photocopying, recording, or by any storage and retrieval system, without permission in writing from the Publisher.

CAUTION:
The author has taken extreme care to provide the most accurate and reliable charts possible for use in this edition, nevertheless, the charts in this guide are designed to be used in conjunction with DMA, NOAA, and other government charts and publications. The Author and Publisher take no responsibility for their misuse.

Edited by Jeremy McGeary.
Book design, chart design, and layout by Stephen J. Pavlidis, *Nightflyer Enterprises*, Melbourne, Florida.
Cover design by Ken Quant, *Broad Reach Marketing & Design*, Mequon, Wisconsin.
Title page photo of Don Street on *Sincerity* by Alison Langley

Library of Congress Cataloging-in-Publication Data

Street, Donald M.
Street's guide to the Cape Verde Islands / by Donald M. Street.
p. cm.
Includes index.
ISBN-13: 978-1-892399-34-2 (pbk. : alk. paper)
ISBN-10: 1-892399-34-2 (pbk. : alk. paper)
1. Yachting--Cape Verde--Guidebooks. 2. Cape Verde--Guidebooks. 3. Pilot guides--Cape Verde. I. Title.
GV817.C36S87 2011
797.124'6096658--dc22
2011014398

Introduction

The majority of cruising sailors who make the wintertime trade-wind passage westward across the Atlantic follow the traditional route from the Canary Islands to the Windward or Leeward Islands of the West Indies. For them, the Cape Verde Islands are little more than a notation on the chart. The few that do sail to the archipelago, whether by choice or because of encountering an obstinate southwesterly after leaving the Canaries, have regarded it as simply a way station where they can stop briefly to top off with fuel, water, and provisions. In my view, more yachtsmen should view the Cape Verde Archipelago as worthy of a much longer visit.

In late November and early December, when most transatlantic passages are made, the trade winds have not really filled in, and can be unreliable. The possibility exists also of a late-season tropical cyclone, as in 2005 when the season extended into January 2006 and the National Hurricane Center of the United States National Oceanographic and Atmospheric Administration (NOAA) ran out of names for tropical storms. Rather than risk having your ears blown off by a hurricane, or your teeth rolled out of your head in a mid-Atlantic calm, why not forget the rush to spend Christmas in the Caribbean and spend it instead in the Cape Verdes? Then, when the celebrations have worn off, cross to the Caribbean in early January when the trades have really settled in and you can expect a solid breeze all the way across, with no surprises.

I have cruised the Canaries in 1956, '79, '85, '86, and 2005 (and visited them by air in 2002 and '10). I have also cruised the Cape Verde Islands, on *Iolaire* in 1985 and '89 and on *Sincerity* in 2005 (and visited them by air in 2002 and '09). On all occasions, the crew that sailed with me in both island groups much preferred the Cape Verdes over the Canaries, mainly because the Cape Verdes are still largely unaffected by tourism.

In the Canary Islands, boats are funneled into marinas surrounded by developments for tourists. In the Cape Verdes it's easy to meet local people over a beer and get into conversation with them. And if you don't want to be around other boats, you can find any number of places to anchor where you'll be by yourselves.

As I explain in this book, the Cape Verdes are not the Virgin Islands. While there are several good harbors with interesting towns and villages ashore, the coastlines are unreliably charted and largely undeveloped and unexplored and offer the yachtsman who is skilled in coastal piloting and eyeball navigation a wonderful opportunity to venture off the beaten track.

On *Iolaire*, on *Sincerity*, and in local fishing boats, I have visited several anchorages that are not described elsewhere. I have viewed over a dozen more potential anchorages from land and, by the grace of modern technology, through *Google Earth*. On my most recent visit, in November 2009, with Indira Dom as my guide and interpreter, I hiked to some bays and hired fishermen to take me to others I had only viewed on Google Earth or from the shore. As I approach 80, I find these exploits more challenging than they once were.

My *Cruising Guide to the Lesser Antilles*, which was published in 1966, opened the Eastern Caribbean to the cruising yachtsman and made bareboat chartering possible in those waters. My 1980 *Cruising Guide to Venezuela* in turn opened that area and its offshore islands to the cruising yachtsman.

I hope that *Street's Guide to the Cape Verde Islands* will change the perception of these islands, and that adventurous yachtsmen and women will see them not as simply a way stop en route to the Caribbean but as a cruising area to be enjoyed for several weeks. Those that do will also benefit by crossing the Atlantic at the proper time of year — January or early February — when the trade winds have filled in and are consistent.

Donald M. Street Jr.

Street's Guide to the Cape Verde Islands

Table of Contents

Introduction 5

List of Charts 8
    Legend 9

Background and Acknowledgements 10

Don Street Through the Eyes of Long-Time
    Associates 14

Chapter 1
The Case for Cruising the Cape Verde Islands 17
    A Cruising Ground with Choices 17
    Waiting for the Trade Winds 18

Chapter 2
Cape Verde in a Capsule 22
    Political History 23
    Cape Verde Today 27
    Foreign Aid Fiascos 28
    Cape Verdeans Abroad 29
    Fishing and Fishing Boats
        in the Cape Verdes 30

Chapter 3
Infrastructure in the Cape Verde Islands 34
    Marine Infrastructure 34
    Chartering 36
    Formalities 36
        Port Captain, Customs, and Immigration 36
        Visas 37
    Ground Transportation 37
    Air Transportation 38
    Inter-Island Ferries 39
    Provisioning and Stores 39
        Food Supplies 39
        Water 40
        Fuel 40
        Ice 40
        Cooking Gas 41
    Communications 41
    Language 42
    Medical Emergencies 42
    Money 42
    Search and Rescue 42

Chapter 4
The Mariner's Essentials 43
    Landfalls in the Cape Verde Archipelago 43
    Sailing Directions 43
    Cape Verde Charts and Sketch Charts 45
    Wind, Weather, and Tides 47
        Wind 47
        Tides and Currents 47
        Predicting Tides 48
        Northwest Groundswell 50
        Hurricanes 50
    Navigation Matters 51
        Harbors 51
        Navigational Warnings 52
        GPS, Chartplotters, and
            Eyeball Navigation 53
        Beware of Waypoints 54
    Anchors and Anchoring 55
        Anchors 55
        Anchoring 57
        Tripping Line 57
        Becued Anchor 58
        Bahamian Moor 59
        When the Windlass Dies 59
    Safe Practices for the Ship's Boat 59
        Landing and Launching in Surf 59
        Under Outboard 60
        Under Oars 60
        Hauling the Boat up the Beach 60
        Safety While Exploring in the Ship's Boat 60

Chapter 5
Sal and Boavista 62
    Ilho do Sal 62
        Baia da Palmeira 62
        Baia da Mordeira 64
        Santa Maria 65
        Baia de Pedra de Lume 66
    Ilha da Boavista 67
        Porto de Sal-Rei 69
        South Coast of Boavista 70
        Departing Boavista 71

Chapter 6
São Nicolau and Santa Luzia 72
    Ilha de São Nicolau 72
        Anchorages on the South Coast
            of São Nicolau 73
            Carrical 75
            Baia Gombeza 76
            Boca da Praia de Falcão 76
            Baia da Chacina 77
            Ponta do Ilhéu 77
            Aquada da Garça 77
            Ponta Posson 77
            Porto da Lapa 78

Preguica	78
Bahia de Fidalgo	79
Bahia debaixo da Rocha	79
Tarrafal	81
Ponta do Galeão	81
Ilha de Santa Luzia	83

Chapter 7
São Vicente and Santo Antão	86
Ilha de São Vicente	86
Porto Grande/Mindelo	87
Other anchorages in São Vicente	90
Puerto de São Pedro	90
Bahia das Gatas	90
Ilha de Santo Antão	90
Porto Novo	94
Tarrafal de Monte Trigo	94
Mar Tranquilidade	95
Monte Trigo	97
Ponta do Sol	98
Porto do Paúl	98

Chapter 8
Santiago and Maio	99
Ilha de Santiago	99
Getting to Santiago	102
Tarrafal	103
From Tarrafal South Along the West Coast	104
Ribeira da Barca	105
Porto Rincão	106
Ilhéu dos Alcatrazes/Bahia de Inferno	110
Porto Mosquito	110
Porto Gouveia	111
Cidade Velha	111
Calheta de São Martinho	111
Porto da Praia	112
Unexplored Harbors on the East Coast of Santiago	116
Baia de Angra	116
Porto Formoso	117
Mangue de Sete Ribeiras	117
Cove East of Ponta da Ribeira Brava	117
Veneza	117
Calheta de São Miguel	118
Porto Coqueiro	118
Ponta de Santa Cruz	118
Porto de Pedra Badejo	119
Ponta Pinha	120
Monte Negro	120
Ponta Porto	120
Ponta Salameia/Ponta Inglez	122
Praia de Moia Moia	122

Ponta Bomba	122
Porto Lobo	122
Ponta Leste and Porto de São Francisco	123
Portete Baixo	123
Ilha do Maio	123
Vila do Maio/Porto Inglez	124
Calheta	125

Chapter 9
Fogo and Brava	127
Ilha do Fogo	127
São Filipe	129
Vale de Cavaleiros	130
Ilha Brava	131
Porto da Furna	133
Fajã da Agua	136
Porto dos Ferreiros	136
Ilhéus Secos ou do Rombo	137

Chapter 10
Setting up for a Trade-Wind Passage	138
The Proper Downwind Rig	138
Preventer	138
Reaching Sheet	140
Boom Vangs	140
Twin Headsails	142
Hanked-on Sails	143
Mizzen Staysails	143
Spinnaker Poles	144
Sail Inventory	145
Sailing the Angles Downwind	146
Seeing Ahead	147
Generating Electricity	147
Water-Driven Generators	147
Wind Generators	148

Chapter 11
After the Crossing	150
Landfalls in the Caribbean	150
A Guide to Cruising Guides	151
Cruising Guides to the Eastern Caribbean	152
Off the Beaten Track in the Eastern Caribbean	153
Street's Boast	164

Appendices	165
Appendix 1: Contacts and Resources	165
Appendix 2: Cape Verdean Words and Phrases	166
Appendix 3: Listing of Approach Points	167
Index	169

Street's Guide to the Cape Verde Islands

List Of Charts

CAUTION:

All charts are to be used in conjunction with the text. Projection is *Transverse Mercator*. **Datum** is WGS84. North is always "up" on these charts. The Index charts are designed strictly for orientation, they are NOT to be used for navigational purposes.

The prudent navigator will not rely solely on any single aid to navigation, particularly on floating aids.

The author and publisher take no responsibility for errors, omissions, or the misuse of these charts. No warranties are either expressed or implied as to the usability of the information contained herein. Always keep a good lookout when piloting in these waters.

Chart #	Description	Page
Ilho do Sal - Index Chart		62
S1	Baia da Palmeira	63
S2	Baia da Mordeira	65
S3	Santa Maria	66
S4	Baia de Pedra de Lume	67
Ilha de Boavista - Index Chart		68
BV1	Porto de Sal-Rei	69
Ilha de São Nicolau - Index Chart		72
SN1	Carrical, Baia Gombeza	75
SN2	Boca da Praia de Falcão	76
SN3	Baia de Chacina	76
SN4	Ponta do Ilhéu	77
SN5	Aquada de Garça	78
SN6	Ponta Posson	78
SN7	Porto da Lapa	79
SN8	Preguica	80
SN9	Baia de Fidalgo	80
SN10	Tarrafal	83
SN11	Ponta do Galeão	83
Ilha de Santa Luzia - Index Chart		84
SL1	Ilha de Santa Luzia	85
Ilha de São Vicente - Index Chart		86
SV1	Porto Grande/Mindelo	88
Ilha de Santo Antão - Index Chart		91
SA1	Porto Novo	94
SA2	Tarrafal de Monte Trigo	94
SA3	Monte Trigo	96
SA4	Ponta do Sol	97

List of Charts

Ilha de Santiago - Index Chart		100
ST1	Tarrafal	103
ST2	Ribeira da Barca	105
ST3	Porto Rincão	109
ST4	Ilhéu dos Alcatrazes/Bahia de Inferno	110
ST5	Porto Mosquito	110
ST6	Porto Gouveia	111
ST7	Cidade Velha	112
ST8	Calheta de São Martinho	113
ST9	Porto da Praia	114
ST10	Baia de Angra	117
ST11	Porto Formoso	117
ST12	Mangue de Sete Ribeiras	118
ST13	Veneza, Calheta de São Miguel	118
ST14	Porto Coqueiro	119
ST15	Ponta de Santa Cruz	119
ST16	Porto de Pedra Badejo	119
ST17	Ponta Pinha	119
ST18	Monte Negro	120
ST19	Ponta Porto	120
ST20	Ponta Salameia, Ponta Inglez	122
ST21	Moia Moia to Malhada	122
ST22	Ponte Leste	123
ST23	Portete Baixo	123
Ilha do Maio - Index Chart		124
M1	Vila do Maio/Porto Inglez	124
Ilha do Fogo - Index Chart		127
F1	São Filipe	129
F2	Vale de Cavaleiros	130
Ilha Brava - Index Chart		127
B1	Furna	134
B2	Fajã da Agua	135
B3	Porto dos Ferreiros	136

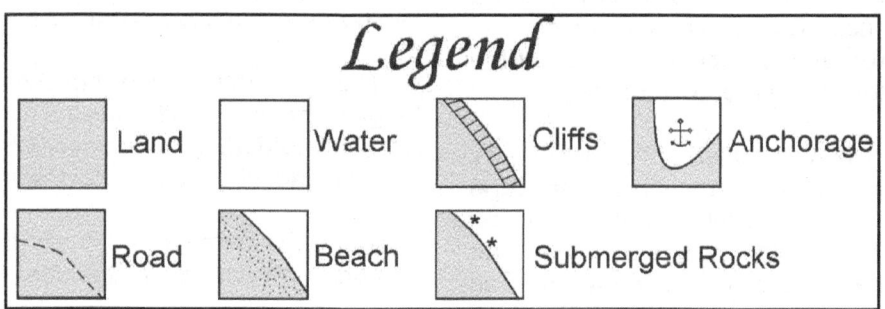

Background and Acknowledgements

I explored the Cape Verdes on *Iolaire* in 1985 and again in 1989. Then, when I decided to completely rewrite and expand my 1986 *Transatlantic Crossing Guide* that was also a cruising guide to the Atlantic Islands, I explored the Cape Verdes once more, this time by flying to Sal and traveling around the islands by plane and ferry. On this trip, which was in 2002, I stumbled upon some postcards that were satellite photographs of the individual Cape Verdean islands. These gave me a fresh view and some valuable information.

The available navigational charts of the area are drawn to such a large scale that small harbors and coves don't show up. The satellite photos, even at postcard size, showed much more detail. Wherever waves were breaking along the shore, the white surf showed up clearly. Where there was no white, that suggested no surf and the possibility of a calm anchorage.

On this same trip, I discovered that walking maps had been made up to useful scales. A number of coves showed up on them that looked to be worth exploring. The maps were especially useful as they were keyed to the WGS 84 datum, which is the standard used for a majority of navigational charts. This meant information from the maps could be easily correlated with the Imray-Iolaire chart of the Cape Verde Archipelago. Map in hand, I investigated some of the potential anchorages on the east coast of Santiago.

In 2005, I made further explorations of the islands while sailing on *Sincerity*, and also explored Santiago again by car.

In 2009, I flew to the Cape Verdes once again and visited every island except Brava via air. On this visit, I spent seven and a half hours exploring the south coast of São Nicolau in an 18-foot outboard powered fishing boat. With Indira Dom as chauffer, guide, and translator, I explored and re-explored almost all the possible anchorages on the island of Santiago.

Indira is the second generation of the Dom family to have helped me gather information on the Cape Verdes. I don't know anyone who knows the Cape Verdes better than her father, Gerry Dom, and he has been an invaluable asset to me, first when I was putting material together for my *Transatlantic Crossing Guide* and more recently for this book. Gerry is from Belgium, and how he came to settle in the Cape Verdes is a tale worth telling.

In 1978, Gerry's parents sold everything, bought a 48-foot Camper and Nicholsons sloop, and left with their three sons to go cruising. Gerry was 17 and his brothers were 15 and 13. They had made it as far as the Azores when Gerry's grandfather became very sick. His mother and father flew back to Belgium to take care of grandfather, leaving Gerry and his two brothers in charge of the boat.

Gerry being a bit of lad, six feet tall and good looking, began to cut a wide swath through the young ladies of Horta. He evidently was throwing some momentous parties on board the boat.

The conservative harbor master took a dim view of this, and announced to Gerry that the harbor authorities were going to haul the boat with a crane and store it ashore. Gerry and his brothers would have to live in a bed and breakfast ashore where they could not have their riotous parties and lead the young ladies of Horta astray.

Gerry figured this would cost his father a lot of money so, that night, he upped anchor and took off for the Cape Verdes. It was November, so a good time of year for the passage. Gerry knew how to take a noon sight and how to keep up his dead reckoning, and Ilha do Sal had a good direction-finding radio station.

Thirteen days and 1,440 miles later, they arrived in Praia, Santiago. An average of 111 miles a day wasn't bad for a bunch of teenagers!

Needless to say, the parents were more than a little upset when the harbor master in Horta notified them that Gerry and his brothers had taken off. They were relieved when Gerry notified them that they were all safely in Santiago. Gerry placated his father by pointing out to him how much money he saved him by leaving Horta.

The grandfather died, but the parents stayed in Belgium for nine months and the two younger brothers went back to join them. Gerry stayed on to take care of the boat, and acquired a beautiful Cape Verdian girlfriend.

When the parents had finally finished sorting out grandfather's papers, they and the younger boys flew

Background and Acknowledgements

to the Cape Verdes. The family then took off cruising again, augmented by one: Gerry's wife. They cruised until 1982 when, off the coast of New Guinea, Gerry got his wife pregnant.

Gerry and his wife flew back to Santiago and, not long after that, Gerry discovered that the U.S. Embassy had acquired a 38-foot ketch. It seems the ketch, which had shown up in the Cape Verdes in about 1981, had been stolen. Its owner managed to repossess it and sent a delivery crew down to take it back to Europe. They turned back two days after they departed, saying it was impossible to deliver a boat from the Cape Verdes back to Europe.

The boat sat in Santiago until somehow the U.S. Embassy ended up with it. By then, it was very run down, but Gerry, being a fast talker as well as a very competent sailor, told the embassy he could re-commission the boat.

He was hired. He had the boat hoisted out of the water with a dockside crane and spent a year refitting it. It was re-launched in 1983.

In 1983, the political situation was not particularly stable. The Republic of Cape Verde had only gained its independence from Guinea-Bissau in 1982 and its government was communist. The U.S. Embassy justified the yacht's acquisition by designating it an "escape boat," in case things went really bad.

The ambassador at the time, Vernon Brenner, was a yachtsman. Travel among the islands was difficult. Few islands had airstrips and the local airline was small and its schedule erratic, so the ambassador, with Gerry skippering, made regular visits to the islands in the 38-foot ketch.

In 1985, when *Iolaire* was in Praia, the USAID officer at the embassy was Tom Ball, a yachtsman, and he took us under his wing. He arranged for us to get water from a U.S. Navy ship that was in the harbor and he introduced me to Gerry Dom. I was preparing my *Transatlantic Crossing Guide* at the time and Gerry supplied me with a good deal of information.

In 1989, when we visited the Cape Verdes again in *Iolaire*, the embassy let Gerry go sailing with us for about a week. Needless to say, I was picking Gerry's brain the entire time. Gerry ran the embassy boat as full-time skipper until 1997, when he moved to Boavista, but he continued to run it part time until 2002. He had picked up a 40-foot bare hull in 1991 and spent the next five years completing it as a fishing boat for commercial fishing. He fished commercially from 1991 to 1996, when he switched to sport fishing. He did this until 2009 when he sold his fishing boat. He obviously used his boat hard, as when he sold it, it had over 13,000 hours on the engine meter.

In 2008, he found a South African-built 48-foot double-headsail sloop in Casamance, Senegal, where it had been semi-abandoned by its French owner. It took Gerry half a day to get down the river, after which it was a fast reach to Boavista for two and a half days averaging 6 knots — not bad for a boat with a foul bottom.

Gerry Dom obviously has intimate knowledge of the Cape Verdes, and I am very grateful for all the help he has given me over the years as I've put together the information in this book. He has read, reviewed, and corrected all the navigational and piloting sections.

I also want to thank Kai Brosmann for the help he has given me. Kai is from Germany. As a youth

Photo by Indira Dom
Gerry Dom

Indira Dom

he learned to sail on lakes. He spent 11 years in the German navy and continued his sailing career on the navy's sailing yachts and on private yachts. On getting out of the navy as an electronics specialist in 1990, he went to university to study electronics and civil engineering.

In 1997, Kai ended up in the Cape Verdes when he was as skipper of a Gibsea 44. He returned to Germany where he rounded up financial backing to set up a bareboat charter operation in Mindelo, São Vicente. The charter company opened for business in 1998 with a fleet of about five boats, and for a couple of years operated from a 120-foot Baltic ferry that had managed to get itself stranded in Mindelo.

In 2003, Kai, in partnership with another German, Lutz Meyer-Scheel, who provided most of the financing, obtained permission to build a small floating marina just east of the main shipping pier. His intention was to service his little bareboat operation there, but it immediately filled up with sport fishermen. Kai kept two berths for his own bareboats and as a place to moor transient yachts that he was working on so they could continue on across the Atlantic.

In my 1986 *Transatlantic Crossing Guide* I stated that the broken down dock in front of town should be rebuilt and set up as a marina for visiting yachts. Kai saw the same potential, and his dream of creating a proper marina by rebuilding this same old dock finally came to fruition in June 2008 when he and Lutz opened a 120-berth facility.

In 1999, in order to keep his bareboat charterers out of trouble, Kai wrote a cruising guide to the Cape Verdes. When he created his website he gave waypoints for anchorages throughout the Cape Verdes.

With Kai's permission, I have cross-checked all my information with his waypoints, and have added to my list some anchorages that I did not know of.

The first cruising guide I wrote was the *Yachtsman's Guide to the Virgin Islands*. It was privately printed in 1964 on a hand operated copying machine, which the English would know as a Roneo and Americans a mimeograph.

I followed that guide in 1966 with the hard-covered *Cruising Guide to the Lesser Antilles*, the book that opened up the Eastern Caribbean to the cruising yachtsman and made bareboat chartering possible.

Over the years, I expanded and re-published the Lesser Antilles guide, and it finally became a three-volume work that covered all the islands from Trinidad to the western end of Puerto Rico.

In 1980, my *Cruising Guide to Venezuela and the Offshore Islands* was published, and opened another area to the cruising yachtsman.

In the middle 1980s, I stated in print that if anyone could come up with an anchorage in the Eastern Caribbean that I had not mentioned in my guides, I would buy the drinks. So far, I have never had to pay off.

I'll make that challenge again, with regard to the Cape Verde Islands. Based on my own explorations in the Cape Verde Archipelago, backed up by information given me by Gerry Dom and Kai Brosmann, I believe I have located every harbor in the Cape Verdes that can provide a reasonable anchorage. If anyone can come up with an anchorage in the Cape Verdes that is not mentioned in this guide, I will buy the drinks.

Further, if anyone comes up with good information on anchorages that expands or corrects the information in this guide, I will happily pay for the drinks.

Author's Acknowledgements

Needless to say, this guide would not have come to fruition if it had not been for the help of a large number of people.

Tom Ball, the USAID officer at the U.S. Embassy in the Cape Verdes, knew of my writings and spotted *Iolaire* on our first cruise through the Cape Verdes, in 1985. He made contact with me and put me in touch with Gerry Dom, who had for a number of years been running the U.S. Embassy's escape boat (see page 8 for more information on Gerry). In our first meeting, Gerry gave me a complete run-through of the Cape Verdes, describing the weather and marking up my British Admiralty charts.

As we had been discovering, the British Admiralty charts were out of date and inaccurate. This, and the added experiences from our second Cape Verde cruise, in 1989, prompted me to work with Imray, Laurie, Norie and Wilson to develop the Imray-Iolaire chart of the Cape Verdes.

Background and Acknowledgements

At the time of the 1989 cruise, Vernon Brenner was the U.S. Ambassador. He was, and still is, an enthusiastic sailor and gave Gerry a week off to sail with us on *Iolaire* to explore Fogo and Brava.

While in the Cape Verdes in 2002 (this time I arrived via the big bird), I met Kai Brosmann, who was running a small bareboat operation and planning a small marina in Mindelo, São Vicente. He had written a small cruising guide (in German). He not only gave me a copy of his cruising guide but, when I visited again in 2009, gave me the waypoints for all his recommended anchorages. I have included many of these anchorages in this guide but left out some that I was not happy with. In some cases, I felt I had discovered better anchorages nearby; others I eliminated as I felt they were too dangerous.

Lutz Meyer-Scheel, Kai's partner in building and operating the marina, was helpful in supplying photos and answering e-mails that Kai was too busy to answer.

In 2005 I met the chief firefighter at Praia airport, Patrick Rodriguez Nascimento, and he provided me great services as interpreter and guide when I explored the east coast of Santiago by car.

In 2009, Indira de Vasconcelos Dom, Gerry's daughter, was of invaluable support in Santiago. With her help, I re-explored Santiago, checking anchorages from shore. Some of the coves were barely accessible from the land side but we were able to reach them as she is a "bush driver" par excellence.

Fifty four years in the Caribbean, and starting my career there as a land surveyor when I had to do a lot of driving on semi-completed roads, made me a good bush driver, but Indira was fantastic. She knows the island well and speaks both Portuguese and the local Crioulo, so was able to talk about anchorages with the local fishermen.

Indira also provided the small, English/Portuguese/Crioulo dictionary in Appendix 2 on page 166.

I also must thank the two fishermen who enabled me to explore the south coast of São Nicolau, and the fishermen who enabled us to explore Honeymoon Cove and the anchorage behind Punta Tuna in the Rinção area of Santiago's west coast.

Susi, who with her husband, Frank, owns and runs *Mar Tranquilidade*, a small guest house hotel on the southwest corner of Santo Antão, supplied wonderful information on the west coast of that island and its anchorages. Her stories reinforced what I believed, as Kai, Lutz, and the RCC guide seemed to view the anchorages through rose-tinted glasses.

Needless to say, I thank the crews of *Iolaire* who were aboard on our 1985 and 1989 cruises and explorations in the Cape Verdes.

Finally I must thank Trygve Bratz the owner and skipper of the 88-foot ketch, *Sincerity*, who invited me to join him and his crew to cruise Madeira, the Canaries, and the Cape Verdes, where we did a lot of exploring before crossing the Atlantic.

And for his help in turning my ramblings into a book, I want to thank my editor, Jeremy McGeary. Jeremy's career has taken him from Caribbean charter skipper, to yacht designer, to yachting writer. He spent several years as an editor on the staff at *Cruising World*, where his job was to coax articles submitted by sailors like me into publishable form. He edited many of my articles, and sailed on *Iolaire* in 2005, when we celebrated her 100th birthday by racing in the *British Classic Yacht Club Regatta* in Cowes.

Jeremy has gathered together all my information on the Cape Verdes and assembled it into an excellent guide. Most important, he convinced *Seaworthy Publications* that publishing the Cape Verde Guide was a viable proposition.

I must also thank Stephen J. Pavlidis who, as well as laying out the entire book, has taken the various harbor charts I provided - some from the Imray-Iolaire chart, others copied from a variety of topographical maps - and incorporated my notes to create handsome charts in a uniform style.

Finally I must thank everybody at Seaworthy Publications, Inc., for making this project a reality.

Donald M. Street, Jr.

Don Street Through the Eyes of Long-Time Associates

Tom Cunliffe Crosses Tacks with Don Street

My first visit to the Caribbean was in 1976. I was 42 days out from Rio de Janeiro when the mail drop in Bridgetown, Barbados, served up a letter from my father and a copy of Don Street's then relatively new Cruising Guide to the Lesser Antilles, ordered from London. I was relieved to find this publication because a general shambles in Rio meant I'd arrived with no charts at all. All I had was a lat/long for Barbados, some notes culled from a friend's Admiralty Pilot, a sextant, and a Nautical Almanac. I bought myself a rum in the yacht club and settled down to read.

Dad's letter took half an hour, and I spent the rest of the afternoon getting to know Don though the salty pages of his book. Every leaf turned was a relief and an inspiration. Transits ('ranges' if you are the American persuasion), eyeball navigation, and reef-spotting from the spreaders (plus a tutorial on how to master this vital art of the tropics) took the place of mumbo-jumbo. Even more important, it was immediately obvious that this was a pilot book written by a man without an engine. It's one thing driving into an anchorage under power. It takes seamanship of a higher caliber altogether to beat up a narrow, unmarked channel, so I knew I'd struck gold.

The wry asides about so-and-so's beach bar, the insights into the local schooner culture, and the obvious message that the writer was a man who respected the islands and loved their inhabitants showed me the way. Armed with that book, I not only dodged the reefs, I thoroughly enjoyed everything the area had to offer.

"God bless Don Street," I thought, and then I met him. A week later, my gaff cutter – also engineless – was anchored in Grenada when in swept Iolaire. She jinked past the reef and into the Lagoon, rounded up and anchored, a distinctive figure in a battered sunhat at the helm. To my delight, he rowed over, admired my little boat and gave me a chart of the islands that looked as though it had been regurgitated by the local barracuda. We've been friends ever since.

To most passing sailors, the Cape Verde Archipelago is an area of dark mystery. Charting scale and survey quality does not encourage cruising off the beaten track, and yachts entering its remoter anchorages have been rare and adventurous. For Don Street, at the age of 80, this presented a challenge to be grabbed rather than a safety issue best avoided. Typical of this one-off buccaneer, he sailed into the islands, he visited them virtually via Internet mapping systems, he used road transport and he hiked over mountains. He struck deals with local fishermen and penetrated far-flung roadsteads with them as his guide. In the way that only he can, he has produced a unique pilot that will open a rich cruising ground for many.

Don Street's books are not always the glossiest, but anyone who is fooled by this is making a sorry mistake. It sometimes seems to me that Don has more sea miles than the rest of us put together. And remember, almost all of them have been run off under sail alone. His delivery of information shoots straight from the hip and, my goodness, he tells us how it is. May the old sea gods give him long life to inform and entertain us through many a trade-wind winter yet to come.

Tom Cunliffe

Patience Wales: On a Parallel Course with Don Street

It was in 1967, at the end of a four-year circumnavigation, that I first had sightings of Don Street on the (even then) venerable yacht, *Iolaire*. He had already been cruising in Grenada and the Grenadines for five years and had written the first of his many guides: *A Cruising Guide to the Lesser Antilles*. My boat partners and I had made landfall in Barbados and were planning to sail to Grenada and then up the Caribbean on our ketch, *Kismet*, a tad venerable herself, before taking off for Bermuda and home to New England, and we were relieved to be able to rely on a real cruiser's recommendations for passages and anchorages. Then, in 1970, something happened that changed the world of sailing: bareboat chartering began. Charter companies unleashed fleets of boats all over the Caribbean and introduced tens of thousands of sailors to warm water, eyeball navigation, and the art of anchoring.

Street and I sailed a parallel path in those days. He began writing guides with some seriousness as well as articles for the various sailing magazines one of which was *SAIL*, whose staff I joined in 1973. As managing editor, I spent a lot of time on charter boats in the Caribbean and no matter where I went, there was the galloping grandmother *Iolaire* with Street aboard, his beard glistening in the heat and his hand firmly grasping the best heat-reducer known to man— a cold, green Heineken.

Iolaire was always anchored in the choice spot, her Ampair wind generator whirling atop the mizzen mast, and Street was invariably tweaking her rig (early on, he changed her from a 7/8 cutter with small headsails to a masthead yawl with large headsails, smaller main, and a mizzen) or tending to her large collection of anchors and attendant gear.

This inclination for invention complemented Street's explorer side. Very early, he cruised and wrote about the east coast of Martinique, Venezuela and its offshore islands, and, in ways especially useful to charter skippers, the offbeat anchorages of the Virgin Islands. In those days, passagemakers used sextants and single-sideband radios, so Street's early guides focused on inter-island interests — where to anchor for lunch but not overnight, where to anchor for a month, where to be hauled, what rock to avoid (sometimes he knew this from firsthand experience), and when to get out because hurricane season was on the horizon.

As anchoring equipment became easier to use, roller-furling showed up on almost all boats, and satnav, then GPS, became common on cruising boats in and out of charter, Street began to expand the range of his guides.

He is a consummate sailor. For 37 years, he sailed *Iolaire* without an engine not only throughout the Caribbean but also seven times across the Atlantic and 12 times up and down the Thames River to St. Catherine Dock. *Street's Transatlantic Crossing Guide* was published in the mid-1980s; it was also a guide to the Atlantic Islands and it opened a new cruising area to both new and experienced sailors. By then, cruisers were used to the Caribbean and needed new island playgrounds — Cape Verdes, Azores, Canaries, and Madeira. The transatlantic guide really did change things. I was in the Canaries in 1967 in the days when you played by ear and by chart. Now here was a guide that spelled things out in the same way as his guides of the Eastern Caribbean had.

What makes Don Street's guides worth reading is the fact that he's been there done that. And he's still out there, his beard a bit whiter but just as real.

Patience Wales

Street's Guide to the Cape Verde Islands

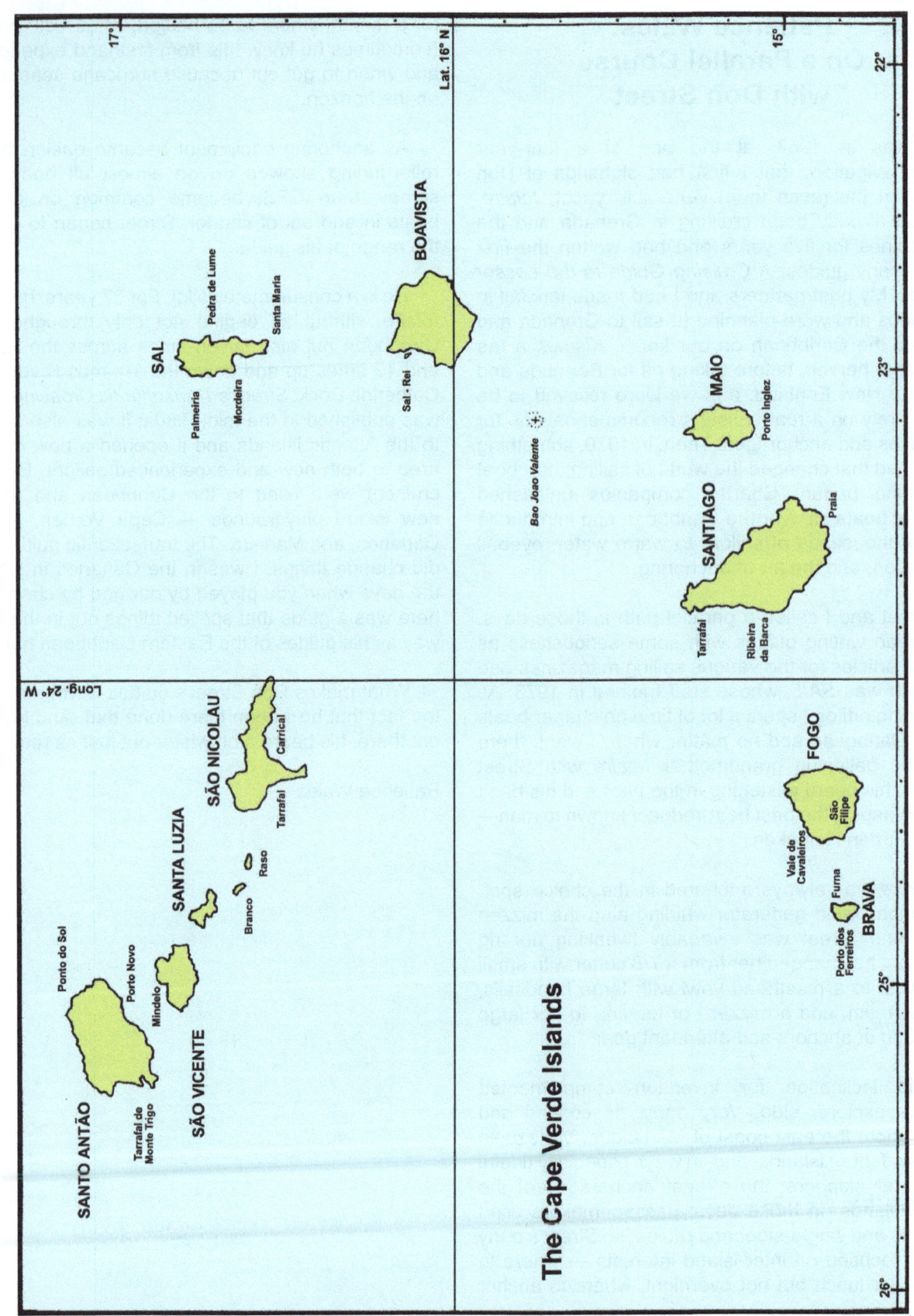

The Cape Verde Islands

Chapter 1
The Case for Cruising the Cape Verde Islands

In the past, the Cape Verdes were not popular with yachtsmen. For years, the islands had a reputation for being short on food and water, expensive, unfriendly, and too far south of the traditional east-west tradewind route across the North Atlantic. Until 1990, the representatives of the communist government who performed clearance formalities were officious, obstructive, unfriendly, and generally a pain in the backside. And, for the longest time, the islands had absolutely no infrastructure to cater to yachts.

Of the sailors who did visit the Cape Verdes, most stopped in Mindelo, on São Vicente, and judged all the Cape Verdes from what they experienced there. This was unfortunate, because the other islands of the Cape Verdes are quite different from the dry and arid São Vicente. Also, for many years, Mindelo was very run down. The magnificent market building that stood as a reminder of the town's prosperous past was in such bad shape it was scheduled for demolition.

On top of all this, very little cruising information had been available from published sources. Even so, many yachtsmen who have visited them, myself included, shared the opinion that the Cape Verdes were worth going to and writing about.

With this book, I hope to fill the information gap, at least for the purposes of cruising the islands (I provide some suggestions for further reading on the islands in *Chapter 11* on page 150). And I am pleased to report that in the Cape Verdes today, yachtsmen can expect a warmer welcome than in the past from officialdom and more facilities for servicing their yachts, at least in Mindelo.

When I arrived in Mindelo in 2002 via the big bird, one of the first people I met was the skipper of a 100-foot Swan sloop that I had met a few months previously in the Azores. As we chatted, he told me he was on his way to clear in. I asked if I could join him to see what the routine was like. He said, "Fine, come ahead."

The port captain was efficient and helpful and gave us directions to the immigration office. The immigration officer was friendly, and busily stamped the crews' passports until he came to two crew members who didn't have passports; they only had seamen's papers. The immigration officer stated in no uncertain terms, "Every crewmember must have a passport," to which the skipper replied, "But they only have seamen's papers."

Again the immigration officer said, "They must have passports."

This went back and forth three times. The fourth time, as he said it, he stamped the seamen's papers. As he handed back the stamped passports and the stamped seamen's papers, he said one more time, "Everyone must have a passport!" He then stood up, shook the skipper's hand, smiled, and said, "I hope you enjoy your stay." What a difference from my experience in 1989!

In the 1970s and 1980s, thievery and burglary was rife. That, too, has changed. Kai Brosmann at Marina Mindelo reported in 2009 that in the last two years there has been a little minor pilferage from yachts but no burglary. Nor have there been any attacks on yachtsmen. And now that the new marina in Mindelo is fully open, yachts now have a secure place to moor and get almost any work done they might need to complete an Atlantic crossing (see *Marine Infrastructure*, page 34).

A Cruising Ground With Choices

The islands are certainly isolated, but that's a plus for many cruising folk, particularly those who want to get away from tourists and fellow yachtsmen and who prefer to anchor out rather than cruise from one expensive marina to the next.

I have visited and explored all the Atlantic island groups many times over the last 54 years. I've been to Bermuda too many times to count. I sailed to the Azores on *Iolaire* in 1985, 1989, and 1995, and on *Nimrod* in 1992, and I flew there in 2009. I went to Madeira on *Arabella* in 1956, on *Iolaire* in 1985, 1989, and 1995, on *Sincerity* in 2005, and by air in 2002 and 2010. I sailed to the Canaries on *Arabella* in 1956, on *Iolaire* in 1975, 1985, and 1989, and *Lone Star* in 1984, and flew there in 2002 and 2010. I visited the Cape Verdes on *Iolaire* in 1985, and 1989, on *Sincerity* in 2005, and by air in 2002 and 2009.

In the light of the above, I feel I am in a position to make a good comparison of the island groups. Of all them, I think the Cape Verde Archipelago offers the best cruising.

In the Azores, cruising largely involves sailing from one marina to another. There is only a handful of anchorages outside of harbors, and all of them are "iffy" — you have to be prepared to move on short notice in the event of a change in conditions.

In the Madeiran Archipelago, there are only five anchorages: outside the marina in Porto Santo (weather permitting), Mochico, Bahia de Abra at the eastern end of Madeira, the overcrowded marginal anchorage in Funchal, Isla Deserta Grande. In the Salvage islands, you'll find two more. Again, these anchorages are marginal.

In the Canaries, too, there are only a half dozen places where you can anchor outside of a marina, and you have to keep a sharp eye on the weather. In October, November, and early December, the wind in the Canaries can blow from any direction. Your quiet anchorage with the easterly wind holding you off the shore can, with a wind shift to the southwest, suddenly turn into a deadly one with no protection from the wind and swell and with the lee shore close under your stern. (For relevant weather information, see the back of Imray-Iolaire Chart 100. This is a planning chart for the North Atlantic and is a gnomonic projection, on which a straight line is a great circle course.)

All too often, in the second half of October and all of November, you will find the marinas in the Canaries are so full you can't shoehorn your way in, leaving you with the choice between heaving-to outside or sailing to another island and hoping to find room there. When you do get into a marina, it's in the middle of a concrete jungle and, when you go to a bar or restaurant, you'll be in the company of tourists and hard pressed to find locals with whom to strike up a conversation.

In contrast, in the Cape Verdes, there are dozens of anchorages and only one marina, in Mindelo, São Vincente, a town with colonial origins and a center dating back to the late 19th century. If you don't choose to go into the marina, there is plenty of room to anchor out, and when you go ashore you can easily get to know the local people. The only concrete jungle in the Cape Verdes is at Santa Maria on the south end of Sal. Cruising sailors will probably not use this anchorage unless the crew is into surfing, windsurfing, or kite surfing.

Another good reason to visit the Cape Verdes is that they are closer to the Caribbean by some 500 miles than any other logical jumping-off place on the east side of the Atlantic. From São Vicente in the northern group, or Santiago in the southern group, it's 2,175 miles to Antigua and 2,110 miles to Barbados.

And with the 50 sketch charts presented in this guide, the attractive cruising possibilities the islands offer are available to any sailor with a sense of adventure and a good dose of navigational horse sense. The vast majority of these anchorages are not shown on any chart nor are they shown or described in any other guide.

For those interested in water-based activities, the Cape Verdes have good beaches, diving, surfing, windsurfing, and kite surfing. For those who like to hike, the hills of the high islands offer wonderful walking country. All this comes with an interesting culture set amid dramatic and varied scenery in a very pleasant climate.

Finally, in late October, November, and December, the time of year when most yachts cross to the Caribbean, you have to sail so far south from the Canaries to get into the trade winds that you might as well go a little farther and win the triple bonus of a new cruising ground, a shorter transatlantic hop, and pretty much guaranteed trade winds all the way across.

Waiting for the Trade Winds

When departing the Canary Islands in November, bound for the West Indies, you have to sail southwest at least to 20° N to pick up the trade winds. Even in December, you might sometimes have to go down to 17° N or even 16° N. On the way, around 25° N or even farther south, you might run into southwest or southerly winds. Look at the weather charts and Pilot Charts — it's all there.

That route brings you very close to the Cape Verdes, so why not stop there? You can replenish your stores and then head across, refreshed and ready for a short fast passage. In a boat of about 45 feet, it should take only 14 or 15 days.

The Case for Cruising The Cape Verde Islands

Another reason for visiting the Cape Verdes is that sometimes a southwester fills in south of the Canaries and drives you there — as happened to many boats in December 2002 and again in 2005.

When I visited the Cape Verdes by air in late November 2002, I found Mindelo full of yachts. Boats leaving the Canaries, including many that were taking part in the Atlantic Rally for Cruisers (ARC), had run into a southwesterly wind and some were barely able even to lay a course to the Cape Verdes. Some of them stayed long enough to pick up fuel and continued on across. Others waited a couple of weeks for the trades to fill in.

Similarly, in 2005, the trades were very erratic. Some boats, those that left between December 2 and December 4, had fast passages, but those that left between December 10 and December 12 had incredibly slow passages. The Christmas winds did not arrive in the Eastern Caribbean until the end of the first week in January 2006.

The strong trades along the African coast are created by the Azores high and the Sahara low. Once in a while, strange things happen. In 1985, the Sahara low became a Sahara high. For well over a month, there was virtually no wind in the Canaries. On the route to the Cape Verde Islands, winds were such that *Iolaire* took eight days to sail, or perhaps I should say drift, the 850 miles from the Canaries to the Cape Verde Islands. (This passage is recorded in the *Transatlantic with Street* DVD, which Tom Cunliffe recommends as good viewing.)

At about the time we reached the Cape Verdes, the Sahara high went back to its usual state, as a low, and the trades kicked in with a vengeance. For the entire time we were in the islands of the Cape Verdes, and for the first week we were at sea, heading for the Caribbean, the trades blew a solid 20 to 25 knots, and frequently built to 30 and 35 knots. Be prepared for wind in the Cape Verdes.

As I have noted elsewhere in this book, the trades do not really fill in with reliability until mid or late January; this is illustrated by *Iolaire*'s trips in 1985 and 1989.

Sailing from the Canaries to the Cape Verdes is usually easy, as, the exceptions noted above notwithstanding, you are almost guaranteed a strong trade wind blowing down the African coast to push you along at hull speed.

From the Cape Verdes to Antigua, your course is slightly north of west. Since the trades are usually slightly north of east, when you leave from the Cape Verdes, you can cross the Atlantic on a starboard tack all the way. You shouldn't have to jibe once.

Iolaire has done this on three occasions: in 1949 under gaff rig, when the late R. H. Bobby Somerset owned her, then in 1985 and again in 1989 under my ownership under her present yawl rig. All three passages were sailed on a starboard tack all the way and all were completed in 14 days and a few hours.

On both my passages, we were able rig the spinnaker pole semi-permanently to starboard, with the fore guy, after guy, and topping lift secured to the pole. We then fed a line through the end of the pole. If it was blowing hard, we attached it to a headsail; if the wind went light, to the spinnaker. As the wind went up and down we could switch from headsail to spinnaker or the reverse *without* touching the pole except for minor adjustments. (See page 138, "The Proper Trade Wind Rig.")

Boats traditionally sail across the Atlantic to the Caribbean during late November or early December, with large charter yachts trying to make the Antigua Charter Yacht Show (formerly Nicholsons' Agents Week) and private boats aiming to spend Christmas in the Caribbean. At this time of the year, the trades have not fully filled in and can be very erratic.

Having made this trip six times in the last 54 years, I can speak from experience. I have also listened to the stories told by literally hundreds of yachtsmen who have made the crossing.

In 1975, sailing the engineless *Iolaire*, we left Grand Canaria in early December for the passage to Antigua. It took us 19 days and 12 hours and we worked hard at it all the way. We had to go almost to the Cape Verdes looking for the trade winds. We had the spinnaker up for four or five days, hoisting it intermittently when the wind went light and dousing it when it picked up.

About 500 miles from Antigua, on December 15, the wind went northwest, despite the fact that we were down to 15° North. For 24 hours, we were hard

Street's Guide to the Cape Verde Islands

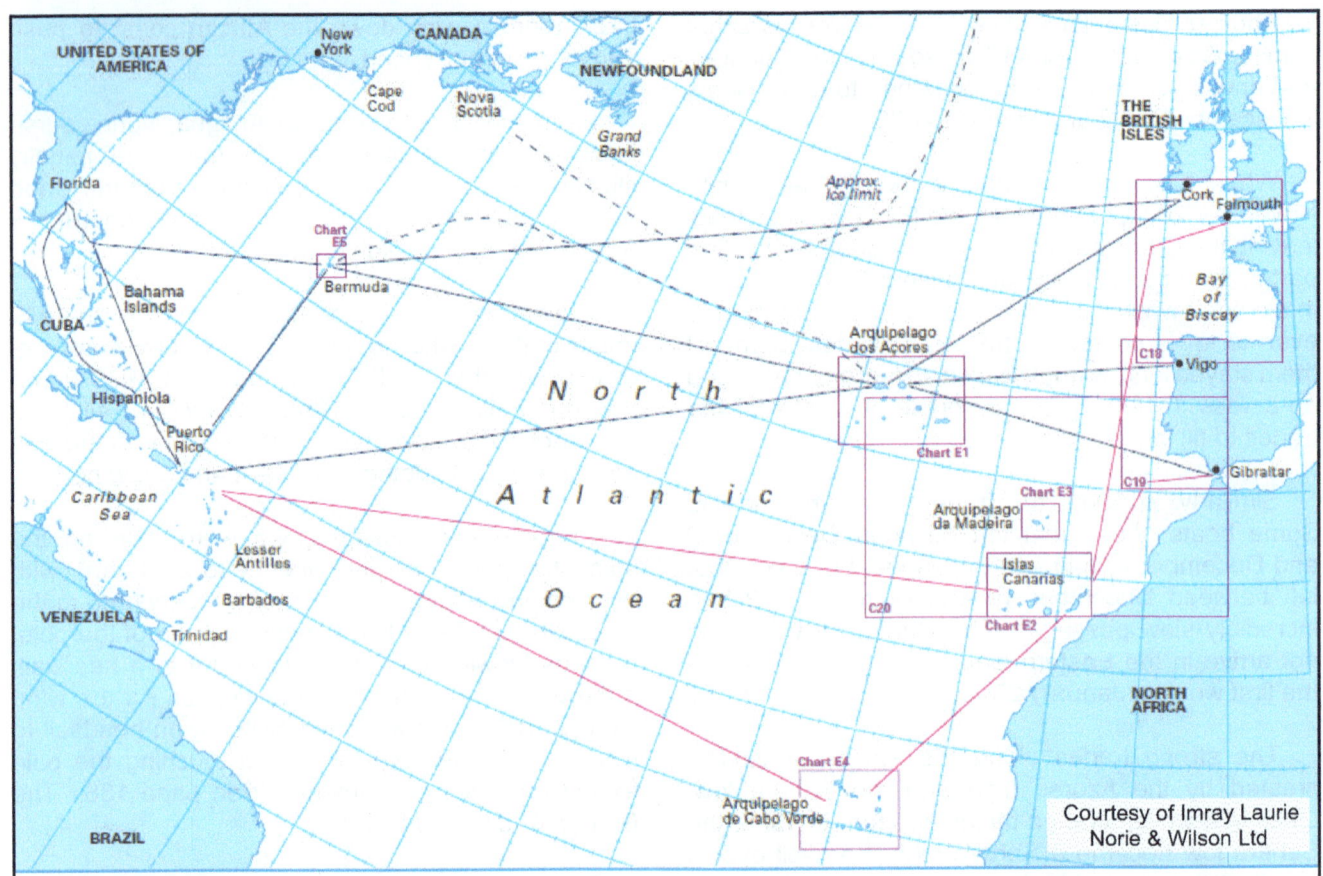

On this gnomic projection of the North Atlantic Ocean, popular great-circle cruising routes appear as straight lines. Imray Chart 100 uses the same projection and is very helpful when planning passages.

This photo taken by the author on December 14 2005 at Latitude 15N illustrates how the trade winds can be fickle during the traditional season for crossing the Atlantic.

The Case for Cruising The Cape Verde Islands

on the wind, rail down, unable to lay west. After 24 hours the wind veered and settled down to the normal east-northeast trades.

In 1985, we departed on December 2 from Mindelo, Cape Verde. We started out getting caught for 12 hours in the wind shadow of Santo Antão, then blasted off beam reaching for the first four days. The wind then went aft and light. We hoisted and doused the spinnaker a number of times and finally arrived in Antigua after 14 days and some hours.

We again left from the Cape Verdes on December 2 in 1989. This time, we set off from Brava, hitting the trades immediately. However, four days out, the wind eased, and we slowed down drastically. We set the spinnaker and carried it for the next 10 days, only dousing it as Antigua's Shirley Heights came abeam. This trip again took us 14 days and some hours. It was so light we could have been sailing in Long Island Sound, and if we had not set the spinnaker, it would have been an extremely slow passage.

On December 10, 2005, this time on the 88-foot ketch, *Sincerity*, we once again left from Brava, this time from Porto dos Ferreiros. We picked up the trades immediately and had a wonderful 36 hours. The wind then died. We powered, or motorsailed, or sailed, struggling hard to get the best out of her yet we still took 13 days and 15 hours, and six of those days were under power as there was virtually no wind. The trades had not filled in and the Christmas winds did not show up in Antigua until January 7th, when they arrived with a vengeance. They blew 20 to 25 knots, often up to 30 and gusting to 40, and continued that way for a full two weeks.

However, I later met in Tortola the crew of a 52-foot boat that had left Mindelo a week before we left Brava. They carried the trade winds all the way, sailing from Mindelo to Antigua in 12 days and a few hours.

I also met in Antigua, the crew of a 40-foot boat that I had originally met in Palmeira. They had left Mindelo January 4 and for the first week had more than enough wind, after which it eased off to a boisterous trade of 18 to 25 knots. They did the whole trip from Mindelo to Antigua in a 40-foot boat in 14-days and hours. They apparently came across on the trades that arrived so forcefully in Antigua on January 7. Obviously, during December, the trades are not reliable.

Sincerity's slow mid-December passage was due in part to two intense lows that formed in the Atlantic and caused winds that briefly reached hurricane force. One of them, Tropical Storm Delta, hit Tenerife, in the Canary Islands, late at night and caused havoc in a well sheltered marina. Pontoons and boats broke loose and many boats were damaged and some sank. According to one magazine report, the damage was so bad that when the marina manager arrived in the morning, he took one look at the carnage, disappeared, and was not seen for a week.

Boats that were caught in these lows had plenty of wind but elsewhere the storms sucked all of the wind out of the normal trade-wind route.

The two really fast passages I made were in 1956, on *Arabella*, and in 1984, on *Lone Star*. *Arabella*, a 46-foot cruising ketch, departed the Canaries on May 1. Under her cruising rig, with one of the twin headsails on a pole, main, mizzen, and big mizzen staysail, we averaged 194 miles a day for 11½ days until we turned north to head for Newport. If we had continued on to Antigua, we would have set a record for the passage that would have stood for 40 years.

On *Lone Star*, a 53-foot heavy-displacement ketch, we left in early June, and had a proper trade-wind rig (see photos on page 144.) We covered the 2,701 miles from Puerto Rico, Gran Canaria, to Antigua in 14 days and 20 hours, at the time a record for a boat of that size.

On both those passages, the trades had really settled in. The northern limit had moved up above the Canaries, so a direct great-circle course could be sailed at hull speed. In the light of this, if you want a really fast passage across the Atlantic, you should go in May or June, jumping off from Madeira or the Canaries.

For the normal fall/winter passage, I recommend cruising sailors not rush to be in the Caribbean for Christmas. Instead, they would do well to spend a month to five weeks cruising in the Cape Verdes, then depart for the Caribbean in early or mid January, thus being almost guaranteed a fast passage on a starboard tack all the way across. Why hurry to the Caribbean with its crowded anchorages when you can enjoy the uncrowded ones in the Cape Verdes?

Chapter 2
Cape Verde in a Capsule

The Cape Verde Archipelago is located in the Atlantic Ocean between 14° 50' and 17° 15' N and 22° 40' and 25° 20' W. This puts the islands about 700 miles south of the Canary Islands and 300 miles west of Cap Vert, on the coast of Senegal, Africa.

You'll find that these islands are referred to by a number of different names. In Portuguese, they are the Ilhas do Cabo Verde. In English, they are called the Cape Verdes, and this the term I will use, except in passages, such as that below where I present political history, when I think it's clearer to use the term Cape Verde when referring to the islands as a nation rather than a geographical location.

Because the archipelago was under the control of Portugal for four centuries, the islands bear Portuguese names. They fall into two groups, named by the sailors that discovered them as Ilhas do Barlavento (Windward Islands) and Ilhas do Sotavento (Leeward Islands). The Ilhas do Barlavento are the northern group, made up of Santo Antão, São Vicente, Santa Luzia, São Nicolau, Sal, Boavista (sometimes written Boa Vista), and a few small islands. To their south, Brava, Fogo, Santiago (sometimes written São Tiago), and Maio comprise the Ilhas do Sotavento. To be consistent with the Imray-Iolaire chart, I will stick with the first spellings of the islands that have two.

While the islands are volcanic in origin, only one volcano, on Fogo, has been active in recent times. From 1540 until 1740, Fogo erupted with a fair degree of regularity and was so active that seafarers used the fire at its peak as a landmark. It then went into a period of dormancy until a series of major eruptions in 1847, 1952, and 1957. It then went quiet again until erupting in 1951 and again in 1995. In the most recent event, the village that had grown up around the fertile soil in the volcano's crater was evacuated. Once the volcano quieted down, everyone went back to their homes and continued to cultivate grapes for wine making.

Agriculture is difficult in the Cape Verdes because rain is scarce. Fogo, Santiago, São Nicolau, and Santo Antão are high enough to benefit from some rainfall from the clouds that form over them, but the air generally comes off the deserts of Africa and doesn't carry much moisture. In this respect, although the Cape Verdes occupy the same latitudes, their climate differs from that of the middle islands in the eastern Caribbean, which are wetter even in the dry season because of the moisture the air picks up as it crosses the Atlantic. It's interesting to observe that, in the Cape Verdes, the windward sides of the islands that are high enough to gather rain are the green sides and the leeward sides the dry sides (see the illustration). In the Caribbean the opposite is true: The heaviest rain falls on the leeward sides of the islands and the windward sides are the dry sides.

The Cape Verdes are definitely cooler than the eastern Caribbean, and, like the West Indies, they have a dry season from December to June and a wet season from June to early November. Dry season temperatures are 25°C/78°F during the day and 18°C/66°F at night — definitely cool. In the wet season, daytime temperatures are 27°C/80°F during the day and 23°C/73°F at night. During the dry season it is normally clear, but occasionally a sandstorm — the harmattan — blasts out of the Sahara, reducing visibility and giving everyone a sore throat.

The wet season produces sudden heavy rains and flash floods and the wind can come from any direction. All the walking maps carry warnings for hikers to get out of ravines whenever it rains and to be wary of rock slides for even weeks after a heavy rain.

Heavy rains can muddy the normally crystal-clear waters for many weeks. They also wash out roads and cause landslides. On the high islands of São Nicolau, Santo Antão, Santiago, and Fogo, the rainy season severely damages the roads, to the extent that the entire dry season is spent repairing them. The roads are finally repaired just in time to be torn up again by the next rainy season. Repairing roads provides a lot of employment on those islands.

There is an old saying in the Cape Verdes: "We pray for rain and when it comes we sometimes drown. But if the rain does not come, we starve."

From the earliest times, the Cape Verdes have periodically suffered horrific famines during which large portions of the population have died of hunger. The last one is referred to as the "Great Famine of 41-44." It was followed by another famine combined with sickness in 1946-48. Reputedly, from 1941 to 1948, the combination of famine and sickness killed 60,000

Cape Verde in a Capsule

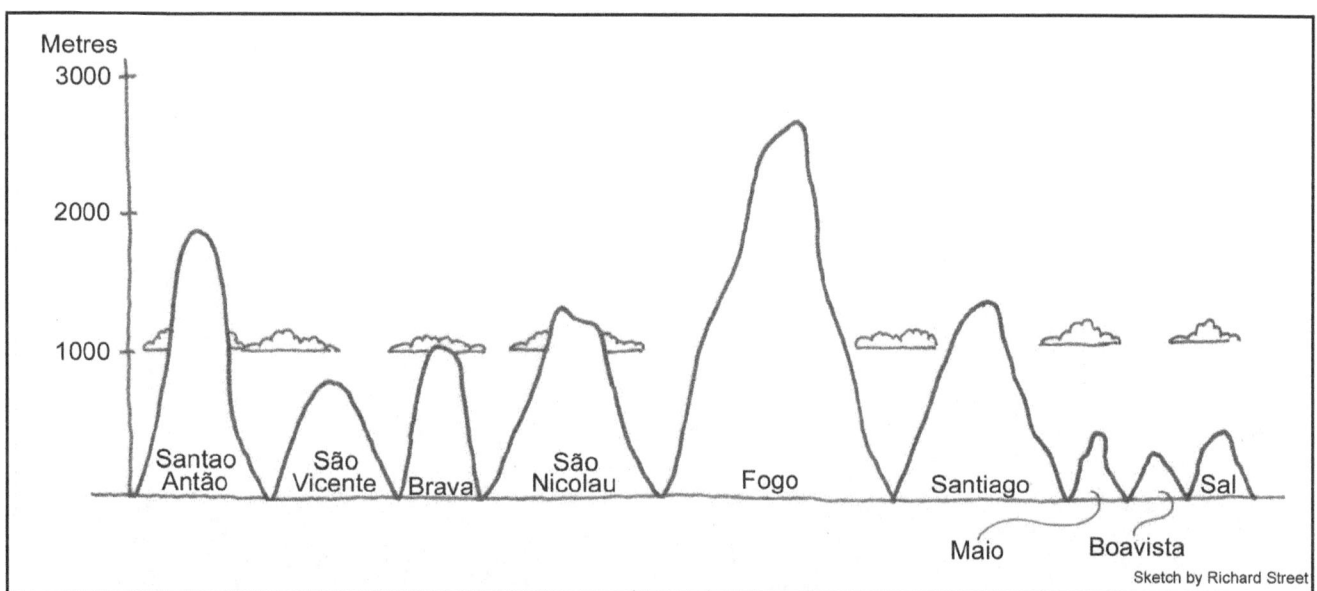

Only the higher islands in the Cape Verde Archipelago reach elevations where they can gather moisture from clouds. The lower islands receive small amounts of rainfall, only in the wet season, and often in downpours.

in the Cape Verdes out of a population of around 400,000. This is a rather horrific loss of life.

In the *1948/1949 Yachting World Annual*, which my parents bought in England in spring of 1949, is the story of *Iolaire*'s 1948/1949 transatlantic crossing via Gibraltar, the Canaries, and the Cape Verdes to Barbados. *Iolaire* was in Mindelo December 26 to 28, 1948. The crew reported that everyone there was destitute and 20 people a day were dying of starvation.

Political History

Although known in Roman times, as far as the modern world is concerned, the Cape Verdes were discovered in 1456 by Alvise Cadamosto, a Venetian who was at the time working for Prince Henry of Portugal. By 1462, the Portuguese had begun to establish settlements in the archipelago, which turned out to be strategically located on the trade routes that subsequently developed between Europe and the Americas. Although the English and French both fought over the islands, Portugal retained control and established them as a colony.

Ribeira Grande (now Cidade Velha), on Santiago in the southern group of islands (Ilhas do Sotavento), rapidly became the center of everything as it had a decent anchorage and a supply of drinking water from the river. It rapidly developed into a very wealthy city, attracting the interest of pirates who periodically raided the town and at times sacked it completely.

Exactly how often, when, and by whom Ribeira Grande was attacked is difficult to ascertain. Sir Francis Drake certainly raided it in 1584 and again in 1586. These regular attacks prompted the Portuguese to build the fort of San Filipe above the town. Construction began in 1687. Although it's a large fort and in an excellent location, it was captured in 1712.

Local legend has it that pirates, led by Jacques Cassard, captured the town and fort, but a little investigation reveals a different story. Jacques Cassard came from a French shipping family. He went to sea at age 14 on a family ship and became a captain by the age of 20. When he was 24, he had progressed up the line to command a privateer that captured 25 English ships in two years. He was then commissioned into the French navy and given command of a small ship of the line. A brilliant career followed, in which he regularly escorted important convoys, defending them successfully and capturing English ships in the process.

In 1711, while in command of the *Parfait*, a 72-gun ship of the line, and leading a squadron of six ships, he was sent out to raid English, Dutch, and Portuguese colonies, including the Cape Verdes. When Cassard

Even on São Vicente, which is largely arid, some agriculture is possible at higher altitudes on the windward (eastern) side. This view is looking east toward Santa Luzia.

Salt was the basis for the economy of the Cape Verde Islands for centuries. The ruined salt works on Sal are now a tourist attraction.

arrived in the Cape Verdes, he was a commissioned officer leading a sizable French squadron.

The story of how he captured the fort, which because of its location and construction looks to be impregnable, would make interesting reading. It may well have similarities to that of the "impregnable" fort on the Dutch island of St. Eustacia in the Eastern Caribbean during the War of 1812. Statia was an important transfer point for shipping arms to the United States, so the British sent Lord Rodney with a powerful force to capture it. He succeeded, but shortly after, the French recaptured it. I relate the whole story on pages 59 and 60 of the Anguilla to Dominica volume of Street's Cruising Guide to the Eastern Caribbean.

The War of Spanish Succession, which had given legitimacy to all these privateering and military activities, was ended by the Treaty of Utrecht in 1713, so Cassard's raid on the Cape Verdes must have been one of the last naval actions of the war.

At about this time, Praia, built on a plateau overlooking a more sheltered harbor five miles east of Ribeira Brava, became the principal city of Santiago and to this day is the capital of Cape Verde. Ribeira Brava was renamed Cidade Velha to avoid confusion when the town with the same name on Santo Antão became the seat of government for the Ilhas do Barlavento in 1850.

The Portuguese got into the slave trade with a vengeance and by the early years of the 17th century had a virtual monopoly on it. Salt was abundant in the archipelago and easily mined. The Portuguese dug it out and shipped it to Africa where they established trading posts where they traded it for slaves, whom they then sold off to slave traders of all nationalities. They were able to establish a hammerlock on the trade because Sal-Rei — "King of the Salt" — was virtually a mountain of salt.

The Portuguese also shipped large numbers of slaves to the Cape Verdes. Ribeira Grande became a major transfer point where the slaves were sold to the slave ships that carried them across the Atlantic.

At one point early in the middle of the 17th century, when Ribeira Grande was at its peak as a slave transfer point, there were thousands of slaves in the city yet only a few hundred Europeans. By the end of the 18th century, the city had grown so much that it was said to be home to 24 churches, chapels, and seminaries.

Long after the U.S. and England outlawed the slave trade and tried to suppress it, the Portuguese and Spanish continued to trade in slaves. Slavery was not abolished in Portugal until 1879, in Brazil until 1883, or in Cuba in 1882. Interestingly, slavery was abolished in the Portuguese colonies in 1838, many years before it was abolished in mainland Portugal. This was probably as a result of a slave uprising in the Cape Verdes in 1835. Whether it was a real rebellion or a violent strike I do not know, but I think is was probably the latter.

Slaves were used in the Cape Verdes but not to the same extent as in the islands of the Eastern Caribbean. A 1771 census shows Fogo with the highest proportion of slaves, at 25 percent of the population. On the other islands the proportion was considerably lower: Santo Antão 15 percent, São Nicolau 10 percent, Brava 5.5 percent.

A lot more Caucasian blood was introduced in the first half of the 19th century as Portugal shipped out large numbers of criminals to the Cape Verdes rather than imprison them in Portugal. Many more males were shipped out than females, and the resulting shortage of women led to extensive intermarriage between Caucasians and Africans, producing a very attractive mixture. Cape Verdeans today come in all colors and shades, and the population breaks down roughly into 10 percent white, 60 percent *mesticoi* (mixed blood) and 30 percent African.

Abolition could have dealt a severe economic blow to the Cape Verdes but, at about the same time the slave trade was dying out, coal-burning steamships began to take the southern route across the Atlantic from Europe to the Americas. The first coaling station was established in Mindelo in 1838. In 1854, 157 ships coaled there; in 1898, 1,504 ships coaled — that's four a day. It was the fourth largest coaling station in the world, after Port Said, Malta, and Singapore. The joint must have been jumping. Ships coaled in Madeira or the Canaries, then topped off in Cape Verdes for the voyage across the Atlantic or to Cape Town.

As well as coal, ships took on water barged from Santo Antão, fruits and vegetables grown on Santo Antão, and meat from animals raised on São Vicente.

Amílcar Cabral, who led the Cape Verde independence movement, was raised in this house on Santiago.

After decades of decay that followed the abandonment of Mindelo as a coaling station for ships, many of the colonial-era buildings have been restored.

An undersea cable terminus was established at Mindelo in 1885, with cables going to Cape Town and, later, across the Atlantic to South America. By 1912, Mindelo had become a major cable terminus. This kept the islands moderately prosperous until after World War I when oil-burning ships began to supersede the coal burners. The coaling business slowed down dramatically during World War II, finally drying up in the late 1940s.

Cape Verde was a Portuguese colony until 1951, when it became a Portuguese overseas province. In the late 1960s, an independence movement spread through all the Portuguese colonies. In Cape Verde, the leader of this movement was Amílcar Cabral. He was assassinated in Guinea-Bissau in 1973, but Cape Verde did gain independence, in association with Guinea-Bissau, in 1975. After a coup in Guinea-Bissau in 1980, Cape Verde separated from it in 1981 to become its own nation, the Republic of Cape Verde.

The first government after independence was communist. To the visitor, it certainly felt like a police state in 1985 and pretty much so in 1989. After an election in 1990, a capitalist government took control, but was replaced 10 years later by the communists. However, they had by this time seen the light of day and said to hell with communism, and stuck to the capitalist route. Cape Verde began to make economic progress.

Another big change occurred with the election in 2001. Since then, Cape Verde has made amazing progress.

Cape Verde Today

Two rival think tanks rate African governments on honesty, free elections, friendliness to business, educational system, and so forth. For the past five years, Cape Verde has been in the top 10 of all African governments.

Another group rates the nations of the world on how free their economies are. Year after year, Hong Kong is number one. Cape Verde has been rated at 77, above many nations in the EU.

The government is trying to move Cape Verde out of the third world. In 2010, it planned to distribute 13,000 computers to students, with the ultimate goal of giving every student access to a computer by 2013.

I'm told that a corporation can be set up in a matter of hours. In one way this is good, as it makes it easy to for someone who wants to invest in the islands to set up. It's bad in that it's all too easy for real-estate developers to set up a company, promote development, and collect deposits on vacation homes that have not been built and in some cases will never be built. In some ways, Cape Verde is like the Virgin Islands in the 1960s, "a sunny place for shady people."

The islands are seeing a revival in their fortunes with the advent of tourism, through yachting and eco-tourism from Germany. The eco-tourists come to walk the hills and dales of the higher Cape Verde islands, such as Brava, Fogo, Santo Antão, and São Nicolāu equipped with the topographical walking maps now available for those islands.

Also, tourist developments are springing up rapidly on Sal, Boavista, Maio, and Santiago. In 2005, Santiago looked like one massive construction site, with cranes everywhere, but in 2009, it appeared that many projects had come to a halt. Direct flights that had been initiated from Dublin in 2006 and London in 2007, presumably to deliver prospective buyers of vacation homes, were no longer operating.

Fishing is also an important money earner for the islands, especially offshore fishing for tuna for export. They fish for tuna in the proper way, with hook and line rather than big nets. Lobsters are also caught, for local consumption and for export, frozen, to Europe. Inshore fishing provides for the local market. A magazine article I read when I was in the Cape Verdes in November 2009 stated that there were 1,300 fishing boats in the Cape Verdes and 4,000 fishermen actively employed in the fishing industry.

Although agriculture is a challenge because of the lack of rain, all of the mountainous islands have extensive terraced fields that suggest it wasn't always so. In all the Atlantic Islands the Portuguese settled — the Azores, Madeira, and Cape Verdes — they terraced the hillsides. In the Azores and Madeira the work was done by free labor, in the Cape Verdes by a combination of free labor and slaves, but they were built so long ago, the true history of how they came to be and for how long they were used is unclear.

The rugged terrain and lack of rainfall make large-scale agriculture uneconomical, and today, agricultural

Terraces like these on a hillside on Santiago are to be found on all the mountainous islands of the Cape Verdes and suggest agriculture was once very productive.

products are grown strictly for local consumption and sold within the Cape Verde Archipelago. The islands depend on imports for much of their food and almost all manufactured goods.

Cape Verde is fortunate to have one of the most stable governments in Africa, and is well positioned to exploit its rich history in the service of tourism. Like the government offices of many island nations, those of Cape Verde operate with varying degrees of efficiency, and while the local officers appear to handle yacht clearances quite efficiently, getting information from other departments can be a trial.

It seems to me the Cape Verdes are getting into the tourist business by accident rather than by any effort on the part of a department of tourism, if there even is one. I have yet to find a website or phone number for a department of tourism. Such an office existed at one time because I have maps published (admittedly in 1993) by the Instituto Naçional de Turismo de Cabo Verde.

The staff of the U.S. office of Transportes Aéreos de Cabo Verde, or Cape Verde Airlines (TACV), felt, in the light of my background and the fact I was writing this guide to the Cape Verdes, which will certainly encourage tourism to the islands, that the ministry of tourism should help out. They gave me the e-mail address of the Minister of Tourism. My e-mails went unanswered.

I sent e-mails to the Hydrographic Office explaining what I was doing and asking for information on updates being made to nautical charts. These too went unanswered.

I also e-mailed the U.S. Embassy in Cape Verde with a similar result.

Foreign Aid Fiascos

Because of the archipelago's strategic position, a sort of crossroads in the North Atlantic, many nations have tried to obtain a foothold in Cape Verde through aid programs. The Cape Verde government has received aid from the United States, Belgium, Iceland, Britain, the Soviet Union, France, Holland, Norway, Germany, Austria, and even China, sometimes, it would appear from the results, whether it was wanted or not. Currently, numerous projects are under way aided by grants from the E.U.

In years gone by, I thought that England, Canada, and the U.S. took aside their bad engineers, those they didn't want fouling up their own infrastructure projects, and sent them as advisors to the Eastern Caribbean. Many crazy projects in the Eastern Caribbean are not a result of the local engineering but, rather, the result of misdirected aid programs. In the course of my five trips through the Cape Verde Islands, I have come to the conclusion that the Cape Verdeans are suffering from the same problem: aid programs funded by foreign countries and designed by engineers not wanted in their home countries.

Two prime example are the airports in Brava and Santo Antão. In Brava, Germany spent a veritable fortune carving an airfield out of the hillside on the leeward side of the island. The airfield was completed, and everything set up. Then the planes tried to use it. After 10 landings, all the pilots in the Cape Verdean airline refused to fly in or out of the airport. The mountain to the east of the airport created such erratic wind eddies that it was just too dangerous to try to use it. The airport now sits abandoned.

Unfortunately, a local who figured there was going to be a lot of tourism and air passengers, built a very nice small hotel in Fajá de Agua, the village near the airport. This also now sits totally unused. There are no planes, so no customers.

In Santo Antão, a German engineering company did a massive landfill operation in the northeast corner of the island to create a runway with its axis running northwest to southeast. This location is fully exposed to the winter trades that will blow at 20 kts and more day after day. Because the prevailing wind direction is northeast, the runway would always have a crosswind, much of the time at 90 degrees. It was a case of the pilot being good or dead!

In August 1999, a flight from São Vicente, unable to land because of limited visibility, turned back to São Vicente and crashed into a mountainside, killing all 18 aboard. The runway has not been used since.

In Maio, as the result of some aid program or another, a 900-foot dock has been built. This seems rather over the top, as the freighter that uses the dock is only about 200 feet long. By the time cruise lines begin to send big cruise ships to Maio, the dock will have fallen apart. It's already beginning to crumble.

In the 1980s, the government of Iceland sent a steel trawler to bolster the fishing fleet. Unfortunately it was useless to the Cape Verdeans as it wasn't suited to the kind of fishing that actually catches fish in those waters and it was too expensive and complicated to maintain.

However, some aid money is well directed and well spent. The Chinese built a dam in Santiago creating a lake a full half kilometer long. If more dams were built in the ravines throughout the islands, it might go a long way to easing the water shortage and increasing their agricultural production.

Norway sent rugged-looking ferryboats, that seem to still run fairly regularly despite their age, and a number of motor fishing boats that are used to transport patients from remote coastal settlements to medical facilities.

Cape Verdeans Abroad

The Cape Verdean people have close ties to America. Records exist of American ships stopping at the Cape Verdes and picking up crew as early as 1740. Whaling ships came out from New Bedford to hunt for whales in the waters around the Cape Verdes. Other ships came to pick up fresh supplies and fill out their crews before heading to the Pacific and South Atlantic whaling grounds. So many men from Brava went to sea that in 1920 there were 188 women and only 100 men on Brava!

Ties between New England and the Cape Verdes were strong enough that, during the 1853-1855 famine caused by failure of the rainy season, the Massachusetts legislature voted money to buy wheat and charter ships to take relief supplies to the Cape Verdes.

Enough Cape Verdeans signed on as crew on whaling ships it was inevitable that some would work their way up from seaman, to leading seaman, to bosun, and finally to mate. In the last days of U.S. commercial whaling under sail, a fair number of them became captains. Later, they captained whalers that had been converted to passenger freighters and plied between the Cape Verdes and New Bedford, Massachusetts.

As whaling died out, a whaling ship could be bought for a song, and many of them were purchased and put into the Cape Verdean Packet Trade which started about 1892. Whalers were built for seaworthiness and carrying capacity, not for speed. The average trip took 35 days from the Cape Verdes to the States; 45 days back to the Cape Verdes.

This packet trade carried on until the middle 1930s, when a change in U.S. immigration law made it difficult for Cape Verdeans to immigrate to the States, so they started going to Canada and Northern Europe.

The *Ernestina*, the last of the Cape Verdean packets and originally built as a fishing schooner, has been restored and is on exhibit in New Bedford, Massachusetts.

Cape Verdeans who settled in New England also provided cheap labor for the Cape Cod cranberry bogs, fishing boats, and shipyards. There are now about 100,000 Cape Verdeans in the Boston area alone. The money they send back to relatives is a considerable chunk of the Cape Verde economy.

Fishing and Fishing Boats in the Cape Verdes

When *Iolaire* arrived in the Cape Verdes in November 1985, our landfall was Palmeira, Ilha do Sal. One boat was anchored there, sailed by a singlehander from Iceland named Toby who pointed us in the right direction to buy a sack of lobsters at what we thought was an incredibly cheap price.

We invited him on board for our lobster feast. The crew was busily eating only the lobster tails and ignoring the feelers where the best meat is found. In a clawed lobster, the meat in the claws is so far superior to the meat in the tail that, in the days when Diamond Jim Brady and Lillian Russell had their feasts at Delmonico's, lobsters were brought out, the claws were cracked and their meat eaten, but the tails were sent back to the kitchen to be used in lobster thermidor.

When chartering *Iolaire* in the old days, we would have a lobster feast whenever we were in the Tobago Cays. The charter party would eat all the meat from the tails and Trich and I would grab all the feelers, crack them open with pliers and gorge ourselves on their meat.

I was doing that in Palmeira, but Toby said, "No, that is too much work." He was picking the feelers up and eating them shell and all like sticks of candy! All I could think of was the next morning, when he went to the head: What were those shells like coming out the other side?

It brought to mind the football song of Georgia Tech:

We're the rambling wrecks of Georgia Tech
We drink our whiskey clear,
We wipe our ass with broken glass . . . .

Over dinner, we gleaned from Toby a tremendous amount of information about the Cape Verdes.

It seemed Toby was supporting himself by writing about the Cape Verdes for the leading Icelandic newspaper. He said he was making himself very unpopular in some circles in Iceland as he was pointing out in print that the aid money Iceland was sending to Cape Verde was being wasted. They had sent down a typical steel Icelandic trawler, which was totally useless in the Cape Verdes as, in the state the economy was in at the time, the Cape Verdeans could never afford to maintain a steel trawler and all its equipment. More important, by trawling in the Cape Verdes in the same way they did in Iceland they were catching no fish.

The Cape Verdeans were mainly hand lining from 16- to 24-foot boats launched from the beach plus a few tuna clippers. They fished for tuna using the traditional method employed for many years by the tuna clippers from San Diego that fished the Galapagos. A gang of men lined the sides of the tuna clipper fishing with bamboo poles. The lines were of a fixed length, with barbless hooks. It was one man to a pole for medium tuna, two men with two poles to one line for larger tuna, and occasionally, if they ran into a school of really large tuna, three men, three poles, one line.

Nets are not used in Cape Verde except for small fish. The only places I saw nets spread out to dry were in Porto Mosquito and Porto Rincão, on Santiago. The nets had very small mesh. They shoot the net from the boat outside the school of fish, take lines from each end of the net ashore, and haul in. They catch small fish, about 6 inches long, called cicharo and babrada.

In 1985, the only place we actually observed boats out fishing was in Mindelo, where in the afternoon we would occasionally see a boat beating to windward back into the harbor under lateen rig. The boats were incredibly crude. I reflected at the time that they must be good seamen as, if they lost a mast or broke their flimsy oars made up of two or more short pieces of wood scarfed together with nails and wire, their next stop would be the islands of the Caribbean 2,100 miles to leeward.

In 1985, and again in 1989, we saw no outboards.

In 2005, on *Sincerity*, we were under power, heading from the southwest tip of São Nicolau heading for Tarrafal, when we came up on a lateen-rigged fishing boat, about 25 feet long. In 15 to 18 knots of wind in smooth water, the fishing boat was very close reaching and making at least 5 and probably 6 knots — going like hell. We overtook her very slowly.

Cape Verde in a Capsule

We arrived at Tarrafal before she did and watched her as she made her final approach to the harbor. The lateen sail was dropped, an outboard clamped on the stern, and she proceeded into the harbor under outboard.

In 2002, again in 2005, and especially in 2009, I had a chance to visit many of the small harbors and take a good look at the Cape Verdean fishing boats that launch from the beach. These beach boats appear to be all either strictly for rowing, or for rowing but with an auxiliary outboard that is used only to get back into the harbor. The outboards all appear to be 8-horsepower Hondas, but they are few and far between.

In all my explorations in 2002, 2005, and 2009, I only saw one boat on the beach that had a sail. It was a lateen rig, with the spar slightly longer than the boat.

In general, the boats were well shaped, well built, and fairly well maintained, but nothing like the well kept Azorean fishing boats, most of which are finished almost like yachts.

The Cape Verdean boats have a relatively narrow beam, about 4.5 feet, a nice tucked-up stern with a heart-shaped transom, a pleasing but not pronounced sheer, and, except in two ports on the west coast of Santiago, all had wall-sided bow sections with little or no flare. However, in Porto Mosquito and in Porto Rincão, the boats not only had much more sheer but they had very distinctive flaring bows. I maintain that the flaring bows are to make it easier to launch through the surf, and Gerry Dom agrees.

The oars on the Cape Verdean beach boats are interesting. The most common oar is 12 to 14 feet long, has a long normal blade, and the shaft is two pieces of wood scarfed together. The scarf joint is held together by seizing wire tied off to a couple of nails. This is the same system I encountered among the local fishing boats when I first arrived in the Caribbean in 1956. The blades are fairly narrow as, both in the West Indies and in the Cape Verdes, feathering the oar is unknown. The narrow blade facilitates rowing to windward without feathering the oar.

However, in Porto Rincão and Porto Mosquito, the oars were a full 16 to 18 feet long and made up of three pieces. The third piece is a really big blade. It's a flat piece of wood, sometimes plywood, shaped in area like the blade you would see on the oar of a racing shell. The blade looked like a giant Ping-Pong paddle.

Gerry Dom says that, because it is normally calm in the lee of the islands, the fishermen are not rowing into the wind, so a narrow blade is not needed.

In Fogo, I was amazed to see that the oars, though a full 14 to 16 feet long, were made from a single piece of wood. The only ones I saw that were two pieces of wood scarfed together were ones that obviously had been broken and rather than being discarded had been scarfed.

In the case of most boats, the oars were sweeps — one man one oar. The exception was in Porto dos Ferreiros, on the southwest corner of Brava. This harbor is so superbly sheltered there is no surf. The boats were smaller than I have seen in other harbors of the Cape Verdes. They were about 16 feet long and set up to be rowed by a man pulling two oars "Portuguese style," i.e. with crossed hands. This technique gives more power as the distance from the loom to the oarlock is greater than it is when the arms are not crossed. All the fishing boats in Porto dos Ferreiros had outboards, but they were obviously used only to get home. All the boats went out to sea and fished under oar.

Tuna is, or was, widely caught throughout the Cape Verdes as is witnessed by the fact that there were tuna canning factories in Carrical on São Nicolau, Puerto Inglez on Maio, Porto Rincão on Santiago, and Tarrafal de Monte Trigo on Santo Antão. Most of these canneries have been closed down and converted to factories that produce ice for the fishermen. This allows the fishermen to ice their fish and sell it fresh even if it takes a day or so to get it to market. The larger fishing boats that have inboard engines will take on board enough ice to last three days.

Tuna are in the Cape Verdes all year, but are most prevalent from September to the end of the year. The locals fish for them with hand lines, with an interesting variation at Porto Mosquito and Porto Rincão. It seems they frequently catch tuna as big as 100 kilograms, which is too much fish to boat alive and kicking in their comparatively small boats. Thus, when they have hooked a big tuna and hauled it either alongside or close aboard, they harpoon it.

The harpoon consists of a wooden shaft about 1.5 inches in diameter and 8 feet long to which is attached a 3/8-inch-diameter iron rod about 6 feet long. Four feet or so of the rod extends beyond the end of the wooden shaft. A dart fits over the end of the shaft. The dart has an eye in it to which is attached a 4-foot wire leader connected to about 200 feet of 3-strand line. The harpoon is thrown or stabbed, depending on how close they can work the fish, and when the tuna has been darted, the fishermen let it tow the boat around and wear itself out in the same fashion as the old-time whalers did (and the Bequia whalers still do). Once worn out, the tuna is hauled alongside the fishing boat and heaved on board. It all sounds like something out of Hemingway's *The Old Man and the Sea.*

I encountered two boatbuilders in the Cape Verdes. In Praia, Santiago, about 300 yards south of the Harbor Police office, which is at the head of the two docks on the western side of the harbor, you will find a boatbuilder in a small shop. He has been building boats for about a half century and claims the numbers are in the thousands! His shop is a bit of a mess, with holes in the galvanized roof (but it seldom rains) and chickens running to and fro.

He and his two apprentices had three boats in frame. The apprentices were about to commence planking up one boat. The construction looked good. They were using natural crook frames, which were not yet painted so I was able to examine them closely. I found the grain followed the curve of the frame exceptionally well, with little cross grain.

Amazingly, the frames were all cut out by hand with an H-frame saw. The tension on the blade was set up by a Spanish windlass. There was a big stack of timber sliced to the thickness of the siding of the frames for the boats that he was building. The timber was carefully stacked so it was air drying.

The stem and sternpost were natural crooks, as were the floor timbers, one at each frame tying the frames together really well. The planking was nailed in place with long thin galvanized nails, without pre-drilling.

In Porto Rincão, we found another boat in frame, being built out in the open. The builder said he laid out his frames on his wood and took the wood to Assomada, Santiago's second city, where there was a band saw. He cut the frames there and brought them back to Porto Rincão to install them. That must have been a rather tedious procedure as Assomada is a good half-hour drive from Porto Rincão.

If an aid program would really like to help the Cape Verdean fishing economy, it should give the boatbuilders heavy-duty battery-powered sabre/jig saws with a number of spare batteries, some buckets full of bronze anchor-fast nails, plus a 20-foot container load of Douglas-fir planks. Twenty-foot-long 3 x 8s would make really good oars. That would be aid money well spent.

In a number of anchorages I've seen lying at anchor a few fishing boats with cabins. They are wooden, ranging in size from 30 to 40 feet, and inboard powered. Also, I spotted in various places the odd fiberglass inboard-powered boats about 25 to 30 feet long, all similar in appearance. These apparently came from Norway as part of an aid program. They are fiberglass replicas of the standard Scandinavian-style inshore fishing boat, and are probably powered by a simple hand-start diesel. I saw one close up in Carrical, São Nicolau, and they look ideal for any harbor where the boats can be left afloat.

Some of these boats go fairly far afield from Santiago to Boavista, well supplied with ice, a handheld GPS for navigation but no safety equipment of any kind — sort of the same situation as exists in the Caribbean today.

Sport fishermen come to the Cape Verdes after blue marlin and sailfish, which are in the area from August to the end of the year.

Humpback whales arrive in the Cape Verdes in February and and depart in May to return to their feeding grounds off Norway.

According to published figures I saw while I was in the Cape Verdes, there are over 1,000 fishing boats crewed by slightly over 4,000 fishermen. Obviously, fresh fish is readily available on all the islands.

After trying meat and chicken, I decided that, in restaurants in the Cape Verdes, one does best to stick to fish.

Cape Verde in a Capsule

Fishing boats are still built in the traditional way in Praia, Santiago.

A fisherman in Porto Rincão, Santiago, demonstrates the technique used to harpoon a tuna after it has been brought alongside the boat.

Chapter 3
Infrastructure in the Cape Verde Islands

Marine infrastructure

Until recently, any kind of resources for servicing yachts were virtually nonexistent in the Cape Verdes. Kai Brosmann, a young German, began operating a small fleet of bareboats in Mindelo, São Vicente in 1998, and the fact that he was able to maintain the boats at all is a tribute to his skill at doing a lot with nothing. He certainly has a first class degree as MBLU (master of the bastard lash-up). I began my apprenticeship toward earning this degree while serving on the submarine USS *Sea Leopard* during the Korean war, and completed it maintaining *Iolaire* in the Caribbean in the late 1950s and early 1960s, and I have great respect for my fellow graduates.

With Kai pushing, things in the Cape Verdes slowly changed. In January 2003, he and his partner, Lutz Meyer-Scheel, who contributed the lion's share of the financing, installed a 50-meter floating dock for a small marina, complete with electricity, water, showers, and toilets. This did not prove of much advantage to visiting yachtsmen as the Cape Verdes have become a popular sport-fishing venue. There were 10 slips in the marina. Eight of them were permanently taken up by sport fishermen, the other two were occupied by boats while Kai worked on them, repairing gear so that they could continue on across the Atlantic.

Kai Brosmann spent 12 years in the German navy as an electronics specialist, he has been a sailor all his life and is typically German. He is very efficient, and knows how to get things done.

Lutz Meyer-Scheel, was in the German merchant marine for 11 years and followed that with a successful career in IT and communications. When he left that professional world, he wanted to do something connected with recreational boating. He looked at several opportunities around the world where he might invest and settled on the Cape Verdes as a location with great potential but little existing infrastructure.

Marina Mindelo

Photo by Lutz Meyer-Scheel

Infrastructure in The Cape Verde Islands

In my 1986 *Transatlantic Crossing Guide* (which was also a guide to the Atlantic Islands), I pointed out that if the derelict dock in Mindelo harbor was rebuilt it would make a perfect marina and bring much needed money into the economy. It only took 20 years for something to happen. In late 2007, Kai and Lutz opened up the first stage of a 120 berth marina which is now capable of taking boats up to megayacht size stern-to.

Marina Mindelo was officially opened in a big ceremony in June, 2008, and while other infrastructure to support visiting yachts and their crews is still minimal, it will no doubt expand in years to come as Kai reports that in 2008-2009 more than 1,000 yachts visited Mindelo (although I think that is a rather optimistic estimate).

Cape Verdeans are good apprentices too. From the earliest days, Kai has hired and trained Cape Verdeans to support his bareboat fleet and to work for his yacht maintenance company, boatCV. They have a good work ethic and are eager to learn and, like people in many Third World areas where resources are limited, they are wonderful at improvisation. They are so good Kai says, that given two to two and half weeks, there is no piece of yachting equipment that cannot be repaired in Mindelo. He says that the electricians he has trained solder connections faster and better than he has ever been able to.

For rigging, he can swage on wire up to 12mm; above that he uses either STA-LOK or Norseman fittings. After 50 plus years in the Caribbean and 47 years in the marine insurance business, I can say without fear of contradiction that the life expectancy of a swaged fitting is not particularly long. I recommend anyone replacing rigging on a boat that will be staying in the tropics to spend the extra money and install Norseman or STA-LOK mechanical fittings. I've heard high praise for Hi-MOD fittings, too, but until they have been around for 30 years I cannot give them my absolute recommendation (I've been on the yachting scene for 68 years so, for me, the "test of time" is a long yardstick.)

For sail repair, he has three machines, one for light work, another for medium work, and a heavy-duty machine that can sew through anything.

He tells the story of repairing a sail for a megayacht. The sail was so big that it took eight men to feed it through the machine: three pushing the sail, three pulling it, and two men running the machine. At that point one wonders if they should not have gone back to old-fashioned hand sewing, making lead holes for the thread with a battery powered drill with a very small bit.

Franklin of A and F sails in Antigua earned the undying love of the skipper of the 110-foot ketch *Sojana*. They were getting ready to race when they blew the clew out of the headsail. They thought that was the end of the day's racing but Franklin asked for a battery powered drill with a small bit and a length of Dyneema. He set a couple of the crew to work unraveling the Dyneema while he drilled a series of holes. He then took the strands of Dyneema, threaded them onto a big sail needle, and proceeded to re-sew and rebuild the clew. In 45 minutes or an hour, he had the clew rebuilt. They hoisted the sail and raced. The clew looked a little bit rough but it held. This is a story that all sailors should remember, and so should Kai's boys next time a really big sail comes in for repair.

There are about 10 or 15 sport fishermen based in the marina, so Kai's crew is getting plenty of practice working on generators and engines.

Kai points out that any parts they don't have in stock, they can have shipped in from England, Spain, Portugal, or the States as regular flights come to the international airport in Ilha do Sal from the far corners of the world. By the time you read this, the airport in Mindelo will also be operational as an international airport.

When getting parts shipped into the Cape Verdes, do not rely on courier-service promises of 48- or 72-hour delivery. As in the Azores, almost all courier packages are routed through Lisbon. Goodness knows exactly what happens in Lisbon, but there is often a hold-up. If your courier package arrives within 10 days, consider it a victory. If a package comes direct from the States, the U.K., or Germany you may have it in three or four days.

Kai has access to the excellent machine shop in the commercial shipyard that the Dutch set up in the 1980s that is equipped to work on both steel and aluminum boats. This yard is capable of welding in stainless steel and aluminum and can haul large vessels up to megayacht size. The railway is the Dutch type on which boats are hauled and launched sidewise rather than lengthwise. Because of the size of the platform and the cost of hauling, it doesn't work very well for boats under 80 or 90 feet.

Medium sized boats, up to about 20 tons and about 7 feet of draft, can be hauled on the old-fashioned railway. This is more than a bit of an operation, and reminiscent of hauling in the Caribbean in the 1950s and early 1960s, but it can be done. The yard looks like something out of the last years of the 19th century.

Because this railway has no side track and hauls local commercial boats, there could be a long wait. Between holidays and another boat being already on the railway, a friend of mine had to wait three weeks for an emergency haul.

John Eyre, the electronics genius behind Cay Electronics in Antigua, with his wife, Ann, on *Swanhilde* (which *Iolaire* raced against in Cowes in the 2005 British Classic Yacht Club Regatta) hauled in Mindelo in 1969. The yard hauled *Swanhilde* on a huge cradle winch that was powered by an ancient steam engine and boiler dating back to the mid-19th century. Amazingly, it is still operational, although the boiler has since died and the winch is now powered by a steam engine running on compressed air! This is the same setup as the ancient steam winch for the big cradle in St. George, Bermuda. In both cases the steam boiler died and was too expensive to replace.

John and Ann had some stories to tell as the Cape Verdes at that time were in the depths of depression. There was plenty of coal in Mindelo and the labor to load the coal, but there were no coal-burning ships to load. It had not rained for seven years, and there were no distillation units in the islands, so water had to be barged from Santo Antão to São Vicente.

Outside Mindelo, marine infrastructure of any kind is practically nonexistent. You might find an outboard mechanic and a few spares for an 8-horsepower Honda, but little else. Marinas have been proposed and promised on some of the other islands, but none has progressed beyond the billboard stage.

Chartering

Kai Brosmann moved to Mindelo in 1999 to start a bareboat fleet. He started small with six boats and the fleet today has both monohulls and catamarans. He can also arrange captained charters. Contact him through boatCV (www.boatcv.com).

Sailing in the Cape Verdes is for the adventurous who want to get off the beaten track, visit uncrowded anchorages, and explore an environment ashore that is completely different from what they are accustomed to.

No one should think of bareboat chartering unless they are good sailors, have cruised on their own boats, and are not afraid to beat to windward under shortened sail in 30 knots of wind.

Resources
Kai Brosmann, boatCV: www.boatcv.com
Marina Mindelo: www.marinamindelo.com
Imray-Iolaire chart E4

Formalities
Port Captain, Customs, and Immigration

When arriving in the Cape Verde Islands from foreign waters you *must* enter at one of the three main entry ports. These are Palmeira on Ilha do Sal, Mindelo on São Vicente, and Praia on Santiago. Failure to do so can result in a fat fine as the Cape Verdes are having problems with boats smuggling people in from the even poorer African nations.

Upon arrival at your first port, you must see Cape Verde Immigration and the harbor police. It is not necessary to see customs unless you are discharging dutiable items ashore or importing gear for the boat.

The best procedure is, immediately upon arrival, to send the captain with the passports and ship's papers around to the harbor police.

In Palmeria, offices of both authorities are near the dinghy-landing dock.

In Mindelo, the harbor police and immigration have their offices in the Marina Mindelo.

In Praia, the office of the harbor police is at the head of the rebuilt dock on the western side of the harbor. Immigration, unfortunately, is on the main dock on the other side of the harbor.

At the present time, it is necessary to clear in and out with the harbor police when sailing from island to island. You only need to see immigration again to obtain outward clearance to an island in the Caribbean, or wherever your next destination may be.

Visas

According to the website of the U.S. State Department, a passport and visa are required for entry into the Republic of Cape Verde. However, when I flew there in November of 2009, I had no visa, I was not asked to present one, and I was charged no fee by Cape Verde Immigration. Visas have never been required for those arriving by boat.

In the past, a visa was required but was automatically granted after I filled out some papers at the airport and paid a fee. What it amounted to was a landing fee for tourists. Exactly when it was scrapped I have no idea.

Resources

Government of the Republic of Cape Verde: www.governo.cv

Cape Verde Embassy to the United States: 3415 Massachusetts Avenue, NW, Washington DC 20007; 202-965-6820

Cape Verde Consulate in Boston: 535 Boylston Street, Boston MA 02116; 617-353-0014

U.S. State Department, Cape Verde pages: www.state.gov/r/pa/ei/bgn/2835.htm

The U.S. Embassy to Cape Verde: Rua Abílio Macedo, 6, Praia; C.P.201; tel. (238) 260 8900; fax 2611 355; http://praia.usembassy.gov

Ground Transportation

Most Cape Verdeans get around by *aluguer*, the local version of the collective taxi found in many developing countries. Aluguers run to a rough schedule and the vehicles vary from pickup trucks with lids and wooden benches (for which you are advised to bring a cushion) to VW buses, which are more comfortable but not as well ventilated. You may be sharing the aluguer with live chickens, occasionally a goat, and passengers loaded with parcels. This form of transportation is ridiculously cheap and a great way to see the islands and meet the people.

Taxis range from pickup trucks with lids, to VW buses, to modern taxis, these last found at airports. At taxi ranks, try to find a driver who speaks your language, but give him a quiz first as some claim they can speak the language when they only know five or 10 words.

In some places, you'll find big modern buses. These are usually organized by tour companies but, while they are comfortable and often air-conditioned, they are not as picturesque as the aluguers or as much fun.

Rental cars are available on all the islands. On Sal, Boavista, Maio, and São Vincente a normal car will get you around. On São Nicolau, Santo Antão,

Most of the permanent roads on the islands are surfaced with stone blocks, like this one on São Vicente. The view is over Mindelo looking toward Santo Antão.

Santiago, Fogo, and Brava you need a 4 x 4 to handle the roads. Do not rent a car on these islands unless you are a good bush driver and brave. You are better off with a taxi and a driver who speaks your language. The pickup with the lid is the best taxi as it's easier to hop in and out of when you want to take pictures.

Air Transportation

For many years, a large source of income for Cape Verde was landing fees Russia paid for the use of the airport on Ilha do Sal when it was flying troops and supplies to Angola. South African Airways also used Sal as a layover on flights to and from Cape Town. Sal has a wonderful long runway. It was originally built by the Italians in anticipation of flights from Sal to South America. The Portuguese finished it in the early 1940s. Exactly when and why it was extended to its present length is a bit of a mystery. According to one story, the extension was built by the Americans in anticipation of possible space shuttle emergency requirements.

Today, the terminal at the Sal airport is more than adequate, and it provides free WiFi which is nice to have while you sit and wait for your delayed flight to take off. It also allows townspeople and transient sailors to take care of their business in an air-conditioned building with a bar and restaurant at hand.

Sal receives scheduled and charter flights from various European cities plus weekly flights from Boston. South African Airways flights to and from Europe still stop here. Schedules change frequently, so check the Internet for current information.

For years, international flights only landed at Sal, but several of the airports on other islands have been expanded. Santiago's airport, outside Praia, has been completely rebuilt and is fully certified to handle international flights. It has an interesting new terminal. Its main lobby is covered with a perfectly fitted tent made of some type of white sailcloth. From the fit, and the way in which the corners and stress points where it rests on the supporting pillars are reinforced, it was obviously made by a sailmaker. I wonder who that was. A gap between the edge of the canvas roof and the wall allows the wind to blow through, creating a venturi effect. The main lobby is comfortably cool without having to be air-conditioned.

A similar design would have worked well on the new airport on Beef Island in Tortola, in the British Virgin Islands.

The runway on São Vincente has been extended to accept international flights and the word in November 2009 was that certification was expected in the near future. However, the terminal is nowhere near big enough to handle the number of passengers a really large aircraft would bring.

Boavista also has an international airport but the terminal again is much too small. In its first year, the airport handled 5,000 passengers. The airport authority thought the number of passengers would double in the second year of operation. That turned out to be a bad guess: In its second year of operation, the airport handled 77,000 passengers.

Maio, São Nicolau, and Fogo only handle inter-island flights. Their terminals are miniscule but everyone is friendly and cold beer is available at one euro per bottle.

In all three airports, the fire truck that is supposed to stand by whenever a plane lands was noticeable by its absence. Visiting them reminded me of flying into Grenada in the old days, at Pearls airport except that there the fire truck was always in attendance. It was an ancient American LaFrance, started by hand. It could have been sold in the States as an antique for enough money to buy a modern fire engine. Every bit of brass on the vehicle and the end fittings on the hoses were beautifully polished, but the ancient hoses were useless because rats had eaten through them.

I was pleased to discover that, unlike LIAT in the West Indies, the local Cape Verde airline, TACV, seems to keep track of baggage, even if its baggage-handling procedures and lack of equipment mean that, on inter-island flights the wait for baggage is a long one. On international flights, make that a very long wait. When flying to and from the islands, and flying inter-island, make sure you have a good supply of reading material.

Finally, the most wonderful feature of flying inter-island is the fact that there is *no security check at all*. I think it must be 30 years or more since I last boarded a plane without having to go through a security check.

Infrastructure in The Cape Verde Islands

Be forewarned if flying to the Cape Verdes from Boston. TACV, has an office in Quincy, Massachusetts. In October 2009, I found it impossible to book a flight through the company's website. My efforts to obtain a flight to the Cape Verdes were further complicated by the fact that TACV does not return calls when you leave messages on their answering service, nor does it answer e-mails.

At one point, I did get through by telephone. When I asked to talk to the manager, I was told he worked from home, and was given his phone number and e-mail address. Despite my calling at least 10 times, getting his phone message, and leaving a call-back number, he never called back. I sent at least five e-mails and received no reply.

I finally got in a car and made two four-hour round trips from Jamestown, Rhode Island, to Quincy just to obtain my ticket. I also had to make a side trip to TACV's bank in Weymouth, Massachusetts, because the airline only accepts payment by American Express card or by bank draft. All in all, I shot two full days buying the tickets. On the positive side, by buying your inter-island flights before you arrive in the islands, you save 50 percent of the ticket price.

Resources
Cape Verde Airlines (TACV): www.flytacv.com

Inter-Island Ferries

The inter-island ferry schedules are also a movable feast. From November until late May, the Cape Verdes are subject to the North Atlantic groundswell. Frequently, the inter-island freighter cannot stop at Fogo because the groundswell makes it impossible to lie alongside the dock at Cavaleiros. This knocks the schedule into a cocked hat.

The same happens at Sal-Rei on Boavista, where the ferry sometimes cannot visit for days on end.

Further, ferry operations come and go. In Mindelo in November 2009, there was one Russian hydrofoil washed up on the beach on the western side of the harbor; another had been hauled out in the big shipyard for years. Three high-speed ferries were moored in the middle of the harbor. Kai Brosmann said they had not been operational for three or four years.

The most reliable ferry service seems to be the one that runs between Mindelo, on São Vicente, and Porto Novo, on Santo Antão.

In Mindelo, I was told the only way to reach Brava was by the combination passenger/freight vessel whose schedule as mentioned above was very erratic. I was also told that the only way to get to Fogo was by air.

The first day I was in Fogo, as I sat in a nice bar/restaurant having a mid-morning beer, what did I see but a Russian hydrofoil departing the island heading south and a large fishing boat heading west.

Subsequent inquiries with Zebra travel in the Colonial B&B (see page 128) revealed that there was daily service between Fogo and Praia, Santiago, via the Ukraine-designed and built hydrofoil — if it is running. These vessels have a reputation for being hard to maintain. It takes two crews keep them running reliably: one to run the boat during the day and another that includes a couple of good mechanics to overhaul the engines and mechanical gear at night. There is also daily service between Fogo and Brava. Zebra Travel calls the boat a sport fisherman, but the photo on the bela-vista website (see below) shows a rugged steel trawler that looks as though it could go on forever.

The misinformation I got probably has something to do with the fact that, as in New Zealand, the residents of the northern and southern islands have little to do with or anything good to say about each other. The lesson is to check independently.

Resources
One of the more reliable sources of information on ferries (and other general Cape Verde activities for that matter) is bela-vista. It's part of the same German group that produces the walking maps and seems to keep on top of what's going on: www.bela-vista.net.

Provisioning and Stores
Food Supplies

The variety and availability of provisions in the Cape Verdes has improved dramatically over the past 10 years. It is not up to the standard of the Canary Islands but it is adequate. In Mindelo, São Vicente, there are three small supermarkets on the waterfront and two much larger ones on the outskirts of town. By visiting all of them, you should be able to adequately stock your boat for the transatlantic passage. Since the stores are scattered around town and none of the streets are signed, I strongly urge you hire a "gopher" to serve as a guide.

The magnificent central market in Mindelo has been restored, and while other markets in the Atlantic Basin have a better selection of produce, in none of them will you buy it in more beautiful surroundings. Go early to get the best produce.

Eggs are readily available, but bring your own boxes. You'll also find lobsters, but they are not as widely available or as cheap as they were in the past, although the price is still reasonable compared to European prices.

Right next to the main market in Mindelo is a butcher's shop which is now in the hands of the second generation of the family that owns it. The butcher speaks English, Portuguese, and a couple of other languages. He will happily cut meat to your specifications and vacuum pack and freeze it solid for you to pick up just before your departure.

In Santiago, the stocking situation is easier than Mindelo at the two large, real supermarkets in Praia that have just about everything you need. Meat of all kinds is available, from beef and lamb imported from Argentina, to local beef, and pork with all the parts of the pig — trotters, ears, snouts — that you don't often see in America north of the Mason Dixon Line.

There is a good supply of fresh fruit and vegetables available in the main market and also along the roadside.

Fogo produces wine, and, according to some, the best coffee anywhere.

Water

In Mindelo, water is available at berthside in Marina Mindelo. You can also collect it in jerry cans when you pay the fee for use of the dinghy dock. Large yachts that might have difficulty maneuvering alongside the fuel dock can pick it up at the main commercial pier.

In Boavista, you can take on water alongside the dock at Sal-Rei but you have to arrange for the truck to deliver it. You buy it by the ton (about 250 U.S. gallons), and in 2009, the price per ton was €15.

In Praia, Santiago, water is available alongside via a hose.

Everywhere else it is strictly a case of carrying it in jerry cans from whatever source you can find.

Fuel

For diesel fuel, the situation is essentially the same as for water. It's available at the fuel dock in Marina Mindelo and large yachts can go alongside the commercial pier and have it delivered by tanker truck.

In Praia, if the floating dock has been repaired, you can pick up fuel alongside. Elsewhere, you have to fetch it in jerry cans from a gas station.

Ice

Ice isn't easy but in many places you can buy or beg slush ice from the fishermen, then leave it overnight in their deep freeze. When we were in Santiago in 1985, the USAID officer, Tom Ball, told us that ice was so scarce that when you were invited to a cocktail party you were not asked to bring your own bottle but your own ice!

In the summer of 2005, while we were celebrating *Iolaire*'s 100th and my 75th birthday in England, we had a problem: Both our refrigeration units died of old age. Each unit chilled a box, and because both boxes were originally built to each hold 100 pounds of ice in the tropics, they are well insulated with four inches of urethane foam on all sides including the tops. So, it was back to the ice.

At first I was buying cube ice and keeping a cool box. It subsisted well on one 2-kilogram bag of cubes a day. However, when I was in Cowes, I got smart. I bought two 2-kilogram bags of ice and dumped them into a plastic bucket, then managed to persuade the Somerfield supermarket to fill the bucket with water and put it in the deep freeze overnight. Hey presto! I had about 8 kilos of good block ice, which lasted a week.

This system will work anywhere in the world.

I also discovered that, because the boxes are so well insulated, if I put 20 pounds of shaved ice in each box to cool the boxes down, then the next day filled them with shaved ice, the shaved ice froze itself into a solid block. We used this system in the summer of 2008, mostly topping off with shaved ice for free, sometimes paying for it (but it was cheap), and sometimes buying cubes from the supermarket. Our total cost for ice for nine weeks of cruising was £15.

Cooking gas

LPG bottles can readily be filled at the bottling plants at Mindelo or at Praia. In both ports it is a short taxi ride from the anchorage to the plant. You may find they fill your bottles with butane rather than propane, but both will work in your stove without your having to make any changes. British boats should bring or make up an adaptor. American and European bottles (and in fact the entire world's) have the same thread but the British bottles are different. They will need an adaptor that's a length of high-pressure hose with a British fitting on one end and the international fitting on the other end. The international fitting can be purchased anywhere in the world except in the U.K.

Communications

For phone calls you can use your mobile as the coverage is very good. But, as is to be expected, on the high islands you will run into dead spots.

For long phone calls, go to an Internet café and get on Skype.

Fax machines are hard to find and the post office seems to be the best place to track one down.

Forget about using the mail system. I sent an important envelope from Tarrafal, São Nicolau, by registered mail and it never arrived at its destination. I have the receipt, but it appears that there is no way of tracking the envelope.

DHL or FedEx are the only reliable methods for both incoming and outgoing mail. For incoming mail, make sure the sender e-mails you the tracking number.

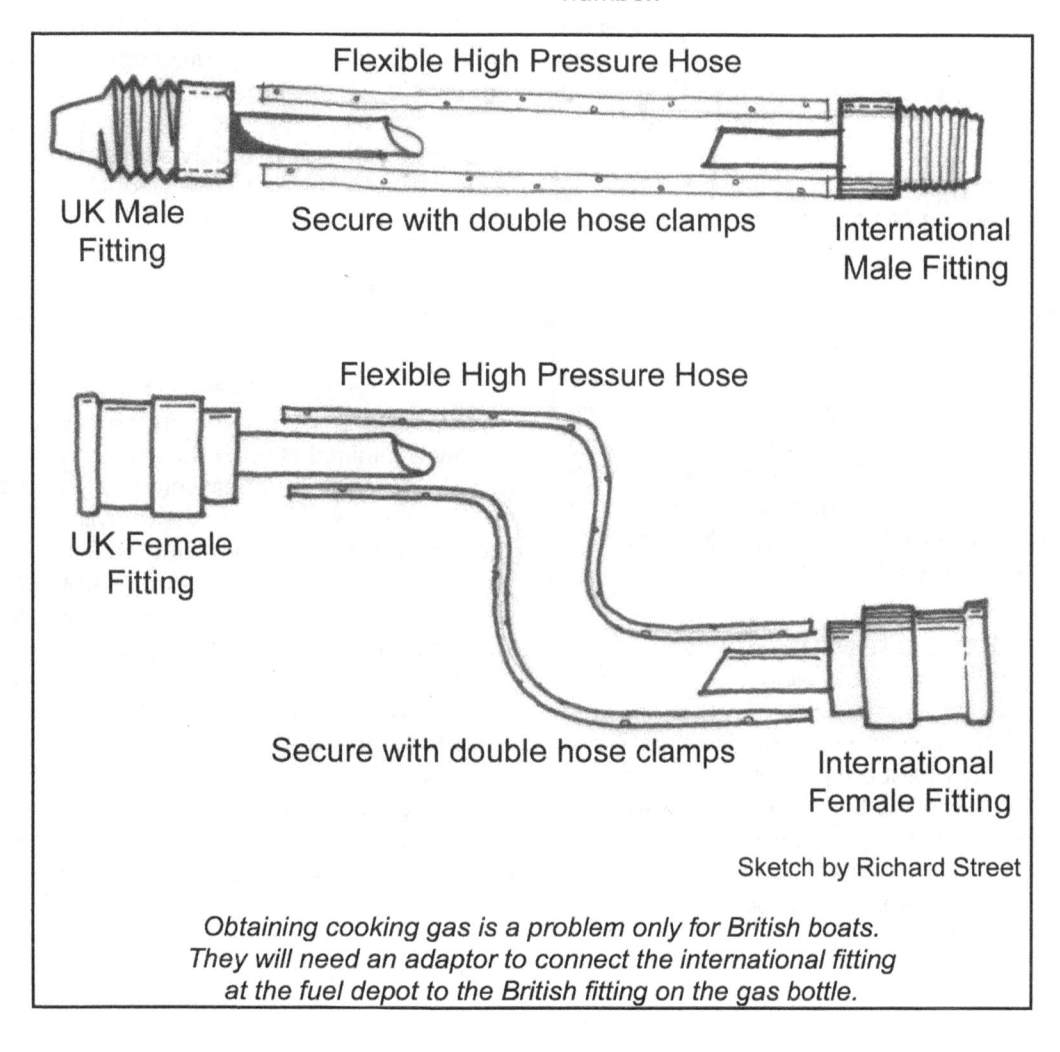

Sketch by Richard Street

Obtaining cooking gas is a problem only for British boats. They will need an adaptor to connect the international fitting at the fuel depot to the British fitting on the gas bottle.

Cyber cafés with Internet access are in every town, it's just a case of finding them. Charges vary but in general it seems to be €2 per hour.

Marina Mindelo has an excellent WiFi system that can be activated for boats moored in the marina and for those anchored out that are paying the dinghy-landing fee.

Free WiFi is available in some of the airports and will probably be in all the international airports by the time you read this.

Language

The official language of the Cape Verde Islands is Portuguese, and the local patois, Crioulo, is spoken everywhere. A Spanish speaker can usually get by.

In the eastern islands, the foreign languages most commonly spoken seem to be French and Spanish, and practically no English. In São Nicolau, the most common language is German, which I suppose is on account of all the German tourist walkers venturing over hill and dale. But in São Vicente, Fogo, and Brava it's not hard to find an English interpreter.

In Santiago, French and German seem to be the most common foreign languages and relatively few people speak English.

Regarding the speaking of English, this will change in years to come as, by law, all children must attend school until the age of 16. We were told in 2005 that English is a compulsory language from the earliest age, but when I asked about this in 2009, it did not seem to be the case. I am not sure just how much this will be enforced anyway, as we saw a lot of children who should have been in school happily fishing off the piers or rowing around in beat-up rowboats.

Medical Emergencies

As you would in most of the islands of the Eastern Caribbean, avoid the local public hospital like the plague as, if you are admitted, you may not come out alive! If a crew member is injured or is taken ill, contact the manager of the biggest hotel on the island and ask for the name and phone number of the best doctor. Then contact the doctor and hope he can take care of the sickness or injury in his surgery.

Also, get on the radio and call for help, you may be lucky and discover there is a doctor or nurse on a nearby boat.

Money

The currency in Cape Verde is the Cape Verdean Escudo (CVE) which is more or less tied to the euro at a rate of €1 for approximately CVE110.

Access to money has improved in the last few years. There is an ATM in every major town but you can only take out CVE20,000 in one shot. For greater amounts, you must go to the bank and stand in line - and make sure you have your passport.

On long weekends, the ATMs will run out of money. I discovered this in Mindelo, with the result that I was almost completely out of money when I flew to Sal. Luckily, in the airport there I found an ATM that had money.

Do not overload with local currency as it is virtually impossible to change your excess escudos back to negotiable currency except in the black market, which is illegal and you'll probably get a poor exchange rate. Euro paper money is widely accepted but discounted about 10 percent. Very few people will take pounds sterling or U.S. dollars.

Practically no one takes credit cards, and when they do, often only cards issued by local banks.

Search and Rescue

In the Cape Verdes you are on your own, as there is only a minimal chance that any of the government patrol boats will be operational. If you activate your EPIRB, the data from the signal will be forwarded to the Canary Islands where the Rescue Coordination Center (RCC) covers the Canaries, Madeira, Morocco, the West African coast, and the Cape Verdes. Don't expect to be picked up by a helicopter. As of 2005, a couple of helicopters were based in the Canaries but in Cape Verde you are beyond helicopter range. They sometimes leapfrog the helicopters down the African coast when they are needed beyond their operational range, but that takes time. A search by fixed-wing aircraft would be the most likely response, followed by a call to direct shipping toward the source of the signal.

Chapter 4
The Mariner's Essentials

Landfalls in the Cape Verde Archipelago

Boats arriving in the Cape Verdes must check in at one of the three ports of entry: Mindelo, São Vicente; or Palmeira, Ilha do Sal; or Praia, Santiago.

If fuel and water are needed, Mindelo would seem to be the logical first stop, but if you do this, it will be very difficult to visit the wonderful anchorage at Ilha de Santa Luzia and the interesting island of Ilha de São Nicolau. Rather, unless you don't mind beating to windward in 20 to 25 knots of wind so as to visit them, it would be a case of skipping these islands and heading south to Maio, Santiago, Fogo, and Brava.

The logical landfall when sailing to the Cape Verdes is Palmeira, Ilha do Sal (see page 62), as from there, you can zig-zag through the islands and visit all of them with sheets eased.

Sailing Directions

From Palmeira it's a 34-mile fast broad reach south to Boavista, on a course of about 196°M. The distance is less if your take-off point is Bahia do Modeiro or Santa Maria.

From Boavista to São Nicolau, Santa Luzia, São Vincente, Santiago, Fogo, and Brava, you'll be sailing broad off or downwind.

From Sal it's better to head south to Boavista before going west to São Nicolau. From Boavista to São Nicolau you will be on a good fast broad reach, but if you head directly to São Nicolau from Sal, the course is dead downwind.

At Boavista, you can either anchor in Sal-Rei or continue down the coast inside Baixo Vauban, round the southwest corner, and to the south coast where you'll find an anchorage off the abandoned house and mile after mile of deserted sand beaches (see page 68).

From Boavista, the course to São Nicolau is approximately northwest, depending on whether you leave from Sal-Rei or from the southwest corner of the island. It's 70 miles to Carrical or, better, to nearby Baia Gombeza (see page 76). From there, you can explore the numerous anchorages on the south coast of São Nicolau, then round the southern tip and head up to Tarrafal, where you will be able to buy locally grown fresh fruit and vegetables that are not available on the dry islands of Sal and Boavista. If you want to explore the island, find a taxi in Tarrafal with a driver who speaks your language.

From São Nicolau, it's a fast broad reach of 25 miles to Santa Luzia with its incomparable three-mile-long white sand beach (see photo on page 85).

En route to Santa Luzia, you pass Ilhéu Raso and Ilhéu Branco, both bird sanctuaries and both with anchorages suitable for sailors who have more guts than brains. I recommend you give them a bye.

From Santa Luzia to Mindelo, São Vicente, it's a distance of 20 miles. The course starts off with a very close reach of 15 miles on about 320°M to Ponta do Recanto da Prainha, the northeasternmost point of São Vicente. It may be a little lively between Santa Luzia and São Vicente as there is a shelf between the islands that's only 25 meters deep, with depths of over 1,000 meters on each side. If the tide is running to windward, it will give you a nice lift, but it will be bouncy. If the tide is running with the wind, the sea will be smoother but the current will be sucking you off to leeward.

Once the northeast corner of São Vicente is abeam, it's only 5 miles to Mindelo. When Punta J. de Evora is abeam, bear off slightly and ease sheets until the Canal de São Vicente opens up. It's then a fast downwind run to Mindelo (see page 87 for piloting instructions).

If you're thinking of sailing direct from São Nicolau to Mindelo and passing south of São Vicente, do not do it. You will start off on a 20-mile beam reach, but from the southwest corner of São Vicente up into Mindelo, although it's only 6 miles, it may be the longest 6 miles you ever sail in your life. With the high land on either side of the channel, the wind funnels through and accelerates, tending to blow 20 knots and more. Plus, the current runs westward through the channel at 2 knots and occasionally, during times of spring tides, up to 3 knots. Beating to windward against a 2-knot foul current means very slow progress to windward; against a 3-knot foul current it's an impossibility unless you have a racing machine.

Street's Guide to the Cape Verde Islands

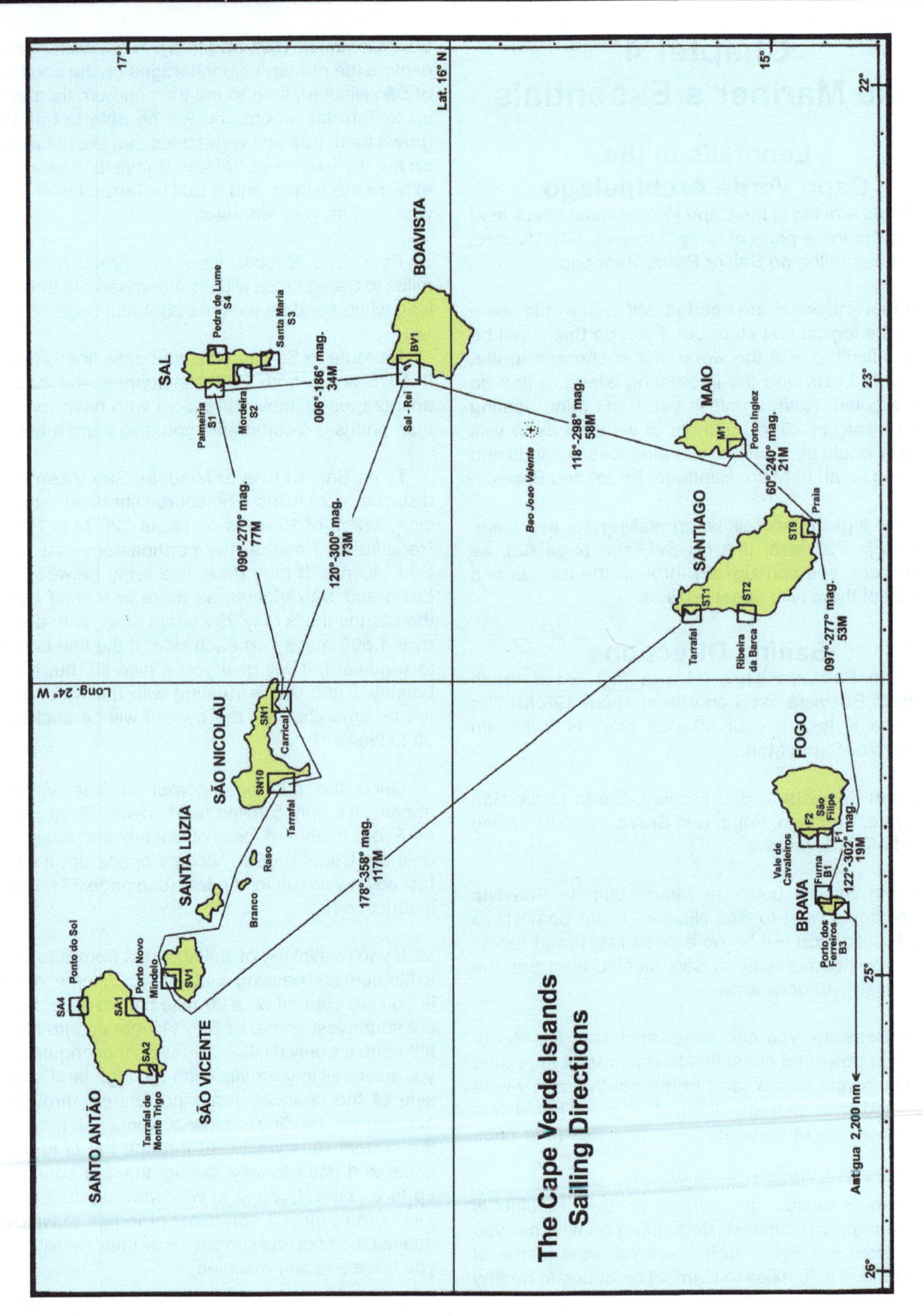

The Cape Verde Islands Sailing Directions

44

If you sail from São Nicolau to Mindelo over the top of São Vicente, the course leads right by Santa Luzia, so you might as well stop and enjoy the island.

From Mindelo to Tarrafal on the northwest corner of Santiago it's a wonderful 130-mile run. You start out sailing dead downwind from Mindelo to the southwest corner of São Vicente and from there it's a glorious 120-mile reach on a course of about 150°M to Tarrafal. Organize your departure for a mid-morning or noontime arrival at Tarrafal (see page 103).

Once you have enjoyed Tarrafal, you have to make a decision: Do you continue down the west coast of Santiago to Praia (see page 112), do you do a short beat over the top and work your way down the east coast of Santiago (see page 116), or do you go over the top and fight your way eastward on a course of about 120°M to Maio (see page 123)? It's about 27 miles to Maio from Baia da Angra on the northeast coast of Santiago (see page 116). Needless to say, it will be longer if you sail directly from Tarrafal to Maio.

In Praia (see page 109), you will be able to stock up for your transatlantic. As of November 2009, Praia has two real supermarkets, and may have more by the time you read this. Praia is a much better place to stock for the transatlantic than Mindelo. Neither Fogo nor Brava are good places to stock up. Both islands will be able to provide some fresh fruit, vegetables, and eggs but that is about all.

From Praia, it's about 64 miles dead downwind to Fogo, where you can anchor off São Filipe. Fogo, like Santo Antão, is an interesting island but, also like Santo Antão, the anchorages are poor (see page 88). Thus I recommend, when sailing from Praia, you bypass Fogo and sail on to Brava and anchor in Furna (see page 133). From Praia to Furna is 70 miles. In Furna, if you are shorthanded, arrange for someone to look after the boat so you can take the ferry to Fogo, visit the volcano, and spoil yourselves with a night or so in the Colonial B&B (see page 128). If the boat is fully crewed, the crew can take turns doing boat watch so everyone can visit Fogo.

It's only 10 miles from Furna to Fogo. In November 2009, a converted trawler carrying 20 people was leaving Cavaleiros, on Fogo, at about 1000, returning to Cavaleiros at about 1600, probably taking 45 minutes to an hour for the trip.

From Furna, sail to Porto dos Ferreiros on the southwest coast of Brava to relax, make final preparations for the transatlantic, and buy some really fresh fish as the fish sold in Furna may not be really fresh (see page 137 for that story).

Cape Verde Charts and Sketch Charts

In years gone by, charts of the Cape Verdes presented a bit of a problem. Many were based on British surveys of 1819-1821 updated by Portuguese surveys of 1931, 1954, and 1971. Often there were disagreements between the British, U.S., and Portuguese charts. I also discovered some German charts that detailed a number of harbors not covered by the British, U.S., and Portuguese charts.

One major anomaly was the location of Baixo João Valente, whose position on the BA chart did not agree with that on the Portuguese chart. This is a dangerous reef as it is very close to the course from Boavista to Maio. I was able to verify its position with the help of my good friend Gerry Dom (see page 11) who has often fished on it (the Portuguese chart was correct).

With great difficulty, over a two year period, I managed to obtain all the British, U.S., Portuguese (with the help of the Portuguese-born yacht designer Tony Castro), and German charts covering the Cape Verdes. Cross checking these charts, together with the information supplied by myself and Gerry Dom, Alan Wilkenson the then head of Imray's chart department, compiled Imray-Iolaire chart E4, *Arquipelago de Cabo Verde*.

Imray-Iolaire E4 is the only chart needed for cruising the Cape Verdes as it shows all the islands on a single sheet. It also has nine harbor charts, one for each of the populated islands. To fully explore and enjoy the Cape Verdes, though, a cruising sailor needs to consult the 50 sketch charts found in this book. These charts are the product of a long (and sometimes physically rigorous) research program.

While in the Cape Verdes in 2002, touring the islands via air to gather information for the complete rewrite of my 1986 *Transatlantic Crossing Guide*, I stumbled across some French-made postcards that were aerial photographs of the individual islands. Looking at the photos, I noticed a number of small coves that did not show on any chart because of the small scale to which the charts were drawn. I could see from where there was white water and, particularly, a lack of white water, that some of these might be possible anchorages.

On the same trip, I discovered walking maps drawn to a scale of 1:50,000 that had a WGS 84 grid superimposed on them. This allowed walkers equipped with a handheld GPS to find their way over hill and dale.

I saw on these maps a large number of coves that might be suitable for anchoring for experienced sailors who are accustomed to eyeball navigation and prepared to send a crewmember aloft to the spreaders.

The maps were compiled by two Germans, Dr. Attila Bertalan and Dr Pitt Reitmaier. Dr. Bertalan was most helpful and cooperative. He sent me electronic scans of the potential coves that I felt might make suitable anchorages. The scans were done from 1:25,000 topo maps of Brava and Santiago, two of the three islands for which Dr. Bertalan had made the walking maps.

Dr. Reitmaier, who had made the walking maps of Santo Antão and São Nicolau, was uncooperative in the extreme. He gave the impression that he had received special permission from the Cape Verdean military to use their secret maps of the islands to make his walking maps. He stated if he sent me any scans of sections of the secret maps he had managed to obtain permission to use, he would be thrown in jail.

Regarding secret maps, nothing could be farther from the truth. Dr. Bertalan told me to go up in the hills of Santiago to the little village of São Jorge dos Orgãos where, in November 2009, we found topo maps covering all of the islands of the Cape Verdes. They were to a scale of 1:25,000 and scattered in dust-covered stacks three feet high, completely uncatalogued. They had been prepared by the Portuguese Air Force from aerial surveys made in the mid-1950s, about the same time as the British made aerial surveys of all the British islands in the Eastern Caribbean. So much for Dr. Reitmaier's secret military maps.

Prior to securing the topo maps of Santo Antão and São Nicolau, I had made some preliminary sketch charts based on images from Google Earth, which covers the Cape Verdes rather well. In fact, I recommend *Google Earth* as a valuable source of visual information on any anchorage. It shows the topography clearly, as well as details of buildings and other features on the shore. You can manipulate the image on the screen so that you can view a region from different angles and elevations — to mimic your approach to an anchorage, for example. Google Earth images are not always reliable as a substitute for eyeball navigation, as water depths can be disguised by runoff from rivers and froth washed back from surf breaking on beaches.

These sketch charts are the end product of investigations I made during cruises through the islands on *Iolaire* in 1985 and 1989 and *Sincerity* in 2005, together with information I gathered on two tours of the islands by land by looking at harbors from shore, interviewing fishermen who use the harbors and coves, and exploring the south coast of São Nicolau in an 18-foot fishing boat. I have cross checked all my information with Gerry Dom and Kai Brosmann (see page 11), both of whom have lived in and sailed among the islands for many years. A note about the source of the information shown appears on every chart.

In some of the anchorages, obviously, the mariner should proceed with extreme caution, using eyeball navigation, taking bearings with a hockey-puck compass, and keeping one eye on the fathometer. At the very least, a crewmember should be standing on the bow pulpit and, in some cases, on the lower spreaders.

Boats that have one could first send in a big RIB to explore. Check depths with a built-in fathometer if the RIB has one or with a handheld if not. Best, of course, is to use an old-fashioned lead line and arm it so you can check the nature of the bottom.

Needless to say, I would greatly appreciate any information sailors are able to forward to me, as it can be included in the next printing of this guide.

At ages 80 and 105, my and *Iolaire*'s exploring days together are over. However, if a yachtsman who likes to explore were to invite me to cruise the Cape Verdes, I would jump at the chance.

The Mariner's Essentials

The author employed fishermen to take him to anchorages on the west coast of Santiago.

Wind, Weather, and Tides
Wind

In the Cape Verdes, be prepared for wind — it blows. A normal sailing breeze seems to be about 20 knots, sometimes easing off to 15 knots but also frequently going up to 25 to 30 knots and staying that way for days on end. One look at the trees and bushes on the eastern side of any island is enough to show you how the wind blows in the Cape Verdes and blows all the time.

During the dry season, December to June, the wind is continually out of the east to northeast. Very occasionally, as we experienced on Iolaire in 1985, it can go all the way around to north, but if it does, it will only stay there for a few days.

Occasionally in November, it can go to the southwest or die out completely. It did this in both 2002 and 2005.

During the wet season, July to November, although it will generally stay in the easterly quadrant, you must be prepared for winds from the southeast, south, and southwest. This wind shift arises when a tropical wave moves off the coast of Africa and begins to develop into a tropical depression. Usually, the winds from this quadrant are not very strong, but if the low develops quickly, they can become tropical-storm force — 35 to 63 knots.

Tides and Currents

My first piece of advice on the subject of tides is to be wary about what you believe and to not always trust what you read. For instance, the modern tide tables say there is only one high tide a day in the Virgin Islands. Nuts. There are two high tides a day, a major and minor high tide.

At one time of the year, the high tide is during the day; at another time, it is in the evening. Robert

Schombergk, a Danish naturalist who lived in St. Croix, figured this out in the 1850s. He also noted that in late May, June, and July the Caribbean is 18 inches, and occasionally two feet, lower than it is in winter.

I found this information in 1957 in my Norie and Wilson Guide to the West Indies that was published in 1867.

Both Jol Byerly, with the 72-foot deep-draft Alden schooner, *Lord Jim*, (twice), and John Clegg, with the converted 12-Meter *Flica*, (once), forgot about this and left the Lagoon in St. Georges, Grenada, at low-water springs in June. They got stuck firmly in the channel they had been going through all year with no trouble. Until high tide, they were like the proverbial cork in a bottle: No one could get in or out of the Lagoon until they floated free at high tide.

In the Caribbean, the tidal current starts running east about one or two hours after moonrise and ceases to do so about the time of the meridian passage of the moon. So, basically, it's running or trying to run east for four hours of the 12-hour tidal cycle.

The east-running flood tide is always fighting against the westerly Equatorial Current, but this current is affected by the strength of the wind so, if the wind is light and it is spring tides a few days *after* new or full moon, you can get a strong easterly flowing tide.

I was most amused the year I wrote an article titled "Hitchhiking in the Caribbean" for *Sailing World*. I sailed on a different boat every day in the Antigua Classic and Antigua Sailing Week (ASW).

After the race I sailed on *Titan*, we were having lunch on *Titan*'s mother ship when Campbell Field, a young but very experienced hotshot navigator, came on board and said to Peter Isler, "I have sailed ASW about eight times and today for the first time I found an easterly current of one knot instead of the one knot or more westerly current."

Peter replied that he had sailed ASW more than a dozen times and he had also discovered an easterly current for the first time.

I pointed out that, with no instruments, I had figured out over morning coffee at about 0630 that there would be an easterly current! They were amazed, and very interested when I explained how to try to figure the current.

The rule of thumb I follow in the Eastern Caribbean is that high water comes about one and a half hours after the moon passes overhead (or underneath), i.e., the upper (and lower) passages of the moon as listed in the *Nautical Almanac*. An oversimplification that helps give a clearer view is that the tidal current tries to flow toward the moon, i.e., when the moon is east of you after rising, the current turns to the east (floods); after the moon has passed overhead and moves to the west, the tidal flow also changes and also runs to the west (ebbs).

On the day I sailed on *Titan*, it was a couple of days after new moon, the trades had been light for almost a week, and moonrise was about two hours before our start. So, given that the strongest tides are three to five days after new and full moon, everything lined up for an eastward-flowing current. If I am sailing almost every day, I figure I can get it right 80 to 90 percent of the time.

Inside the Virgin Islands, where the Equatorial Current has little effect, the current runs six hours one way and six hours the other and there are all sorts of back eddies which, if you can take advantage of them, will considerably ease any passage to windward through the islands.

I discovered this in the late 1950s and early '60s when a large number of Tortola sloops still carried cargo between the BVI and St. Thomas. Going to windward, you would sail by a Tortola sloop heading the same way and not think too much of its speed. An hour later, you would again overtake the same sloop. The local skipper knew of the eddies and took advantage of them. His local knowledge made his Tortola sloop just as fast to windward as a modern cruising yacht. At times, before I learned to take advantage of wind and tidal eddies, I remember passing the same sloop *three* times between St. Thomas and Road Town.

Predicting Tides

Once observations have been made of the times of high and low tide at a location, it is possible to predict these times well into the future. Over the course of centuries, mariners have made observations for hundreds, if not thousands, of places worldwide. One of the most important data points, to use an in-vogue term, is the time of high water at full (full moon) and change (new moon).

The Mariner's Essentials

At full moon, the moon crosses the local meridian at approximately midnight and at new moon at noon. The interval between meridian passage of the full moon or the new moon and the time of the next high tide is called the time of high water on full and change days (HWF&C) for that location.

In the 1986, *Street's Transatlantic Crossing Guide*, I printed the table of (HWF&C) that I copied from a 1912 edition of *Bowditch* I found in the Library of Congress. The information in it for the Eastern Caribbean really does not make sense.

From Martinique south, the time of high water (HW) varies from 2h. 30m. to 3h. 50m. after meridian passage of the moon. Going from my description above in relation to the moon, which does work, this means the current is turning west well before high water.

In the northern islands, HW is 7h. 30m. to 9h. after meridian passage but the old rule of current running toward the moon still holds.

Ask any old time fisherman or good diver, as divers only dive on a weather-going tide.

Now to the Cape Verdes. Jeremy McGeary found a website with tidal information for Mindelo, São Vicente, in three-day predictions, which he fed me via e-mail. Then Paul Adamsthwaite, who became famous by rescuing and rebuilding *Stormy Weather* when she was well on her way to becoming an irreparable wreck, sent me a full month's tide table for Mindelo.

With two months of tide tables in front of me, I compared the times against the meridian passage of the moon and came up with the following figures, which come close to those in the 1912 Bowditch. (Bowditch gives the time of HW *after* meridian passage. Subtract 12 hours and you have the time of HW *before* meridian passage, so you can work it either way. Because of the shorter time difference I think it's easier to use the time before meridian passage.)

At Mindelo, high water at full moon is 5h. 20m. before meridian passage. This time difference becomes smaller as the moon wanes, until at new moon it's down to 3h. 12m., then it goes back up to 5h. 20m. at full moon again.

In the days before GPS, all navigators had on board a copy of the *Nautical Almanac*. Thus looking up the time of meridian passage was simple. Today, although very few boats will have an almanac on board, all is not lost.

Most calendars and good diaries note the days of new and full moon. On days of new moon, meridian passage is roughly 12 noon, give or take 20 or 30 minutes. On the days of full moon, meridian passage is approximately midnight. The meridian passage of the moon and high tide are approximately 50 minutes later every day, so there you have the information to approximately figure the time of high tide each day of the month.

The 1912 *Bowditch* tables list nine tide stations in the Cape Verdes and the time of HWF&C varies among them from 7h. 54m. to 7h. 22m before meridian passage.

From looking at the chart, it appears that most of the islands are far enough apart that it should be reasonable to figure on the Equatorial Current running at ½ to 1 knot toward the west. However, between São Vincente and Santo Antão, the axis of the channel runs NE/SW and the current runs to the southwest at 1½ - 2 knots. With an ebb tide also running it can get up to 3 knots.

Between São Nicolau and Santa Luzia there can be a strong current running against the Equatorial Current. Trig, the Norwegian skipper of *Sincerity*, told me that, from the hill on western end of São Nicolau, he could see a very strong tidal current running against the wind and the Equatorial Current.

The passage between Santa Luzia and São Vincente is like the Anegada Passage in that there is very deep water northeast and southwest of the channel but the channel itself is relatively shoal, only 60 to 70 feet. That means a strong tidal current will flow through this passage. On the ebb tide, the water will be relatively smooth, but the combined tide and current will be sucking you to leeward at as much as 2 knots, thus the course to steer to make good will have to be probably 20 degrees above your desired course.

When the tide is flooding, it will be rougher. Keep your GPS going, plot your course every 30 minutes, and ascertain what course you have to steer to compensate for the set of the current. Back up your GPS calculations by checking bearings with the hand-bearing compass.

As previously mentioned, the passages between the other islands are wide enough that the tidal current effect is minimal, and you can normally expect a ½ to 1 knot current setting you west or southwest. However, at the tips of the islands, you may run into fairly strong tidally affected currents, just as in the Eastern Caribbean. Keep your hand-bearing compass handy, take bearings, and back them up with GPS fixes and you will stay out of trouble.

It would be nice to be able to suggest sailors in the Cape Verdes try the "tide toward the moon" rule of thumb, but it doesn't seem to hold. I hope that, as more and more yachtsmen start sailing in the Cape Verdes, they will make observations of how tidal currents affect the generally southwesterly set of the wind-driven current. I would be very grateful to receive information regarding the behavior of tides and currents in the area and how they correlate with the time of moonrise or meridian passage of the moon.

Northwest Groundswell

While I was putting together the finishing touches of this guide, I received an e-mail from Mar Tranquilidade, a small hotel in Tarrafal de Monte Trigo on the west coast of Santo Antão. Susi, who with her husband, Frank, built the hotel, wrote that they had unexpected guests the day before. A party of seven had swum ashore from a yacht anchored in the bay to have dinner at the hotel. By the time they were ready to return to the yacht, the groundswell had built up to the point that they didn't want to risk swimming back out. The skipper alone swam out to the boat and the rest of the crew crashed in the one unoccupied room in the hotel.

The next morning, the hotel received a phone call from the skipper. He had swum to the boat, picked up the anchor, and spent the night drifting in the lee of the island. At daylight, he got under way and motored to the Canal de São Vicente, where he could get cell-phone reception. He told the crew to hire an aluguer to take them to Porto Novo (three hours over a rough mountain road) where he picked them up at the dock.

Like the Caribbean islands, Madeira, and the Canaries, the Cape Verdes are exposed to the northwest groundswell produced by North Atlantic storms. Remember, this swell has absolutely nothing to do with local conditions; it can come in at any time without any notice and give you grief if your anchorage is open to it. All anchorages exposed to the northwest are subject to the northwest groundswell, so anchor accordingly and have an escape plan. The swell can become dangerous and at times has severely damaged the combined dock and breakwater in Cavaleiros on Fogo

When the groundswell comes in, you can find shelter in a number of harbors that are not exposed to the west.

On Sal, the northwest corner of Baia da Mordeira is your best bet. The swell might hook around the corner, but should be much reduced.

All the harbors on the south coast of São Nicolau east of Preguica should remain calm.

Mindelo on São Vicente is protected by Santo Antão, and you should be reasonably comfortable hanging on an anchor. Time will tell if the marina remains tenable in a really big swell.

In the southern group of islands, all the harbors on the east coast of Santiago will be sheltered from the northwest groundswell but, depending on local conditions, more or less exposed to the trade winds. Fortunately, they are close enough together that it shouldn't be hard to find the right one on any given day.

Several of the harbors on the west coast of Santiago will provide shelter, including the cove east of Ponto do Atum near Porto Rincão, Ilhéu do Alcatraz, the cove west of Cidade Velha, and Praia.

On Brava, neither Furna nor Porto dos Ferreiros is exposed to the west.

Hurricanes

The Cape Verde islands are in the North Atlantic hurricane belt. Very few actual hurricanes form east of the Cape Verdes, but the lows that become tropical storms, some of which subsequently develop into hurricanes, do form east or southeast of the Cape Verdes, and they occasionally pass over or close by the islands with winds of up to hurricane strength.

In early September 1979, a rapidly developing storm passed close by the north of Sal and the Ilhas do Barlavento as a tropical storm and became Hurricane Gloria a day later. At the same time of the following year, TS Frances, heading west northwest, passed just south of Santiago, Fogo, and Brava, causing considerable damage.

Even tropical disturbances that have not reached "named" status can drive southerly or southwesterly winds and seas toward the islands, rendering many harbors that are normally well protected in summer untenable and dangerous. The wrecks in the harbor at Praia, Santiago, are clear reminders of this.

Because these storms form so close to the Cape Verdes, there is little or no advanced warning of their arrival. The Caribbean islands, on the other hand, have the benefit of watching these same storms for days as they cross the Atlantic.

The U.S. National Climatic Data Center (NCDC) publishes detailed histories of tropical storms and hurricanes. Anyone who is interested in tropical storms should spend some time with the "Hurricane Book." (That's my short name for the publication put out by NOAA, *Tropical Cyclones of the North Atlantic Ocean, 1871 - 1998*, see below.) It contains a map for each year showing the tracks of that season's tropical cyclones. It's due to be updated but the maps post 1998 are available on the website of the National Hurricane Center.

The Hurricane Book shows that the Cape Verdes received direct hits from hurricanes in 1892 and 1893. Over the years, six hurricanes have passed to the south of the islands. Forty two tropical storms have passed close enough to the islands to cause problems with winds and swell. Most of them passed to the south, a couple passed to the east, but eight have passed through the islands, affecting all of them and giving individual islands a good whack.

It must be remembered that the hurricane season doesn't end in October — the line "October, all over" in the old rhyme no longer holds. The Hurricane Book reveals that there have been more November and December hurricanes in the last 20 years than in the previous 120 years. Prior to 1998, no hurricanes or named storms are on record that would have troubled a yacht making a transatlantic passage in November or December. Then, in 1998, there was Nicole (November 24 to December 1) and, in 2003, Hurricane Peter (December 7 to 11) that sprang up about 300 miles west of the Cape Verdes and headed northeast right across the track of boats sailing from the Canaries to the Caribbean.

In late November 2005, Tropical Storm Delta crossed the route followed by boats heading to the Caribbean. Those near the storm, which approached hurricane strength, had their ears blown off while those well away from it discovered it had killed all the wind to the south. The same storm went on to cause considerable damage in the Canary Islands, particularly in Tenerife where it dismantled a marina. That season, the busiest on record (with so many storms the National Hurricane Center ran out of A to Z boys' and girls' names and had to continue with the Greek alphabet), saw its last tropical storm, Zeta, form on December 30 and keep up a head of steam until January 6 2006.

A little time spent browsing the Hurricane Book will open your eyes to how frequently the Cape Verdes, too, are in the crosshairs. I've spent a lot of time studying it, and it's my conclusion that the prudent yachtsman should avoid the Cape Verdes in August and September. The earliest time to arrive is October, and even then you should keep a close eye on the National Hurricane Center (NHC website).

Resources
Tropical cyclone information:
National Hurricane Center: www.nhc.noaa.gov
Historical data is online at www.nhc.noaa.gov/pastall.shtml.
Tropical Cyclones of the North Atlantic Ocean, 1871 - 1998 is downloadable at www.aoml.noaa.gov/general/lib/lib1/nhclib/index.htm

Navigation Matters
Harbors
The Cape Verdes have only one natural all-weather, year-round harbor, and that is Mindelo in São Vicente. The northwest groundswell can get in the harbor but not enough to be dangerous, just enough to make it uncomfortable. When you are walking on the marina (built of floating pontoons), it makes you feel as if you have had one too many drinks.

Praia is sheltered from the winter northwest ground swell but wide open to the southwest. The August and September storms have put two steel freighters up on the beach in the northeast corner. The other harbors, coves, and anchorages are each discussed in detail in the chapters on the islands.

Navigational Warnings

Abnormal magnetic variations are reported to exist in the vicinity of the Cape Verdes, especially near Fogo and Brava and also off the eastern side of Boavista and the western side of Ilha do Sal.

A particularly dangerous phenomenon is the harmattan, the wind that blows from the Sahara Desert and fills the air with dust. You can be at sea on what appears to be a clear day but the dust in the air has actually reduced visibility to three miles! This means the horizon is moved way in and your sun sights are completely haywire. Combined with the presence of strong and erratic currents around the islands, in the days of celestial navigation, this led to a tremendous number of wrecks.

How many wrecks there are in the Cape Verde Archipelago I don't know, but there are certainly hundreds of them.

The Pilot Books have always warned that often the first sighting you will have of a Cape Verdean island will be the surf. That is especially true of the low islands of Sal, Maio, and Boavista.

Great care must be taken when sailing and navigating within the Cape Verdes. Now, with GPS, there is really no excuse for being surprised, so long as you do an *hourly* plot with your GPS and actually *plot* your position on the chart and compare it with what you see around you. If you do this carefully, you should stay out of trouble, and you have to do it because the lack of accurate tidal current tables and the presence of magnetic anomalies will throw your DR completely off.

Niki Perryman tells a story about a cruising couple sailing to Sal from Gran Canaria some years ago. Just before dark, when their GPS told them they were 12 miles from the waypoint they had entered for Sal, they saw land. They then got busy with a radio net and when one of them next went up to the cockpit for a look around, they were in breakers. They were lucky: They tacked, sailed back into safe water, and had a think.

The waypoint they had set for Sal was the anchorage in Palmeira. Unfortunately, their track toward it led across the island for 5 miles, so when they were 12 miles from the waypoint they were only 7 miles from the island. Today, they might have had a chartplotter on which they could have spotted their mistake a little earlier.

They made other errors, like not getting out the hand-bearing compass to take bearings on the land so as to better identify it (they thought the two peaks they saw were on Sal and São Nicolau when in fact they were both on Sal). Their principal error, though was that they had neglected to enter an "approach point" that they could have safely approached from any likely direction and from which they could have then plotted a safe route to the anchorage, even in the harmattan.

In the Cape Verdes you can forget about buoyage, and navigational lights are totally unreliable. In December 2005, the Norwegian captain of a cement carrier that regularly calls in Palmeira, Ilha do Sal, reported that the lights in Palmeira *never* work. He also reported that the lights in Mindelo are reliable, but the harbor is littered with derelict freighters that may sink at any moment creating navigational hazards that will never show up on any chart or in any notice to mariners.

We try to keep the Imray-Iolaire charts up to date but, all too frequently, harbor authorities in the Atlantic Islands and the Caribbean will extend breakwaters or build new ones and never send out any notice to mariners, cartographers, or anyone else. In Praia, Santiago, back in the early 1980s, they extended the dock and breakwater but never changed the leading lights! If you were to come in at night following the leading lights, you would end up right on top of the breakwater.

At the present time, the breakwaters in Praia and Boavista are being extended but no one has been told. These developments have been noted in the Imray-Iolaire notice to mariners that covers all the eastern Caribbean and the Atlantic Islands only because I was in the Cape Verdes in November 2009 and discovered that work on the extensions was about to start.

The moral is, do *not* try to enter any harbors in the Cape Verdes at night. Wait until dawn. Remember the old adage, "When in doubt, stay *out*."

There are basically only three off-lying navigational dangers in the Cape Verdes.

Baixo Vauban is halfway down the west coast of Boavista. There is a passage between it and the shore.

Baixo João Valente is very close to your course when heading from Boavista to Maio or to Santiago.

The position on the Imray-Iolaire chart is correct. It has been verified by my friend Gerry Dom who fishes in the area.

The third danger is off the northeast coast of Santiago. It's a reef about 300 yards offshore about ¼ mile southeast of Calheta de San Miguel.

GPS, Chartplotters, and Eyeball Navigation

The number of sailors off exploring the far corners of the world has increased greatly since the introduction of GPS and chartplotters. Unfortunately, the convenience of these electronic aids has led all too many to believe that it is not necessary to learn navigation the old-fashioned way. Why bother, when all you have to do is push buttons?

The art of celestial navigation is rapidly disappearing. More important, all too many modern sailors who are cruising the oceans of the world have not learned the art of DR navigation and eyeball piloting using a hand-bearing compass and judging the depth of water by the color.

Many years ago, as I wrote my guides in the 1960s and '70s, I continually warned against over reliance on watching the fathometer. I pointed out that in that era, a number of serious collisions occurred between large ships in clear weather. These "radar-controlled collisions" were caused by watch officers conning strictly by radar and misinterpreting the information on the radar screen when, as the old hillbilly would say, "If dey looked out de window," they would have seen the other ship and avoided the collision.

Similarly, in the Caribbean and other tropical areas, numerous fathometer-controlled groundings have taken place as a result of crews continually watching the fathometer rather than the color of the water. Coral reefs frequently come up as vertical walls and coral heads will rise abruptly out of 20 feet of water. The fathometer is reading 20 feet as the bow hits the coral head!

One of the major limitations of GPS is that the GPS may be getting a correct position from the satellites but the chart you are working on has not been recalibrated to WGS 84. Many government charts in many parts of the world have not been recalibrated to WGS 84. Whenever you are in an area where the chart data is suspect, and the Cape Verde Islands fall into that category, you have to think about where the data came from that is being displayed on the electronic chart. Remember the warning issued by computer geeks everywhere: "Garbage in, garbage out."

In 2002, we discovered that the new chart of Boavista produced by the Cape Verdean HO was out by 1,000 meters.

Even in areas where you could expect the chart data to be accurate, accidents happen when navigators put too much faith in the electronics. In October 2009, the mini maxi *Pricewaterhousecoopers* (ex *Shockwave*), racing in the Cruising Yacht Club of Australia's Flinders Islet Race and crewed by a group of high-caliber professionals, ran aground on Flinders Islet, the turning mark of the race. The boat sank and its owner and his partner drowned. Apparently, the navigator cut the corner too fine. An official investigation into the incident was under way as this book went to the publisher.

In January 2010, the yacht *Cork*, sailing in Sir Robin Knox Johnston's Clipper Round The World Race, struck a reef in the Java Sea. The yacht was declared unsalvageable but the crew were all rescued. The navigator claimed the chart was wrong, but expecting charts of those reef-infested Indonesian waters to have been recalibrated to WGS 84 strikes me as the height of optimism.

Twenty or so years ago, the 95-foot steel schooner *Antares* was lost off the east coast of Central America as the navigator was relying exclusively on electronic navigation and hit a reef that was two miles from its charted position.

When planning a passage, go over every inch of your route on a paper chart, or on the electronic chart at the highest resolution, to make sure there are no surprises in store that don't show up when you zoom out the display.

Plumb along the route between New Zealand and Fiji lie the North Minerva Reef and South Minerva Reef. While a good number of yachts seek them for the spectacular experience of anchoring in the middle of the ocean, several have found these reefs by accident because they didn't know they were there and plotted a course right over them, thus ending their cruising dreams in a sickening crunch in the middle of the night.

Sometimes navigational errors boggle the mind. In April 2009, the 24-meter ketch *Axia* was leaving Gustavia, St. Barths, when she T-boned the brand-new 55-meter expedition yacht, *Steel*. The story going around was that the skipper of *Axia* had set his autopilot to retrace the course taken on arriving in Gustavia. Unfortunately, *Steel* had come in and anchored after *Axia* entered the harbor.

No tide or current tables are available for the Cape Verdes, although I have made some educated guesses (see page 47), and the chart warns of "magnetic anomalies" in some areas that can throw your compass off by 10 or more degrees. When sailing inter-island in the Cape Verdes, therefore, the navigator should run a continuous plot of GPS positions as well as maintaining his DR and keeping a sharp lookout.

GPS is an excellent *aid* to navigation as long as it is backed up by that wonderful navigational instrument, the "eyeball; Mark I", a hand-bearing compass, an eye on the fathometer, and a good lookout.

When entering harbors, a bow lookout is essential. By standing on the bow pulpit, the bow lookout can judge the depth of water a lot better than from standing on deck. To a lookout on the lower spreaders, all becomes clear.

In the days of external halyards, climbing to the lower spreaders was easy. I was still doing it fairly regularly on *Iolaire* until my late 60s. However, in 1996, when I started sailing *L'il Iolaire*, the 28-foot yawl with an aluminum mast and internal halyards, I quickly discovered climbing to the lower spreaders was a major feat. I therefore installed steps up to the lower spreaders.

As I have stated elsewhere, I feel that if a boat is to sail anywhere in tropical waters where eyeball navigation is necessary, it should have steps installed up to the lower spreaders. If this is done, it will be so easy to send a crew member aloft it will become second nature to post a lookout at the spreaders whenever the boat is entering a new or difficult anchorage.

Remember that the vast majority of the anchorage charts in this guide are *sketch* charts. While some are based on old charts, most of them have been prepared from topographical maps. I have sailed into several of these anchorages, viewed many from shore, and visited some in small fishing boats. I have obtained some depths by sounding with an improvised lead line and a few from local fishermen.

Therefore, when entering any of these harbors in the Cape Verdes, it is essential that you use eyeball navigation while keeping a good eye on the fathometer and on the color of the water.

None of the anchorages or harbors should be entered at night: *When in doubt, stay out!*

In 1985, I discovered that in Nanos on Lanzarote (in the Canary Islands), Palmeira on Sal, and Praia on Santiago, the breakwaters had been extended but the leading lights had not been changed. In all three harbors, the leading lights led right into the extended breakwater. In all three cases, we waited for dawn before entering. I only discovered that the leading lights had not been changed when I checked them the night *after* we entered.

In Palmeira on Sal, in 2005, *Sincerity*, bounced off a wreck marked by a Clorox bottle! Luckily, she was going very slowly. In Mindelo, half a dozen derelict freighters are anchored, semi abandoned, and any one of them could sink at any moment, creating a hazard to navigation that could not possibly be spotted at night. Even while they are afloat, I doubt they reliably show anchor lights. *When in doubt, stay out!*

Beware of Waypoints

Electronic navigation systems have taken a lot of the guesswork out of figuring a boat's position. They also make it easier to plot and sail courses. All you have to do is enter a waypoint into a GPS enabled instrument and say, "I want to go there." The instrument will then tell you its bearing from your present position, and you can use that as a course to steer. If it's connected to an autopilot, it will even take care of the steering for you.

But, and this can sometimes be a very big *but*, the value of that waypoint depends on several factors, the first of which is its accuracy.

For example, you might read a waypoint in this book and think it would be a good idea to punch that into your GPS or chartplotter so you can use it when you visit that location. How do you know it's accurate?

While we, and by we I mean my editor, my publisher, and I, have done everything possible to provide sound information, we are not infallible. Errors can creep into waypoints in several ways. I may have misread my GPS or the scale on the chart. My editor may have transposed a digit when working on the manuscript.

Even if the waypoint is correct as printed, you might make a transposition error when you enter it into your navigation device. It's even possible that the original waypoint was taken from a chart or GPS device that was calibrated to a datum different from the one you are using, or from that of the chart you are using. Given all these possibilities for error, the prudent navigator will treat all waypoints with suspicion.

The only way you know you have a rock-solid, guaranteed-accurate waypoint in your GPS device is when you are on the spot and punch the "Make Waypoint" key. Even then, in some parts of the world, while you can see your boat is surrounded by water, your chartplotter may indicate that you are anchored on a mountainside.

Even when you have absolute confidence in your waypoint, you can get into trouble on another occasion when you decide to revisit it. Before you tell the GPS to "Go To" that waypoint, make sure there is nothing between your current position and that waypoint that could interrupt your passage — like an island. The story told by Niki Perryman and related above illustrates this point all too clearly.

In this guide, I provide an approach point (AP) for each anchorage. Depending on the characteristics of the coast, these APs are between a half mile and a mile off the entrance to the anchorage. In many cases, the APs have been taken from a 1:50,000 or 1:60,000 topographical map calibrated to the WGS 84 datum. Where these maps were not available, I have used the Imray-Iolaire chart, which is also WGS 84 but drawn to the much larger scale of 1:510,000. These APs are to be used as guides only, and then only for the specific anchorages or harbors to which they are referenced. The prudent navigator will approach them from seaward, with caution, and with eyes wide open.

Anchors and Anchoring
Anchors

Sailors continually ask me, "What is the lightest anchor I can use?" and then proceed to describe to me their boat and anchoring gear. My immediate response is to say, "You are starting at the wrong end of the scale. You should be asking yourself what is the *largest* anchor you can handle in the light of the size of your boat, your anchoring gear, and your physical capabilities".

As to the number of anchors needed, three is a bare minimum, more is better. I recommend four. With four anchors, space is a problem, but not an insurmountable one.

Iolaire carries seven, which sounds like a bit of overkill until you get caught out. In 1984, we were caught by Hurricane Klaus which, at that time, was only the third hurricane ever recorded to head east in latitudes below 20° N. We were anchored in the lee of St. Martin, off the north coast. However, as the hurricane came east, our shelter disappeared as the wind slowly veered and our sheltered lee became a deadly lee shore.

We were anchored on two anchors set in a V out ahead. As the wind clocked, the port anchor line went slack and the load came on the starboard anchor. We dropped a third anchor under the bow and slacked the starboard anchor line until we were again anchored with two anchors out ahead in a V.

As the wind continued to clock, we repeated the procedure, using six of our seven anchors. When it was all over, despite having no engine, we picked up all six anchors in half an hour with no problems as we did not have a crossed hawse.

The aggravating thing about this episode was that no English-language yachting magazine would publish an article on how we stayed off the beach when 35 boats went ashore in St. Martin. All, however, printed articles about boats that went on the beach because their anchoring gear was inadequate.

Extra anchors are easily stored. The Fortress anchor, an aluminum anchor shaped like a Danforth, disassembles and stows in a very small place.

A Pekney anchor, a stainless-steel Northill-type anchor, also disassembles and stows in a small space.

A Danforth anchor can be made to stow in a small space. Cut off the stocks, then use a tap to cut threads in the stocks you cut off and in the blades where you cut them off. Take a couple of lengths of threaded rod and fit them to the cut-off stocks. The Danforth will now fit in a very small space.

The next question sailors always ask is, "What is the best anchor?" to which I always reply, "When going into battle, the military always wants a mix of weapons. Regarding anchors, the smart yachtsman does the same."

Iolaire carries a variety. Our standard old faithful is a 50-pound Wilcox Crittenden copy of a Herreshoff, which looks like a fisherman anchor but is not. Like the Herreshoff, instead of having palm-shaped flukes, the Wilcox Crittenden has diamond shaped flukes, that are *sharp* — and as the anchor gets older the flukes get sharper.

The Luke three-piece anchor, which looks like the Herreshoff/Wilcox Crittenden anchor, is highly regarded by the Pardeys and sailors on the northeast coast of the States, but our experience with it in the Caribbean was disastrous. In hard or semi-hard sand it would not dig in. By diving in just as the anchor was dropped, I figured out why. It was a combination of factors. The flukes were thick and dull, not sharp, and the cross arm had no balls on the ends. An end would bury in the sand, and instead of pushing the fluke over so it would dig in, it held the anchor flat.

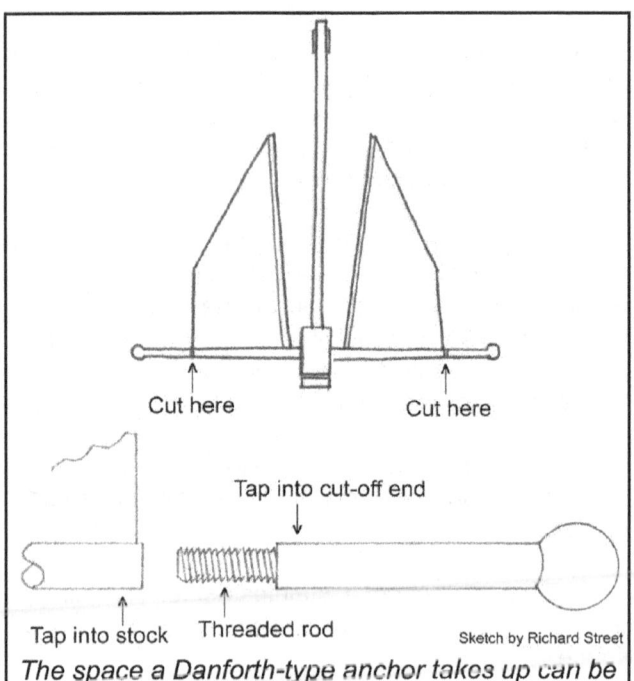

The Nicholson anchor is similar to the Wilcox Crittenden/Herreshoff/Luke type but does not have big palms, like a fisherman anchor, but rather has narrow flukes. It is an excellent rock pick but has very little holding power in sand or mud because of a lack of fluke area.

The CQR and its variations are well thought of and work well in certain bottoms.

The Bruce has superb holding power once it digs in.

The Pekney is a Northill type that disassembles, and is an excellent anchor.

The FOB anchor is the perfect stern anchor as, on the one that weighs about 34 pounds, the total height from the bottom of the anchor to the top of the stock is about 24 inches. This means it can be stowed standing up in the stern pulpit with 15 feet of anchor chain attached and coiled back and forth on the tips of the flukes, and 100 feet of ½-inch line attached, coiled and secured by a light lashing, all ready to go at a moment's notice.

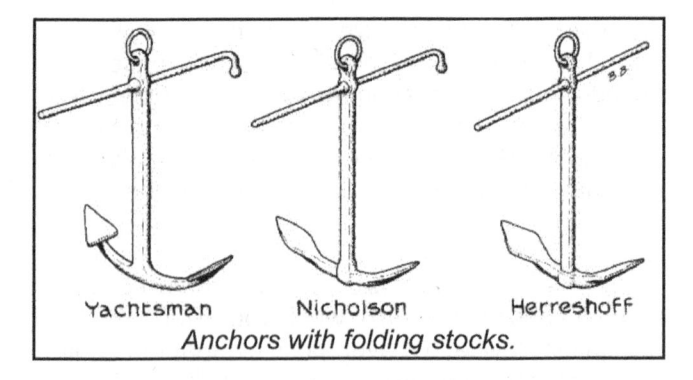

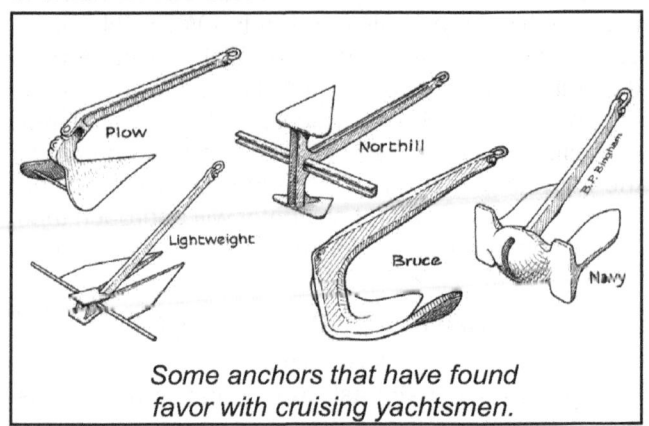

Anchors with folding stocks. (Yachtsman, Nicholson, Herreshoff)

The space a Danforth-type anchor takes up can be much reduced if the stocks are cut off. The stocks can be made replaceable with judicious drilling and tapping and two lengths of threaded rod.

Some anchors that have found favor with cruising yachtsmen. (Plow, Northill, Lightweight, Bruce, Navy)

The aluminum Fortress anchor has amazing holding power once it is dug in. It will hold incredibly well as long as it has about 15 feet of 3/8-inch chain between it and the rope rode. That gives the anchor some weight and helps get it down to the bottom. When setting this anchor, great care must be taken, sort of like setting the hook in a fish. Once in, the Fortress is great, but if not set carefully, it will skid across the bottom and not dig in.

Anchoring

Anchoring in the Cape Verdes is a serious business — this is not the Grenadines where you can watch from the deck as your anchor buries in deep sand. Off the high islands, the shelf in most places will be only 100 to 200 yards wide and to seaward the bottom will drop almost vertically to very deep water. If you are mooring bow-and-stern, if at all possible, drop your stern anchor over the edge of the drop-off. Your anchor line will then be pulling uphill and the angle between the anchor and the anchor line will be so small the anchor will develop tremendous holding power.

Wherever possible, in the descriptions that accompany the sketch charts, I describe the bottom. In some places it's a sandy shelf, especially if the anchorage is off the mouth of a ravine or a *ribeira* (a river that usually only has water in it during wet season). In other places, especially at the mouths of ravines, it will be mixed rock and sand or mud. The rocks are usually loose boulders that have been washed down the gulley in rainy season. If your anchor hooks on one, it may be big enough to hold you, but a medium sized rock will just cause you to drag. Whenever you anchor, back down hard with the engine to make sure your anchor will hold.

When coming in to anchor, use a combination of eyeball navigation (trying to judge the depth by color of the water) and the fathometer. Feel your way in and anchor in a suitable depth.

When anchoring on a shelf that is exposed to the west, be sure to use two anchors set in a V ahead because, if your boat drags anchor while you are ashore, the next stop will be an island in the Caribbean.

In any area where you are exposed to the northwest groundswell, unless you are moored well offshore, set a stern anchor so if the swell comes in it will not pivot you around on your anchor and put you in the breakers and up on the beach.

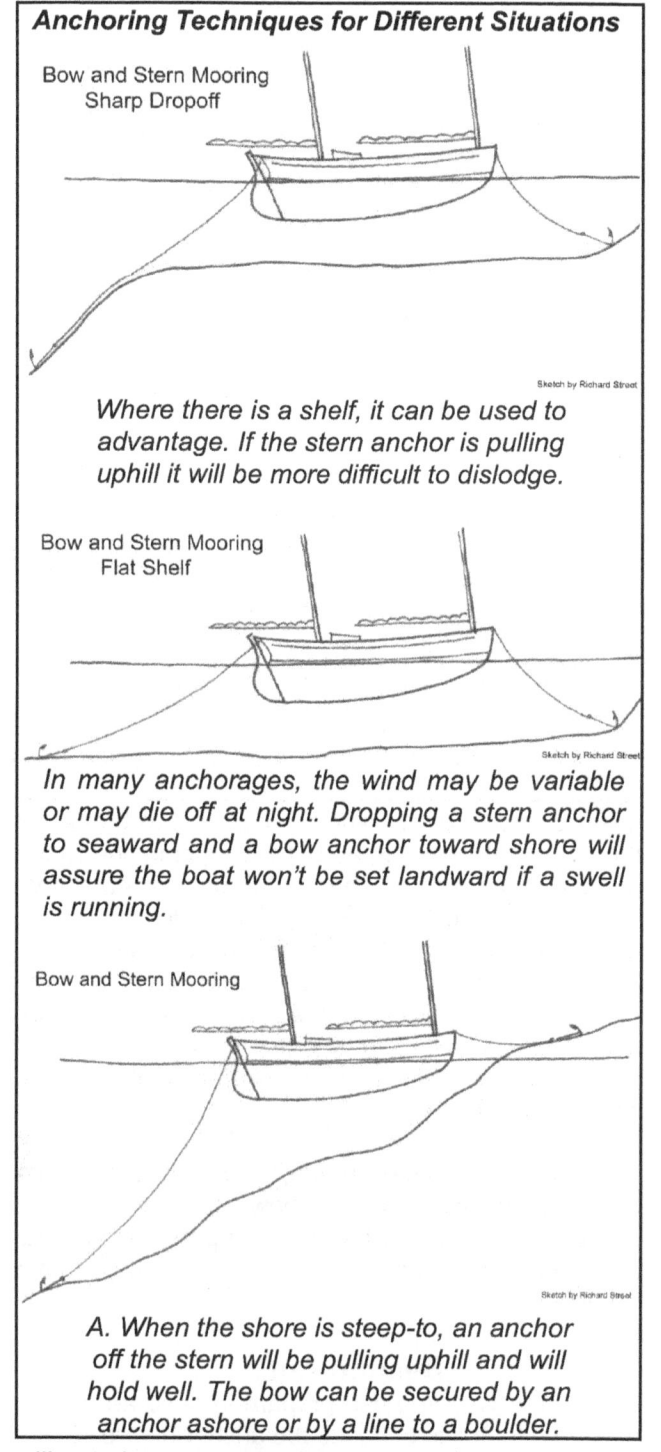

Anchoring Techniques for Different Situations

Bow and Stern Mooring — Sharp Dropoff

Where there is a shelf, it can be used to advantage. If the stern anchor is pulling uphill it will be more difficult to dislodge.

Bow and Stern Mooring — Flat Shelf

In many anchorages, the wind may be variable or may die off at night. Dropping a stern anchor to seaward and a bow anchor toward shore will assure the boat won't be set landward if a swell is running.

Bow and Stern Mooring

A. When the shore is steep-to, an anchor off the stern will be pulling uphill and will hold well. The bow can be secured by an anchor ashore or by a line to a boulder.

Tripping Line

If you are anchoring in water you feel is too deep to dive, rig a tripping line. The line does not have to reach the surface. If it is 10 or 15 feet down, you can

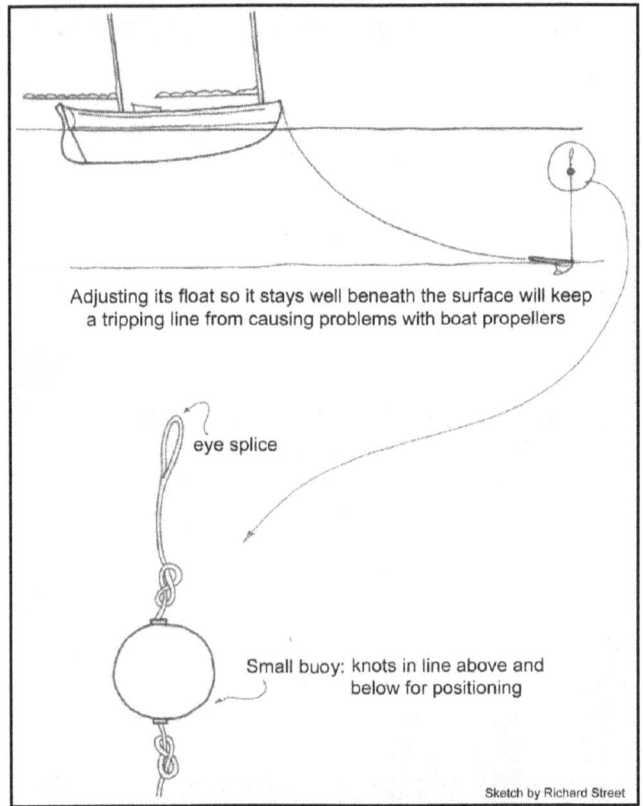

Adjusting its float so it stays well beneath the surface will keep a tripping line from causing problems with boat propellers

eye splice

Small buoy: knots in line above and below for positioning

Sketch by Richard Street

dive down and attach another line to it to break out the anchor. Attach one end of the tripping line to the anchor, and pass the other end through a *small* float with a hole in it. (If you use polypropylene line, you won't even need a float.) Place a knot above and below the float and make an eye in the end of the tripping line, either by tying a bowline or splicing an eye in the line. You can then dive down and attach a line to it by tying a knot into the eye or clipping a snap shackle into the eye.

A safety tip: Make the tripping line 5 feet shorter than the distance from the bow of the boat to the propeller. Then, if you are picking up the anchor and the tripping line is trailing aft, it cannot get around the propeller.

Becued Anchor

Another way you can prepare in case an anchor becomes fouled is to becue the anchor before setting it. Take a CQR or similar anchor, disconnect the anchor chain from its normal attachment point, and re-shackle it to the eye where a tripping line would normally be attached. Lay the chain along the top of the anchor and seize the link that lines up with the normal attachment point to it with four or five turns of ¼-inch braided-nylon flag halyard.

Anchor in the normal fashion. The nylon lashing is amply strong to hold in normal moderate-weather anchoring and will certainly withstand a 500-pound load before breaking.

If, when the time comes to hoist it, the anchor is fouled, bring the boat up to a short stay and secure the rode. Use engine power or the anchor windlass to apply load to the anchor rode. The lashing should break and, because the anchor rode is now attached to the lifting eye, the anchor will upend and come free.

When all else fails, apply BFANDI (brute force and intelligence). If you come up to a short stay and the anchor will not break out via the tripping line, or the lashing of the becued anchor is too strong, all is not lost. Using a chain hook or a rolling hitch, secure a line to the anchor rode, run the line back to a two-speed cockpit winch, put two crew members to work on the handle, and usually the anchor will break out. Two people operating a two-speed winch should be able to pull well over 1,000 pounds.

If that doesn't work, attach a good strong block to the anchor rode by means of chain hook or a short line and a rolling hitch. Run a line through the block. Attach one end of the line to a strong point and lead the other end to a two-speed winch, and put two crew on the winch handle. This effectively doubles the pull, and either the anchor will break out or the anchor rode will break!

If you don't have two-speed cockpit winches, rig a three- or four-part tackle and again you can develop enough line pull to break out the anchor (or break the rode!).

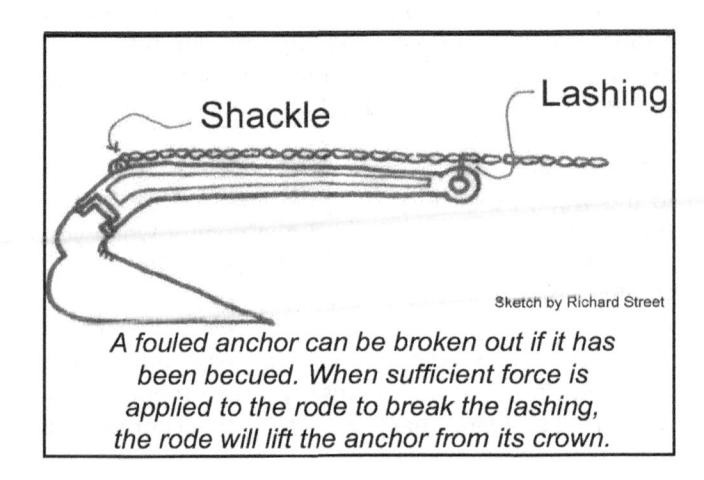

Shackle — Lashing

Sketch by Richard Street

A fouled anchor can be broken out if it has been becued. When sufficient force is applied to the rode to break the lashing, the rode will lift the anchor from its crown.

Bahamian Moor

In small harbors where swinging room is restricted, either moor bow and stern or use a Bahamian moor (known to the British as a proper moor). I learned it from a charter party who had learned to use it in the Bahamas in areas that have a reversing tidal current. You set two anchors in opposite directions so the boat swings in a circle whose radius is the length of the boat.

One way to set the anchors is with the "flying moor." Have two anchors made up and ready with plenty of line faked out on deck ready to run. Approach your spot heading into the tide, slow down, and drop your first anchor (if you drop it off the stern, you won't have to worry about running over the rode). Keep going in the axis of the tide, paying out the rode quickly, until you coast to a stop or run out of line on the first anchor. Drop the second anchor and let the tide set you back. Once you have set the anchor, let out the normal amount of scope, then take up the slack on the first anchor and set it. Give it the proper amount of scope and secure both rodes at the bow. You should be lying evenly between the two anchors and free to swing in a circle as the tide changes.

Sometimes it's easier to put out one anchor, get settled, then run the second one out in the dinghy in the direction from which you think the tide will come when it changes. You can also drop the bow anchor first, let out twice the normal scope as the tide sets you back, then drop the stern anchor and haul back on the bow anchor until you are evenly between them.

This mooring technique is usually problem-free on boats with traditional full keels, but when a boat has a separate keel and rudder, a rode can get wrapped around one or both of them. A solution is to secure a small weight to each rode about 20 to 25 feet down the rode from the bow.

Remember that, especially in the high islands, the wind may die out at night, it may reverse direction, or it may blow from all over the map. Also, as I emphasize throughout this guide, from November until May, the Cape Verdes are subject to the storm-generated northwest swells. Anchor accordingly.

When the Windlass Dies

The technique described above for rigging lines to the anchor chain to break out the anchor, or to get the anchor up if the electric windlass has died, is well illustrated, along with a lot of other tips in the DVD *Streetwise*. This DVD is made up from the very popular Streetwise tips that appeared in *Sailing Quarterly*, the video magazine that appeared four times a year back in the late 1980s and early 1990s. They were so popular that some yacht clubs would hold Street look-a-like or Street talk-a-like contests at their winter parties.

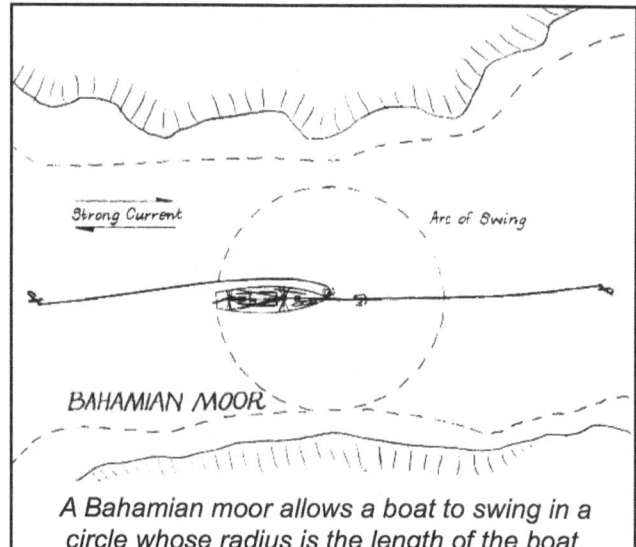

A Bahamian moor allows a boat to swing in a circle whose radius is the length of the boat. This makes it very useful in narrow places and in anchorages subject to current reversals.

The DVDs are available for $30 US from streetiolaire@hotmail.com. Go to www.street-iolaire.com for a list and description of the five Street DVDs.

Safe Practices for the Ship's Boat
Landing and Launching in Surf

When cruising the Cape Verdes, you will often be anchored off beaches that will require running the surf to get the dinghy ashore.

Surf must be treated with respect. The United States Lifesaving Service, which became part of the United States Coast Guard, launched surf boats through the surf from open beaches on both coasts of the States. The service had a motto: "You *have* to go out; you do *not* have to come back."

Surf always looks more benign from seaward than from the shore. If you are in any doubt about the surf conditions, before sending in the dinghy, have a crewmember swim ashore and take a look.

You will encounter two types of surf: rolling surf and surf that breaks abruptly with a crash. With care, you can land and launch a boat through rolling surf, but unless short-breaking surf is small, you cannot safely negotiate it with a boat.

When running surf, the most important thing to remember is that you must prevent the boat from being drawn back into the sea in the backwash of the wave you ran in on. After you ride in on the back of a wave, as soon as the boat runs up on the beach, or even before that when the water is shallow enough, the crew must jump out of the boat, grab hold of it, and keep pulling it toward the beach. If you don't do that, the boat will be sucked back toward the sea and into the next breaker, which will either swamp it or capsize it or both. If anyone is in the boat when this happens, not only will they get wet but they can be seriously injured if the boat capsizes on top of them.

Under Outboard

If coming in under outboard, heave-to just outside the surf line and unlatch the outboard so that when the boat grounds the outboard will kick up. Pick your moment, then give it full throttle and run in on the back of a wave. As soon as the boat grounds, make sure the crew jumps out and holds the dinghy so the backwash doesn't suck it back and into the next wave. At the same time, the driver must kill the motor.

When launching, pull the dinghy bow first into water deep enough that the outboard can be lowered and started. Have one or two crew hold the boat's bow into the surf. When the right moment comes, the motor operator tells the crew holding the bow to jump in (or stand aside and swim out through the surf and be picked up outside), gives her full throttle, and hopes to make it out through the surf.

Under Oars

When running the surf in a rowing dinghy, the procedure is the same except you'll go in stern first. Instruct the crew who are in the stern that they have to jump out as soon as the dinghy is in shoal water, grab the dinghy, and pull it toward the beach, or at least hold it in place so that the backwash does not get hold of it.

If the boat has two rowing positions, row from the forward position. Row in and heave-to just outside the line of breakers, then spin the dinghy around so you are stern-on to the beach. Pick your time, and when it comes, backwater like mad and run in on the back of the breaker. As soon as they can, the crew must jump out and prevent the dinghy from being drawn back into the surf.

When the time comes to launch the boat, again row from the bow position. Have crew members hold the dinghy bow-on to the surf and push it out as far as possible without getting into the surf. They must then watch the waves, and when they think the time is right, push like mad, then jump aboard while the oarsman pulls like hell and hopes the dinghy makes it through the next wave.

Hauling the Boat up the Beach

Once the dinghy, inflatable, or RIB is on the beach, if it is too heavy for the crew to lift and carry, it will stick to the sand like glue. However, a comparatively small crew can move a rigid dinghy or a RIB up the beach with the method used by the West Indian fishermen. They lay a series of sticks in the sand about 4 feet apart, pull the boat onto the sticks, and slide it up the beach. Four or five sticks are sufficient. As you slide the boat up 10 feet or so, you pull the sticks from astern and place them ahead of the boat. Keep the sticks in the dinghy all the time and you are all set whenever you go ashore. In an emergency, lay the oars down and use them.

When landing through surf, make sure you tie anything you are carrying with you to the boat. That way, if the boat does capsize, at least everything will be attached to it when you finally get it ashore. It's very difficult to retrieve bits and pieces when they are rolling around in the surf.

Safety While Exploring in the Ship's Boat

Whenever you set off in a ship's boat in the Cape Verde Islands, you must keep in mind that, if the outboard quits and you have no backup plan, your next stop, unless you are in a rowing dinghy and can row to shore, will be an island in the Caribbean 2,200 miles to leeward.

You should always have aboard the boat a decent-sized dinghy anchor on at least 100 feet of line, a couple of gallons of water stowed in separate containers, a handheld VHF (preferably waterproof), a man-overboard strobe light, and the ship's EPIRB.

Before you leave the mother ship, make sure you have adequate fuel. If you are leaving crew aboard the yacht, tell them where you are going and when you expect to be back, and ask someone to keep an eye on your progress.

If the outboard quits and you have a handheld VHF, hopefully you can call the mother ship and she will get under way and find you. Spotting a dinghy from the mother ship is difficult, but you will likely be able to see the mother ship from the dinghy and you can call her to you using the VHF.

If the crew on the mother ship does not find you by dusk, they may see the strobe light. If not, their chances of finding you are zero as, with the wind and westbound current, you will be drifting toward the west at 2 knots. By dawn, you will be 24 to 30 miles to the west of the Cape Verdes. Your only salvation then will be the ship's EPIRB as the signal it transmits goes to a satellite and the position information will eventually be forwarded to the SAR center in the Canaries. You will be too far away for a helicopter ride but ships directed toward the position given by the EPIRB should find you within a couple of days. If you have water you will be fine, other than being hungry and sunburned.

Over the years, the experiences of many people have shown that if you have one pint of water a day, even with no other food, you can survive an incredibly long time. So, with a couple of gallons of water in the dinghy, plus the ship's EPIRB, your chances of survival if you drift off to the west are very good.

Chapter 5
Sal and Boavista

Ilho do Sal
Imray-Iolaire Chart E4

Ilha do Sal is the northernmost island of the Cape Verdes and the obvious landfall for any yacht coming from the north because of its port of entry in Palmeira. The presence of the international airport is an added convenience for boats that plan on changing crews in the Cape Verdes.

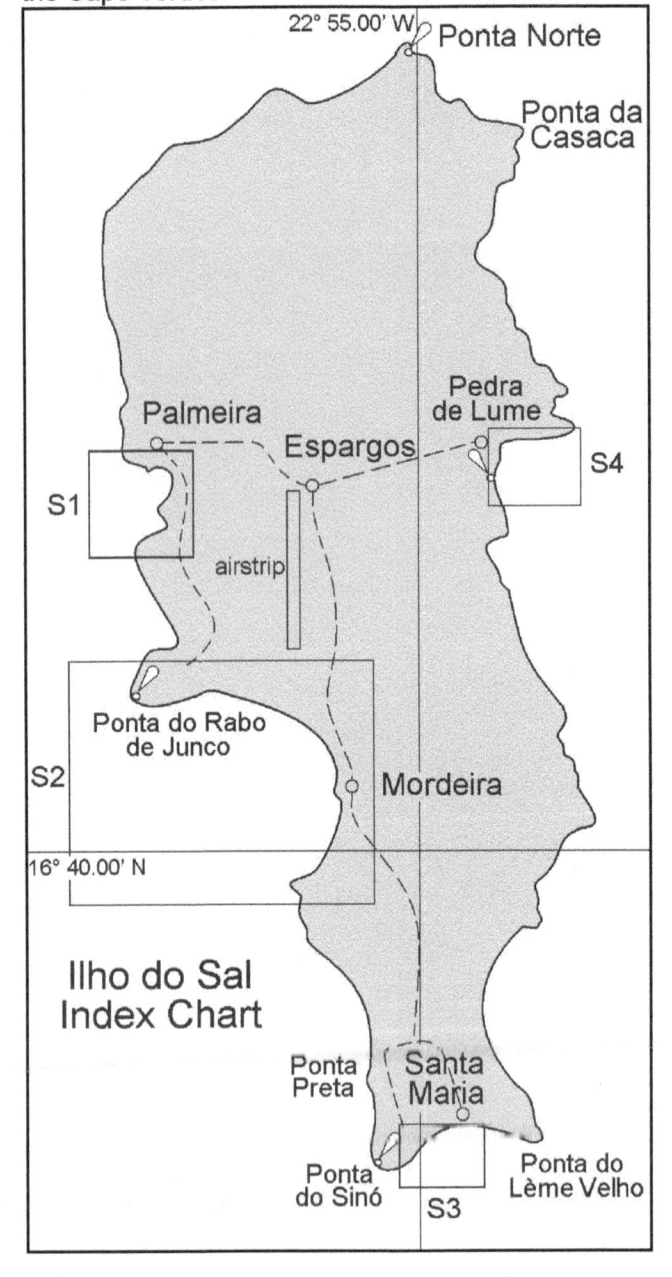

In years gone by, the economy of Sal was largely driven by the export of salt, dug from a salt mine on the east coast. The salt was inside the crater of an extinct volcano. To access the salt, miners dug a tunnel through the volcano's cone. Mining ceased about 25 to 30 years ago and the rusted out equipment can be viewed at Bahia de Pedra de Lume. The area has recently been cleaned up and the tunnel opened, so you can walk through it and take a swim in the salt lake. You will float high because of the density of the water. After your swim, you can shower and visit the restaurant inside one of the administration buildings of the old salt works. Until recently, salt was also gathered by evaporation in salt pans, a practice found worldwide but rapidly dying out.

Water on the island comes from a distillation plant. Unless you are lucky and manage to get alongside and con the water-truck driver into selling you some water, you'll have to take it aboard in jerry cans. The problem is that Sal is expanding so rapidly that three or more ships are anchored off at all times waiting to get alongside to unload. Yachts are not welcomed.

Sincerity did get alongside in December 2005 to load fuel and water, but the story of how she managed that is too long and complicated to relate here.

Abnormal magnetic variations are reported west of the island so approach with care and in daylight.

There are four anchorages in Sal, but only two of them are any good.

Approach Points (AP) are taken from Imray-Iolaire E4 and are approximately 1 or 2 miles off the anchorages.

Baia da Palmeira
Harbor chart S1
AP 16° 45.0' N; 23° 01.0' W

Baia da Palmeira, on the island's west coast, is an excellent anchorage in all normal conditions, but it will definitely be uncomfortable if the groundswell starts rolling in.

The lights do not work, even those on the mooring buoys for the tankers. When maneuvering around the bay, stay outside the box formed by the four buoys. The pick-up buoy for the fuel line is in that area. It's unmarked and is usually a couple of feet under water.

Sal and Boavista

A mixture of locally owned and visiting boats will be found in the anchorage at Palmeira on Sal.
Photo by Pitt Reitmaier

**Chart S1
Ilho do Sal
Baia da Palmeira**
Soundings in Meters
Source: Imray-Iolaire Chart E4

Note: Lights are Unreliable

Caution
Do **NOT** pass between the tanker mooring buoys, submerged obstruction. Pass either north or south.

The dangerous wreck east of the breakwater is only about 1·8m below the surface.

To allow ships to maneuver alongside the quay, stay out of the no-anchoring area marked on the chart.

There is an unmarked wreck of a small steel freighter with about 6 feet of water over it (which we found by hitting it on *Sincerity*, luckily going dead slow). I went back to it with the dinghy and noted its position by GPS as 16° 45.255' N, 22° 58.836' W. It's about 180 meters east of the dock.

The anchorage within the harbor is tight; exactly how many boats can be squeezed in I don't know. There is a dinghy landing where they also land fish. We received plenty of offers of help, but no one asked us to pay them to guard the dinghy. The office of the harbor police is easy to find and they take care of everything. In November 2005, there was no need to see the port captain. In fact trying to see the port captain to obtain permission to bring *Sincerity* alongside to pick up water and fuel was about like getting into the inner sanctum of the CIA in McLean, Virginia.

We found a few friendly bars here, and a couple of very basic stores. Amazingly, there was one small good restaurant with a single set menu of superb steak. In 2005, it was run by a Venezuelan married to an Italian. When I was there in 2009, I did not have time to check out the restaurant, but a very basic but friendly bar was open on the landing used by the fisherman and where yachts bring their dinghies. One of the visiting sailors reported that there were two restaurants, but he had not tried either.

A small village is nearby and the main town, Espargos, is three miles away. Here you will find some restaurants, bars, a little hotel, some small residencials, and some un-super supermarkets. As of November 2009, there was one quite modern hotel, Hotel Atlantica. According to my guide while I was on Sal, the only way to find good meal on Sal is to drive to the south end of the island to Santa Maria. After eating dinner at the hotel I agreed with him.

When I arrived in Palmeira in 2005, I discovered my old friend Barney Barsdell of Shanklin, Isle of Wight, stranded there — his propeller had fallen off, and he was stuck with no wind! He had done some exploring and had met a man who was putting the finishing touches to a Laundromat in Espargos. The town is small enough, just by asking around I am sure you will find the Laundromat.

If you want to use the Internet, go to the airport where there is free WiFi. Hop aboard an *aluguer*, the Cape Verde version of an unscheduled bus or communal taxi (most likely a pickup truck with benches and a lid on top), from Palmeria to Espargos. It's then a short taxi ride to the airport.

Baia da Mordeira
Harbor chart S2
AP 16° 41.0' N; 23° 00.0' W

Bahia da Mordeira, south of Baia da Palmeira and Ilha do Rabo de Junco, is an excellent anchorage and is described in the *British Admiralty Pilot* as the best in Ilha do Sal and one of the best in all the Cape Verde Islands. It is sheltered from all directions except south through west, so it's exposed only in the wet season. In the dry season, which is when most yachts visit, it is best to tuck into the northeast corner and anchor in 15 feet of water, where the anchors are on the sketch chart.

Be sure when anchoring that you are clear of the cable area noted on the sketch chart and on the Imray-Iolaire chart. I also recommend you use a trip line on the anchor in case you hook into a rock ledge.

The diving, snorkeling, and fishing are superb. In years gone by, so was the lobstering, but today the lobsters are all fished out. There is a fair beach, and, except when planes pass overhead on their way to landing at the airport, you will be completely by yourself as there is no road to this part of the bay, only a dirt track. We were debating who might drive on such a track when we saw two 4 x 4s go by with surfboards on their roofs. The surfing is good in the northwest corner of the bay but the swell did not get into the northeast corner where one boat was happily anchored in splendid solitude.

A spur off the main road leads down to the development in the south end of the bay. There are no bars or restaurants here, but in 2005 there was small, exclusive hotel in the southeast corner, surrounded by a high wall. In 2009, the southern end of the bay was quite developed and a big billboard displayed pictures of a completed marina with boats moored in it. In actuality, there was neither a marina nor any sign of anything being built.

One wonders why this bay did not develop as a port in the early days, unless it was too far to easily transport the salt there from the salt mines and salt pans.

Sal and Boavista

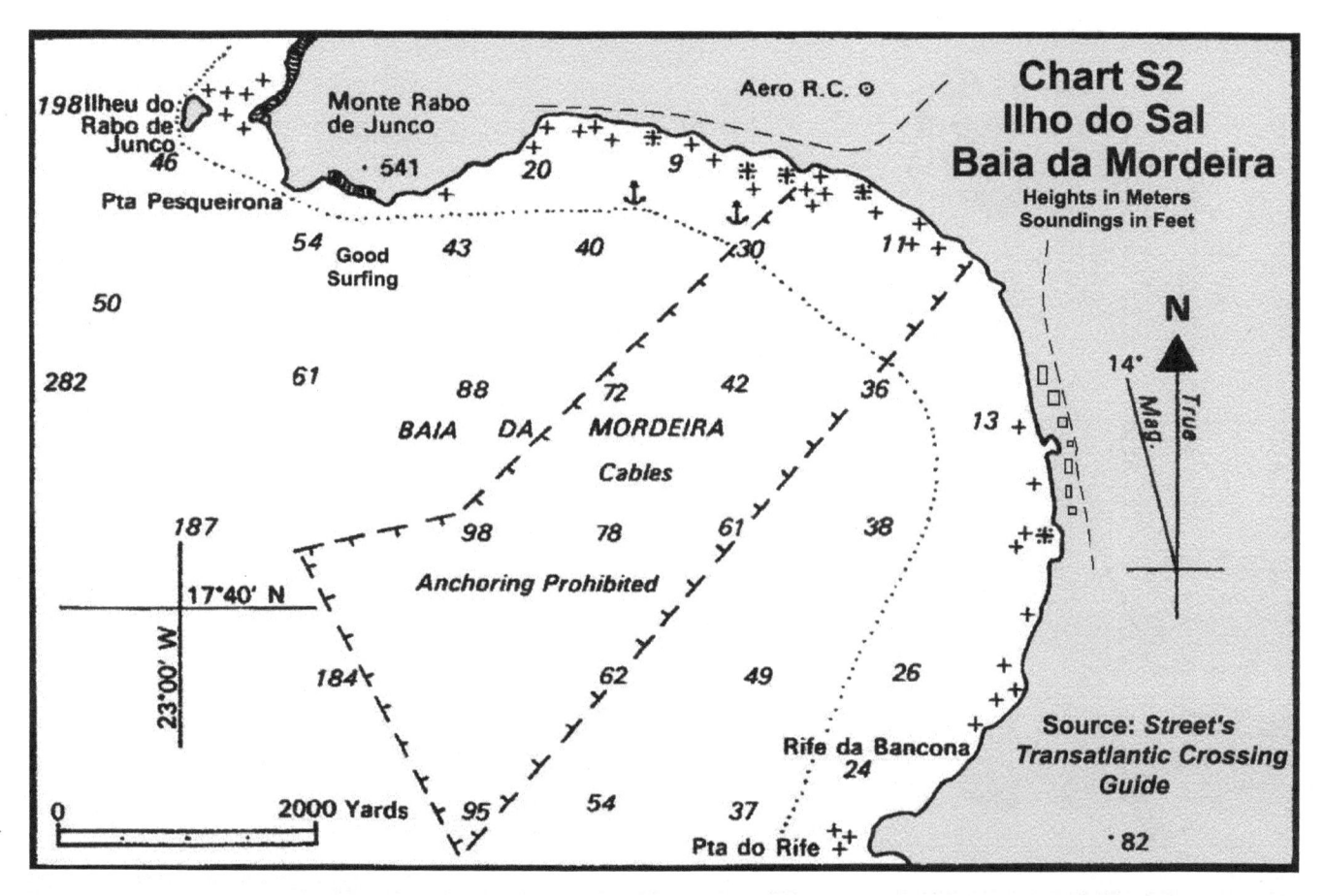

**Chart S2
Ilho do Sal
Baia da Mordeira**
Heights in Meters
Soundings in Feet

Source: *Street's Transatlantic Crossing Guide*

Santa Maria

Harbor chart S3
AP 16° 35.0' N; 22° 54.5' W

This anchorage on the extreme southern end of the island is rather exposed, as the sea seems to sweep around the point off Santa Maria. On approaching the anchorage from the west, you should note that the light is a good 600 yards inside the end of the island and a reef extends another 600 yards or so farther from shore.

The bay is a paradise for windsurfers, kite surfers, and surfers. Needless to say, if the surfers like it, landing a dinghy on the beach is always a bit difficult and can sometimes prove impossible.

However, in 2009, I discovered that the old dock by the harbor master's office had been extended to about 150 feet, and was being used by the fishermen to land fish and nets. It has ladders, so you can come alongside a ladder, unload the crew, put out a stern anchor, and leave the dinghy tied to the dock.

When I first visited Santa Maria in 1985, there were only two relatively small hotels on the beach, the Moraboza and the Bolo Norizonte. Their main income came from accommodating Russian, South African, and German flight crews. There may have been political differences between their countries, but the flight crews managed to forget about all of that at the bar and pool table and while swimming.

On my subsequent visits, I saw the village evolve into a full-on holiday resort. First, a few hotels began to line the beach, then a grid of beautiful cobblestone roads appeared behind the beach. As of January 2005, an example of the ubiquitous Irish pub had already sprung up and by 2009, the town had become a veritable concrete jungle full of poorly designed and poorly constructed small hotels.

It would appear that the building code required the walls of the ground floors to be set back 10 feet from the property line, but set no such rule for the upper stories. Consequently, these have been built right out to the property lines, so those of adjacent buildings are just inches apart. If you sit on your balcony and

Street's Guide to the Cape Verde Islands

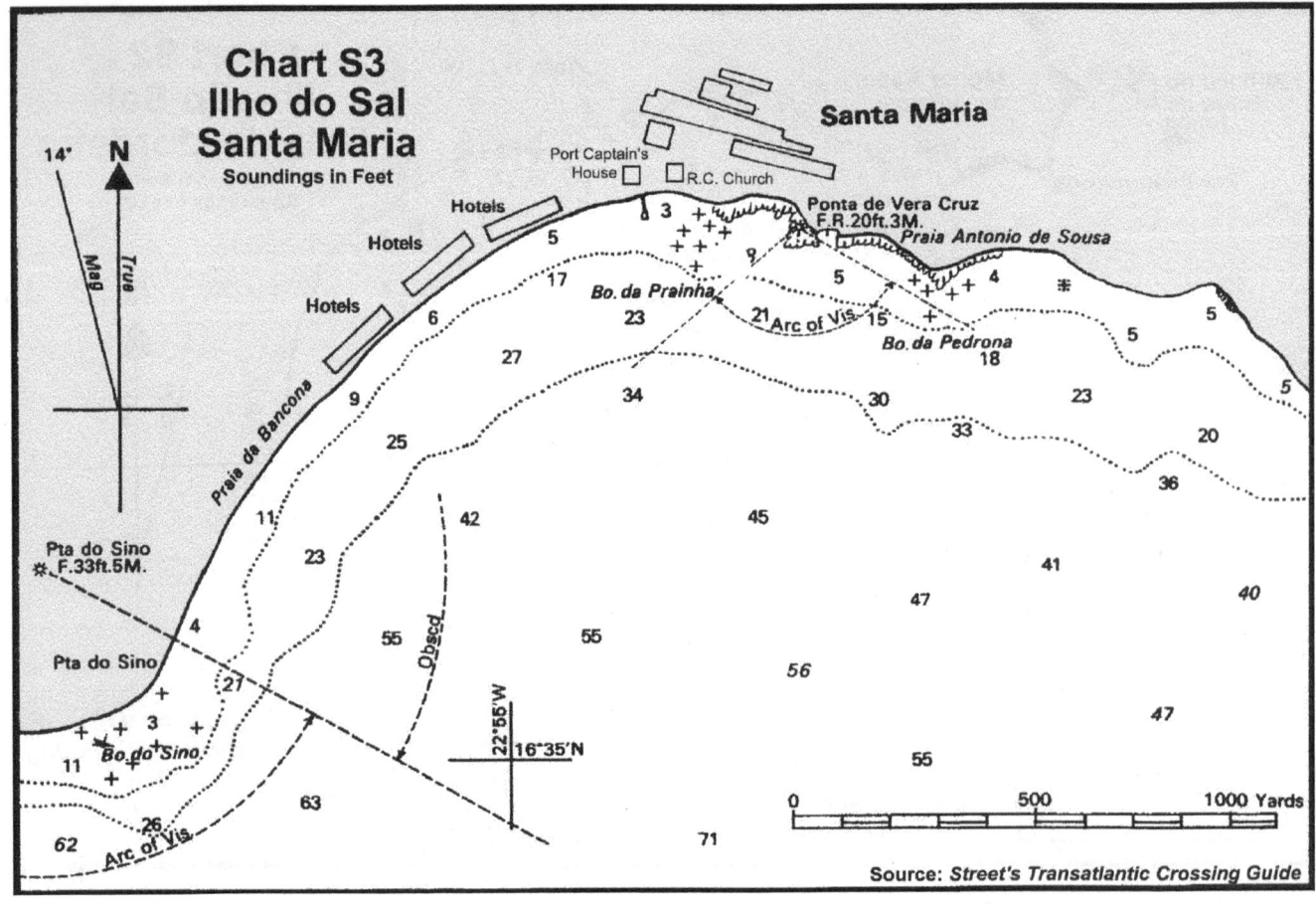

**Chart S3
Ilho do Sal
Santa Maria**
Soundings in Feet

sneeze, you could infect everyone on the balcony of the adjacent hotel.

In the old village, just northeast of the harbor master's office, there is a small, beautifully kept Catholic church, possibly the best maintained church in the Atlantic Islands. When we were there in 2005, I just missed mass, but the crowd that left the church was unbelievable, and I wondered how they all fit in. From the condition of the church, I imagine the tourists must support it well.

You will find moderately good shopping in the un-super supermarkets but forget about obtaining water or fuel in Santa Maria as the surge makes it impossible to lie alongside the dock.

The old Harbor Master's House, that dates from the days when Santa Maria was a major salt-exporting area, has been magnificently restored.

The place is loaded with restaurants and my friend Jose Bravo, a refrigeration expert who spends a lot of time on Sal maintaining the refrigeration systems of the fishing boats, reports that many of the restaurants are excellent.

Baia de Pedra de Lume

Harbor chart S4
AP 16° 44.0' N; 23° 53.0' W

Baia de Pedra de Lume is a former salt-loading port on the island's east coast. The old breakwater is still there and provides shelter to a few local fishing boats. I cannot imagine any yachts approaching the east coast of Sal, much less anchoring off, so I doubt if this small basin will ever be improved. It was obviously built to shelter the barges that were used to lighter the salt out to ships anchored off. The abandoned rusty barges and the small tug that was used to tow them are all hauled up on the beach. The salt works had already been closed down when I first arrived in Sal in 1985.

By December 2002, a restaurant had been opened, the roads had been made, and obviously there were plans for a fairly major project. There was even talk about a marina, but knowing how the wind can really blow up in the Cape Verdes in the winter, I can't really see this happening on the windward coast of Ilha do Sal.

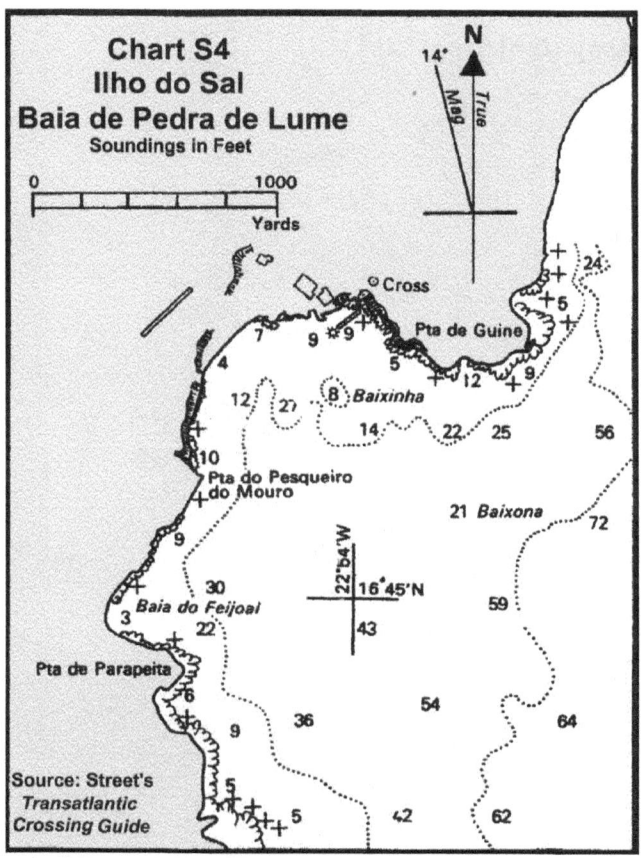

When I visited in 2009, the restaurant was going great guns with busloads of customers arriving from hotels. The salt lake in the volcano, which you reach by a short walk through a tunnel, has become a tourist attraction. The tunnel was dug in the 1850s. In 1919, a Frenchman bought out the operation and installed a high-wire transportation system, the remains of which can still be seen today, that could reputedly move 20 tons of salt an hour. So, while anchoring in Pedra de Lume might not be practical, a visit by car is well worthwhile to view the salt works and take a salty swim.

Near the salt works is an unfinished land development project. A huge wall and an arched entrance between two towers give it the appearance of a medieval fortress, but without the moat, the drawbridge, and the portcullis. A couple of houses were built, but it seems some of the buyers of the yet-to-be-built houses visited the site and discovered that, though the site was indeed near the water's edge, the water's edge was a rocky shore at the base of a 20-foot cliff. They spread the word and everything came to all stop.

Ilha da Boavista
Imray-Iolaire Chart E4
Harbor chart BV1

Boavista's east coast is poorly charted; the island should be approached only from the west and then only in good light. In years gone by, British Admiralty charts carried a warning stating that the island is two miles east of its charted position. Imray-Iolaire charts now have it correctly plotted.

I double-checked the position in December 2002 and came up with an interesting observation. The new Cape Verdean chart of the harbor of Sal-Rei was 1,000 meters out! This was confirmed by an engineer I met on the dock who was using GPS to check the position of the dock and harbor so repairs could be made to a cable that had been cut by a freighter.

This made me wonder how accurately the position of Baixo João Valente was charted. This dangerous reef is about two miles long in a north-south direction and lies 19 miles southwest of the island — almost directly on the course between Boavista and Santiago.

I checked the coordinates of Baixo João Valente as presented on the Imray-Iolaire chart with Gerry Dom, who fishes the area. His GPS coordinates agreed with the position given on the Imray-Iolaire chart.

Finally, the chart warns of strong currents and of abnormal magnetic variation in this area, particularly off the island's east coast. You should therefore keep your GPS going, keep a continuous regular plot, and, most important, keep your eyes open. The reef breaks in most conditions. If you use eyeball navigation, this, and the change in the color of the water, will alert you as to the exact location of the reef and enable you to avoid it.

For the locals, Baixo João Valente provides excellent fishing around its edges. It might be possible, in calm weather periods, for a catamaran to anchor on the edge of the reef and engage in some really good snorkeling, lung diving, and spear fishing.

Street's Guide to the Cape Verde Islands

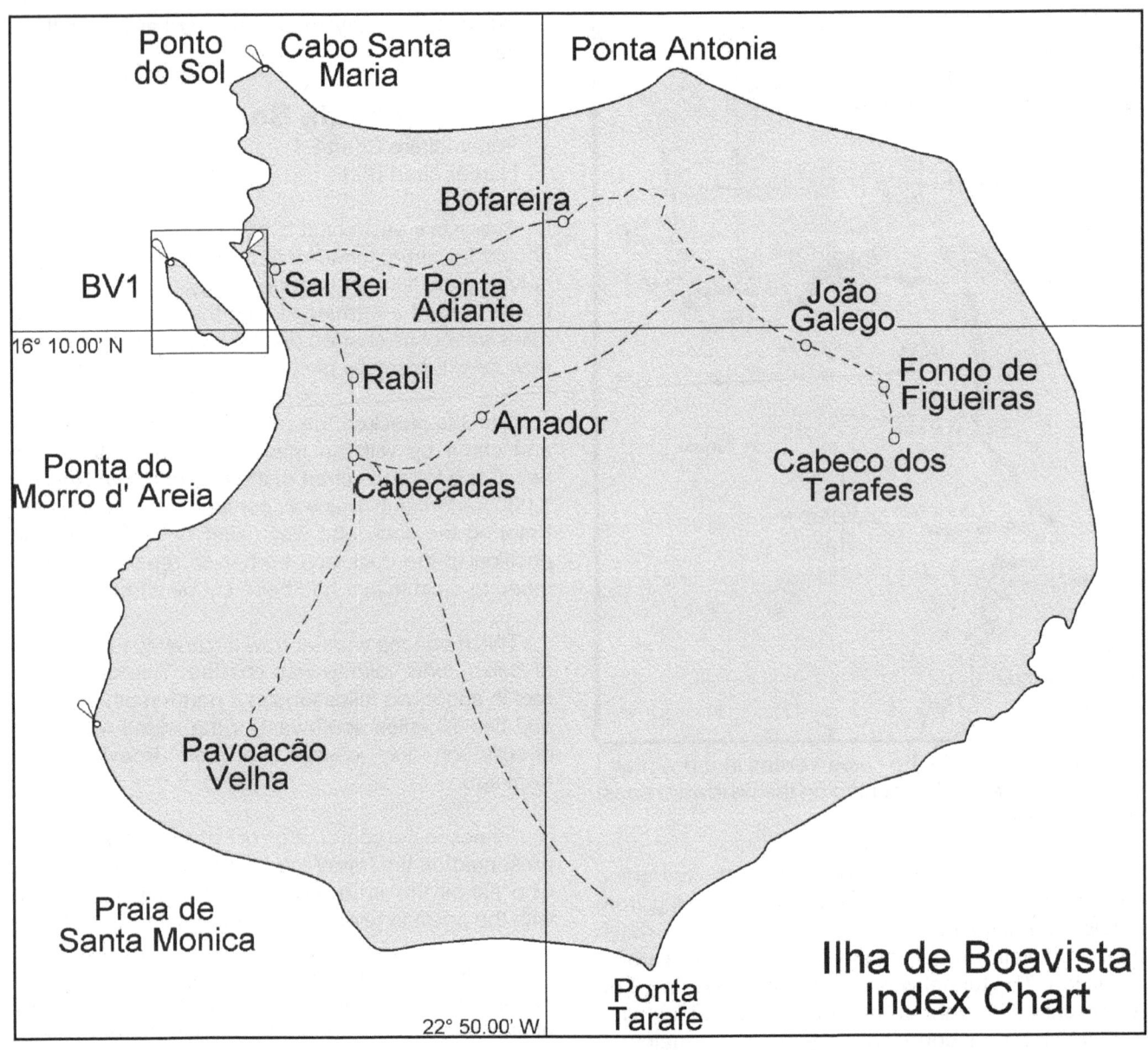

Ilha de Boavista Index Chart

Locations shown on map: Ponto do Sol, Cabo Santa Maria, Ponta Antonia, Bofareira, BV1, Sal Rei, Ponta Adiante, João Galego, Fondo de Figueiras, Rabil, Amador, Cabeco dos Tarafes, Ponta do Morro d' Areia, Cabeçadas, Pavoação Velha, Praia de Santa Monica, Ponta Tarafe. 16° 10.00' N, 22° 50.00' W

Boavista began to develop quite early and by December 2002 a number of small hotels were under construction and a windsurfing school was well established.

We did not visit Boavista in 2005, but by 2009, the number of hotels had grown to the point you cannot count them. My old friend Gerry Dom had also got into the act and had expanded his house, adding another story and making it into a small hotel. If you're in Sal-Rei and looking for meal and a quiet night ashore, book into his hotel (taking a room ashore is the only way you'll get a shower anywhere in these islands). Just ask for him at the dock and the locals will put you in touch.

Gerry (see page 11) has lived in the Cape Verdes for the past 25 years and is an excellent sailor, fisherman, and boatbuilder, so he's a good man to contact when visiting Boavista.

Shopping on Boavista is quite basic but adequate. Interestingly, in the Cape Verde Islands, the idea of a gas station that also supplies food and everything else has taken hold. Even in 2009, the best shopping on the island was at the gas station in the village of Sal Rei. The people could not be friendlier, and a nice though very basic bar, the Te Manche, has been built from a container on the dinghy dock.

Porto de Sal-Rei

Harbor chart BV1
AP 16° 10.5' N; 23° 57.0' W

There used to be two anchorages available in Sal-Rei. One was behind the breakwater on the mainland, but was very restricted with only room for five or six boats. It was mostly taken up by locals.

You approached this anchorage from the northwest. You were all clear once you had passed the dock when you could round up and anchor. You are now not allowed to anchor between the dock and the shoal to the south of it.

In November, 2009, the dock was in the process of expansion, so the area will undoubtedly be full of construction equipment through 2011.

More room is available in the other anchorage, southeast of Ilhéu de Sal-Rei. To approach this anchorage you may pass either east or west of Baixo Inglez (English Reef). If coming from the north or the northwest you should pass between English Reef and Ilhéu de Sal-Rei, avoiding the wreck on the eastern side of English Reef. Leave the island of Sal-Rei to port, round up around the southeast of the island, and work your way northward to a suitable depth for your boat. The best spot to anchor, if Gerry Dom doesn't have his boat there, is off the southeast tip of Ilhéu de

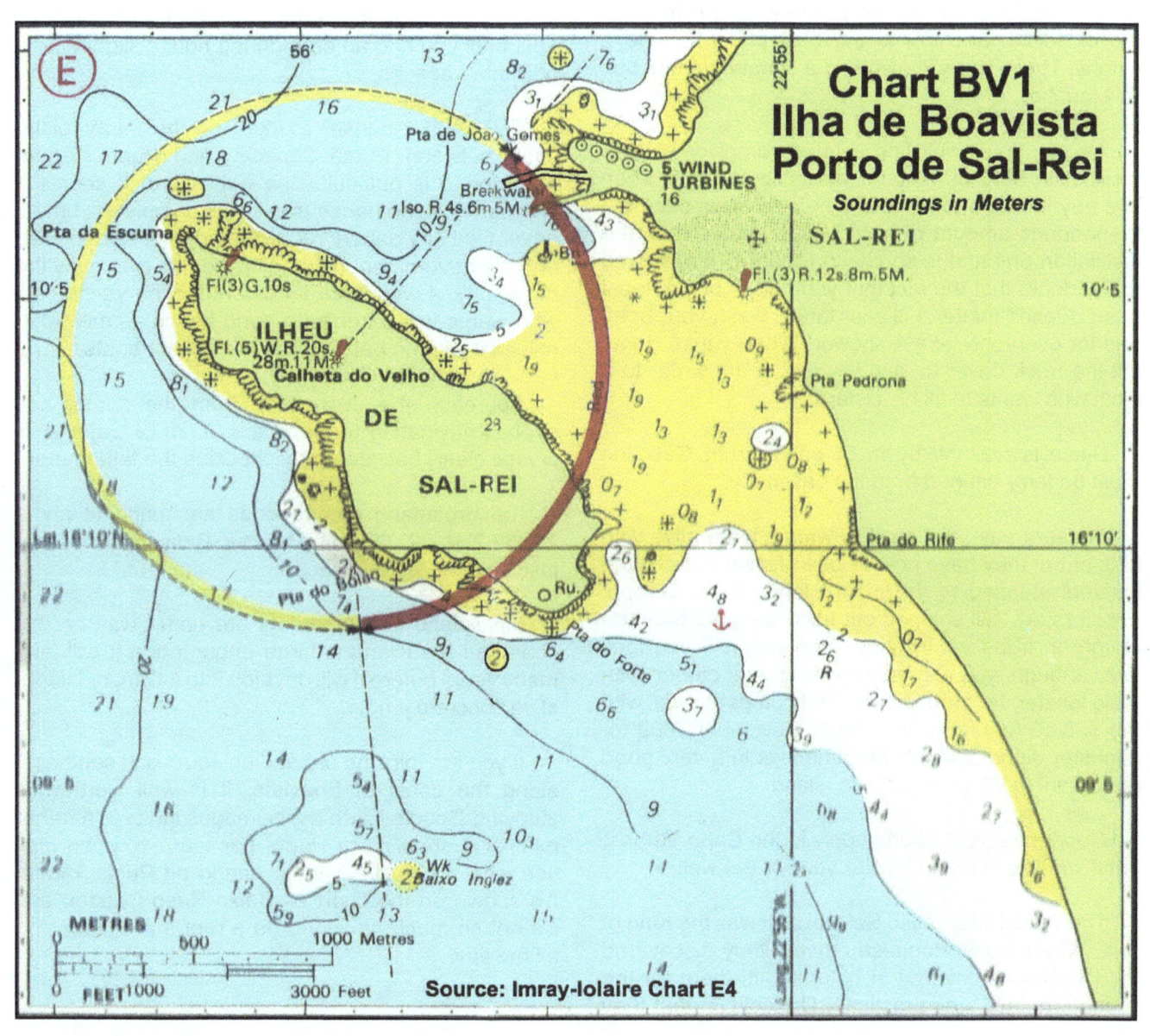

Sal-Rei where the chart shows 2.7 meters. The shoal that extends between the island and the mainland will only allow passage of powerboats or shoal-draft sailboats and multihulls.

This anchorage is safe in all normal weather conditions. While it does not appear to be affected by groundswells generated by North Atlantic storms, very occasionally, the swells from a really bad storm can carry as far as the Cape Verdes and make the anchorage in Sal-Rei untenable. This type of North Atlantic storm usually occurs in the period from January to March when most yachts would have already left the Cape Verdes.

The office of the harbor police is at the head of the old dock, and this is the best place to land a dinghy. There you will also find a simple friendly bar, Te Manche.

As yet, you won't find a Laundromat or shower facilities in Sal-Rei. Water is available, but only when you buy it by the ton in a tanker truck. This seems a tremendous amount of water, but it comes from the distillation unit and is so cheap (about €15 delivered to the dock) that the fact that you had to buy at least a ton doesn't matter. Fill your tanks, wash your boat, and let everyone take a shower. When you're done, tell the truck driver to give the rest of the water to a local who wants to fill his cistern.

Diesel is available by the 55-gallon drum. Gasoline must be jerry-canned from the gas station.

In years past, the shallow waters were alive with lobster but they have now all been fished out and the lobsters shipped to the main islands or to Europe. Lobsters are still shipped out from Maio but they are caught in traps set in fairly deep water. If you look hard enough, you can get a good lobster dinner, with a big lobster, for around €15. That compares well with the $28.50 (about €22) I paid in November 2009 for a lobster dinner with all the trimmings in a very good restaurant in Westerly, Rhode Island.

Good meat is in short supply in the Cape Verdes, but if you like fish and lobster you will eat well.

This island was called Sal-Rei as it was the King of Salt. When the Portuguese arrived, they discovered the island was covered in natural salt, there for the taking. The salt was practically like gold, in that they took the salt to the coast of Africa and traded it for slaves. They brought the slaves back to Boavista to work in the cotton plantations. After the slave trade expanded in the 16th century, they also brought slaves here to be sold for export to the Americas.

South Coast of Boavista

The other anchorage in Boavista is on the south coast. Reach it by sailing down the west coast. When departing Sal-Rei and heading south, you can avoid Baixo Vauban by heading southwest and passing to the west of the bank. Alternatively, you can sail down the coast 200 to 300 yards off the shore, using eyeball navigation, and pass inside the reef. The inside channel has 24 feet (7 meters) of water. Swing around the south end of the island and work your way east until you find an abandoned house slightly west of Punta Lacacão.

This is the "house" marked on the Imray-Iolaire chart between Punta Lacacão and Punta Tarafe. Abandoned is not quite the right word. It seems a German built the house and it was completed, but he never filed any papers requesting permission to build and the government never allowed him to occupy the house. It's a wonderful landmark for the yachtsman who wants to anchor by a sand beach — mile after mile of it with no habitation and no other boats.

Approach the anchorage from the south, use eyeball navigation to judge the depth of water (it is crystal clear) backed up by checking the fathometer.

Kai Brosmann recommends anchoring at about 15° 59.3' N, 22° 53.7' N. This is in Baia do Curralinho, just west of Punta Lacacão.

Major land developments are under way on this coast but the island is large enough that it will take many years before it will develop into a Canary Island-style concrete jungle.

If you are thinking of heading south and southeast along the coast of Boavista, it is well worthwhile studying Google Earth as its images indicate a rather extensive shoaling at Punta Lacacão. You can also see what looks like a small island off Punta Tarafe. It's shown on the chart as Baixo Raso Chegou and it's not so much an island as a reef that is breaking all the time.

Departing Boavista

From Boavista, you can head west to São Nicolau, Santa Luzia, São Vicente, and Santo Antão, stopping in Mindelo if you are in need of supplies or fuel. Alternatively, if you don't have time for those islands and your boat is in good shape and you have adequate provisions, you can sail directly to Maio or Santiago in the Ilhas do Sotavento. Either way, you'll be sailing downwind.

From Sal-Rei to Carrical, on São Nicolau, it's a hazard-free 70 miles, so you might want to plan an overnight passage. That will give you a morning arrival and time to scope out conditions in the anchorages in daylight.

From Sal-Rei to Tarrafal, on Santiago, or to Maio, on Ilha do Maio, is a similar distance, but you need to give Baixo João Valente a wide berth — unless the weather is very calm, in which case it might be possible to anchor on the edge of the reef for some snorkeling and possibly spear fishing. If you choose to approach Baixo João Valente, bear in mind the magnetic anomalies in the area and keep a sharp lookout.

Chapter 6
São Nicolau and Santa Luzia

Ilha de São Nicolau
Imray-Iolaire Chart E4

Ilha de São Nicolau is in the shape of an L. The longer leg is about 30 miles long and lies is an east-west axis, and the shorter leg, about 12 miles long, lies north and south. In contrast to Sal and Boavista to the east, it is a high island. Its highest peak, at 4,300 feet, is Monte Gordo on the western end of the island. A high ridge runs eastward, with several peaks reaching well over 2,000 feet. These mountains are high enough to gather some moisture from the clouds; not enough to make it verdant like the islands in the Eastern Caribbean, but sufficient to support some agriculture. A fair supply of fruit and vegetables is grown on São Nicolau.

If you are looking for small deserted coves with little or no sign of habitation, this is the island for you. There follow descriptions of 11 anchorages, nine of which do not show on any chart and seven of which are not mentioned in any guide. I have explored eight of them myself, either on *Sincerity* in 2005 or in a chartered 18-foot fishing boat in 2009.

An interesting feature of São Nicolau is that the principal town of Vila da Ribeira Brava is up in the middle of the island. It developed in the mountains rather than on the coast for several reasons. It's cooler there than on the coast and it's closer to the water supply — the rain, such as there is, falls on the windward, therefore northern, slopes of the mountains. The town's location inland also made it made it less accessible to raiding pirates.

Until the mid-20th century, Preguica, tucked into the corner of the L, was the principal port. For well over a hundred years, it was a regular port of call for American whaling ships, which stopped there to pick up crew and provisions. The last sailing whaling ship stopped at Preguica in 1924.

Preguica later fell into disuse while Tarrafal on the western side of the island developed into the main port.

One day, I was talking with Gerry Dom, and asked him why Preguica would have been chosen as the location for the main port in the first place, rather than Tarrafal.

"Look at it from the sailor's standpoint," Gerry pointed out. "Preguica is on the southeast coast. The land that stretches out to the east shelters it from the sea and from the worst of the northeast wind. Ships could come around the eastern end of São Nicolau

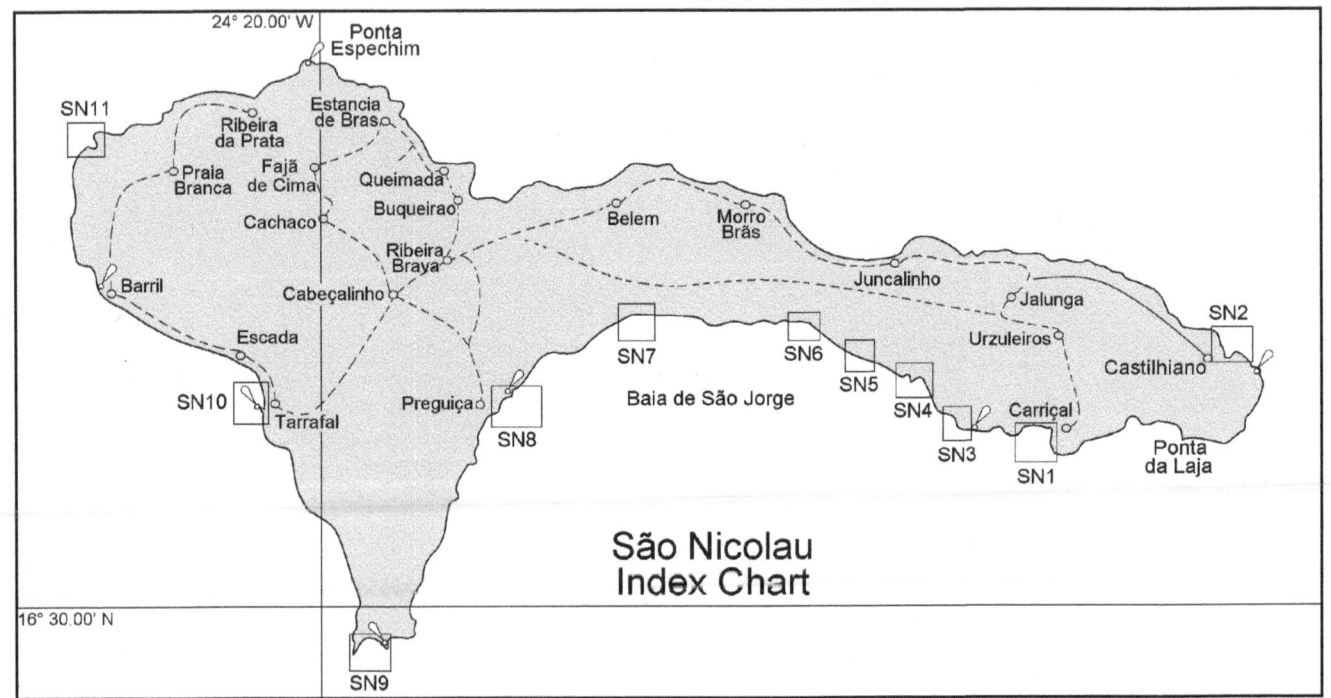

São Nicolau Index Chart

and sail downwind to Preguica, discharge their cargo, and then stand south, still downwind. Once clear of the southern end of São Nicolau, they could head due south or northwest. If they tried to get into Tarrafal, on the other hand, they could be becalmed under the lee of the island, and probably spend days working their way into port."

In the age of steamships and, now, motor-driven ships, Tarrafal makes the better port, but, because of the mountains, it was inaccessible from Vila da Ribeira Brava until a road was built in the 20th century. The straight-line distance from Tarrafal to Vila da Ribeira Brava is five miles or less, but it takes a full 40 minutes driving to get there in a taxi.

The airport was constructed next to the road from Preguica to Vila da Ribeira Brava, and is barely two miles from either one of those towns.

Vila da Ribeira Brava is an interesting town with some very nice small residencials, a bank, a couple of small grocery stores (not even un-super supermarkets), a pleasant town square with a church and government buildings around it, and a very nice Internet café.

The young owner of the Internet café is fantastic. I spent an hour there, paid him off, and went back to the residencial. When I started packing to leave on the afternoon plane, I discovered my notebook, with all my notes of my trips to the Azores and the Cape Verdes, was missing. Obviously, I had left it in the Internet café. I returned to the café. It was closed and would not be open until 1500. A passer by, who luckily spoke English, asked what my problem was, as I guess I looked very distressed. I explained and he immediately pulled out his mobile phone and called the café's owner. He did not get the owner but rather his very cute sister who came and opened up the café. We searched high and low with no success. I returned to the residencial feeling rather discouraged.

About half an hour later, in walks the owner of the Internet café with my notebook. He had gone to all the residencials asking if they had a guest with a white beard and wearing a big white hat. He finally found me.

As I keep saying, the people in the Portuguese islands are the most fantastic people in the world.

The village has narrow streets that are so steep they seem almost vertical in places. Even though they are made of cobblestones, only four-wheel-drive vehicles can negotiate them.

The island does warrant an exploration by car. You can rent a self-drive car, but I wouldn't recommend it unless you are accustomed to narrow winding roads with cliffs that drop vertically from their edges and no guard rails. If you do rent a car, make sure it has four wheel drive. You would probably do better to hire a taxi, as you'll get a local as a guide into the bargain. Taxi drivers on the island speak a variety of languages; find one who speaks yours.

With the aid of Dr. Pitt Reitmaier's walking maps, those who like to explore on foot can visit parts of the island inaccessible even to four-wheel-drive vehicles.

Whether you explore São Nicolau by car or on foot, it's worthwhile bringing along your handheld GPS, as the 1:50,000 topo map is calibrated to WGS 84 and clearly marked with latitudes and longitudes.

Some residents speak English but the principal foreign language spoken is German, possibly brought about by São Nicolau's popularity with German walking tourists. You'll see them on all sorts of roads well off the beaten track, in places they must have walked five or six miles from their starting point to reach.

Amazingly, French seemed to be the most common language among the boys hanging around the dock, but as noted before, more and more of the young people will soon be speaking English as it is a required foreign language in the schools.

The airport is only a 15-minute drive from Ribeira Brava. If you don't visit São Nicolau by boat, it's possible to fly there and stay in a residencial while you explore the island. The scenery is spectacular.

Anchorages on the South Coast of São Nicolau

Looking at the topo map of São Nicolau, and cross checking with Google Earth, I saw several bays on the south coast of São Nicolau that looked as though they might make nice secluded anchorages. So, when I was on the island in November 2009, with the aid of an English-speaking taxi driver I arranged to charter

73

Street's Guide to the Cape Verde Islands

The author hired a local fishing crew to take him on a cruise along the south coast of São Nicolau from Preguica to Carrical and back. The white house in the background is a useful landmark for Preguica.

Fish pots at Carrical take a variety of forms.

São Nicolau and Santa Luzia

an 18-foot fishing boat. I set off with a 1:25,000 topo map, handheld GPS, hand bearing compass, and a lead line made out of some 1/8-inch flag halyard (I always carry it in my sea bag in case the zipper dies) and a chunk of iron supplied by the fisherman. After seven and a half hours in the fishing boat I can truly say that I have explored the southeast coast of São Nicolau in great detail.

After three and a half hours in the fishing boat, we arrived at the small village of Carrical, which I discovered had three different rum shops. But all I could think of was the old Australian song, "The pub with no beer" in which the outback farmer travels 200 miles to the nearest bar to find it was out of beer. I had traveled three and a half hours in a fishing boat to a village with three rum shops, to find all of them locked up and no one could find the keys!

This coast of São Nicolau is long and dry, with virtually no habitation except the occasional house out in the middle of nowhere and the small town of Carrical. Except in the coves, which were at the mouths of ravines that walkers would probably enjoy exploring, the shore is lined with cliffs and offers no chance to get ashore.

Despite a 10- to 12-knot easterly breeze, there was nothing more than a small chop on the sea.

The harbors on the south coast of São Nicolau are listed below from east to west, as you would encounter them when you sail to the island from Sal or Boavista. Some of them are quite small, with room enough only for one boat. I recommend anchoring bow and stern or with a Bahamian moor so as to have enough scope and not swing too close to shore.

Carrical
Harbor chart SN1
AP 16° 32.3' N; 24° 05.2' W

Carrical is moderately well sheltered with 30 feet of water at the entrance and a sand bottom that gradually shelves toward the head of the harbor.

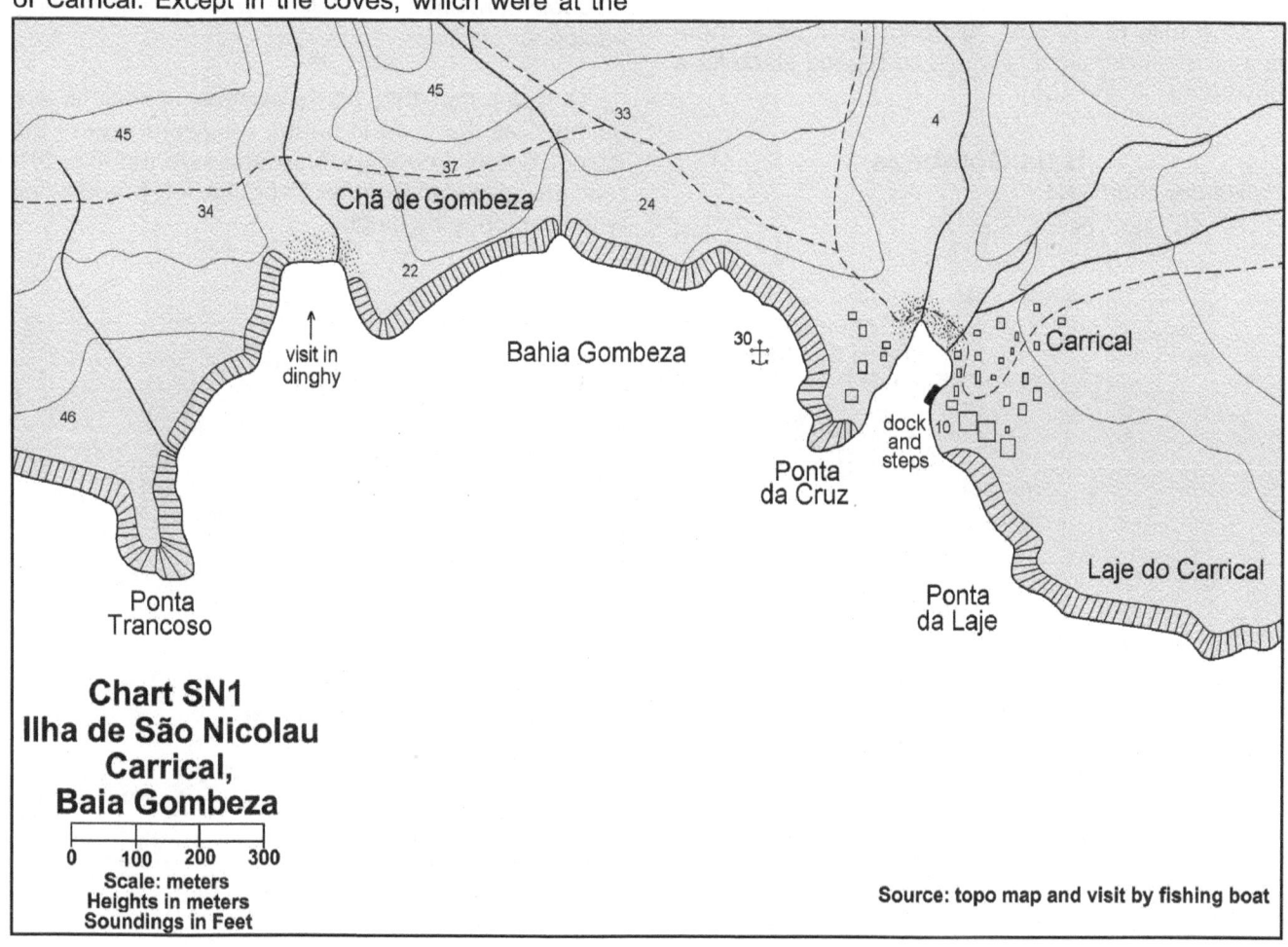

**Chart SN1
Ilha de São Nicolau
Carrical,
Baia Gombeza**

Scale: meters
Heights in meters
Soundings in Feet

Source: topo map and visit by fishing boat

On my visit in 2009, I saw a small inboard-powered fishing boat of about 30 feet anchored in the middle of the harbor and a Dutch cruising boat of about 40 feet anchored at the entrance. A dinghy was pulled up on the beach, so no doubt the crew was exploring the valley that leads down to the harbor.

Despite what the 2004 edition of the RCC *Atlantic Islands Guide* says, there is no float in the middle of the harbor obstructing it with mooring lines, nor is there a weekly supply boat from Tarrafal. Rather, supplies are brought in via 4 x4 when the road is passable or by fishing launches from Preguica. They evidently bring these launches alongside the stone jetty, which was poorly fendered with old tires. This jetty is also a place to land a dinghy.

The village has three rum shops, a church, an abandoned tuna canning factory, and a concrete football field (soccer to Americans). It's a poor village but everyone was friendly and no one was asking for handouts.

One mile to the east, at Ponta Escagarra, there is a nice small cove that would be a good place for a private picnic and swim.

Baia Gombeza
Harbor chart SN1
AP 16° 32.3' N; 24° 05.2' W

This is the first bay west of Carrical, and a much better anchorage in 30 feet over a sand bottom. I recommend anchoring here and visiting Carrical via dinghy.

Although it's a good anchorage, there is no way to get ashore as it is surrounded by cliffs. However, on the west side of the bay, a ravine opens up into a small cove with a few small ruined houses and beach where a dinghy could be landed for the purpose of exploring ashore.

Boca da Praia de Falcão
Harbor chart SN2
AP 16° 35.3' N; 24° 01.0' W

For those with have a taste for adventure, who like to explore and like to hike, and have a good RIB or similar fast launch, an interesting expedition is to head east 4 miles, then north 2 miles to Boca da Praia de Falcão. This is a narrow fjord-like cove 100 yards wide at the entrance and 300 yards long that leads to a couple of ravines that walkers would probably enjoy exploring.

Only attempt this when weather conditions are suitable, as the cove is on the windward side of the island. Before heading off on any side trip like this, read the section in Chapter 4 about safety precautions when exploring by dinghy.

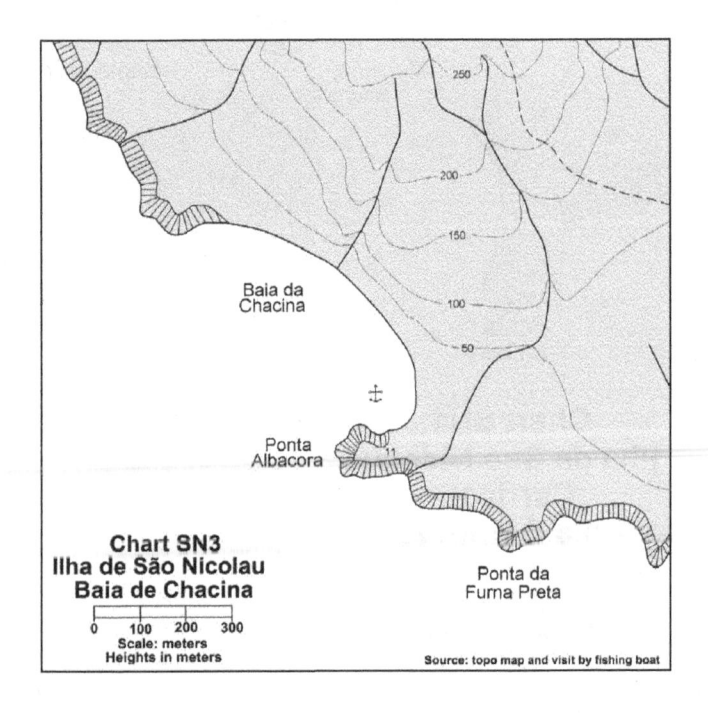

São Nicolau and Santa Luzia

Chart SN4
Ilha de São Nicolau
Ponta do Ilhéu

Scale: meters
Heights in meters
Soundings in Feet

Source: topo map and visit by fishing boat

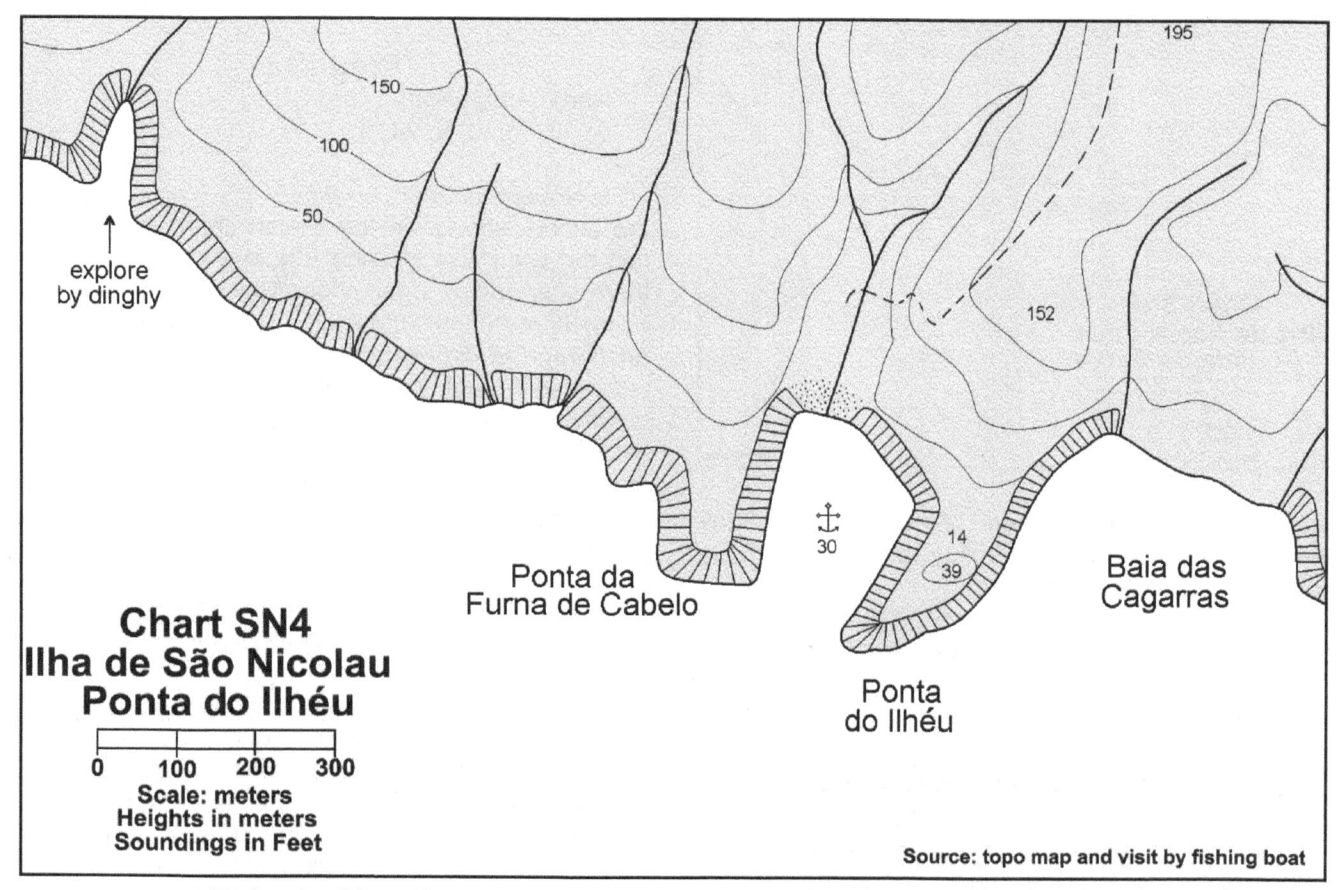

Baia da Chacina
Harbor chart SN3
AP 16° 33.0' N; 24° 07.7' W

Approach from the southwest, tuck in behind Ponta Alcabora, and anchor in 30 to 40 feet. This bay is completely sheltered and there was no sea at all when I stopped by. This makes it a good anchorage, but forget about getting ashore unless you are a mountain climber as the bay is surrounded by cliffs. There is no beach here but the snorkeling is probably good and possibly the fishing too.

Ponta do Ilhéu
Harbor chart SN4
AP 16° 33.7' N; 24° 08.0' W

Between Ponta do Ilhéu and Ponta da Fuma de Cabello is a very attractive cove about 150 yards wide and 300 yards long. There is 30 feet of depth about 100 yards off the beach. The sand bottom gradually shoals toward the head of the harbor where there is a gray sand beach and a ravine that bears exploring by those so inclined.

One half mile to the west is a small unnamed cove that warrants an exploratory expedition in a dinghy.

Aquada da Garça
Harbor chart SN5
AP 16° 34.3' N; 24° 09.35' W

This small cove is only 120 yards wide and 70 yards long, so would only be only useful to boats of 40 feet or less. The depth is 30 feet at the entrance and the bottom is sand, gradually shoaling to the head where there's a gray sand beach and a valley leading out. Cliffs line both sides, and there are two abandoned houses on the top of the cliffs on the southeast side. This would be a tough place to live as it's a long row to the nearest store.

Ponta Posson
Harbor chart SN6
AP 16° 34.9' N; 24° 10.3' W

This narrow cove is only 50 yards wide by 150 yards long. The depth is 24 feet at the entrance and 18 feet inside the cove and it shoals gradually toward

Street's Guide to the Cape Verde Islands

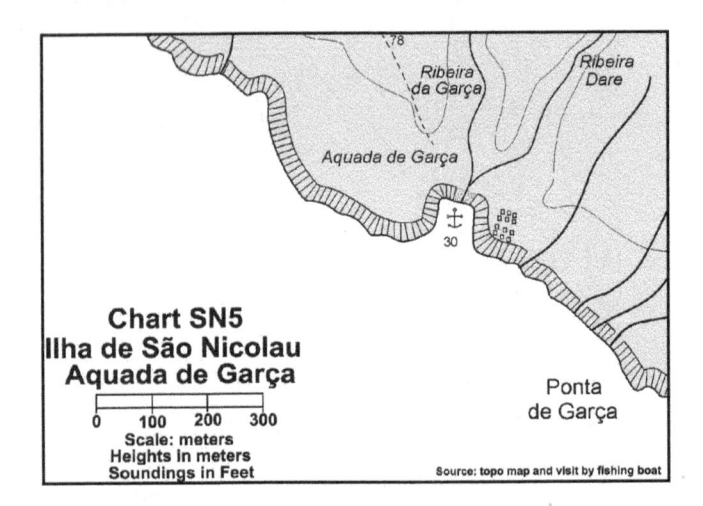

**Chart SN5
Ilha de São Nicolau
Aquada de Garça**

a gray sand beach at the head of the cove. Cliffs flank both sides and a dry river valley might tempt those inclined to take a walk ashore.

Porto da Lapa
Harbor chart SN7
AP 16° 35.0' N; 24° 13.7' W

This doesn't appear to be much of a port today, just an open bay with a shingle beach and a couple of semi-abandoned houses onshore. A small white shrine is visible on the eastern point of the bay. It's deep water fairly close to shore.

Preguica
Harbor chart SN8
AP 16° 35.0' N; 24° 13.7' W

In November 2005, on *Sincerity*, we hove-to where the anchor shows on the sketch chart. Despite the fact the wind was blowing a hooley out of the east, there was only a small chop. The anchorage would be sheltered unless the wind went south of east. The anchorage is exposed to winds from south of east clockwise through to west of south, and it would never be affected by the northwest groundswell. The village did not look all that attractive so, after ascertaining that the chart appeared to be correct and that the anchorage appeared to be in the right place, we moved on.

South of the dock, fishermen haul up their boats on a shingle beach at the mouth of a dry river.

In 2009, the fishermen assured me that the light at Porto Velho, east of town, did work.

Supplies, I would say, are non existent other than the very basics. As of November 2009, there was not even an un-super supermarket, only a couple of what are known in the West Indies as rum shops selling beer and booze and the very basic commodities. The old lady running the rum shop was very friendly.

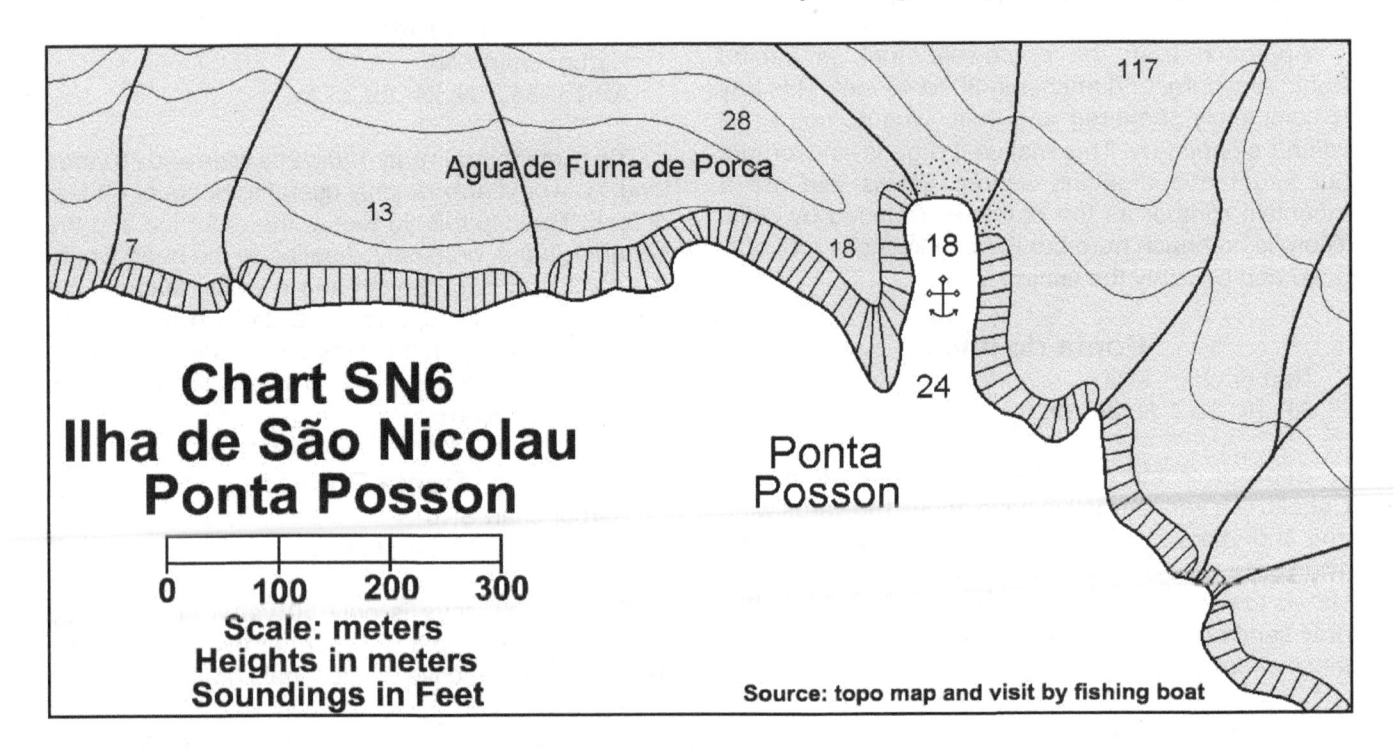

**Chart SN6
Ilha de São Nicolau
Ponta Posson**

Chart SN7 Ilha de São Nicolau Porto da Lapa

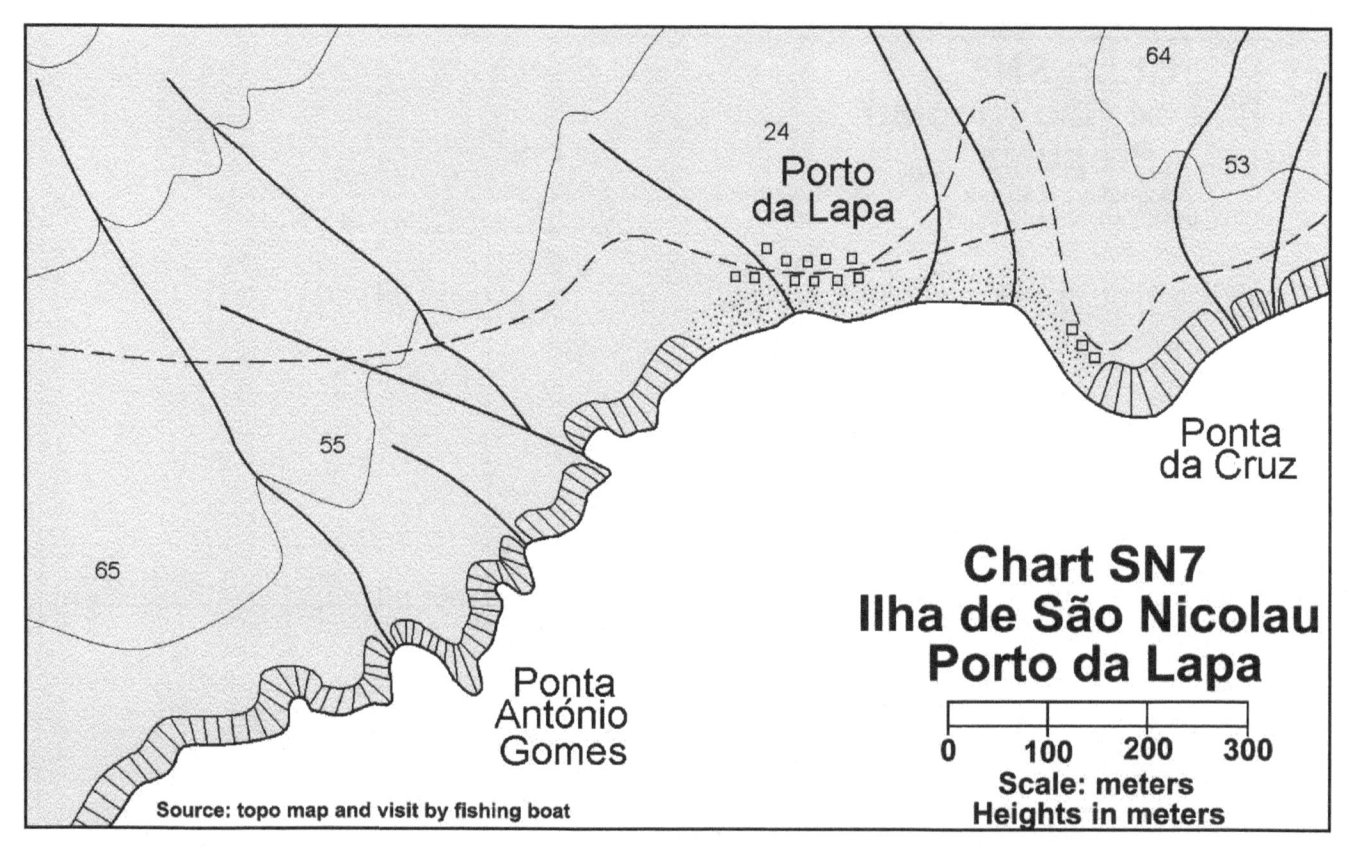

Preguica was for three centuries São Nicolau's main port. About the only evidence that remains to indicate the town's former importance is the remains of bollards that were installed along the cliffs. Ships would anchor off and run lines ashore while they loaded and unloaded. Today, Preguica is linked to Vila da Ribeira Brava by a good road, but in the days before automobiles it would have been a stiff haul for cargo.

When I visited in December 2002, it was obvious that the town had been dying for the last 50 years. The hand-powered crane on the dock was derelict. It might have value as a museum piece, but not any longer for loading cargo.

At that time, what appeared to be a small, very nice hotel with a pool was under construction at the north end of the village. In 2009, I discovered it was a private home. As a young man, the owner had left Preguica and gone to Norway, where he must have done very well. The house is magnificent; it would be considered a small sized mansion anywhere and it really stands out in the Cape Verdes.

Bahia de Fidalgo

Harbor chart SN9
AP 16° 28.4' N; 24° 19.35' W

We explored this bay on *Sincerity* in 2005. We entered the cove but did not anchor. Despite it blowing 25 knots and gusting to 30 knots, 200 yards offshore we found calm water in 30 feet with, apparently, a sand bottom. We could not be sure of the bottom as we did not have an old fashioned lead line we could arm. The shore is rocky and there is no beach, but the water was calm and we would have had no problem getting ashore in a dinghy.

Bahia debaixo da Rocha

Heading from Baia de Fidalgo to Tarrafal, Kai Brosmann reports that there is a beach and anchorage in Bahia debaixo da Rocha at about 16° 31.4' north. Head for the beach watch the fathometer, and anchor in a suitable depth. I suggest either a proper Bahamian moor or bow and stern as under the high land the wind will be very variable and the boat may want to waltz around the anchor.

Street's Guide to the Cape Verde Islands

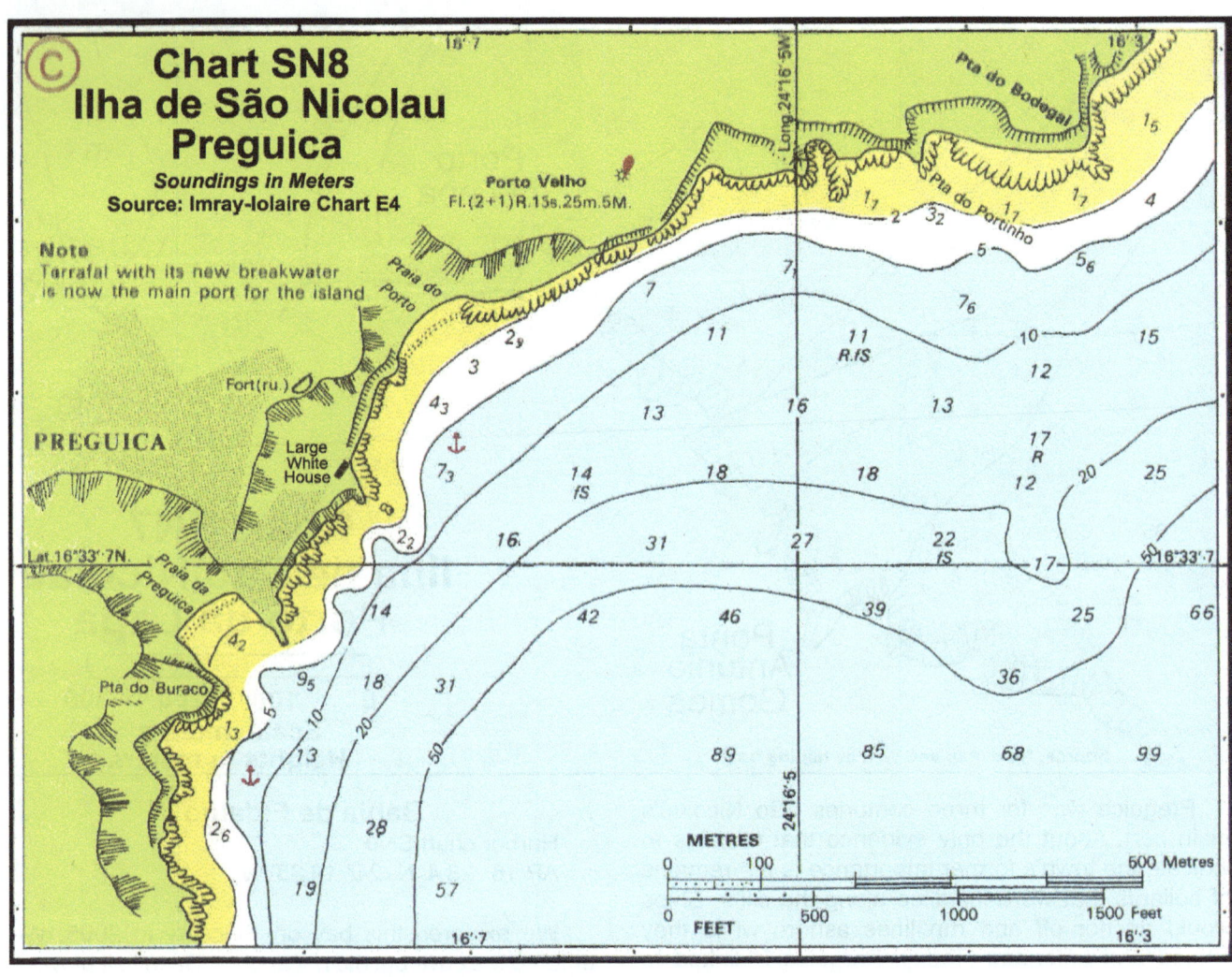

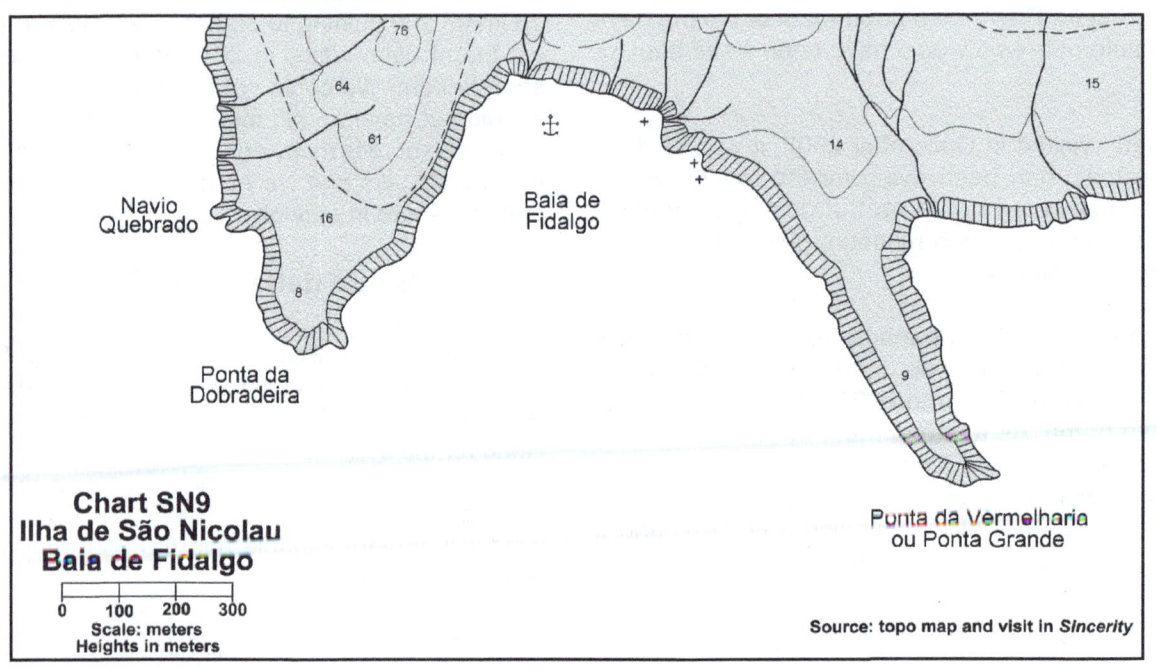

Tarrafal

Harbor chart SN10
AP 16° 34.2' N; 24° 22.3' W

Porto de Tarrafal is protected by a 300-foot-long north–south breakwater. It is used by the local freighters but it might be possible to lay alongside temporarily when no freighters are using it.

There is limited room to anchor behind the breakwater in water 8 to 9 feet deep. Anchor north of the dotted line on the sketch chart and Imray-Iolaire chart E4 to allow room for freighters to maneuver off and on the dock.

Proceed with caution and use a depth sounder or a lead line: The chart from the Cape Verde Hydrographic Office survey seems to indicate more water in the south end of the harbor than my nephew Morgan MacDonald III reported in 2000 when he stopped there in his 40-foot cat schooner, *Ushuaia*.

A Bahamian moor is needed when anchoring in Tarrafal as the wind waltzes around in all directions. Moreover, gusts as strong as 50 knots can blow out of the ravine with absolutely no warning.

We anchored off Tarrafal for two days on *Sincerity*. For the entire time we were there, we observed that, although it was blowing hard where we anchored, it appeared the area about a mile to a mile and a half to the northwest was flat calm. The northwest anchorage would a good anchorage, but a long dinghy ride from town. We were anchored in about 40 feet of water and, despite having the mizzen up; we were tide-rode most of the time by a northwest/southwest (ebb and flood) tidal current. The boats inside of us in 15 to 20 feet of water were inside the tide line.

Kai Brosmann recommends anchoring farther up the coast. His website says 16° 35.07' N, 24° 23.4' W, which is near Lixeira. Head for that waypoint, watch the fathometer and anchor at a suitable depth. Kai says the anchorage has a sand bottom and it's a nice place for a swim. He also says it's quiet, and you won't be bothered by fishermen trying to sell you fish.

When anchoring, remember the bottom drops off steeply. If you do drag in the least, you will be in water too deep to anchor in. I would recommend two anchors toward shore and one offshore, setting basically a Bahamian moor.

Fuel and water are available in Tarrafal but you have to fetch them in jerry cans. Ashore, you'll find a number of small un-super supermarkets. As in Boavista, the un-super supermarket is at the gas station on the main road out of town, a 10-minute walk from the dock. A number of small restaurants serve beer, and a most friendly one is at the head of the dock. I visited it in 2002, 2005, and 2009 and the barmaid and customers were friendly every time.

To my surprise and pleasure, I found fairly good supply of fruit and vegetables. There were two cyber cafés in the village; in one the computers did not work, the other was run by an excellent young man who was most helpful. In 2005, phone cards and fax facilities were available at the Post Office, but the envelope we sent by registered mail never arrived. By 2009, phone booths were hard to find and everyone was using mobiles. There is a bank and a cash machine in town.

To the northwest of town, a big new development is under way. A local taxi driver referred to it as Auschwitz. I drove by it in 2009 and I have to admit the name suits its appearance: The buildings look more like a prison camp than a holiday camp and it's surrounded by a wire fence topped with barbed wire.

My nephew Morgan MacDonald III, sailing *Ushuaia* with his wife and two children as crew, stopped by São Nicolau in 2000 and bought enough fresh fruit and vegetables to carry them across the Atlantic.

Ponta do Galeão

Harbor chart SN11
AP 16° 40.0' N; 24° 26.0' W

This is a possible anchorage on the northwest coast that we did not explore or even look at. It's a big semicircular bay, about 400 meters in diameter between Ponta da Ferra Bráz and Ponta do Galeão.

Approach this harbor from the northwest from the AP, eyeball your way in while watching the depth sounder, and anchor in a suitable depth — if you find it. I am not sure if you will find water shoal enough to anchor.

Street's Guide to the Cape Verde Islands

Looking toward Tarrafal from the north. Sincerity is visible at anchor, mizzen up. — Photo by Alison Langley

This photo is taken from inside the harbor at Tarrafal. — Photo by Alison Langley

São Nicolau and Santa Luzia

Chart SN10 Ilha de São Nicolau Tarrafal
Soundings in Meters

Chart SN11 Ilha de São Nicolau Ponta do Galeão

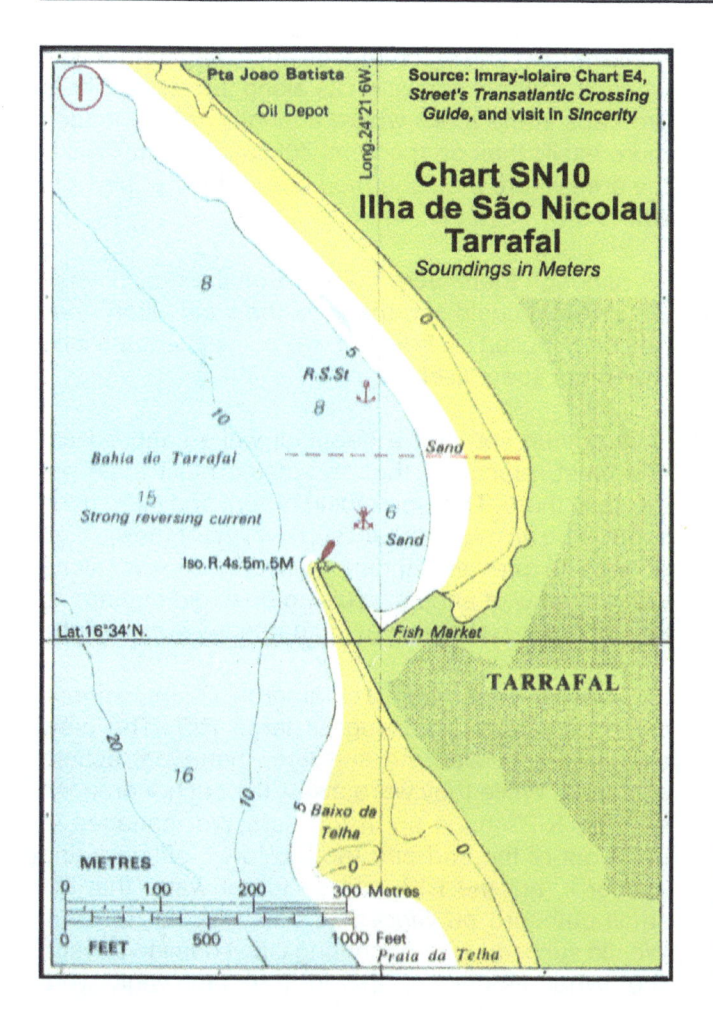

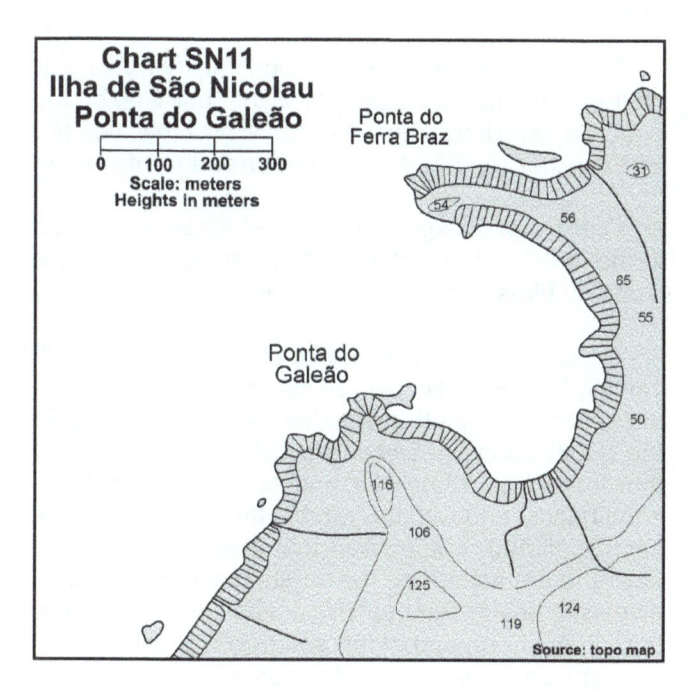

The only structure along the beach in Santa Luzia is this shrine. Fishermen who sometimes stay on the beach keep their matches inside the door. (Photo by Don Street)

The bay is surrounded by cliffs and it should be sheltered in all normal conditions as northwesterly winds are very rare. In normal circumstances, and with the wind in the easterly quadrant, it would be dead easy to stick your nose in and investigate this cove.

There are no roads in this part of the island and no habitation.

Since it is only 25-miles from Tarrafal, Sao Nicolău, to the anchorage at Santa Luzia, an early morning departure from Tarrafal would allow time to take a dog leg north to investigate this harbor. The big question is, is it shoal enough to anchor? If it is too deep to anchor, continue on to Santa Luzia and arrive when the light is still good for eyeball navigation.

Ilha de Santa Luzia
Imray-Iolaire Chart E4
AP 16° 44.0' N; 24° 46.0' W

Ilha de Santa Luzia is seven miles long and uninhabited, although fishermen do periodically camp out on the beautiful three-mile white sand beach on the southwest-facing coast. This is the best beach on the island and the best anchorage is also on this coast, just east of the little island, Ilhéu Zinho. While there are no off-lying rocks to the northwest of this islet, there are rocks along the beach southeast of it, but you can find gaps between them where you can land a dinghy.

The chart of this island on the inset of the 2005 Imray-Iolaire Chart E4 was not quite correct. It was made from an 1820 British survey and the latitude and longitude are slightly off. This has been corrected in subsequent editions of the chart. The position of Ilhéu Zinho, as taken by D. M. Street Jr. by GPS in late November 2005, is 16° 45.12 N, 45° 45´51 W. This makes the chart off by a few hundred yards. Given the numerous sources the Imray-Iolaire chart was made from, all of which were based on old surveys, it's likely that the GPS and chart are not in precise agreement in a number of places. This close in, you should be operating by eyeball anyway.

About halfway between Ilhéu Zinho and the rocky point of Ponta da Laje, at the southeastern end of the beach, you will find a statue in a shrine to Our Lady erected by the fishermen. The best dinghy landing is slightly southeast of this statue. The miniature shrine is protected by a glass door, by means of which the fishermen use it as a cache for matches to use when they camp on the beach.

It obviously seldom rains here as the fishermen have not built a shelter. They just live outdoors out of boxes in which they store their spare clothes and gear.

With *Sincerity*, we spent two days anchored off the southwest coast, just inside Ilhéu Zinho. Despite leaving the mizzen up to reduce the roll, we discovered we were at times tide-rode rather then wind-rode, with the current sometimes running northwest and at other times southeast.

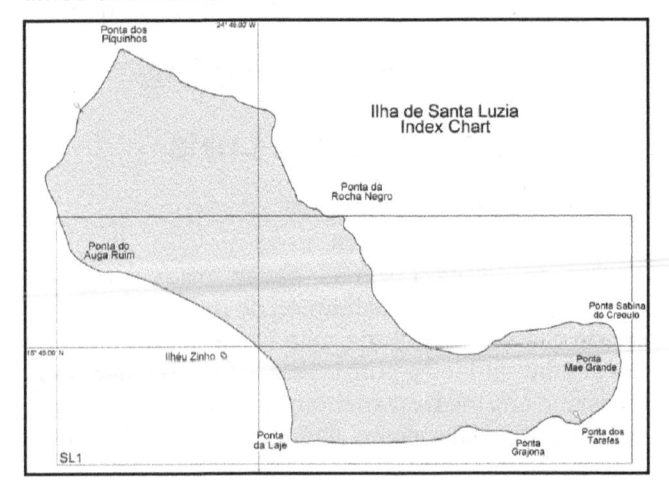

Kai Brosmann recommends anchoring farther east where the charts shows rocks along the shore. There are gaps in the rocks where a dinghy can be landed more easily than on the beautiful sand beach. This is the area where the fishermen pull up their boats, and where they have their shrine.

Although there were no boats on the beach when we visited, I could see marks in the sand where they had been pulled up from the water. I spotted one lone fisherman spear fishing.

Any time you see a beautiful white sand beach, you must remember that something must have put the sand there. That something is surf, and there does seem to be an ever-present surf, which at times is high enough to prevent landing. *Sincerity*'s crew, along with the crew of another cruising boat, did manage to get ashore to have an evening barbecue in moonlight.

During the afternoon, a catamaran, *Orient Express*, came very close to losing its large RIB. The crew anchored it outside the surf line, then went ashore exploring. While they were away, the anchor dragged and the RIB ended up in the surf. We managed to get it out of the surf and tried to tow it offshore and anchor it, but the RIB was so full of water that the small outboard on *Sincerity*'s RIB was not up to it. We did succeed in re-anchoring it just outside the surf line. When its owners arrived, they amazingly were able to get the outboard started.

This was a lesson learned: Don't anchor your RIB off the beach and go exploring. Either pull it up on the beach or send it back to the yacht with a crew member who can then retrieve the exploration party on its return.

One group of explorers reported a freshwater lake in the middle of the island. They did not taste it, but said that birds and goats were drinking from it.

On our approach to Santa Luzia from the east, coming from São Nicolau, we saw a power catamaran anchored on the south coast. Later in the day, we visited the south coast in *Sincerity*'s RIB. We ascertained that there was a shelf for anchoring, with scattered coral heads, and with the wind in the northeast it was semi-sheltered. It appeared that it would have been easier to get ashore on the south coast, which has a nice sand beach. Although it's not as good a beach as that on the north end of the southwest coast, landing a dinghy on the south coast is easier.

São Nicolau and Santa Luzia

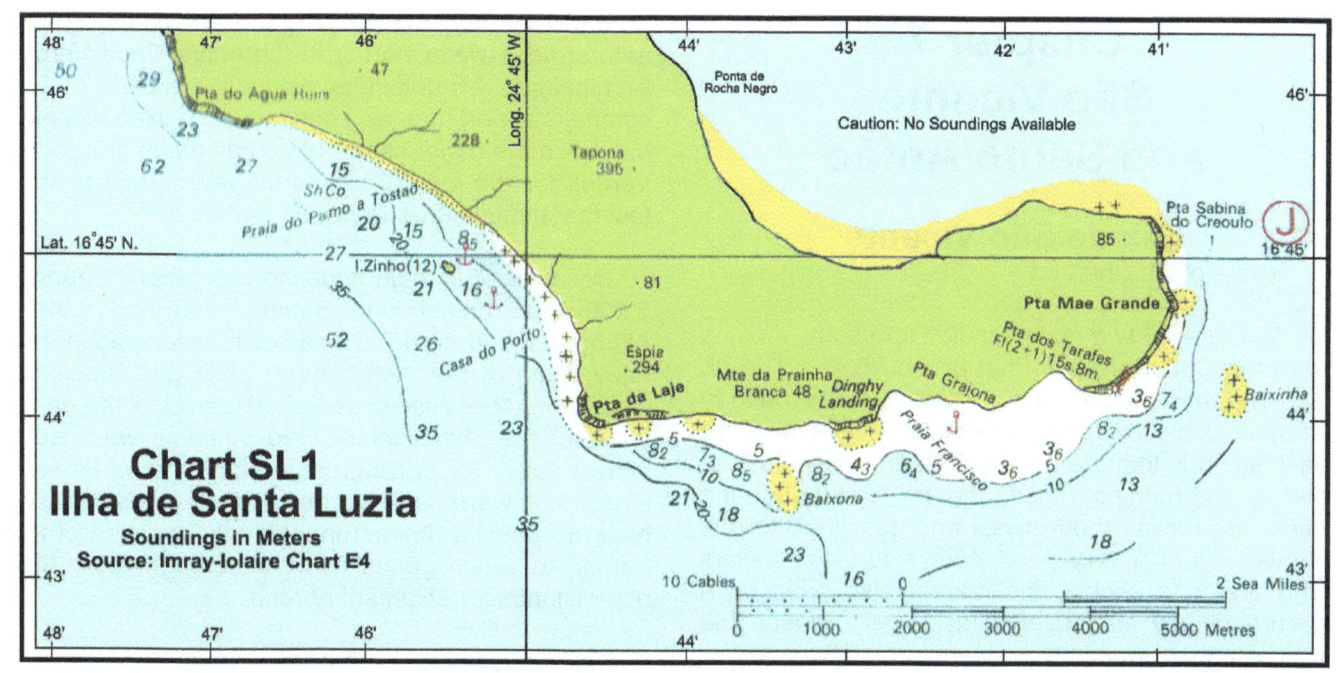

**Chart SL1
Ilha de Santa Luzia**
Soundings in Meters
Source: Imray-Iolaire Chart E4

It's worth noting that there is a notation "Landing Place" on the 1820 British Admiralty chart in the spot on the south-coast beach where the Imray-Iolaire chart says "Dinghy Landing."

The ridge of the island is 1,000 feet high, so I am sure the wind will die in the night at times and come in from offshore, which could swing you ashore. I therefore recommend a Bahamian or bow-and-stern mooring here.

All in all, Ilha de Santa Luzia is a wonderful island to visit and explore. The fishing is good, a good fisherman could probably provide the crew with fresh fish every day either with hook and line or by spear fishing.

If you plan on going to Mindelo, São Vicente, from Santa Luzia, go north about São Vicente so you don't have to beat against the current in the Canal do São Vicente (see Sailing Directions, page 43).

The anchorage at Santa Luzia, shown here looking east toward São Nicolau, is sheltered from the trade winds and gives access to a spectacular sand beach.

Photo by Alison Langley

85

Chapter 7
São Vicente and Santo Antão

Ilha de São Vicente
Imray-Iolaire Chart E4

São Vicente is a major landfall for yachts arriving from the Canary Islands that do not stop in Ilha do Sal. The facilities and services are fully described in Chapter 3 but the most important development for yachtsmen is that the 120-boat Marina Mindelo is at last up and running. Among the services the marina offers are fueling (both diesel and gasoline), toilets, showers, and a very good WiFi setup. For sailors who prefer to anchor, the marina also provides a secure dinghy landing spot at a very reasonable cost. Another great improvement is that Cape Verde Immigration and the harbor police have offices in the marina, eliminating the need to traipse around town looking for them.

Porto Grande, Mindelo, is the only really good natural deep-water harbor in the entire Cape Verde Archipelago. Mindelo has developed into a major commercial port and, as a consequence, São Vicente has been the major center of commerce in the Cape Verdes for the last 200 hundred years, despite the fact that the capital is Praia, on Santiago.

Because of its high ridgeline that reaches above 5,000 feet, neighboring Santo Antão had water. Although it had no decent harbor it developed in the early years of the 16th century while São Vincente was ignored because of its lack of rain. Until the early years of the 19th century, São Vincente was used almost solely for grazing cattle, and most of its few inhabitants were cattle herders. When the island did begin to develop it was undoubtedly because of its harbor, to which goods could be brought from the other islands for shipment abroad.

The development of ocean-going coal-burning steamships necessitated the establishment of coaling stations in strategic locations worldwide. Because of its location on the routes to southern Africa and the

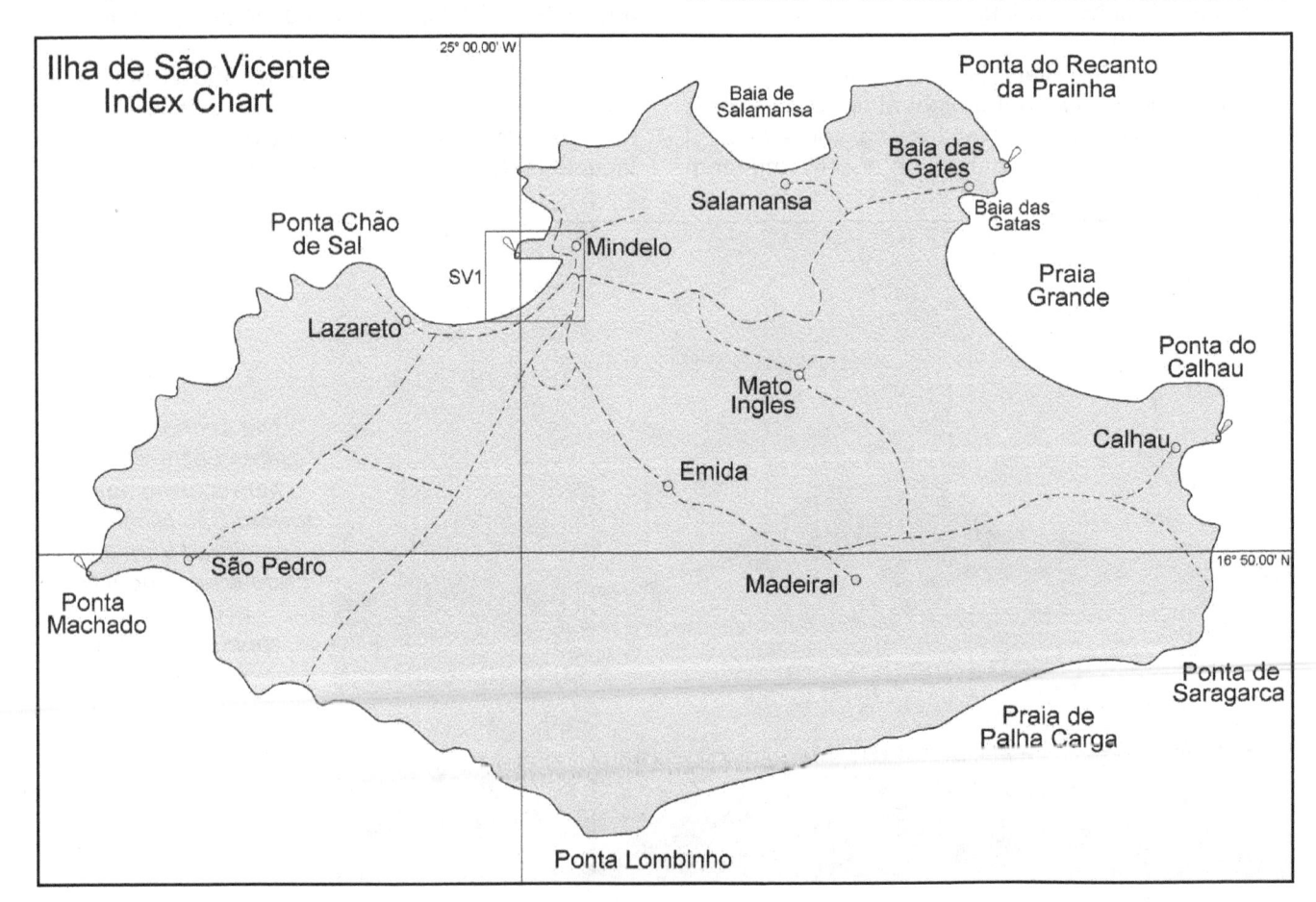

Americas, Mindelo became a coaling station. The first ships coaled there in 1838. In 1854, 157 ships coaled at Mindelo. In 1898, 1,503 ships coaled there, an average of four a day. Coal was stored in vast quantities: 5,000 tons in lighters ready to be passed on board ships and a reserve of 35,000 tons ashore. A 100,000-gallon water tank was kept full with water barged from Santo Antão.

Again, because of its strategic location, beginning in the 1870s, Mindelo became a hub for transoceanic cables. Cables were extended to South Africa and Brazil in 1875.

Coal and cables brought considerable prosperity to the island, and this is apparent in the many examples of beautiful colonial Portuguese architecture that still stand in the center of Mindelo. When I first visited in 1985, the whole place was falling apart, and any new buildings that were going up then were outside the main central section of the old town. In 1989, it was still falling apart and they were talking about knocking down the wonderful market building because it was in such bad shape. Happily, when the economy began to flourish again after the communist/socialist police state was thrown out, instead of knocking down the buildings in the center of the town they began to restore them. The restored two-story central market is without a doubt the most spectacular market building in the entire Atlantic Basin. Markets on other islands may have better produce and be more modern, but none of them can rival the magnificent architecture of the market building in Mindelo.

Throughout the town, in December 2002, in 2005, and again in 2009, we saw building after building being restored. I predict, and many people I have spoken with agree, that, in years to come, Mindelo will develop as one of the most architecturally beautiful towns in the entire Atlantic Basin. Let's hope the government of Cape Verde will declare the town a National Heritage site, along the lines of what was done in the lower end of Christiansted, St. Croix, back in the middle 1950s. There, although you can rebuild the interior of a building, you are not allowed to alter its facade. This policy has created, in the lower section of Christiansted, the most beautiful and attractive town in the entire Eastern Caribbean.

Porto Grande/Mindelo
Harbor chart SV1
AP 16° 54.0' N; 25° 01.0' W

Mindelo is very definitely worth exploring. Any semi-restored colonial building with a sign for a restaurant is well worth investigating. For instance, stop in at Club Naval, where the beer is always cold and the barmaid always beautiful, then walk out the back door. Across the street you will see an old building, a bar, with a door to its left. This is the entrance to an old hotel and restaurant, Pensão Chave d'Ouro. You will go up a narrow staircase to the second floor where you'll discover a magnificent dining room furnished with antiques dating back to the days of Mindelo's heyday in the 1890s (and I think the waiter goes back almost that far). In 2002, a group of us including "Scalpy Nick" (I call him that because I cannot remember his name but he has a little Swan called *Scalpy*), whom I had last seen in Antigua three years before, had an excellent lunch there. In 2005, the crew of *Sincerity* twice had excellent dinners, and in 2009, I again had an excellent dinner, beautifully served in a wonderful atmosphere.

An exploration of the town may turn up equally attractive restored or semi-restored restaurants and hotels.

The easiest entry to Porto Grande is from the northwest, through the channel between Santo Antão and São Vicente. Head generally southwest toward Ilhéu dos Passaros and, once past it (you can leave

Panoramic view of the interior of the restored market in Mindelo, São Vicente

Street's Guide to the Cape Verde Islands

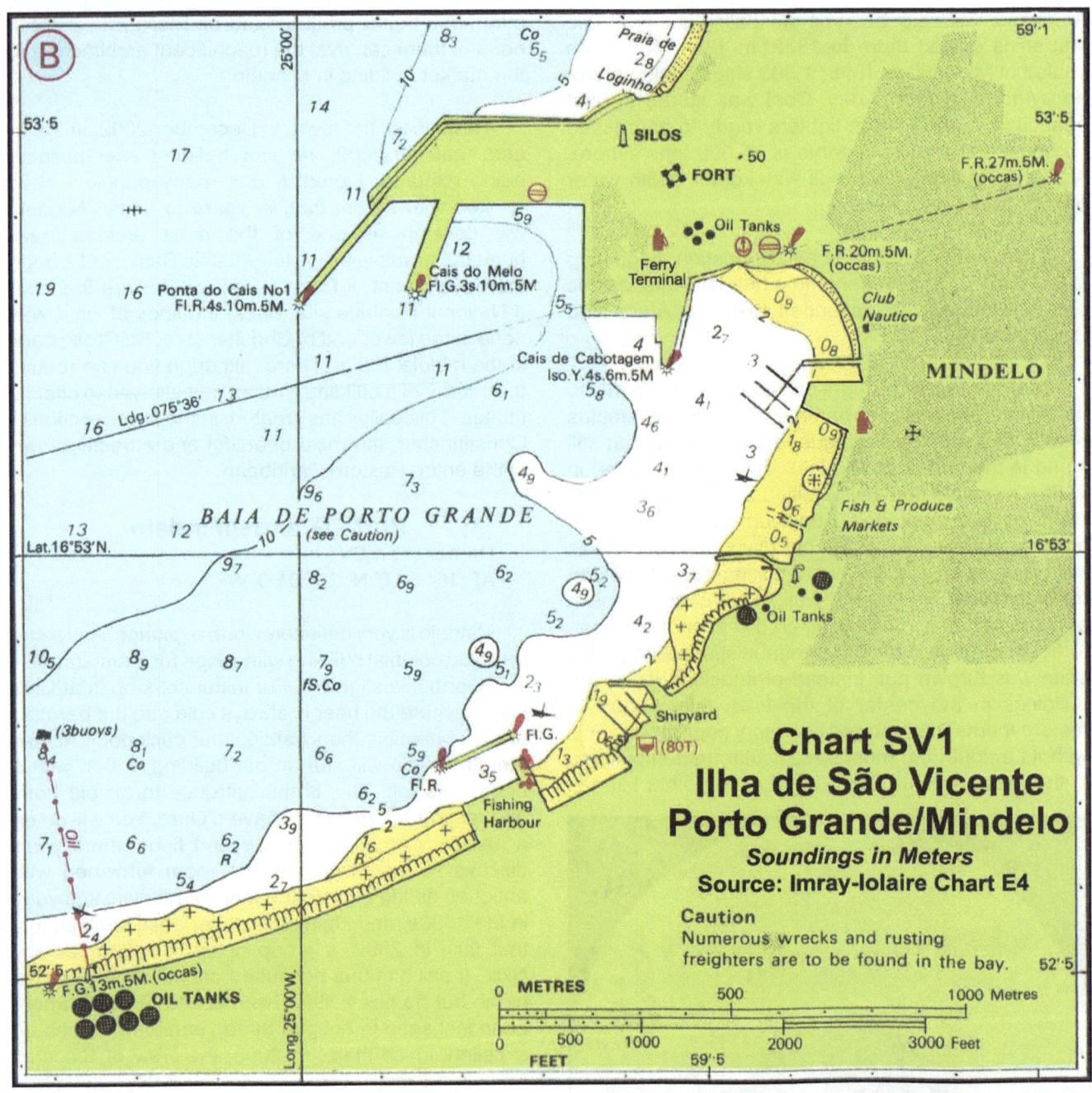

it either side), continue southwest until the city bears about 105°M then jibe over and head east, at about latitude 16° 53' on your GPS. Continue east into the harbor and anchor in the northeast corner, as close to shore as your draft will permit. The bottom in the northeast corner of the harbor is sand and has good holding. Alternatively, contact the marina on VHF channel 16 and arrange a berth.

If you're sailing from São Nicolau, it's best to sail north of São Vicente so that you can slide down the channel between São Vicente and Santo Antão to Mindelo. As mentioned in the Sailing Directions, if you come around the south coast of São Vicente, you'll find it extremely difficult to beat up against the southwest flowing current, especially if the tide is running in the same direction. Coming from the north, Ilhéu dos Passaros can be left on either hand. Its light is listed as being visible 8 miles, but I suspect it's more than that.

Do not enter at night as the lights of the shipyard northeast of town could easily confuse you and lead

88

you into the anchorage off the shipyard, which is not the main harbor. Plus, all sorts of derelict freighters are anchored in the main anchorage off Mindelo. Any one of them could sink at any moment and become another dangerous unmarked wreck to join a good number already there and poorly marked. In this type of situation, it's impossible to keep the charts up to date, so do *not* enter harbors at night.

If there's a chance that by maintaining your speed you will arrive at night, slow down so as to arrive at dawn. I say slow down as it's pretty much impossible to arrive off the harbor of Mindelo and heave-to because, most of the time, the current will sweep you off southwestward at 1 to 2 knots and sometimes up to 3 knots. This means you'll have to beat to windward rather than heave-to. So, slow down well in advance and time your arrival for dawn.

In *Street's Transatlantic Crossing Guide*, which came out in 1986, I suggested, hopefully, that someday, the long derelict dock off the yacht club might be rebuilt as it would certainly make a wonderful marina. It could easily provide space for 70 to 80 yachts if they were shoe-horned in. I'm happy to report that this has happened. As described in Chapter 3, Kai Brosmann and Lutz Meyer-Scheel established a small marina on the eastern side of the main shipping dock in 2003. It apparently filled a need, and on the strength of that, Kai and Lutz were able to proceed with building 120-berth marina. They have since taken apart the small marina.

Kai is very helpful when you talk to him in person, but trying to obtain information from him via email or fax reminds me of my late father's comment about writing to my older sister Mary. He said, "Writing Mary and expecting a reply is like throwing rose petals off the Grand Canyon and waiting to hear an echo."

When doing your entry clearance, if your boat is moored out, you have to sign a paper stating that someone will be on board the boat at all times. This is fine if you have a full crew, but not too good if you are only a couple as that would necessitate hiring a guard. If your boat is pilfered or the dinghy stolen, the police say, "Don't complain to us as you have signed a paper saying someone will be on the boat at all times."

In years past, there has been a security problem, but in November 2009, Kai told me it's a pilfering problem not an armed-burglary problem. Let's hope that, in years to come, the government will sort it out so there's no problem at all.

The crew of *Spirit of Oysterhaven*, a schooner from Oysterhaven in Ireland, reported in December 2004 there was a bit of a problem with boys offering to guard your dinghy. Their feeling was that, if you valued your dinghy, it was best to hire someone to guard it. Needless to say, the quality of these "guards" could vary greatly; some were wonderful, others not. *Spirit of Oysterhaven* ended up with a guard who became a fast friend, guide, and excellent "gopher." The boat's crew also reported that they felt the Cape Verdeans were the nicest people in the world.

The need for a dinghy guard longer exists as, for three euros a day, you can bring your dinghy to the marina and have the use of the showers, toilets, and WiFi, and you can fill jugs with water to take out to your boat. If you are going to be there longer than two weeks, you can arrange a lower fee.

I advise talking to one of the boys who work for Kai in the marina, or to one of the very helpful girls in the office, to find you a gopher who speaks your language. Ascertain from Kai or Lutz the proper wage for a gopher. Hire him by the day to be your gopher and guide.

I recommend this as, in 2005, despite searching for two days, I was only able to find one street map of Mindelo. The printing was so small that I needed a magnifying glass to read the street names. I returned to *Sincerity* and found a magnifying glass only to discover that the map was useless as there were absolutely no street-name signs. In 2009, the same situation existed. Plus there is no such thing as a supermarket but there are a number of un-super supermarkets. You will probably have to visit a half dozen to find what you are looking for, and a guide will be very helpful in finding everything you need.

Oyster XXV, owned by Richard Matthews, the founder of Oyster Marine, lost her mast shortly after the start of the 2005 Atlantic Rally for Cruisers (ARC). She proceeded under power to Mindelo where she was stranded for a month while waiting for a ship to carry her to the Caribbean. The crew found a gopher who was a real entrepreneur — he hired other gophers to do his gophering! They were very pleased with him. His name is Bicauda.

In 2009, I asked one of the Cape Verdeans working in the marina if he knew of Bicauda. He said he did, and that he could be found.

Put yourself in the hands of Kai's Cape Verdean employees and I am sure they will find you a good gopher.

Large yachts can pick up fuel and fresh water alongside the main commercial dock. Smaller yachts can do so at Marina Mindelo.

You can also get fuel and water at the fishing port. In 2005, you had to approach the fishing harbor from the southwest entrance as the northeast entrance was partially blocked by a sunken boat. In 2009, I was told it was still there. It's a steel boat, and it's only rusting away slowly. Reputedly, there is 3.5 meters of water inside the harbor. However, if you draw more than 10 feet, I recommend you send the dinghy to sound the area before you take your boat in. But why bother if you can refuel at the marina?

Resources
Marina Mindelo: +238 9972 322, +238 9915 878, mail@marinamindelo.com
www.marinamindelo.com

Other Anchorages in São Vicente

Mindelo is by far the best anchorage on the island of São Vicente, but Kai Brosmann reports an anchorage south of Mindelo at Ribeira Inha. He gives a waypoint of 16° 50.3' N, 25° 04.8' W. Head south from Mindelo. At Latitude 16° 50.3', head for shore while watching the fathometer and eyeballing the water until you find a suitable depth in which to anchor. Kai describes a gray sand beach and an anchoring depth of 25 to 30 feet.

Puerto de São Pedro
AP 16° 49.0' N; 25° 05.0' W

Puerto de São Pedro is southwest of the airport, on the western tip of the island, and should be sheltered in all weathers from seas but not from the wind. It has a nice beach but it is windy. The wind funnels between the high hills north and south of the airport, reaching gale velocity at times. Your chances of getting your anchors to hold, unless you have a couple of big ones, is minimal.

This is the harbor where the Ro-Ro ships discharge their trailers, and Kai recommends anchoring in the southeast corner of the harbor so as to be out of their way. Eyeball your way in while watching the fathometer and anchor at a suitable depth. The bottom is sand and offers good holding, which you need because of the wind.

In the 1980s, Puerto de São Pedro was highly popular with windsurfers who used the bay's winds in attempts on the world's windsurfing speed record. However, the bar has been raised so high now that anyone trying for the world windsurfing speed record does it in the special canals in the south of France.

Also in the 1980s and 1990s, windsurfers streaked across the channel from Mindelo to Porto Novo on Santo Antão, the fast ones doing it in 20 minutes or so. In the 1990s, an international regatta was held in Mindelo, but as of December 2002, the windsurfing seems to have moved to Santa Maria on Ilha do Sal and the harbor of Sal-Rei on Boavista.

Bahia das Gatas
AP 16° 53.0' N; 24° 53.0' W

There is a possible anchorage in Bahia das Gatas, on the northeast side of São Vicente. This is suitable for shoal-draft boats and only in the summer when the wind is light. Approach using eyeball navigation, preferably with a local pilot on board. Especially in the summer, this bay is popular on weekends with the locals, who light barbeques and lie out in the sun. A music festival is held there in August.

Ilha de Santo Antão
Imray-Iolaire Chart E4
Harbor charts SA1 – SA4

Where São Vicente, despite having peaks of over 2,000 feet, is dry and desert-like, Santo Antão, a mere nine miles away, is totally different. Santo Antão is about 22 miles long and 12 wide, with a ridgeline that tops 5,000 feet. In the mountains, you will find pine trees so large you cannot wrap your arms around their trunks. At the higher elevations, the weather is so cold that, even at the height of the midday sun, you'll need a woolen sweater and woolen hat to be comfortable.

If you are anchored in Mindelo, a visit to Santo Antão is a must. Don't just make a day trip but make arrangements so you can spend two, three, or possibly four days on the island.

São Vicente and Santo Antão

Ilha de Santo Antão Index Chart

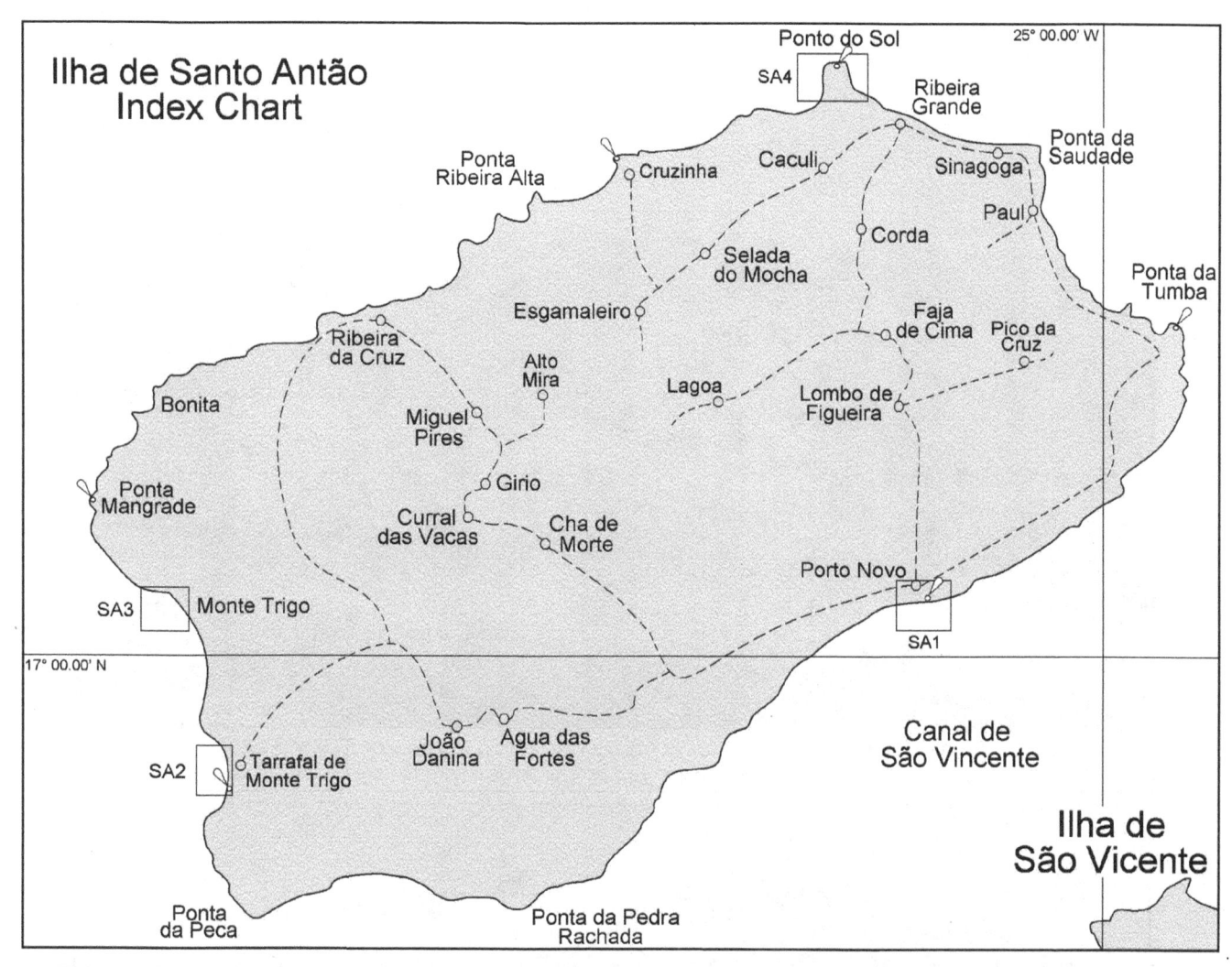

This is difficult, especially if you are a crew of only two, as Santo Antão has no anchorage safe enough that you can confidently anchor the boat and go off for the day or a couple of days.

If your crew is large enough that one or more members can be left on board while the rest of the crew are off exploring, an anchorage can be found on the west coast of Santo Antão. Because of the height of the ridge, the west coast is sheltered from the almost ever-present northeast wind that can get to you in the Cape Verdes. However, any anchorage on the west coast of Santo Antão will be uncomfortable, and very likely untenable, when the northwest groundswell is running.

The only other anchorage is in Porto Novo, opposite Mindelo, and this is not a safe place to leave a boat unattended either.

In 2009, a car ferry was shuttling back and forth between Mindelo and Santo Antão. If you are a two-person crew, the best advice is to leave your boat in the marina in Mindelo, or anchored out with a watchman aboard, and take the ferry to Santo Antão. Find a residencial or hotel to fit your finances and explore the island for two, three, or four days. It will be well worth your while. I've spent over 50 years exploring the Caribbean, made 12 transatlantic passages, and visited the Atlantic islands by sea and by air. After all this, I have come to the conclusion that Santo Antão is the most spectacular island in the Atlantic basin. Go explore it.

Whether you take your own boat or the ferry to Porto Novo, you can take a bus trip across the island to Ribeira Grande and on to Ponta do Sol. The drive via the ridge road is absolutely spectacular.

Street's Guide to the Cape Verde Islands

The road across the mountains from Porto Novo to Ribeira Grande and Ponta do Sol has spectacular views, but is not for those who suffer from vertigo.

Launching and hauling the fishing boats at Ponta do Sol is a community affair.

In 1989, there were two types of buses. One of them was the aluguer, which anyone who has been to Venezuela will recognize as being similar to the *puer puesto*. It's a communal taxi or bus service that runs to a loose schedule. Years ago, the standard vehicle was an open pickup truck with wooden boards and a canvas roof. The drivers we had were friendly and interesting to talk to, and they would stop anywhere we wanted to take photos or wander around. There were also regular tour buses, such as you would find in Europe. How they managed to drive them on the roads of Santo Antão is beyond me!

Today, I am told the pickup truck with a lid is largely but not entirely gone, replaced by 4 x 4s and proper minibuses, which are obviously more comfortable.

On Madeira, taking the bus or self-drive rental car is exciting as in places the road is cut into the side of a vertical cliff. Inboard the cliff rises hundreds of feet above you; outboard, it's a sheer drop of 400 to 500 feet into the sea.

On Santo Antão, the roads are even more spectacular. The old road from Porto Novo to Ribeira Grande follows the ridgeline, from which you can look out over a 1,600 foot drop into a valley on one side and a 400 foot drop into a valley on the other. Along the way, you pass through that wonderful pine forest.

Today, the bus no longer follows the spectacular ridge road but takes the new coast road. It takes less time to get from Porto Novo to Riberia Grande but the drive is not as spectacular. I recommend hiring an aluguer and having the driver follow the ridge road.

If you want to explore on foot, you can avoid the uphill work by hiring a taxi to take you to the top of the volcano. From there, you can walk down one of the valleys to Ribeira Grande, Ponta do Sol, or Vila das Pombas where you can have the taxi meet you to take you back to Porto Novo. If you are contemplating this type of hike, which will be several miles in length, make sure you are equipped with Dr. Reitmaier's walking map, your GPS, cell phone, food and water and, as you will be 5,000 feet up, some warm clothes. There are numerous valleys to explore, and I am told that if you are dropped off at the top of any one of them it will take most of the day to descend to a coastal road.

Ribeira Grande is the principal town, and developed because of the river that provided a moderately reliable source of fresh water. It was important enough in 1732 that the Bishop moved there from Praia, on Santiago. It became the seat of government for the Ilhas do Barlavento in 1850 and only yielded that role to the mercantile center, Mindelo, in 1934.

By any standard today, Ribeira Grande is certainly no metropolis, although it is historically important to the Cape Verdes. Although it doesn't have much else to offer the tourist, it's well worth a visit for its colonial architecture. Since the town is on the exposed northeast coast, getting supplies ashore and sending farm produce out must have been a real test of seamanship.

Ponta do Sol, about a mile northwest of Ribeira Grande on the northern tip of the island, is more attuned to tourists, with cafés, residencials and small hotels. Here you will find an airport which is a classic example of incompetent engineers and planners from the First World being inflicted on the Third World (see page 28 for more examples). Next to the airport, in 1989, we found a nice friendly bar run by a Cape Verdean who learned to speak English in Sweden.

The airport is something to see. The axis of the runway is northwest-southeast. When the wind is northeast, which is most of the time, it blows at right angles across the runway. A pilot attempting a landing is either good or dead. The airport has not been in use since August 1999 when a flight from São Vicente, unable to land because of limited visibility, tried to turn back and crashed into a mountainside, killing all 18 aboard.

A favorite area with visitors and especially walkers is Vila das Pombas, on the east coast. This is at the shore where Ribeira do Paúl meets the sea, and a variety of accommodations can be found all the way up the valley to the top.

Today, a fast and frequent ferry service serves Porto Novo from Mindelo, and the new coast road provides good access to Ribeira Grande. The money spent building a bad airport with the 90-degree crosswind could have built that road a lot sooner and bought a number of fast ferries.

Of course, in 2009, only the big passenger car ferry was operating while three fast ferries sat at anchor in Mindelo. Apparently, they have been out of use for a number of years, and you have to wonder why.

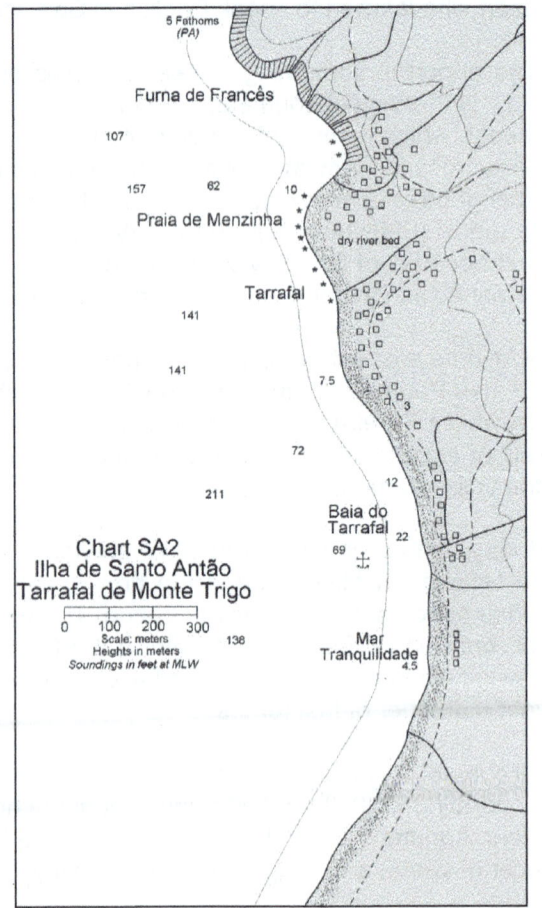

Porto Novo
Harbor chart SA1
AP 17° 00.0' N; 25° 03.5' W

As mentioned above, the brave and skilful can whip across from São Vicente to Santo Antão on a windsurfer in 20 to 30 minutes. On a yacht, the passage to Porto Novo will take an hour to an hour and a half.

The anchorage in Porto Novo is behind the dock and is none too good. In 1989, when we visited this anchorage in *Iolaire*, it took us two or three attempts before we got the anchor to hold. Because the wind dies down at night and the current can swing you into the dock, you need three anchors: two out ahead and a stern anchor or Bahamian moor. Further, if you intend to leave the boat with no one aboard, it's essential that you run a safety line from the boat to the dock. Make sure the line is long enough that it lies on the bottom and does not hinder boats trying to use the dock.

This is an important precaution. Over the years, a number of boats that have been left anchored in the lee of the dock, with no one aboard while their crews went ashore on their expeditions, have dragged, ending up on the beach a total loss.

Tarrafal de Monte Trigo
Harbor chart SA2
AP 16° 57.3' N; 25° 19.5' W

Tarrafal de Monte Trigo is on the west cost of Santo Antão and connected with the rest of the island by a passable road — passable, that is, in a four wheel drive vehicle and even then, in the wet season, sometimes not.

The sketch chart for this anchorage is compiled from an ancient BA survey and a modern topo map. Kai Brosmann recommends anchoring at about 16° 57' N, 25° 18.7' W, which is at the south end of the village. I recommend approaching this approximate position from the west, keeping an eye on the fathometer, and anchoring once you are sure you are on the shelf.

This anchorage is sheltered from the trade winds by the huge mountains, so the sea is usually calm. However, it is exposed to the ever-present Atlantic swell, so any dinghy landing must be made through the surf. This will be anything from easy, to adventurous,

Mar Tranquilidade

At Tarrafal de Monte Trigo, there is a small hotel built by a couple who discovered Santo Antão while cruising in the late 1990s. Frank (who is German) and Susi (who is American) were sailing their 1958, Nevins-built Sparkman & Stephens cutter, *Manatee*, when they dropped the anchor in Tarrafal de Monte Trigo. The quiet village seemed to be in its own time zone, Susi says, and when they learned about a property there they could purchase, they eventually set their anchor there. For a long time, they lived aboard the boat in the bay while they worked on their new home. As time went by and they hired local stone masons, the villagers began to accept them, and the local fishermen who sleep on the beach and seem to have an in-built knowledge of the weather systems, would always warn Frank and Susi if they suspected bad weather was on the way.

Mar Tranquilidade is not a resort hotel. It's more a small collection of guest cottages that grew one by one as Frank and Susi rebuilt old structures. For a long time, even after moving ashore, they kept *Manatee* on a mooring in the bay and used her to ferry building supplies and furniture from Mindelo. The guests, mostly Europeans on hiking holidays, started coming almost by chance and slept in their sleeping bags in the unfinished buildings. Eventually, electricity and running water came to the village and now they have the Internet — but no hot water and no cell-phone coverage. The electricity is on only from 0900 to 1100 and 1800 to 2300.

Sailors are welcome at Mar Tranquilidade, whether it's to have a beer, eat dinner, or pick up a couple of jerry cans of spring water. Susi asks that anyone wishing to have dinner make arrangements the night before or first thing in the morning as they begin planning early. They can also prepare a big lunch for crews that don't want to face a wet dinghy launching after dark.

Tarrafal de Monte Trigo is connected to the outside world by a very rough road over rugged and intimidating terrain — Susi calls it "the filter." The regular aluguer leaves the village for Porto Novo at 0430 and returns in the afternoon, but it's possible to arrange for a private taxi in the village. Because it's so remote, Tarrafal is not a good base for exploring the rest of Santo Antão except for the dedicated. Susi recommends travelers not keen on roughing it take the ferry from Mindelo to Porto Novo where buses are available.

Many boats spend a few days anchored off Tarrafal to wind down from Mindelo and prepare for the Atlantic crossing to the Caribbean or, in many cases, South America. For them, and for boats cruising the islands, I've included some of Susi's and Frank's comments and advice about anchoring in Tarrafal.

There is rarely any wind on this side of the island except when there are disturbances to the south, and that doesn't happen often in winter.

The best place to anchor is on the outer shelf in about 30 meters (100 feet) where it's good holding in sand. If the swell is not running, it's possible to anchor closer to shore on the shallower shelf, but keep an eye on the conditions.

You can anchor off Mar Tranquilidade, which is near a grove of trees south of the village. It's better not to anchor off the village where the fishing boats are. Also, don't anchor near where the river comes into the bay, as your anchor can get caught among big boulders on the bottom, and don't anchor too far south, near the abandoned tuna factory, as it's rocky.

A current runs parallel to the shore and changes direction with the tide, so anchor accordingly.

If you want to stay at the hotel, make a reservation as sometimes they are full. They will give you directions on how to get there. Normally, aluguers meet the ferry in Porto Novo. The drive over the mountain to Tarrafal de Monte Trigo takes two and a half to three hours. It's a bouncy ride, but an interesting adventure through spectacular scenery.

Mar Tranquilidade
+238 2276 012
www.martranquilidade.com
info@martranquilidade.com

A sailing couple settled in Tarrafal de Monte Trigo and restored several buildings on their property to create the little resort hotel, Mar Tranquilidade.

to impossible, depending on the sea conditions. (See page 59 for a discussion of landing a dinghy in surf.)

Since the bay is definitely exposed to the groundswell, and the shelf drops off suddenly to very deep water, I strongly recommend a bow-and-stern mooring or Bahamian moor. If on a bow-and-stern mooring, I recommend taking the stern anchor out far enough that it is over the edge of the drop-off. In this way, the anchor line will be pulling uphill. The angle at the anchor will be very flat, thus it will hold very well. I also advise diving and checking the anchors to make sure they are dug in.

Although this coast is sheltered from the trades, during the summer, the wind can come in from the southwest. Also it can occasionally come in from the northwest and blow hard. Wind from either of these directions makes the anchorage a dead lee shore, hence my recommendations for anchoring the boat securely and not going off exploring unless some of the crew remains on board to move the boat if conditions suddenly change.

Susi of Mar Tranquilidade reports that a blow from the northwest in November 2009 was strong enough to knock down a few trees and remove some of the thatched roofs from the hotel's cottages.

Don't forget that from November until late April, and occasionally into early May, the northwest groundswell can come in completely unannounced, unless you have on board a weather reporting system that enables you to keep track of the weather in the North Atlantic. (See Chapter 4 for further discussion of the northwest groundswell.)

In the light of the above, I recommend that, if you are heading for the west coast of Santo Antão, you first call Mar Tranquilidade on the land line and ascertain the sea conditions. Otherwise, you might arrive and discover that, although you can anchor there, you have no hope of getting ashore in a dinghy.

The satellite photograph at Google Maps was obviously taken on a day the groundswell was running high, and shows just how difficult it would be to land a dinghy in those conditions.

Susi of Mar Tranquilidade makes the interesting observation that it's often easier to land a dinghy on the rocky beach, on the big round stones, rather than the long flat sandy beach. The sandy beach shelves very gently and the waves break far enough offshore that, before the dinghy grounds, the backwash pulls the dinghy back into the surf before the crew can jump out and pull it up the beach. If it gets sucked back into the surf, the dinghy will likely be swamped and probably capsized by the next breaker.

Susi states that the local fishermen are very happy to ferry crews back and forth from anchored yachts, for a small charge. Be forewarned, the fishing boats have no fenders so before calling a fishing boat alongside, hang all your finders over the side you want the boat to come alongside.

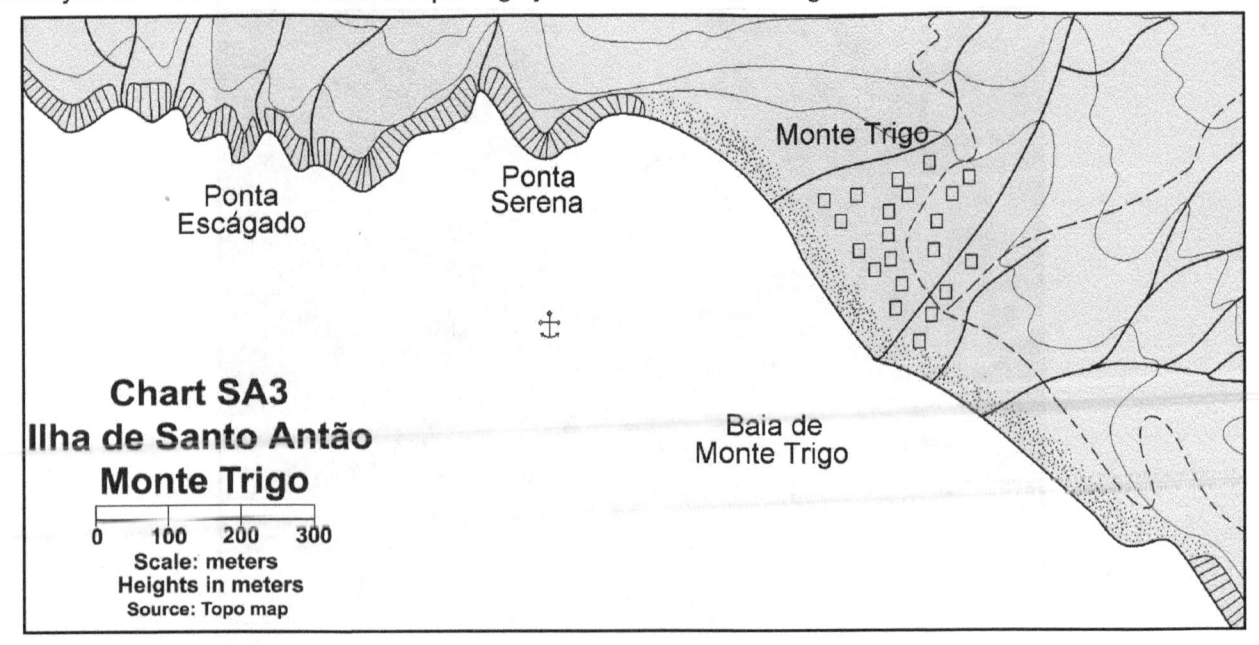

Chart SA3
Ilha de Santo Antão
Monte Trigo

0 100 200 300
Scale: meters
Heights in meters
Source: Topo map

Ponta Escágado
Ponta Serena
Monte Trigo
Baia de Monte Trigo

São Vicente and Santo Antão

And in case I've not provided enough warnings about the groundswell, here's part of an e-mail from Susi in February 2010.

"... by the way, we have a charter yacht crew here right now. They came for dinner, prepared to swim back on board, but the swell picked up and only the skipper swam back. Six crew are sleeping together in the only room we have free tonight — mattresses on the floor, out on the balcony. This isn't the first time ..."

The following day, the skipper called on his cell phone from the Canal de São Vicente (where he found a signal). He had swum to the boat, picked up the anchor, and spent the night drifting in the lee of Santo Antão. His crew had to make their way to Porto Novo, where he picked them up at the dock.

Monte Trigo
Harbor chart SA3
AP 17° 00.5' N; 25° 20.5' W

Monte Trigo is a smaller village, three miles north of Tarrafal de Monte Trigo. Because of the curve of the land to the west, it's possible it may be slightly better sheltered from the swell (it certainly looks so on the satellite photograph). Kai Brosmann recommends anchoring slightly northwest of the village at 17° 01.06'

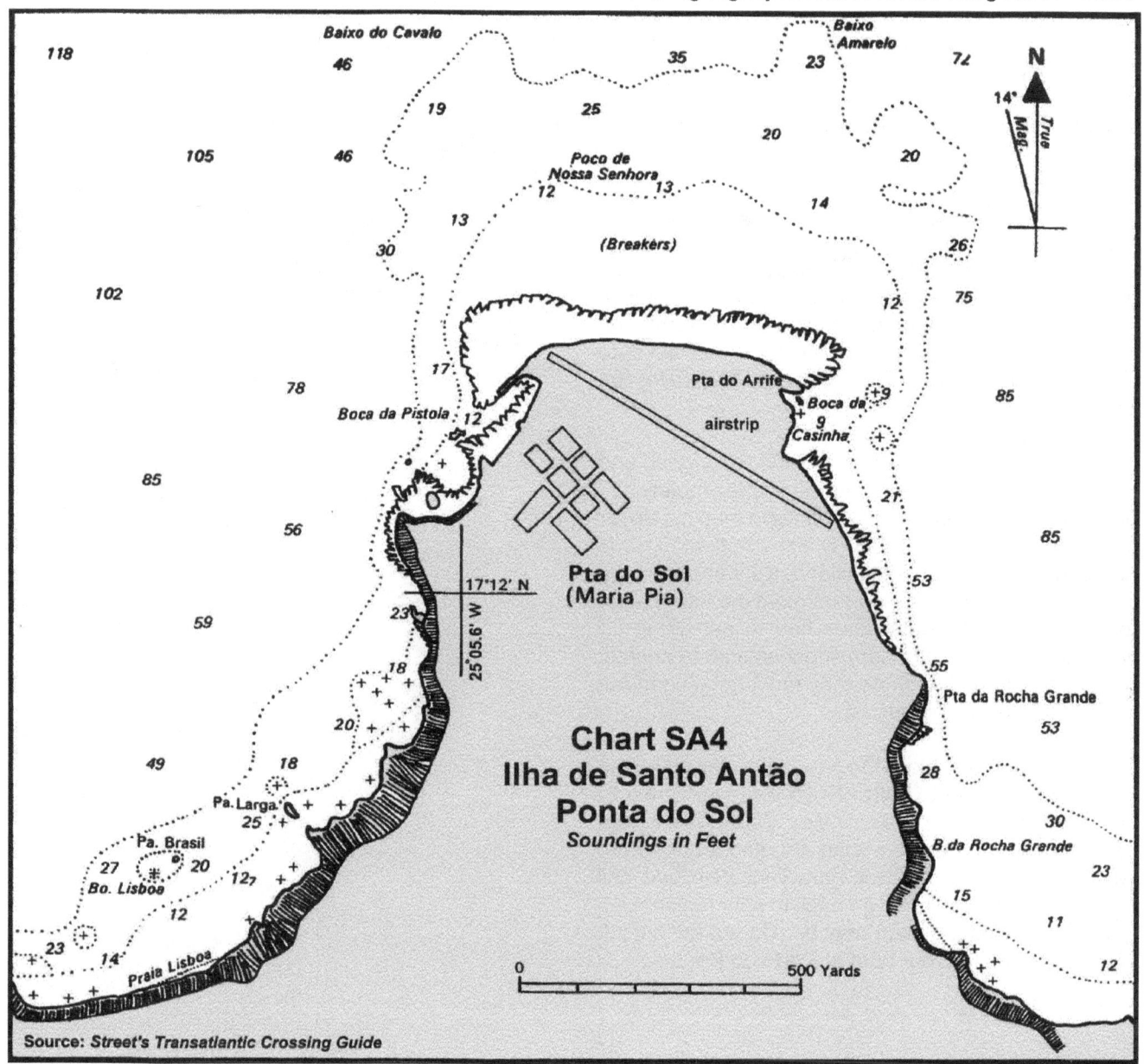

Chart SA4
Ilha de Santo Antão
Ponta do Sol
Soundings in Feet

Source: Street's Transatlantic Crossing Guide

N, 25° 20' W. I recommend a similar approach and anchoring procedure as for Tarrafal de Monte Trigo.

The only advantage this anchorage might have over Tarrafal de Monte Trigo would be some protection from the groundswell. According to Susi of Mar Tranquilidade it's not much of a village.

Ponta do Sol
Harbor chart SA4
AP 17° 13.0' N; 25° 06.0' W

Ponta do Sol is on the extreme northern tip of Santo Antão and completely exposed. It doesn't really have a harbor and there is no beach. A small breakwater provides some protection for a concrete ramp where small fishing boats are launched and retrieved. This is notable, as it's the only place in the Cape Verdes where the boats launch and retrieve from a concrete ramp.

Porto do Paúl
AP 17° 09.5' N; 25° 00.0' W

Porto do Paúl is not a port but a small village with an open beach and a small jetty. In the RCC Atlantic Islands guide, the person supplying the information says that the only reason to visit Porto do Paúl is to visit Figueral de Paúl, the most beautiful valley on Santo Antão.

The anchorage is listed in both the RCC guide and Kai Brosmann's German guide at approximately 17° 08' N 25° 00' W. (On the WGS 84 Topo map it's closer to 25° 01' W, so use the GPS with caution.) This is on the windward side of the island. It's steep-to and a dead lee shore. The person that gave the information to the RCC guide states they had to get within 50 yards of shore to find bottom shoal enough to anchor. Since it is a dead lee shore they must have been out of their cotton picking minds!

If you want to explore the beautiful valley, take the ferry from Mindelo to Porto Novo and hire a taxi to take you up to the top of the valley. Walk down to Vila das Pombas on the coast road and find a bar where you can relax and recover from your hike and call your taxi to pick you up to go back to your residencial, hotel, or ferry as the case may be. Do not even think of trying to anchor your boat at Porto do Paúl.

Chapter 8
Santiago and Maio

Ilha de Santiago
Imray-Iolaire Chart E4

Santiago is the biggest - 30 miles long by 15 miles wide - and most populous - 100,000 - of the Cape Verdes. Its main port, Praia, is also the archipelago's capital. Although it's a city of good size and home to various aid missions, it has no facilities for yachts. However, I expect that to change in the future as the island of Santiago is well worth exploring and, once the word gets out it, will become a sought-after destination.

At present, the charts available to yachtsmen are inadequate for any close-up investigation of the numerous potential anchorages. The scales of the U.S., British, Portuguese, and Imray-Iolaire charts are such that they do not reveal the 24 small coves, harbors and anchorages on the east, south, and west coasts of Santiago. The only harbor chart is that for Praia on the Imray-Iolaire chart. In the following pages, I describe each of these possible anchorages. I emphasize *possible* because few soundings are available for them and a change in wind or sea conditions can quickly render them uncomfortable or untenable.

I have explored Santiago by car on three occasions expressly to investigate these anchorages, first when I flew to the Cape Verdes in 2002, again in 2005 when I was there on *Sincerity*, and most recently in November 2009, this time again via the big bird.

On all three occasions, I made contact with Gerry Dom and, in 2009, his daughter, Indira Dom, accompanied me on my excursions around the island. Indira speaks English, French, and Portuguese, as well as the local dialect, so we were able to obtain a great deal of information from the local fishermen as to water depths in the harbors and the kind of sea conditions to expect during the winter months.

Two of the anchorages I investigated, Santa Cruz and Ponto Pinha on the east coast, are as fine as any in the Caribbean, and I speak as one who has spent over 50 years cruising and exploring in the Caribbean. I trust that yachtsmen, as they explore these anchorages in years to come, will be kind enough to send us further information for inclusion in the Imray-Iolaire charts and in the next printing of this guide. Because Seaworthy Publications uses digital printing, it can print these books in relatively small batches and include such new and corrected information as becomes available in each successive printing.

As soon as I receive information, it will go onto my website (www.street-iolaire.com). Once I am sure of the validity of information about harbors shown on the Imray-Iolaire chart, I will pass it along to Imray Laurie Norie & Wilson and ensure that it's included in online updates to the chart. I have set up the procedure so that long after I have, as sailors say, "crossed the bar for the last time," this guide will still be maintained up to date.

Santiago was settled somewhere in the middle of the 15th Century. The principal town at first was Ribeira Grande, now known as Cidade Velha. It had a reasonably sheltered open roadstead anchorage suitable for the ships of the era and a reliable water supply. It developed rapidly as a slave-trading station but its great wealth attracted the attention of navies and privateers when Portugal was at war and pirates when it wasn't, not that there was much distinction between the three in those days. Sir Francis Drake is revered by the British as a bold seafaring adventurer but the Portuguese and Spanish look upon him as no more than a pirate.

Drake sacked Ribeira Grande in 1582 and again in 1585 so, in 1587, the Portuguese began construction of a large fort above town to deter further attacks. Fort San Filipe did its job until Jacques Cassard overran it 1712 (see Chapter 2). After that, the capital of Santiago moved along the coast to Praia, a village originally built by merchants seeking to unload cargo away from the prying eyes of the King's agents in Ribeira Grande.

Praia was built on a plateau and therefore supposedly easier to defend. However, one wonders if the move was also not instigated to take advantage of the harbor at Praia, which offers better protection than the anchorage off Ribeira Grande. I was surprised when, in December 2005, as we motorsailed past Cidade Velha on *Sincerity*, we saw the massive fort above the town. In contrast, the plateau at Praia bears no sign of defensive walls or gun batteries. I learned later that there were walls and gun batteries at Praia but the walls have been demolished over time and

Street's Guide to the Cape Verde Islands

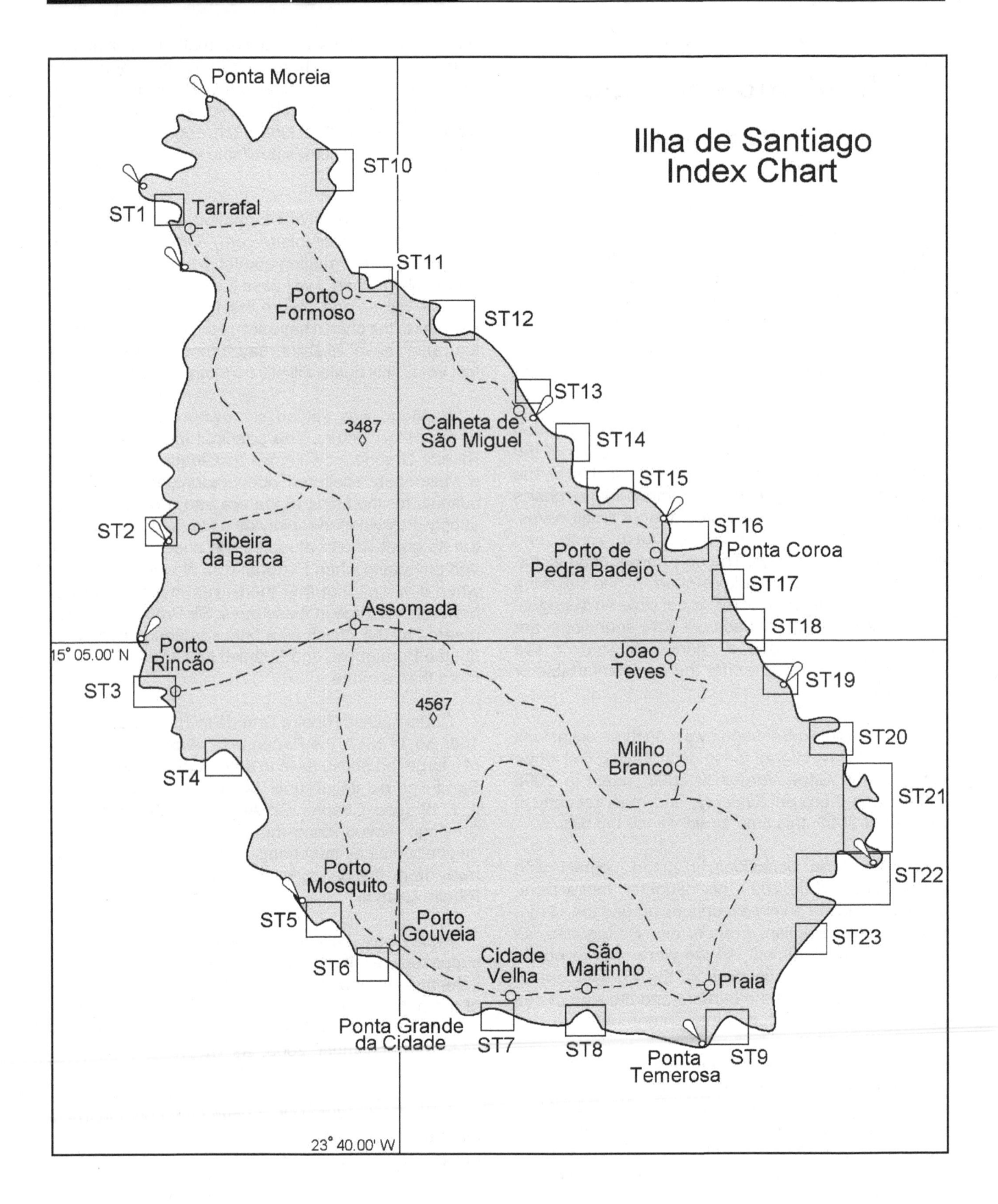

Ilha de Santiago Index Chart

the stone used in other buildings. The harbor was well defended by forts on Ponta Temerosa and where the refinery now stands.

Santiago's highest elevation is over 4,500 feet and much of the island is 1,000 feet high. As a result, it does have rainfall and ground water, though not much. Most of the sweet water is provided by desalinization plants. Santiago's moderate agricultural economy produces provision crops, fruit, bananas, and some sugar cane. The valleys are mostly dry river beds in which the rivers only run in the rainy season. Evidently there is enough subterranean water to allow crops to grow, and a few of the river valleys are veritable green meadows.

In one valley, the Chinese recently built a dam that has created a lake almost half a mile long. It will be interesting to see if, in the future, more ravines will be dammed to create reservoirs.

The island is criss-crossed with roads — until recently all of them cobblestone. Driving around in a car for a full day on a cobblestone road one does get a sore tail, and the car gets shaken up so much that I am sure the auto repair shops do a roaring business replacing suspensions and springs. It is said there are more cobblestone roads in the Cape Verde Islands than anywhere else in the entire world.

On my visit in 2005, I was amazed to discover numerous massive road-building projects. Many of the cobblestone roads had been straightened and asphalted and the main north-south road was being converted into a four-lane divided highway. This road improvement has continued. I saw more massive improvements in the roads in 2009.

The amount of development on the island between my 1980s visits and my December 2002 visit was incredible. Similarly, I saw huge changes between my visits in 2002 and 2005 and again in 2009.

In 2005, Santiago had taken on the appearance of one massive construction site, and it was no different in 2009. Buildings were springing up everywhere, not only hotels and commercial buildings, but also a tremendous number of substantial houses. In the center of the island, where in 1985 and 1989 there was nothing but a small village, there is now a complete city. West of the plateau where Praia stands they had built a whole new modern town, and another new development was being laid out with tarmac roads and services — water, electricity, and telephone — being installed, all underground. In 2005, there was so much new construction that I was unable to find the road that leads westward to Cidade Velha and its massive fort.

North of the airport, which is on the east side of Praia, a British company was in the process of building a complete new town named Sambala. In 2009, it appeared largely completed but, with one vacation house jammed against another, it is not my idea of a vacation home. They talk of a wonderful beach, but to reach the beach you need a car. It is about a quarter-mile walk to the beach. It's a downhill walk, but the climb back up the steep hill in the tropical sun will certainly undo all the benefits of a refreshing swim.

At Ponta de Bicuda, the southeasternmost point of Santiago, an Irish group was in 2005 building a massive residential development with houses starting at €200,000 and going up to €1,000,000. This project was to include a, 18-hole golf course, but I wonder where the water is to come from to keep the golf course green and how golfers are expected to play when the wind is blowing 30 knots. I also wonder how long the buildings will last when they are all built with salt-water sand. The total cost of the project was to be €1.3 billion, or about $2 billion US. It was so heavily promoted in Ireland that, for a while, there were direct flights from Ireland to Santiago.

In 2005, I speculated that it would be interesting to see if they would build a massive marina there. If so, I wondered if guests would take a four-mile trip to town by car over roads that at this point are not too good, or if the developer would set up a water-taxi service for a two-mile trip to town (for which they would have to rebuild the dock by the harbor master's office or build their own landing). Well, as of November 2009, there was no sign of any development at Ponta Bicuda, although in the airport I saw posters advertising the project.

By 2005, the airport had been expanded and the runway extended to receive direct flights from various European destinations and also from Boston.

The airport Fire Department in Praia reminded me of the Grenada Fire Department in the 1950s and early 1960s, which met every arriving flight with magnificent old American LaFrance hand-start truck.

The equipment looked beautiful and all the brass fittings were perfectly polished. However, rats had eaten holes in the hoses, rendering them useless.

In Praia, the equipment is modern. I met an airport fireman who told me he had a wonderful job — he just sat and watched planes land and take off and was paid for doing absolutely nothing! I asked him for his job title, to which he replied he was an airport fireman and an emergency crew. When I asked him where he did his training for handling crashed aircraft, he told me that he only training he has is to train himself in the gym so that he could keep in shape to yank people out of crashed planes. He had no formal fire fighting training at all. Thank god modern aircraft are so reliable.

It appears the economic boom in Santiago has been brought about by the fact that there are more Cape Verdeans living outside the Cape Verde islands than live at home. In the days of the communist government, needless to say, those who were living abroad were not interested in bringing money back home. However, when the regime changed and the capitalists took over, the expatriates began to bring their money home and started investing in their home economy. According to the U.S. State Department, 20 percent of the Cape Verdes' GDP comes from remittances from expatriates.

Something to remember about land development in Santiago: There is no sand on Santiago except in the wonderful cove at Tarrafal. I seems that, just as in St. Thomas and Tortola in the 1950s and 1960s, the locals stripped the beaches for sand until the government stepped in and made the practice illegal. The same situation exists in Santiago.

All the sand for construction must be imported from the eastern islands of Sal, Boavista and Maio. It's loaded into small freighters which take it to Santa Cruz on the northwestern corner of the island. In this wonderful little harbor, which is like a miniature fjord, the sand is liquefied with salt water pumped into the hold of the ship. The slurry is then pumped into a holding pond about 75 feet above the ship where the salt water settles out. From there, the sand is loaded into trucks and carted to the building site.

Everything in Santiago is built with salt-water sand, which builders tell me produces weak concrete. What's more, the salt eats into the rebar and, whenever it rains, which is admittedly rather seldom, all the paint will tend to lift off. As a consequence, the longevity of new construction in Santiago, the quality of which is third-world at best, is definitely suspect.

Anyone who was in the Caribbean in the 1950s will see in the massive tourist expansion of the Cape Verdes a replay of the development of the Virgin Islands in that period. They were, as the sign on one bar in the Virgin Islands says, "A sunny place for shady people."

Now, in the first years of the 21st century, as the Cape Verdes appear to be politically stable, the Cape Verdeans are much more interested in their islands. Many expatriates who have reached retirement age, and who have pensions and savings, have come back to the islands and are building retirement homes. Others who are successful abroad are sending money back to their families and relatives to build their retirement homes or support their various relatives' enterprises at home. International investors are also hard at work. Consequently, things are definitely looking up in the Cape Verde Islands, and especially on the island of Santiago.

Getting to Santiago

Boats arriving in Santiago usually do so from the northern Cape Verde islands or directly from Africa. Boats coming from Africa directly to the Ilhas do Sotavento will have to first go to Praia to clear in; they cannot stop in Maio.

I would recommend anyone wishing to cruise both the northern and southern islands make landfall in Sal, cruise the Ilhas do Barlavento, then head south to Santiago from São Vicente. We went the other way in 1985 — from Santiago to São Vicente — and it was a tough sail for a boat that sailed to windward well. In many modern cruising boats it would be brutal. The course is approximately 345° T, but given the current sets west at up to 2 knots, much of the time you'd be hard pressed to fetch São Vicente.

For yachts arriving in Santiago from São Vicente, to the northwest, or from Sal via Boavista, generally to the northeast, Tarrafal, on the northwest corner of the island, is an ideal first stop, although I say this with a reservation. Tarrafal is a beautiful harbor but it also has a sandy beach. What puts the sand on the beach? The swell! This anchorage always has a slight roll. If the ground swell is running, you will not only be uncomfortable at anchor but you'll find it impossible to get ashore.

A stop at Tarrafal makes a good break in the passage from São Vicente. It's 118 miles from the southwest corner of São Vicente to Tarrafal, so if you depart Mindelo at dusk, you'll have a nice overnight run and arrive in Tarrafal around midday.

The passage from Boavista to Tarrafal is about 75 miles. Because most cruising boats won't be able to cover that within the daylight hours, it means leaving Boavista at night. Be sure to lay a course well north of Baixo João Valente so that current and leeway don't set you down toward it.

Tarrafal

Harbor chart ST1
AP 15° 17.0' N; 23° 46.5' W

On approaching Tarrafal, many feel they have already arrived in the West Indies. The small fishing boats pulled up on a white sand beach backed by palm trees and overlooked by a restaurant perched a cliff give it a very Caribbean air.

Gerry Dom feels there is considerably more water in the cove where the anchor shows on the sketch chart than the chart shows. We also observed, while looking at the harbor from the restaurant above it, that there appears to be more water in the cove than the chart shows. Feel your way in and anchor. In 2009, I saw four yachts and a 35-foot fishing boat anchored off.

While you admire the beautiful white sand beach here, remember that something must have put it there. That something is the northwest groundswell. Another point to consider is that the island is high enough there is a good chance that an onshore breeze can develop during the night. Make sure you anchor on a Bahamian moor or with bow and stern anchors.

There is a small dock, but the surge is such that you would be well advised to pull a dinghy up on the beach rather than leaving it at the dock.

Fishing boats are pulled up on the beach and undoubtedly, early in the morning when the fishermen return, fish can be purchased.

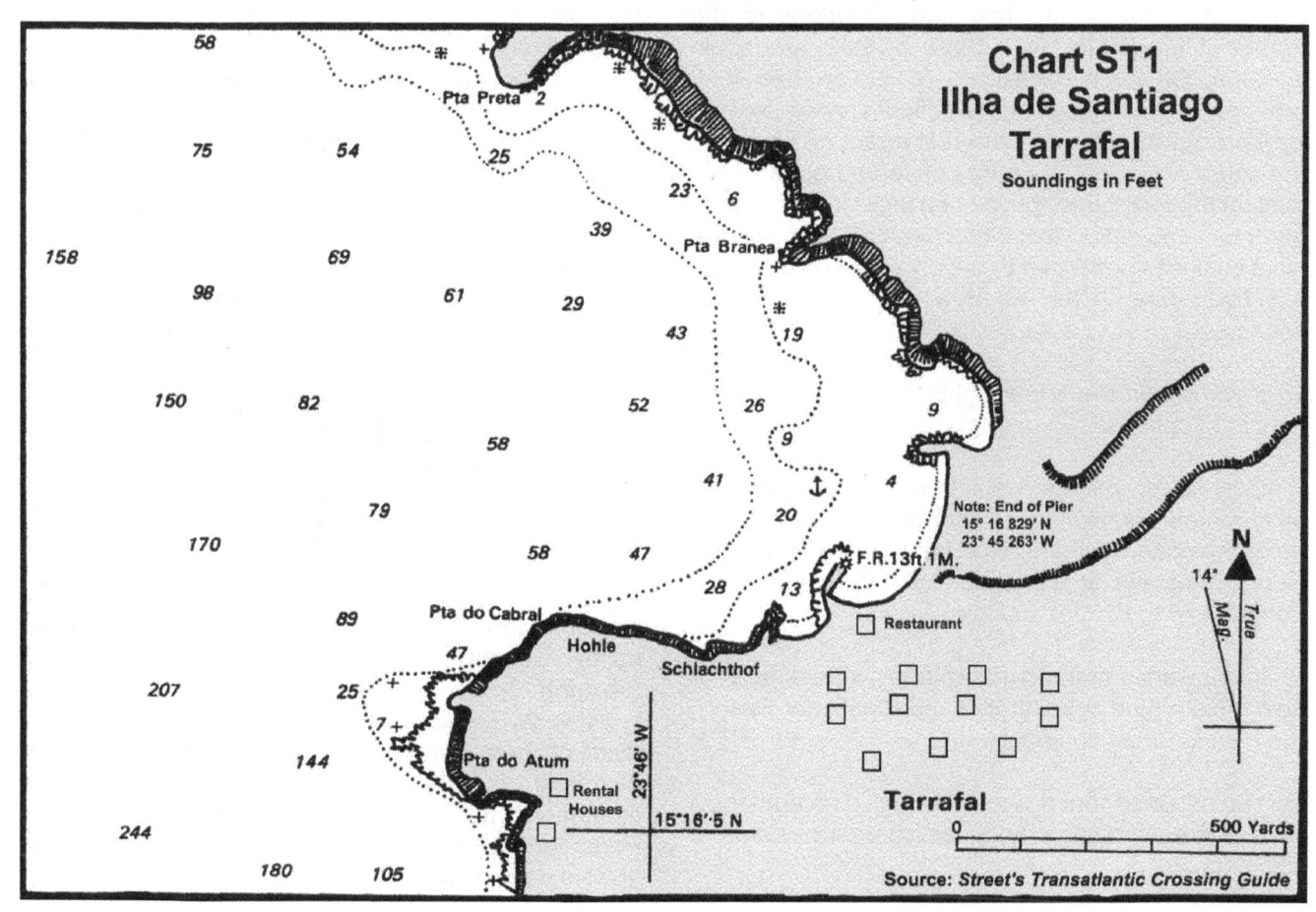

Spear fishing in the area is evidently excellent. In 1989, we met a young Belgian who had been living there for about five months. He had found himself cheap accommodations and was living very simply, supporting himself by the amount of fish he could shoot in a day. He told us he wasn't really making any money, but caught enough fish to have a very pleasant existence.

Since that first visit, when it didn't even have an un-super supermarket, the village has expanded to the size of a small town. Supplies are still really basic, and I would not regard Tarrafal as a place to buy anything other than necessities.

Water is obviously only available by humping it in 5-gallon jugs, and the same goes for diesel and gasoline, so it's important you replenish these in Mindelo if you plan on spending time in these islands before taking off for the Caribbean.

I normally avoid recommending any restaurants or hotels as they are so changeable; what is excellent one month can be a disaster the following month. However, I visited the restaurant overlooking the harbor of Tarrafal in 1985, 1989, in 2002, and again in 2009. On each occasion we had an excellent, reasonably priced meal and excellent service. No one spoke English, but since the restaurant has been in the same place for 24 years, I have had good meals each of the four times I have been there in that period, and I have observed that it has been popular with the local businessmen, I can break my rule: I recommend this restaurant — for the view, the meal, and the service.

If you would like a few nights ashore, you have a couple of options.

Only a 10 minute walk from the harbor is a nice simple residencial, Hotel Sol Marina, that's recommended by Indira, who frequently stays there. Room rates are in the region of €25 to €30 for a double, €18 to €20 for a single.

If you want a more touristy place overlooking your own private tuna cove, there's the Kingfisher Resort, run by a German company.

You can also rent a car in Tarrafal. The company, Baia Verde, also has a hotel, which Indira says is "a little expensive."

Resources
Hotel Sol Marina: +238 266-1219
Kingfisher Resort: www.king-fisher.de
Baia Verde (car rental): +238-266-1128 or 266-1407

Before leaving Tarrafal, hop in the dinghy and head south to Ponta do Tuna and explore the little cove. Another worthwhile dinghy expedition might be to head north around the headland Ponta Preta to Porto Fanzeda, a run of about two miles. I don't know how much of a port it is but a road leads down to the village which lies on an open bay that's about three quarters of a mile north to south. It bears exploring in a dinghy, but read the section in Chapter 4 on safety precautions when exploring by dinghy.

On leaving Tarrafal, you can test your spirit of adventure by exploring the anchorages on either the west coast or east coast of Santiago. Depending on the weather and sea conditions, you have a couple of choices. You can head north from Tarrafal, beat the short distance around the northern end of the island, and work your way south to Praia in stages enjoying the uncrowded anchorages on the east coast. Alternatively, you can head south from Tarrafal and visit some of the anchorages on the lee side of Santiago.

If you plan to visit some of the anchorages described here, you might want to check them out first. Rent a car, or find a taxi (most likely a pickup truck with a lid) with a driver who speaks your language, and explore the island by road. After viewing the anchorages from ashore, you can decide whether or not to visit them by boat.

From Tarrafal South Along the West Coast

Gerry Dom told me in 1985 and 1989 that there were some small coves on the west coast of Santiago where a yacht can anchor. At that time there were virtually no charts, so entering them was possible only by eyeball navigation. I have since done considerable research and with the help of the topo maps, backed up by excursions by car, I have come up with the following spots as offering potential harbors for cruising yachtsmen. No soundings are available for most of them but what information I have obtained has been backed up with conversations with the fishermen who use the bays on a daily basis. In the Porto Rincão area we also explored in a chartered 20-foot fishing launch.

These harbors on the west coast of Santiago can be visited any time except when the northwest groundswell is running, when probably all west and south coast anchorages would be untenable. Remember that the anchorages on the west coast are deep. Often you will anchor and run a line ashore, secured by an anchor or chain leader around a boulder. Be sure to rig a tripping line or becue the anchor (see Chapter 4), as in many of the anchorages you will be anchoring on a rocky bottom.

As I have said before, this kind of exploring should only be done by experienced sailors with a man (or woman) on the lower spreaders, as standing on the bow pulpit would not provide a high enough perspective. In some areas the water may be murky, especially after a rain, so keep a good eye on the fathometer.

Alternatively, a cruising boat that carries a RIB can heave-to off the harbor entrance and send the RIB ahead to explore. A RIB with a fathometer or fish finder permanently installed would be ideal for investigating these unexplored anchorages without endangering the mother ship.

The island of Santiago is so high, a wind shadow frequently extends out almost 20 miles to the west, so you'll probably power along the coast. In that regard it's similar to the islands of the Eastern Caribbean. Norie Wilson's guides of 1813 and 1867 state, "To sail in the lee of the high islands in the Eastern Caribbean, one must stay 7 leagues, or 21-miles, off or within two pistol shots of shore". The same holds true in the Cape Verde Islands.

In general, the winds will be light in the lee of the island, but be prepared for hard blasts off the high hills and particularly off the valleys. These katabatic winds (called williwaws in some parts of the world) can produce gusts that often reach 30 knots and sometimes higher.

Gerry Dom warns that, sailing south from Tarrafal, from Baia de Chão Bom until you have passed a pyramid-shaped rock a couple of miles north of Ribeira da Barca, you should be prepared for occasional violent gusts so strong they pick up water off the surface. He says this is where the mizzen mast was blown out of the 38-foot ketch he skippered for the U.S. Embassy.

The shore is steep-to, in that the edge of the shelf, which varies drastically in width, drops off suddenly to very deep water. Wherever you anchor, moor bow and stern with the bow anchor toward shore. If you can, bury the anchor in the beach or tie a line around a rock.

The harbor descriptions and sketch charts are listed below as you would encounter them going south from Tarrafal along the west coast to Praia. The only one of these I have not personally visited is Ilhéu dos Alcatrazes.

Ribeira da Barca

Harbor chart ST2
AP 15° 08.8' N; 23° 46.7' W

This harbor chart was drawn up from a German chart — why did the Germans draw a chart with all the various small harbors in the Cape Verdes, prior to World War I? It's possible they hoped to hide commerce raiders there in time of war.

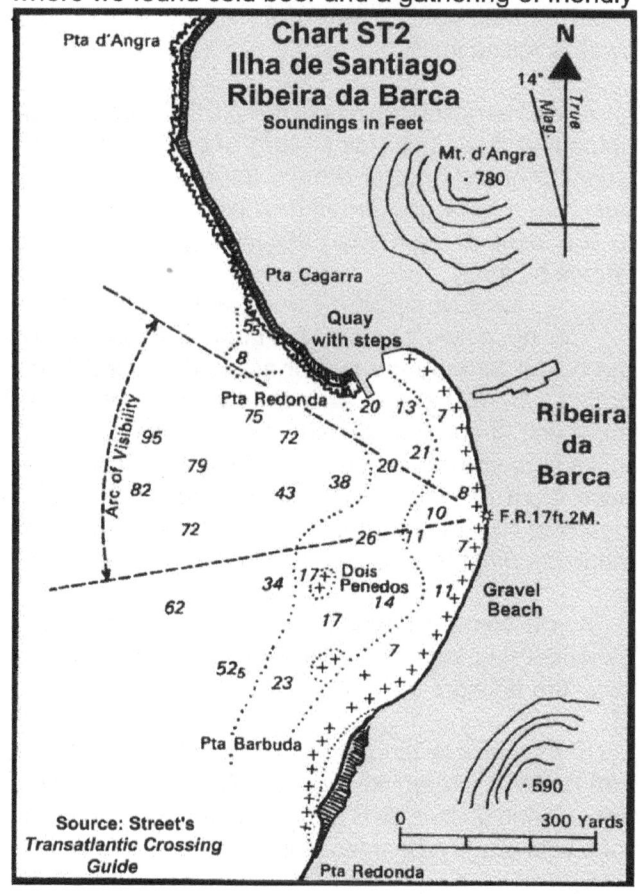

We visited this harbor by car in 1989 and discovered an interesting little village with a small provisions store and the inevitable local rum shop where we found cold beer and a gathering of friendly

active fishing fleet, and the boats pulled up on the beach were without doubt the best designed fishing boats in the entire Cape Verde Archipelago. I visited again in 2009 and must say the village has improved dramatically in the 20 intervening years. Now, there is a small village square with attractive plantings and a bar and restaurant where I bought a beer but not a meal.

Ribeira da Barca looks like a good place to stop when heading up or down the west coast of Santiago.

The best approach is from the northwest on a course of about 120°M. If approaching from the south, continue north until you can steer about 120°M toward the south end of the village, as south of this line is the reef Dos Penedos.

The beach is steep-to and made of shingle and not too much sand. Wind undoubtedly funnels down the ravine and at night god knows what the wind will do, so the anchorage is obviously bow and stern. You'll be best off with two anchors ashore and a stern anchor set so that if a big swell comes in you'll be hobby horsing to it, not rolling your guts out. This anchorage clearly should not be used when a northwest ground swell is rolling in.

Anne Hammick reports in the *RCC Guide* a cargo unloading float, but I didn't see one in 1989 and it wasn't there in 2009. Perhaps there was one in the past, but a fairly good road now connects the village to the central main road so I imagine everything comes by truck.

You have two choices for landing a dinghy: on the beach through the surf or at the north end of the harbor where there is a long jetty with steps at its outer end. If you use the jetty, tie off by the steps but make sure you have a good anchor to hold the dinghy away from the jetty as the shingle beach is a sure sign of a constant surge. Stone jetties eat RIBS and inflatable dinghies.

If you venture beyond the village to explore, it's essential you leave someone on board the yacht in case the anchors drag off the shelf.

If you have a dinghy with a good outboard, you can make an expedition south to Aguas Belas where you will find a cave filled with water into which you can take your dinghy. Besides being beautiful, this cave is historically important as it was used as a rendezvous point by Amílcar Cabral, who led the Cape Verde Islands in their fight for independence from Portugal and was assassinated in 1973.

It is also interesting that on the back of the walking map is a photo of Acha da Falcão, the home of Amílcar Cabral's family, now a small museum. It is very distinctive in that it is the only house I have seen in the Cape Verdes that is built like the old houses in the Caribbean, with a porch on all four sides. This keeps the sun off the walls of the house, making it much cooler than houses that do not have a porch. Why more houses are not built that way is very puzzling.

Porto Rincão

Harbor chart ST3
AP 15° 03.0' N; 23° 47.0' W

This bay appears to have a couple of coves and since it is named Porto it must have been a port in years gone by. A secondary road connects it to the main road. This anchorage could be difficult as it is open to the northwest groundswell from November to April. However, about 1,200 meters to the northwest and just east of Ponta do Atum there appeared, from the map, to be a nice harbor that would be sheltered from the worst of that groundswell. It is shoal enough for anchoring.

This is a fishing port with very good vibes. On my visit to Santiago in 2009, I was lucky enough to have Gerry Dom's daughter, Indira, as a guide. The road to the village is fairly good but the track from the village down the hill to the fishing village was so bad that even Indira, whom I rate as an extremely good bush driver, said, "This road is dangerous." Nevertheless, she still drove down the road to the beach.

We had long discussions with the fishermen, who sent us off on foot to visit the wonderful cove to the south of the harbor that they said was white sand. They said it was just a short walk, so Indira and I took off, or I should say, Indira, aged 27 and six foot one, took off while I, aged 79 and five foot eight, struggled to follow. After 20 minutes of walking over very rough ground, we gave up and headed back to the beach where we found a primitive bar. It was built of skinny upright sticks, their ends driven in the ground, and had a thatched roof. It gave good shelter from the sun, the breeze blew between the small sticks, and the beer was cold.

Santiago and Maio

A round of refreshments was in order after a tour of Porto Rincão and its surroundings by fishing boat. (Photo by Indira Dom)

Aguas Belas, on the west coast of Santiago, not far from Ribeira da Barca, was reputedly used as a meeting place by Amílcar Cabral and his associates during the struggle for Cape Verde's independence. (Photo by Pitt Reitmaier)

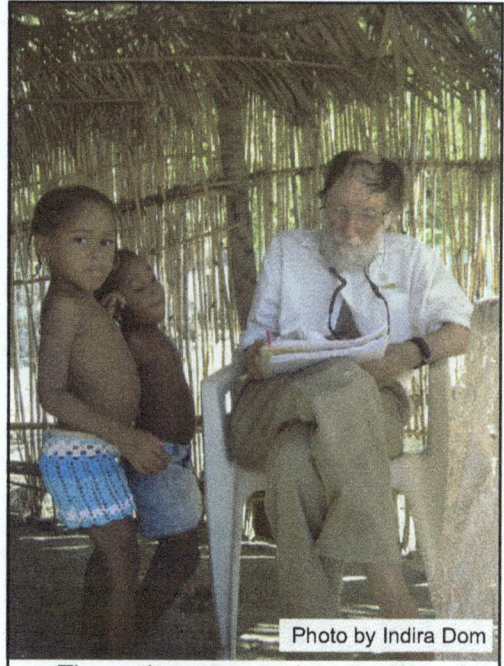

The author attracts the attention of the younger set as he compiles notes in the fishing village of Porto Rincão. (Photo by Indira Dom)

107

Street's Guide to the Cape Verde Islands

The fishing boats at Porto Rincão have the flared bows and paddle-blade oars typical of Santiago's west coast.

Santiago and Maio

Besides the two small friendly bars, we also found a boatbuilder who had a boat in frame, almost ready to start planking (see page 33).

We got into conversation with some fishermen and managed to arrange a charter. For €10, they launched a 20-foot skiff with an 8-horsepower outboard.

There was no groundswell that day, just what is evidently the normal surf. I took off my sandals and pulled up my trousers (wondering, "Why can't you buy bell bottoms any more? They would make this so much easier."). It turned out to be unnecessary as they insisted we get in the boat while the stern was still on dry beach. Then, about eight guys launched the boat, four piled in, and two of them immediately grabbed the sweeps and pulled us free of the surf. They then stood easy on the oars while the outboard was rigged.

We headed south to find a magnificent cove, with vertical 50-foot cliffs on all sides, a gray sand beach, and a white sand bottom. It was absolutely perfectly sheltered, there was no sea, and it was cool — I think the sun could only reach into it at high noon.

I have named it Honeymoon Cove as it's an ideal place to have a barbecue and swim *au naturel* with no chance of any Peeping Toms being around.

On the way back to the beach, we discussed the cove to the east of Ponta do Atum. They said in even the worst ground wells the anchorage there is fine. It has 30 to 40 feet of water over a sand bottom with good holding — and plenty of tuna!

They also said that anchoring off the beach was fine, again in 30 to 40 feet of water. They say it's a safe anchorage when the groundswell is running if you anchor fairly far offshore. Check the fathometer and make sure you are on the shelf before anchoring (see "Anchors and Anchoring," page 55).

In the lee of Santiago there is little wind and the sea is calm. You only get a sense that there's any swell at all when you launch or land through the small breaking waves.

The fishermen did advise us that the groundswell comes in so big at times that they have to move all the boats off the beach and carry them up a good 100 yards into the village.

Chart ST3
Ilha de Santiago
Porto Rincão

0   100   200   300
Scale: meters
Heights in meters
Soundings in Feet
Source: topo map and visit

Ponta do Atum

Porto Rincão

Porto Rincão

Honeymoon Cove

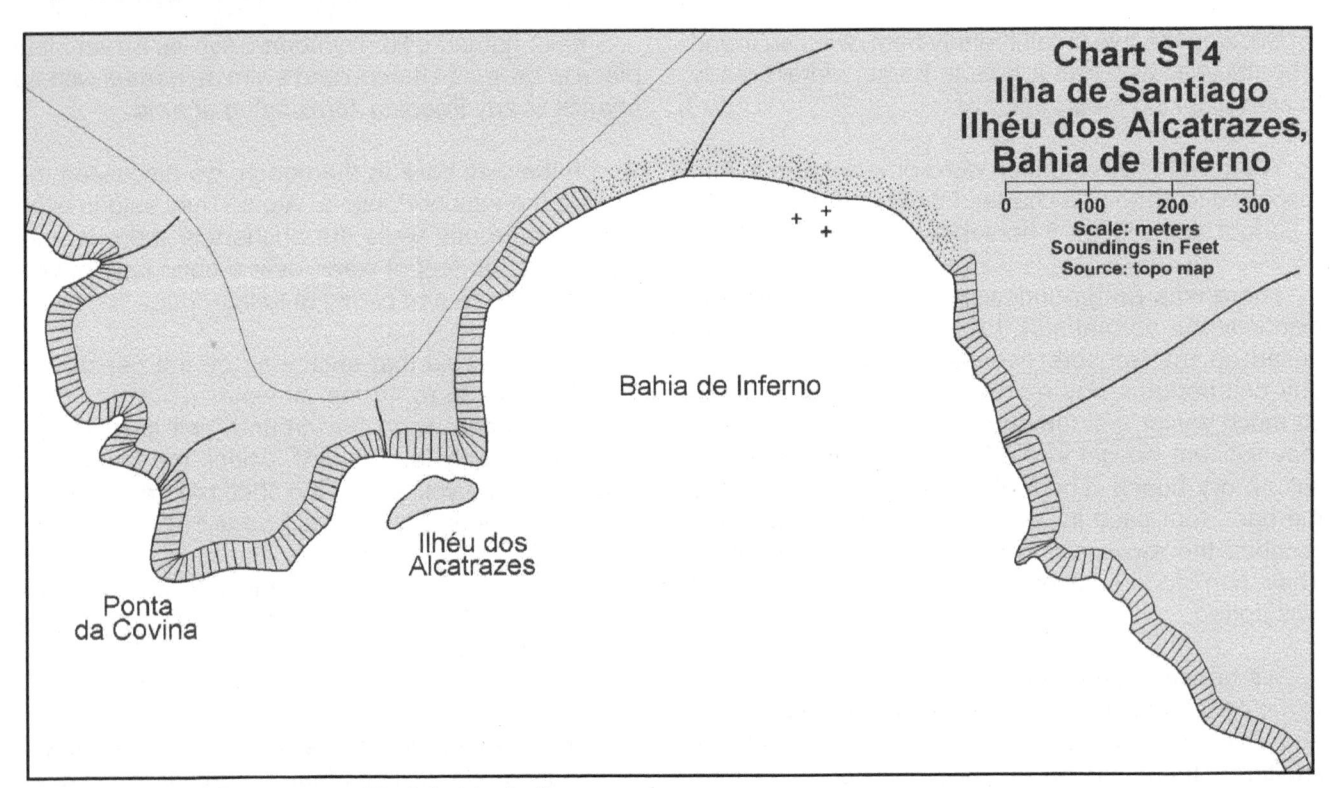

Ilhéu dos Alcatrazes/Bahia de Inferno
Harbor chart ST4
AP 15° 01.5' N; 23° 45.0' W

This harbor should be approached from the southwest to avoid the island and possible rocks on the southwest corner of the harbor. When coming from the north, make sure you are well south of the harbor before turning to enter.

I have not visited this bay but Kai Brosmann says this is an excellent anchorage as you can tuck your boat up into the northeast corner where you will be sheltered from the groundswell. Be sure to tie a tripping line on your anchor or rig it as a becued anchor as the bottom is rocky and it could get caught under a rock. Indira says it is a beautiful bay, but we were unable to visit it as it was too soon after the end of the rainy season and the road was impassable. You will find high cliffs, a ravine, and a gray sand beach.

Porto Mosquito
Harbor chart ST5
AP 14° 56.5' N; 23° 42.0' W

The name doesn't seem too encouraging, but it would appear that there might be an anchorage in the cove west of town. Obviously the fishing must be good as I counted 60 boats pulled up on the beach. The boats were notable for their high flaring bows. They also all had a 10-foot pole with a 4-foot by about ¼-inch iron rod attached to it. Indira was able to ascertain that they used these to harpoon big tuna. I describe the tuna-fishing method used here in Chapter 2.

The fishermen report the shelf is wide enough for anchoring. Yachts anchored 200 yards offshore appear to be safe even when the groundswell comes in.

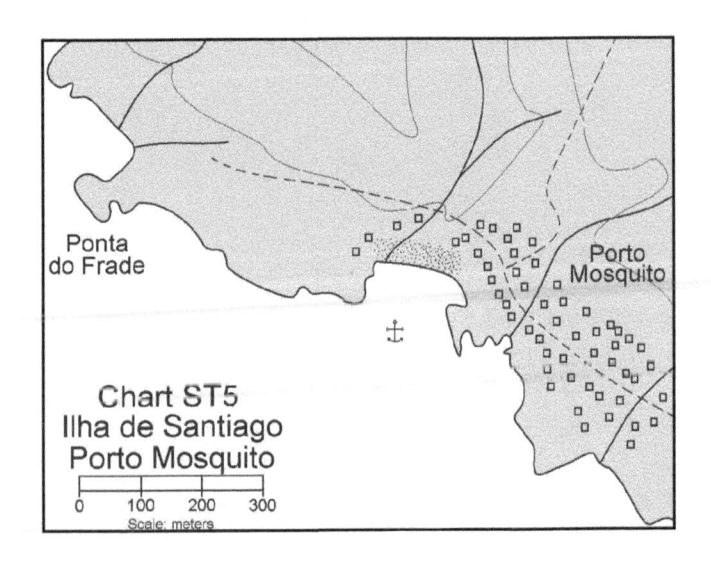

Porto Gouveia

Harbor chart ST6
AP 14° 56.5' N; 23° 42.0' W

The cove to the east here is a possible anchorage. It is an open beach. It was fairly calm on the day we saw it and a small number of fishing boats were pulled up on the beach. Note that between Ponta do Lamisqueiro and Ponta do Alcatraz there is an island. I am not sure how many rocks there might be in the area, so eyeball navigation it essential. I would stay clear of this area and anchor off the beach.

Cidade Velha

Harbor chart ST7
AP 14° 54.0' N; 23° 36.5' W

Cidade Velha is the original settlement on Santiago and was the capital until the early 18th century, when that function was moved to Praia.

This is a good harbor but there are apparently some off lying rocks (or very small islands) along this coast, so make sure you only approach in daylight. There is a shelf off town and anchoring is easy with reputedly good holding in sand. The best anchorage, according to Kai Brosmann, is in the northwest corner of the harbor. Eyeball your way in while watching the fathometer and anchor in about 40 to 50 feet.

There is a small rock island and reef in the middle of the harbor with deep water on all sides. When viewing the harbor from the fort that overlooks it, I noted two fishing boats about 40 feet long anchored east of this reef.

The best dinghy landing is on the southeast corner of the beach. Within 50 feet of where you land the dinghy you will find a pleasant bar and restaurant, adjacent to the main square. Cidade Velha has been declared a World Heritage site, and in the restaurant you will find flyers of the various historic sights that are worth a visit.

A frequent bus service runs between Cidade Velha and Praia. The route goes by Forte San Filipe so, on the way to Praia, you can get off the bus, tour the fort, then pick up the next bus to Praia.

I recommend, and Kai agrees, that it's best to anchor in Cidade Velha and visit Praia by bus. Sail to Praia only to take on fuel water and stores just before you leave for Fogo, Brava, and the Atlantic crossing.

Calheta de São Martinho

Harbor chart ST8
AP 14° 53.7' N; 23° 34.2' W

Calheta de São Martinho is about 2 miles east of Cidade Velha. This is a supremely well sheltered cove

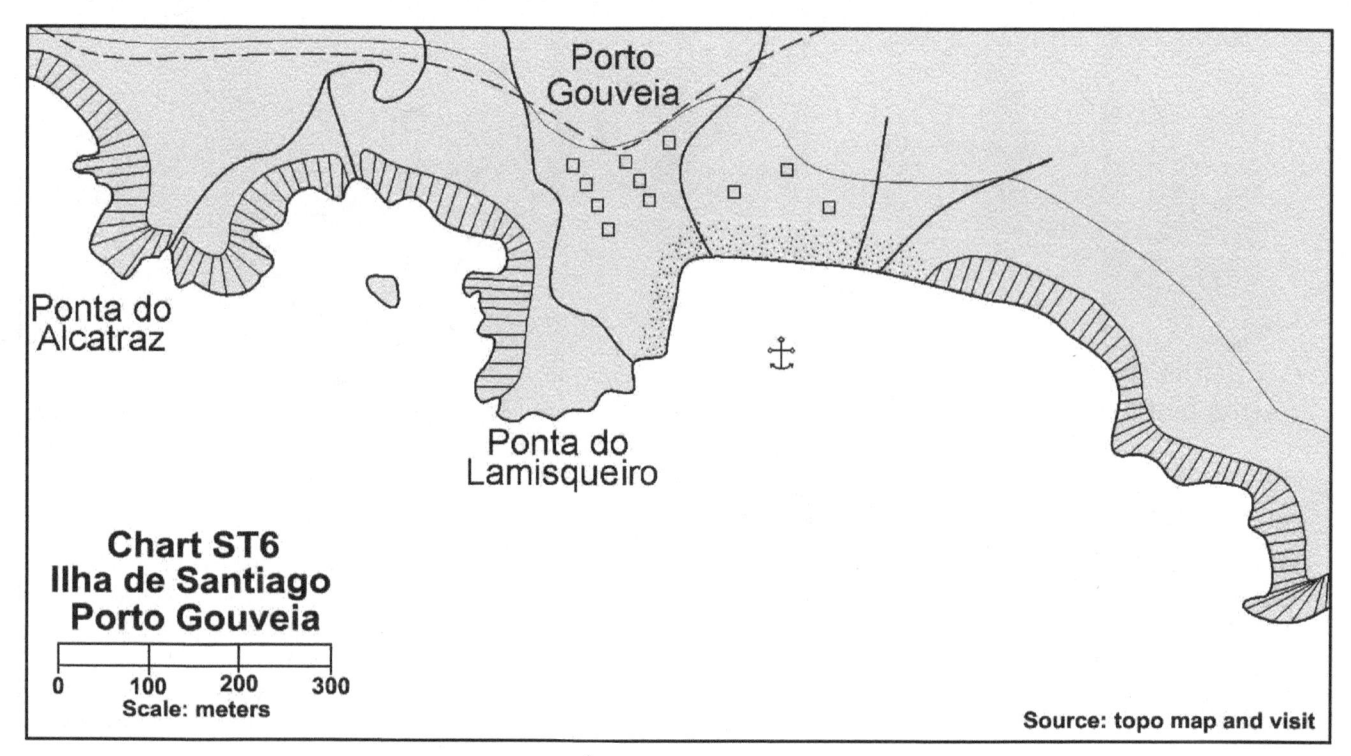

**Chart ST6
Ilha de Santiago
Porto Gouveia**

0   100   200   300
Scale: meters

Source: topo map and visit

Street's Guide to the Cape Verde Islands

as is illustrated by the fact that, in November 2009, I discovered a small marine railway that has evidently been there for years. When I was there, that's all there was: the railway but no shed and no habitation. However, there are signs of an impending big land development in the future just east of the cove as roads were well on the way to being constructed.

If the anchorage in Cidade Velha is too rocky and rolly, move east to this harbor and enjoy a quiet night.

Porto da Praia
Harbor chart ST9
AP 14° 53.7' N; 23° 30.0' W

The harbor of Praia is sheltered from all directions except southeast. Blows from the southeast are very uncommon and only experienced during hurricane season, June through early December. These southeasters, which have put a couple of medium size freighters ashore on the northwest corner of the harbor, arise when tropical lows form south of the Cape Verdes — the same tropical lows that sometimes develop into hurricanes by the time they have crossed the Atlantic.

The best anchorage for yachts is northwest of the main dock but the holding, in soft mud, is poor. The problem with anchoring in the northern corner is that the wind funnels down through the northern ravine, at times at gale velocity. Avoid the anchorage off the old customs pier, which in December 2005 was derelict but has now been completely rebuilt. The current Imray-Iolaire chart shows two ruined piers in that area.

For clearance, go to the harbor police office, which is at the head of this rebuilt dock. (It should be a good place to leave a dinghy.) From there, you'll have to go to the main dock to find the immigration department.

Be on the lookout for pilfering when alongside the pier. While the crew of *Sincerity* were hoisting the dinghy aboard, four body boards were stolen off the deck — in broad daylight. We took turns standing pilferage watch during the night and had no further problems.

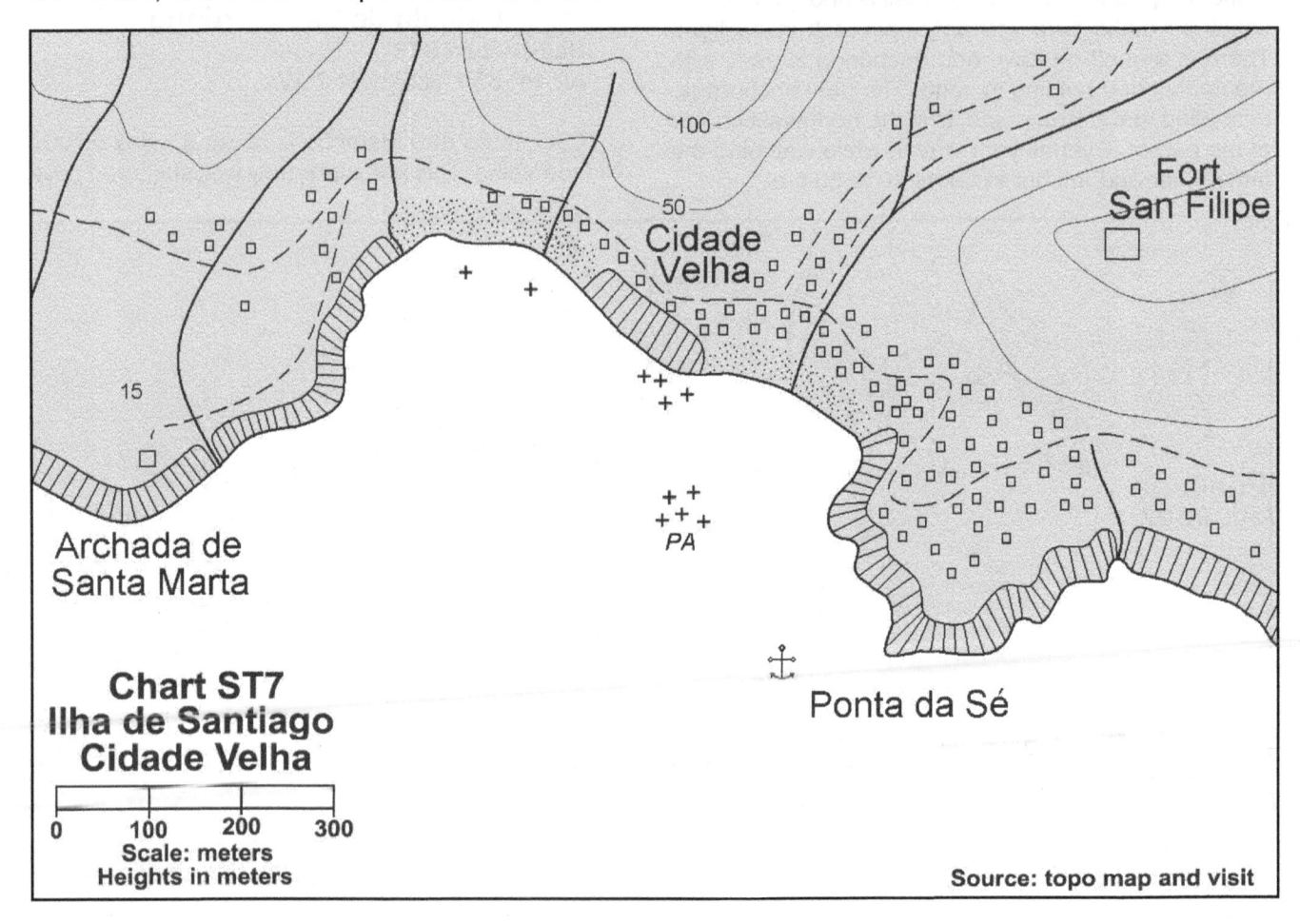

**Chart ST7
Ilha de Santiago
Cidade Velha**

0 100 200 300
Scale: meters
Heights in meters

Source: topo map and visit

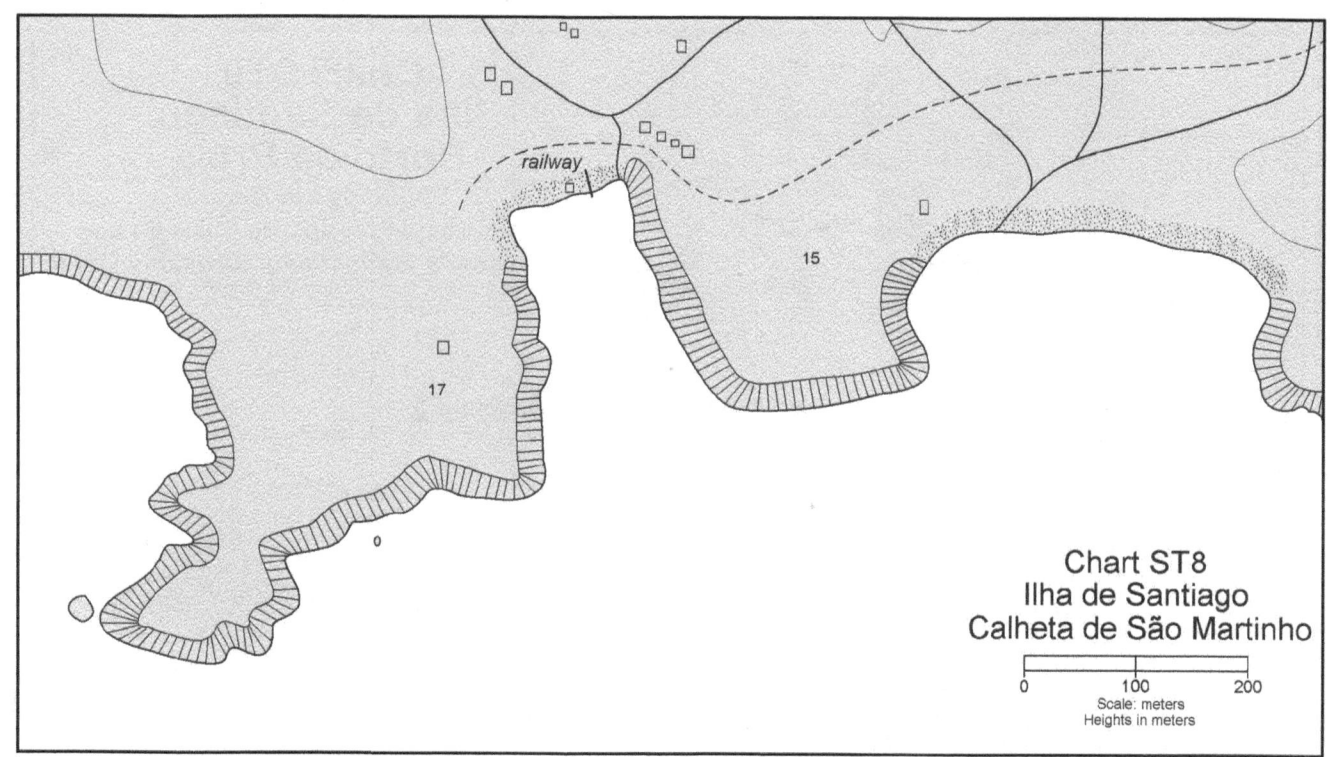

**Chart ST8
Ilha de Santiago
Calheta de São Martinho**

When it comes to landing a dinghy, you have two options. You can land the dinghy on the dock where the harbor police are. Here, you are within walking distance of town or you can flag a cab to take you up to the main part of town on the plateau.

The alternative is to tie up the dinghy at the fishermens' pier or, if it has been reestablished, the float at the fueling pier.

The float west of the fishermen's pier used to be a fueling station, with 15 feet of water alongside. Unfortunately, the fueling pier died in the summer of 2009 of corrosion and being hit by boats coming alongside to fuel. As of late November 2009 it had not been replaced. Until it is, you'll have to carry fuel in jerry cans or arrange a bulk delivery of diesel to the fishermen's pier.

Water is available at the fishermen's pier, and that we took aboard *Sincerity* in 2005 was satisfactory. In 1985, we obtained water from a visiting U.S. Navy destroyer, and in 1989, we carted it in 5-gallon jugs from Gerry Dom's household cistern. This was of course rainwater.

In 2005, when I was in the bank trying to obtain money (where I discovered MasterCards were no good), I met Patrick Rodriguez Nascimento, an airport fireman who spoke Portuguese and French. With his aid, I finally obtained money and rented a car. He served as my guide while we drove over hill and dale. In many cases, we found no roads from which to view the unexplored harbors from shore. His help was invaluable, the best way to contact him is to call the airport fire department (263-3593).

When I was in Praia in both 1985 and 1989, with *Iolaire*, the talk was that the shoal between the mainland and Ilhéu de Santa Maria was going to be filled in and the prison on Santa Maria reconstructed as a hotel and marina complex. However, almost 24 years later, in November 2009, nothing had yet happened.

With the massive developments going on in Santiago, it's probably only a matter of time before a developer takes over the island and the fort, does some dredging, and creates a marina. This is needed as anchoring in Praia is not all that good.

As of December 2005, the port was undergoing expansion, and a section for the fishing boats had just been completed. They had a great collection of massive cranes. I am quite sure a relatively large yacht could be lifted out of the water for emergency repairs if the skipper could tell the right story to the right people.

Street's Guide to the Cape Verde Islands

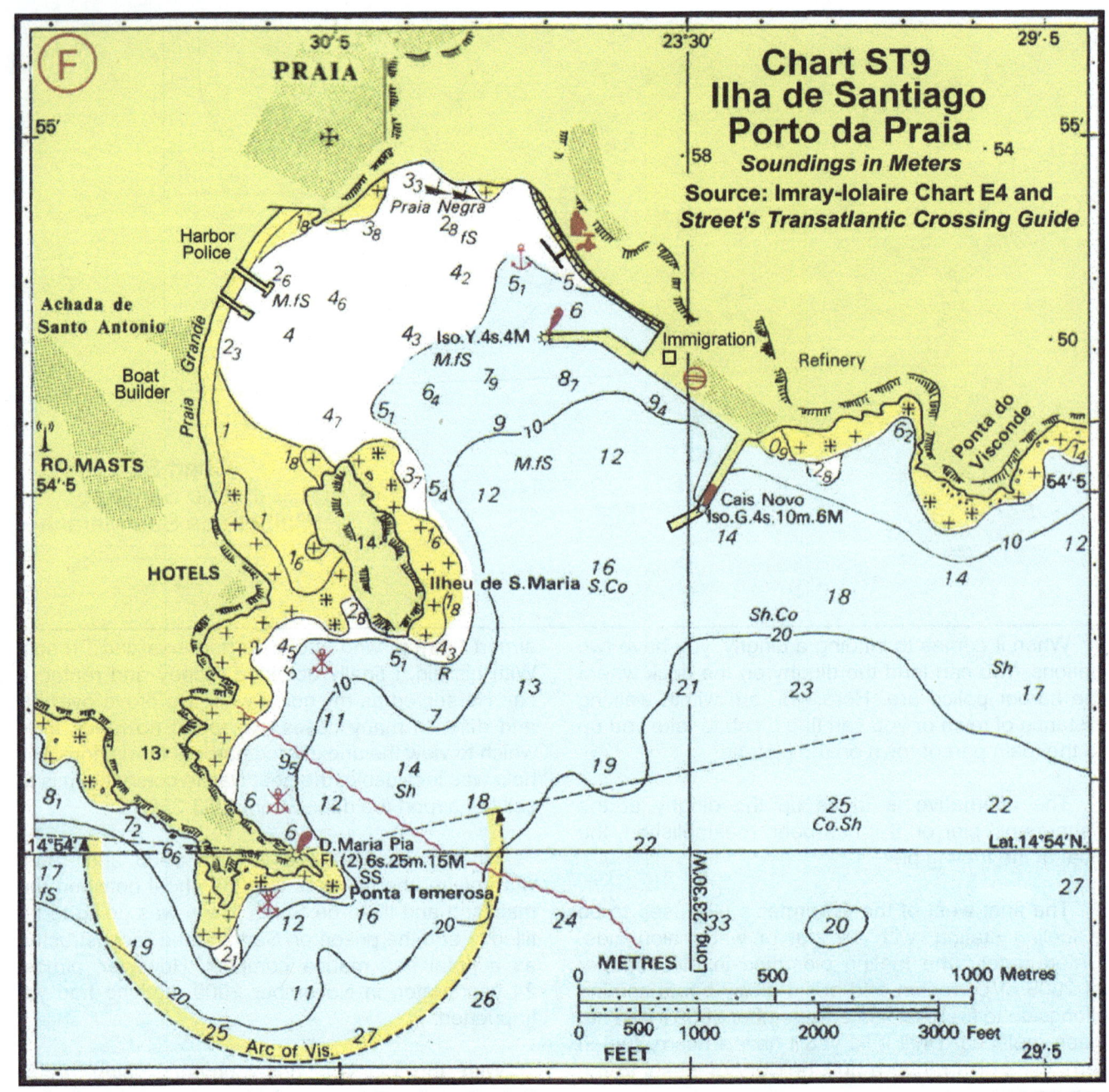

During my visit in November 2009, I learned that the port was about to undergo another expansion in the coming years to handle the large amount of container traffic. The breakwater on the east side of the harbor, which is also the unloading pier, is being widened to make it easier to handle containers. It is also being extended 300 feet at an angle to the southwest from the existing dock.

Over the years, relationships between the harbor police and yachtsmen have improved. In December 2002, Donna Lange, a wandering sailing troubadour, arrived in Praia singlehanding her little 32-foot cutter on which she had numerous problems. She tied up at the fishing pier and later reported that everyone was most helpful. However, in her story as reported in the free nautical newspaper, the *Caribbean Compass*, in the winter of 2003, she is quoted as stating that the main harbor authorities definitely do not like yachts.

In 2005, Trygve Bratz the owner/skipper of *Sincerity*, found the harbor police most cooperative, even though Trig did not have my passport as I had taken it with me to the bank to get money.

Santiago and Maio

On the beach at Porto Mosquito, someone's unfinished dream provides shelter for a fishing boat. (Photo by Don Street)

The marine railway in Calheta de São Martinho is the only one the author has seen outside of Mindelo. (Photo by Don Street)

As long as the groundswell isn't running, the roadstead at Cidade Velha provides a good anchorage, as seen here from Fort San Filipe. (Photo by Don Street)

Food supplies are adequate, and between the roadside stands and the central market a good supply of fresh produce is available. While the selection isn't as good as in the Canary Islands, it's a lot better than in Mindelo.

Also, there are now on the plateau a number of proper supermarkets with good stocks of frozen meat, both local and imported. Some of the cuts of meat are rather interesting — pigs' ears, snouts, and trotters, which are cheap and excellent when properly cooked. Do remember to bring egg cartons, otherwise you'll have to carry eggs loose in a bag — and make omelettes as soon as you get back aboard the boat.

The town of Praia is worth a brief exploration. It has a nice open square with cafés around the corners, an old church, banks, cyber cafés, and pharmacies. Other amenities include a telephone exchange, but between Skype and mobiles, which work well here, you shouldn't have much need for it.

Numerous restaurants can be found in and around the town of Praia. Those at two hotels southwest of town overlooking Ilhéu de Santa Maria obviously cater to an international clientele. They are good, but expensive by Cape Verdean standards — although cheap by European standards. At the other end of the scale are restaurants in town that cater to the locals, serving good but inexpensive meals.

The city of Praia is also well supplied with residencials, which provide perfectly adequate accommodations at a reasonable price.

Praia is the last place where you will be able to do serious provisioning for your transatlantic crossing. It is also the last place to fill gas bottles and get alongside for fuel and water. Let's hope that, by the time you read this, the fueling float will be repaired and back in place. If not, you'll have to squeeze into the fishermen's pier to take on water and carry fuel in jugs from the fuel station. If the fuel float stays out of commission for long, you may find an enterprising guy with a pickup with a couple of 55-gallon drums in the back and a means of siphoning the diesel into the yacht's tanks.

Unexplored Harbors on the East Coast of Santiago

The east coast of Santiago and its numerous harbors, or perhaps I should say potential harbors, can be accessed from either the north or the south. Note that when the trade winds are blowing, the entire east coast is a lee shore, so choose your time carefully to explore it. The island is only 30 miles long, so if you do find conditions not to your liking, you can turn back (or keep going) and head for the west coast.

If you have sailed down the west coast to Praia and have time, you can, weather permitting, turn left and sail up the east coast of Santiago. Once you get past Ponta do Lobo, the easternmost point of the island, you should be sailing on a reach, and the harbors and coves are only a few miles apart.

Because most boats will arrive in Tarrafal from the Ilhas do Barlavento and will then choose which side of Santiago to sail along, the harbors on the east coast appear here in southward order from Tarrafal.

Either way, they should be approached with caution and with someone in the rigging or after a preliminary exploration in a RIB.

As for the west coast, I have given every harbor an Approach Point (AP) taken from the WGS 84 topo map. They are usually about a mile off and in the direction from which it appears the best approach can be made. Approach these APs with due caution and, from each AP on in, rely on eyeball navigation, hand-bearing compass, and fathometer or lead line and have a crewmember standing on the bow pulpit or, if it's a tricky entrance, on the lower spreaders.

Baia de Angra
Harbor chart ST10
AP: 15° 18.0' N; 23° 40.5' W

This is a big open semi-circular bay about 600 meters in diameter. Gerry Dom reports there is a good anchorage in the northeast corner in about 15 feet of water.

Approach this anchorage from the southeast using eyeball navigation backed up by fathometer.

Fishing boats are drawn up on a shingle beach and a goat track leads up to the road.

I suspect this harbor is like Furna in Brava. Although it faces into the trade winds, the hill — almost a cliff — rises steeply behind the harbor to about 600 feet so that the harbor is in a back eddy. This same back-eddy effect is found in Road Town, Tortola, in the British Virgin Islands.

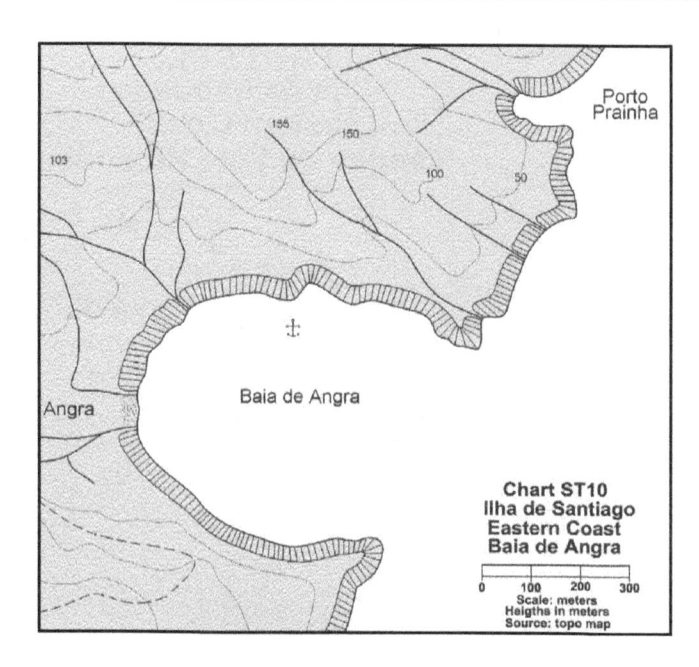

Porto Formoso
Harbor chart ST11
AP: 15° 16.0' N; 23° 40.0' W

There should be complete shelter here unless the wind is due north. The cove is 200 meters wide and 500 meters long. There appears to be adequate water at the entrance, gradually shoaling toward a gray sand beach with about a half dozen fishing boats pulled up on it.

Approach from the north, eyeball your way in along the middle of the harbor, watching, the fathometer, and anchor in a suitable depth.

There is a small village on the main road.

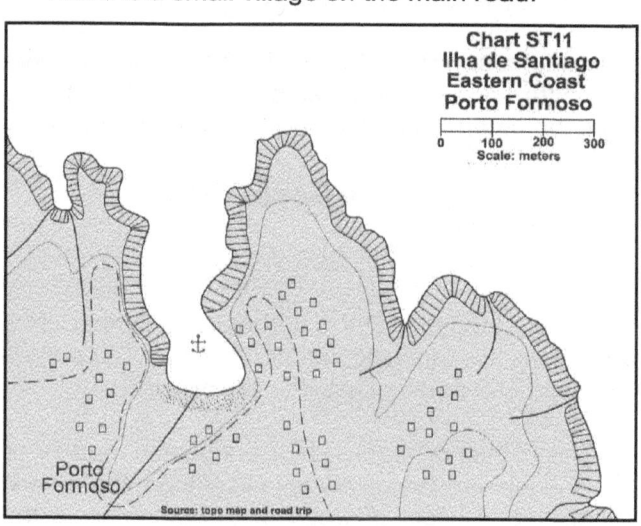

Mangue de Sete Ribeiras
Harbor chart ST12
AP: 15° 15.0' N; 23° 37.5' W

This harbor is also called Porto do Mangue.

You should have good shelter once you are inside the cove but there are a lot of off-lying rocks to the east of the harbor.

The best approach into this bay appears to be from due north midway between a rock about 50 feet high on the port hand and a 3-foot high pinnacle rock on the starboard hand. Continue south until the harbor opens up. There is deep water on the south side of the harbor entrance. Once the harbor opens up, turn west staying in the middle of the harbor and anchor in a suitable depth. It should be a sand bottom.

The entrance is 120 meters wide and the cove is 300 meters long with two separate anchorages. One anchorage on the south side of the harbor, but the better, more sheltered one is at the western end of the harbor.

I worked out these piloting directions standing on the cliffs on the south side of the harbor in November 2009.

Here again, there is a small village on the main coastal road, which runs around the bay.

Cove East of Ponta da Ribeira Brava
Harbor chart ST12
AP: 15° 15.0' N; 23° 37.0' W

I viewed this cove from the shore in December of 2002. The axis of the cove lies 045/225. Approach this cove from the east. When entering, leave the awash rock to starboard then, once past it, turn to the southwest.

The entrance to the cove is 70 meters wide and the cove is 120 meters long.

I would advise anchoring in Mangue de Sete Ribeiras and exploring this cove by dinghy before entering with your boat.

Veneza
Harbor chart ST13
AP: 15° 12.0' N; 23° 35.0' W

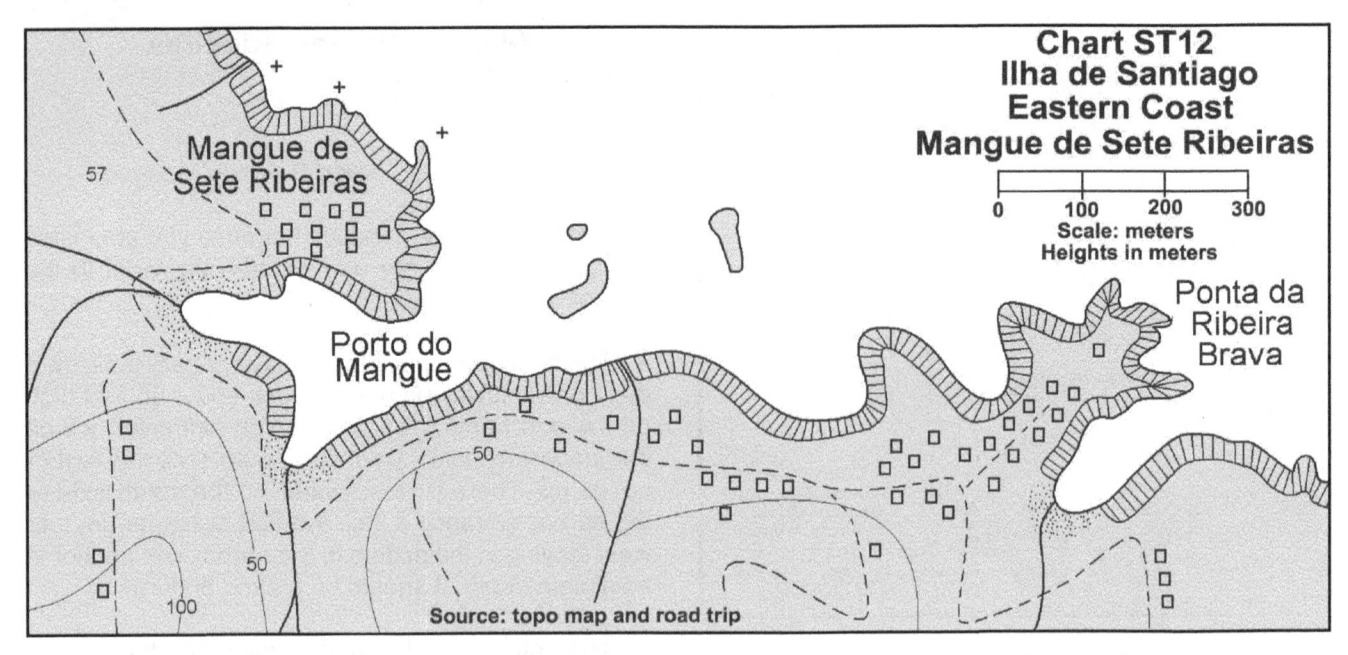

Street's Guide to the Cape Verde Islands

This cove is west of Calheta de São Miguel. The entrance is 120 meters wide and the cove is 180 meters long. I viewed it in November 2009 from shore. It appears to offer good shelter as long as the wind is not right out of the north. At the head of the cove is a pebble beach where a couple of fishing boats were pulled up on shore.

Calheta de São Miguel
Harbor chart ST13
AP: 15° 12.0' N; 23° 35.0' W

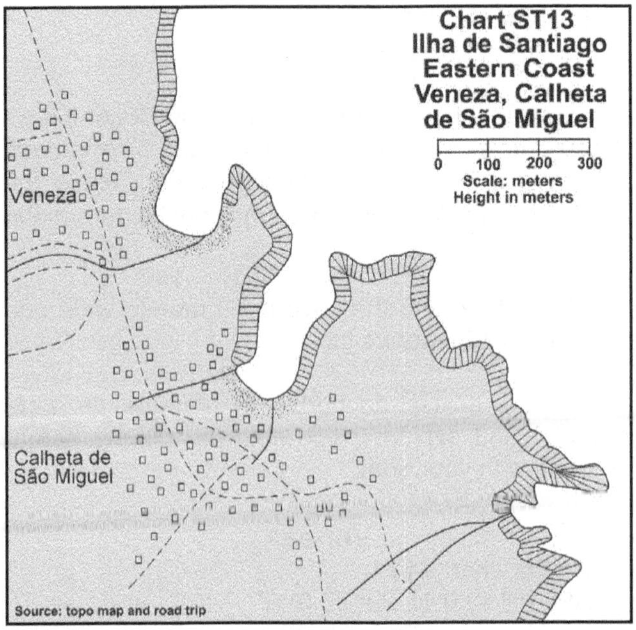

The entrance to the cove is 100 meters wide and the cove 300 meters long. It has a muddy bottom and a shingle beach. São Miguel should be sheltered in all conditions unless the wind is right out of the north.

When approaching from the south, look out for a reef that is breaking water at all times, about 300 yards offshore ¼ mile southeast of Calheta de São Miguel.

There is a small village nearby. Some new houses look as though they have been built for a developing tourist market.

Porto Coqueiro
Harbor chart ST14
AP: 15° 10.0' N; 23° 33.0' W

I did not see Porto Coqueiro, to the west of Ponta de Santa Cruz, but it appears to have a beach and could be an anchorage if the wind is south of east.

Ponta de Santa Cruz
Harbor chart ST15
AP: 15° 09.7' N; 23° 32.0' W

I took a long look at this harbor in December 2005 and I think it is fantastic harbor. It's about 120 meters wide and 600 meters long with deep water.

This is the port where ships bring sand, and since fully loaded sand ships come in to offload, there must be at least 12 feet of water at the entrance to the

Santiago and Maio

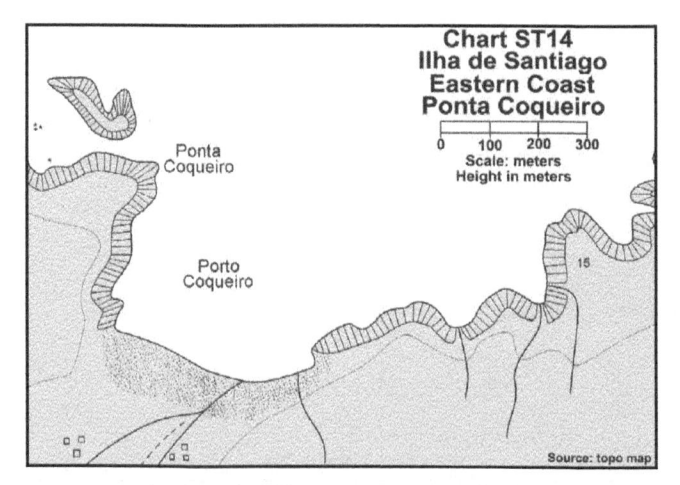

cove, gradually shoaling as you get further into the fjord. It would be essential that you anchor south of where the sand ships unload. Allow enough room for them to do a 180 degree turn.

At the head of the cove, a gravel digging and loading operation moves gravel up to the road on the east side of the fjord.

There is no habitation on the cove as steep cliffs line both sides, but there is a beach, palm trees, and a dry river bed at the head of the cove. This is an area that might bear exploring by those so inclined.

Since the bay is at the outlet of a ravine, the water at the head of the bay will be muddy whenever it rains, but it will probably be clear at the mouth.

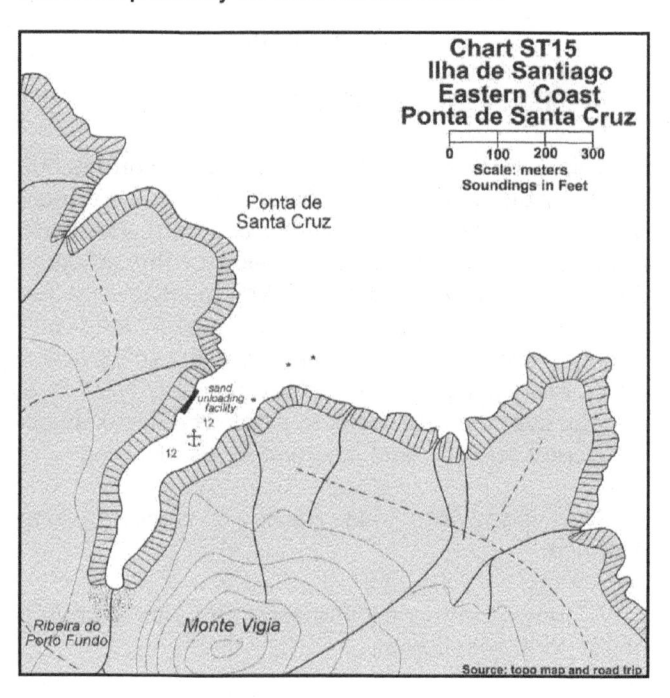

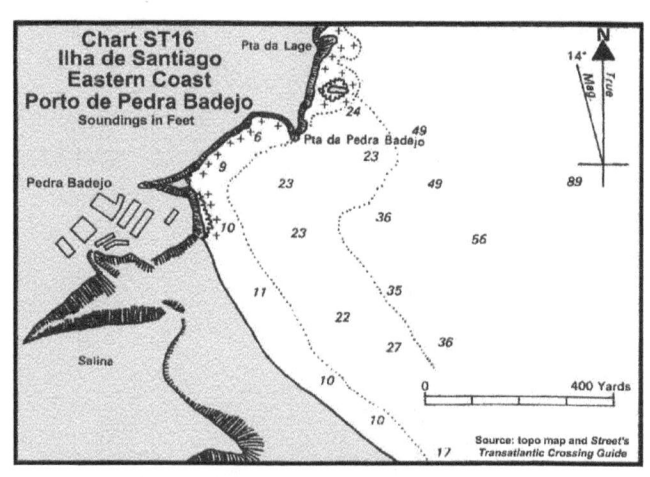

There is a narrow cove with steep cliffs to the west of Ponta de Santa Cruz, that might bear exploring by dinghy from the Ponta de Santa Cruz anchorage.

Porto de Pedra Badejo
Harbor chart ST16
AP: 15° 08.4' N; 23° 31.0' W

The sketch chart is made up from the topo map with soundings taken from an old British survey from the mid 19th century.

Pedra Badejo is a small town with what looks to be a rather exposed harbor. When I visited the town with Indira Dom in November 2009, we were surprised to see three moderate-sized boats anchored off. There was the usual collection of boats hauled up on the beach.

Indira quizzed the fishermen about weather, sea conditions, and anchoring. They said the anchored boats stayed there all year and that they had no trouble except during the winter months of January through March or early April. They also said the bottom is sand and offers good holding.

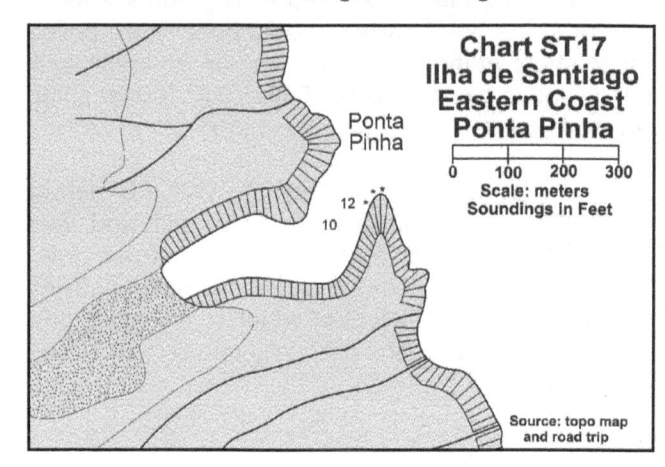

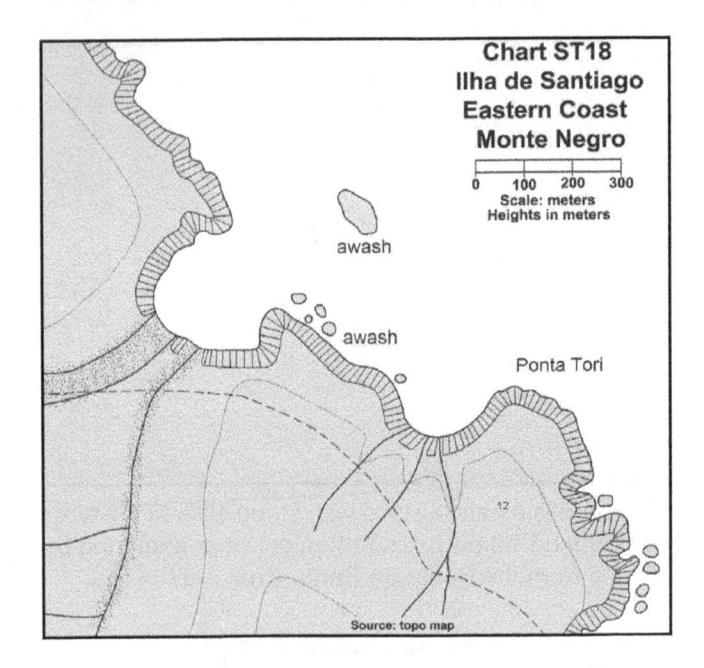

Gerry Dom concurs. He says as long as it's not blowing hard, this is a good anchorage.

Ponta Pinha

ST17
AP: 15° 07.0' N; 23° 29.0' W

The entrance to this cove is L-shaped and may be extremely hard to spot except when you are northeast of it. Enter from the north as there are rocks on the south side of the entrance. Head southwest then due west. The bay is about 400 meters long but only 100 meters wide. Because of the L-shaped entrance, yachts should be completely sheltered once inside the harbor.

As I viewed this harbor I thought it looked fantastic. I estimated the depth in the outer harbor to be 10 to 12 feet. Two 25-foot motorized fishing boats were at anchor in the outer harbor and 20 boats were pulled up on shore at the head of the harbor. An uphill walk brings you to a small village. Cliffs 70 to 100 feet high line both sides.

In November 2009, we tried to visit this harbor again. The road had been washed out and was impassable but we found some fishermen who happened to know Indira's father, Gerry Dom. They told us there was 10 feet of water in the outer part of the harbor and that it gradually shoals toward the head of the harbor.

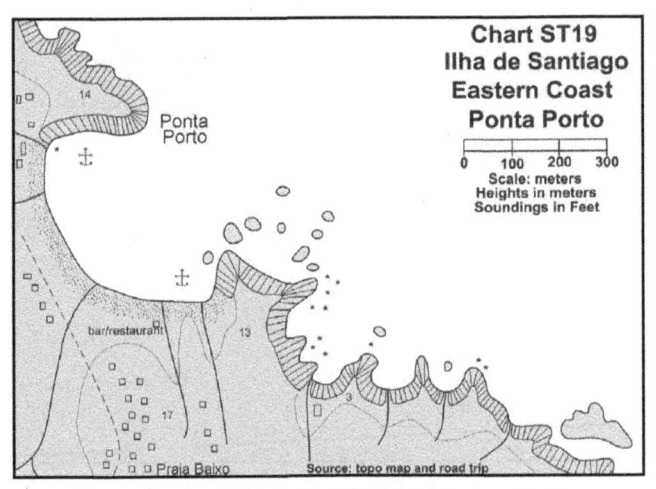

Monte Negro

Harbor chart ST18
AP: 15° 06.0' N; 23° 29.0' W

This cove is about a mile south of Ponta Pinha harbor described above. It is private property. One family owns the whole valley and the road is barred to the public by a locked gate. Indira knows the family and inquired as to how they would feel about of boats anchoring in the cove and people going ashore on beach and exploring the valley. The family told her that they do not own the beach, so yachts are free to anchor in the cove and their crews to walk on the beach. There is always a guard on the property, so anyone wishing to explore farther ashore can ask for permission.

Ponta Porto

Harbor chart ST19
AP: 15° 04.3' N; 23° 27.7' W

This semicircular bay south of Ponta Porto is 500 meters in diameter. It's exposed to the east and would only be acceptable if it is not blowing hard. There are numerous rocks on the south side of the entrance that might provide good diving. A drying river, one that only has water in it during the rainy season, leads into the north side of the bay where there is a small village and a few fishing boats. The south side of the bay is popular over the weekends as it has a beach, a simple restaurant and bar, and it's good for windsurfing.

The village of Praia Baixio is within walking distance.

A Google Earth view showed four boats anchored in the northwest corner.

Santiago and Maio

Ponta Pinha on the east coast of Santiago is very sheltered. Photo by Don Street

In Ponta Pinha the local boats remain on their moorings year round. Photo by Don Street

The sand harbor at Ponta de Santa Cruz is well sheltered even from the trade winds. It gets a little muddy after a rain, but rain is infrequent. Photo by Don Street

121

Street's Guide to the Cape Verde Islands

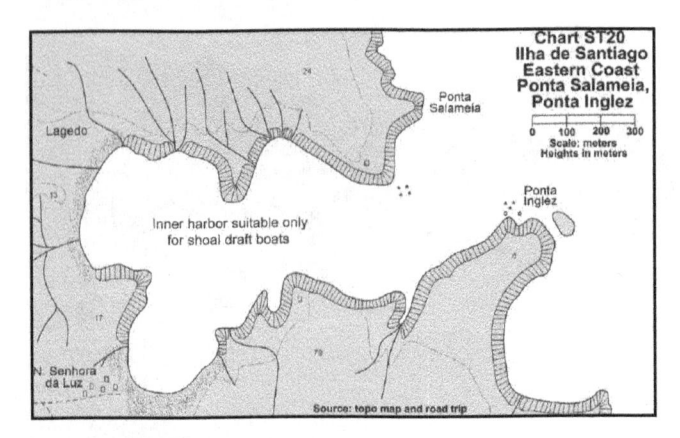

Ponta Salameia/Ponta Inglez
Harbor chart ST20
AP: 15° 03.0' N; 23° 26.0' W

The entrance to this bay between Ponta Salameia and Ponta Inglez is 400 meters wide and the bay is 1,400 meters long. A secondary road reaches the southwest corner of the harbor. As there are two separate coves inside the harbor, shelter should be possible even with easterly winds.

Viewing it from the hill on the southern side of the harbor December 2005, I estimated the depth in the outer harbor at 12 to 15 feet and shoaling in the inner harbors. The water was murky, which made it hard to judge the depths in the inner harbors. I suspect the southern cove is shallow. There is a very small settlement ashore. An abandoned bus landmarks the hill on the south side of the harbor.

I did not visit this cove in 2009.

Praia de Moia Moia
Harbor chart ST21
AP: 15° 02.0' N; 23° 25.8' W

You should find a good anchorage here as long as the wind is not in the northeast. The bay is circular, about 400 meters in diameter, and sheltered if the wind is south of east. It has a gravel beach and possibly good diving around the edges.

Watch out for a breaking rock on the starboard side when entering. The best approach is from the northeast.

Ponta Bomba
Harbor chart ST21
AP: 15° 00.5' N; 23° 25.2' W

South of Ponta Bomba, between it and Ponta Malhada, is a big open bay. You might find shelter behind the north or the south points of the bay but I am not sure whether you will find water shoal enough to anchor. There is a rock 200 meters south of Ponta Bomba. The shore is rocky and I doubt that you could land a dingy, but you'll possibly find good diving there.

Porto Lobo
Harbor chart ST21
AP: 15° 00.0' N; 23° 25.0' W

This is a circular bay, about 500 meters in diameter and with an entrance 200 meters wide, directly south of the Ponta Malhada.

Shelter might be possible behind the points that form the north and south sides of the bay but, again, I am not sure whether you will be able to find water shoal enough to anchor and, as the shore is rocky, landing a dinghy might be difficult. There are better harbors to visit than this. One good thing — if you want solitude you will have it. There are no roads, only tracks, and not even a settlement in the area.

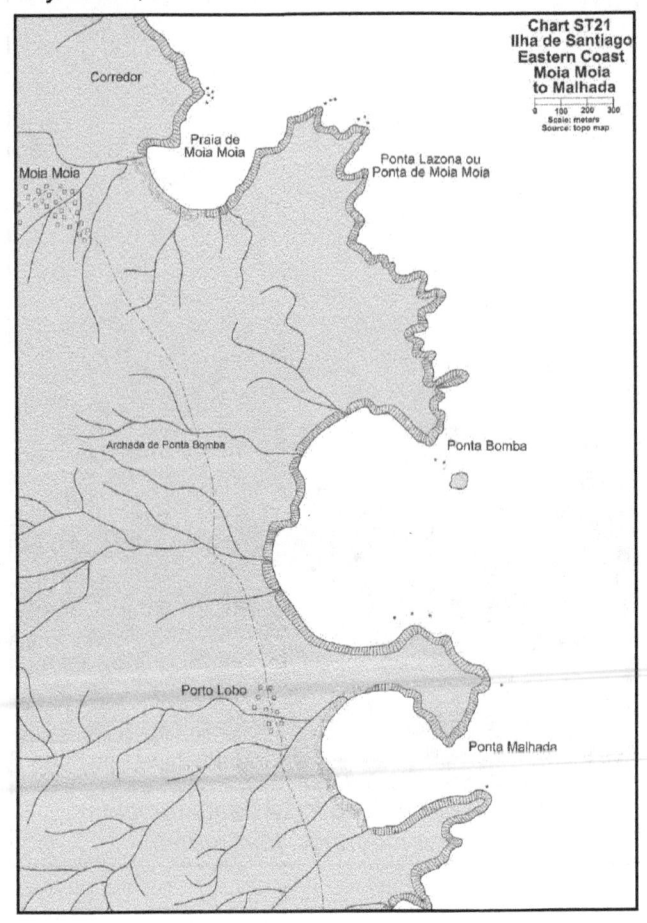

Curiously, on the Reitmaier topo map, Ponta Malhada is shaded like a built-up area and it's labeled "Marina Porto Lobo." Perhaps someone once had a plan for a marina, but they'd have to be nuts to build one here.

Ponta Leste and Porto de São Francisco
Harbor chart ST22
AP: 14° 58.2' N; 23° 26.3' W

As long as the wind is north of east there should be an anchorage under Ponta Leste. I viewed this from shore in December 2005 and I can say you can forget about getting ashore anywhere near Ponta Leste. Kai Brosmann says the anchorage is fine but a little rocky and rolly.

On the west side of the bay, about a mile and a half away at Porto de São Francisco, is a nice beach with, a few hundred yards inland, some ostentatious houses surrounded by high walls.

This is one of the few sand beaches in all of Santiago. It's accessible from Praia by a very good road and it's also used by the new Sambala development on the plateau due west of Ponta Sambala, so I'm sure that in years to come it will be a very up-market area.

The beach is accessible via dinghy from the anchorage behind Ponta Leste, but only if the dinghy is suitable for a semi-open-water passage of something over a mile.

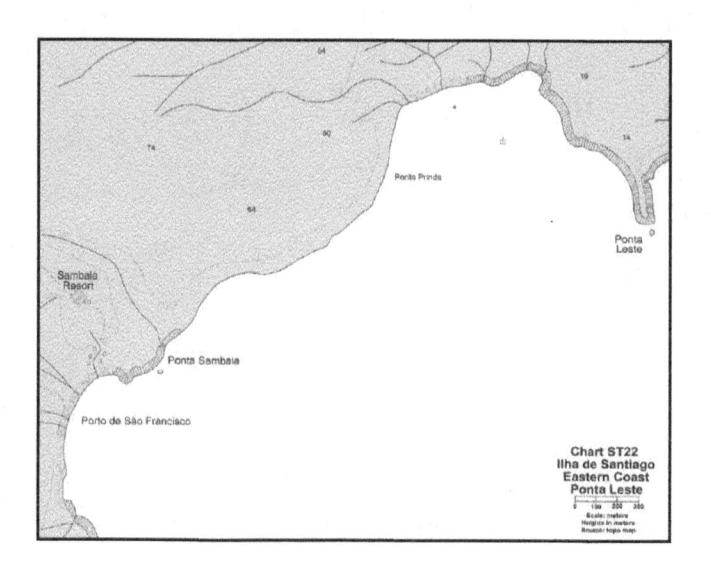

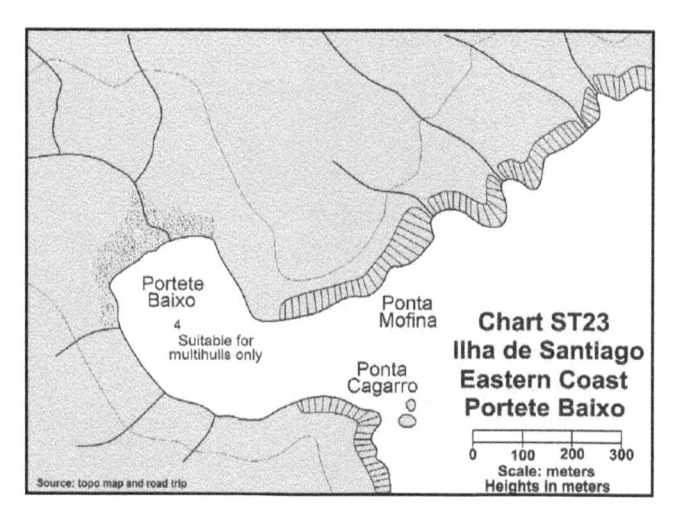

Portete Baixo
Harbor Chart ST23
AP: 14° 57.3' N; 23° 26.8' W

This bay is at the outflow of a wide river valley which is dry most of the year but shows signs of plentiful agriculture. The entrance is 150 meters wide and the bay 400 meters long and should provide good shelter except in strong easterlies.

The problem with this harbor is that, although it looks great on a topo map, there is only 3 to 4 feet of water inside. This, however, is great for powerboats or multihulls.

It's apparently a popular spot with the local fishermen as I saw more than twenty boats pulled up on the beach.

Ilha do Maio
Imray-Iolaire Chart E4
Harbor chart M1.

Maio is low and flat —the island where nothing happens. There is not much to attract the yachtsman except lobster and mile after mile of deserted beach on the south coast.

When traveling by air and inter-island ferry through the Cape Verde Islands in December 2002, I met a very nice young German with whom I explored Brava and Fogo. He said he came to the Cape Verde islands every year for almost a month, spending two weeks of it on Maio. I asked why he spent two weeks in Maio and he said, "I work in a very high-stress business in Germany and I come to the Cape Verdes to completely unwind." He stated that Maio is an

Street's Guide to the Cape Verde Islands

In the 18th century, so many English ships came to Maio to pick up salt that they named the town Porto Inglez — English Harbor.

Vila do Maio/Porto Inglez
Harbor chart M1
AP: 15° 07.5' N; 23° 14.0' W

The best anchorage is north of town, between the town and the 900-foot-long dock.

This is another bit of bad engineering exported from the first world to the third world. I wonder why they built a 900-foot dock when the passenger freighter that uses it is only 200 feet long. The money it cost to build the last 600 feet of unused dock could have better been spent elsewhere.

The shelf is about 300 yards wide and 30 feet deep with a sand bottom. Beyond that it drops off suddenly to 90 feet.

When we anchored *Iolaire* there, in 1989, we discovered that there is a reversing tide and we were tide-rode even with the mizzen up. Also, the presence of a beautiful white sand beach is a reminder that

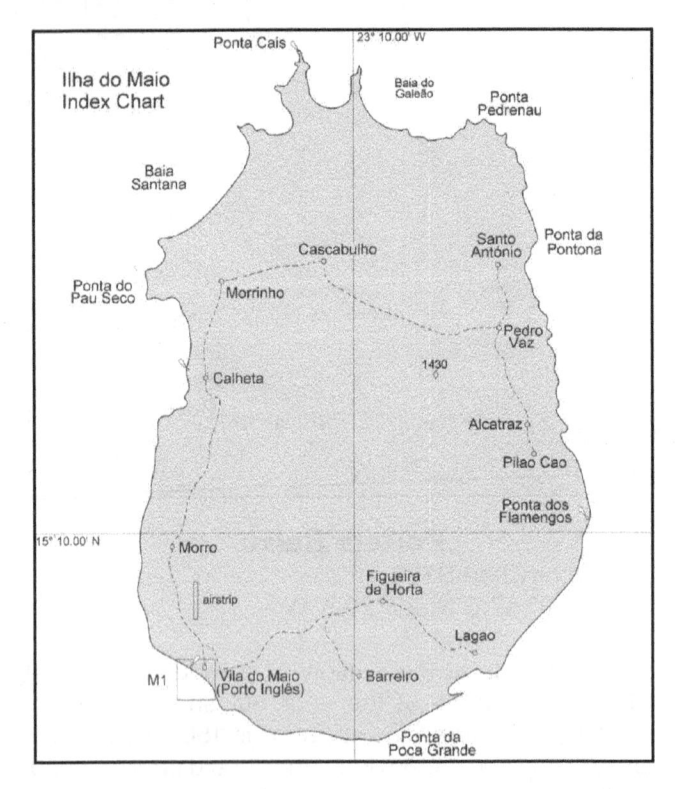

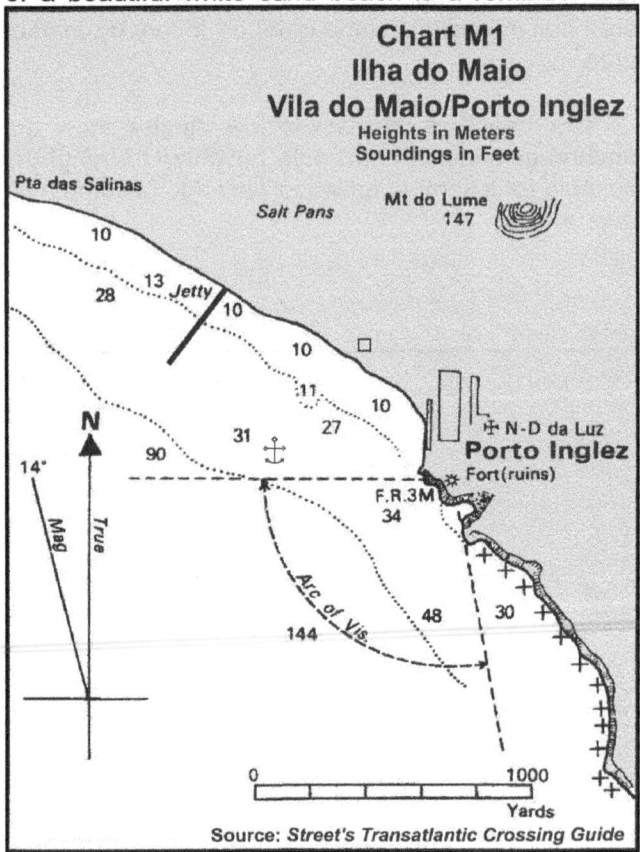

excellent place to unwind, as *nothing* happens. He said so little happens that if a chicken ran across the road, the topic of conversation for the rest of the day is whether the chicken was followed by four chicks or five chicks.

I arrived by air in late November 2009 and discovered that the island was developing. In the town of Vila do Maio, I noticed a large collection of new tourist guest house/hotels. Most, but not all of them, were of very poor architectural design and built in a location that was not very attractive. They were all built on the north edge of town facing out on to a big salt pan. Since it was right at the end of the rainy season it was a big shallow lake. During the tourist season it would be a broad salt flat where they still gather salt.

Gathering salt is a hard-earned living. Two kilograms of true sea salt sell for €0.50.

When I first arrived in the Caribbean, in 1956, they were still gathering salt on both Anguilla and on the French side of St. Martin. I walked out on the salt flats one day to watch them at work. It was an eye opener. Feeling the heat of the noonday sun reflecting off the salt flats despite the cooling effect of the trade winds made me realize why islanders everywhere give up gathering salt as soon as a little prosperity arrives.

the coast is exposed to the northwest groundswell. For both these reasons I advise either a Bahamian moor or bow and stern anchors.

There are various options for landing a dinghy. The first is to go to the north side of the long dock, anchor the dinghy, run a line to the ladder and climb up the ladder. This is evidently the usual method of mooring the local fishing boats that do not haul out on the beach. There is a fence and gate at the head of the dock, but there is a big hole in the fence and a very friendly guard.

From the dock, it's a half-mile walk to town, but only a quarter-mile walk along the beach to a beach bar. Next to the beach bar is a restaurant that opens about 1800 or you can continue on to town were there are a couple of restaurants. One of them has a sign that says "music and dancing." I asked the manager of the small hotel I stayed in about the music and dancing sign. He roared with laughter and said, "Nothing ever happens in Maio, much less music and dancing."

Another option for landing a dinghy is on the beach where the fishing boats are pulled up, but be mindful of the swell, and read the section in Chapter 4 on landing and launching through surf.

The final option is at the steps on the south end of town. Because of the surge, you will have to tie the dinghy off to a dinghy anchor and run a line ashore. The problem is the only ring bolts or securing points are at the top of the steps, so your bow line will have to be at least 50 feet long.

For a nice exploration trip, take the dinghy about 500 yards south of the steps, where you will find a small cove with a white sand beach. It's surrounded by cliffs about 30 feet high which give absolutely no access to the beach except for a single stairway that leads down from one of several very nice private homes. This cove looks like a wonderful spot to have a private beach barbecue.

The village has a long promenade overlooking the beach. On the side of the promenade is a very basic bar. It's not fancy by any means, but the beer is cold, the staff and customers are friendly, the ever-present breeze is cooling, and the view of the beach and harbor is pleasant.

In 2009, I stayed in Hotel Marilú (phone number +238 255-1198, no email or Internet). The manager, Carlos, speaks English and is most helpful.

There is a small un-super supermarket in town but no fresh vegetables are grown on the island, although I was served fresh papaya every morning I was on Maio. The Internet café is wonderfully cheap at €2 per hour, but none of the staff speak English.

I didn't think it worthwhile to hire a car to tour the island as the scenery is dull and flat and in the little villages rum shops, bars, and cafes are noticeable for their absence.

South of town, the coast turns east and presents mile after mile of deserted white sand beach. The shelf does not appear to be that wide, and the surf is not high, but it is not rolling surf but rather the kind that breaks suddenly and makes landing a dinghy treacherous.

The beach begins at Punta das Casas Velhas. Where the rocks end, about a mile farther east, there appears to be a small cove suitable for landing a dinghy. Head for the eastern end of the rocks. As soon as the rocks come abeam turn sharply to port and run up on shore where the surf appeared to be minimal.

At the eastern end of the beach there is an offshore reef with a shelf to the west of it. This might be a good place to anchor and try some diving on the reef. It is not worthwhile sailing east of the reef as, although there is still mile after mile of deserted beaches, the sea comes around the southeast corner of the island, making the anchoring rolly and creating surf on the beach such that landing a dinghy would be impossible.

Calheta

Gerry Dom says that the area off Calheta is excellent for diving. In years gone by it was full of lobsters, but they are probably all fished out by now. In this area, the shelf extends out almost half a mile which means a boat drawing 6 or 7 feet can safely anchor but will probably have a long dinghy ride to reach shore. A boat that draws 4 feet or less, such as a multihull, can get very close to shore. This is an area that should only be explored by a good reef pilot who is willing and able to put someone on the spreaders.

Street's Guide to the Cape Verde Islands

From the dinghy landing at the main pier it's a short walk across a splendid sandy beach to the small town of Vila do Maio.
Photo by Pitt Reitmaier

The white church and "Beau Geste" tower are prominent landmarks in Calheta.
Photo by Don Street

Calheta, north of Vila da Maio, offers some surprises.
Photo by Don Street

From seaward, Calheta should be easy to find as a German from Frankfort has built his dream retirement home at 15° 13.655' north. It stands out as it is painted white and looks like a *Beau Geste* fort transported from the African desert! The area is marked by a light that the German says is working.

The fishing must be good as a fair-sized fleet of boats is pulled up on the beach.

In the village, there's an interesting terra-cotta-colored statue of a girl carrying a basket on her head.

Chapter 9
Fogo and Brava

Ilha do Fogo
Imray-Iolaire Chart E4

Fogo is only 15 miles in diameter but, because it rises 9,000 feet into the air, it stops the clouds, which then deposit rain. The island is incredibly fertile. There is even a village inside the volcano where they cultivate grapes and make wine.

Around Mosteiros, on the northeast corner of the island, they grow coffee which is said to be excellent.

Our Icelandic friend Toby, whom we met in 1985 in Palmeria on Sal, said that the coffee was the best in the world. He and others we met told the story about the village inside the volcano where a lot of the inhabitants have blonde or red hair and blue eyes. They were said to be descended from refugees from the French Revolution.

However, Charles Stammer-Smith, in an article in the travel section of the *Daily Telegraph*, told a different story. According to him, the inhabitants of the crater, some of whom have blonde hair and blue or green eyes along with dark skin, say they are descended from a French nobleman, the Duc du Montrond, who came to Fogo in 1872 because he had an insatiable desire for wine and women. He evidently cultivated vines for wine and the women for offspring. He has the hallmarks of a good old-fashioned remittance man paid to stay far away from France by a noble family who did not want him sowing his wild oats in France. Needless to say, in 1872, news of his sowing his wild oats in Fogo would never get back to France.

One of his descendants evidently followed in his footsteps, reportedly siring 72 children. While this may not be a world record (several Middle-Eastern potentates with large harems have claimed that) it certainly indicates a high level of activity on an island as small as Fogo.

Charles Stammer-Smith wrote of the exceptional fertility of the soil inside the crater. Not only are grapes cultivated there for winemaking but also enough excellent coffee and provision crops to make the settlement within the volcano completely self-sufficient. He also described finding a small guest house there where he spent the night.

It all sounds very attractive, but Fogo does not have an anchorage where a boat can be left unattended for any length of time, so where do you moor the boat while you make an expedition to the mountains?

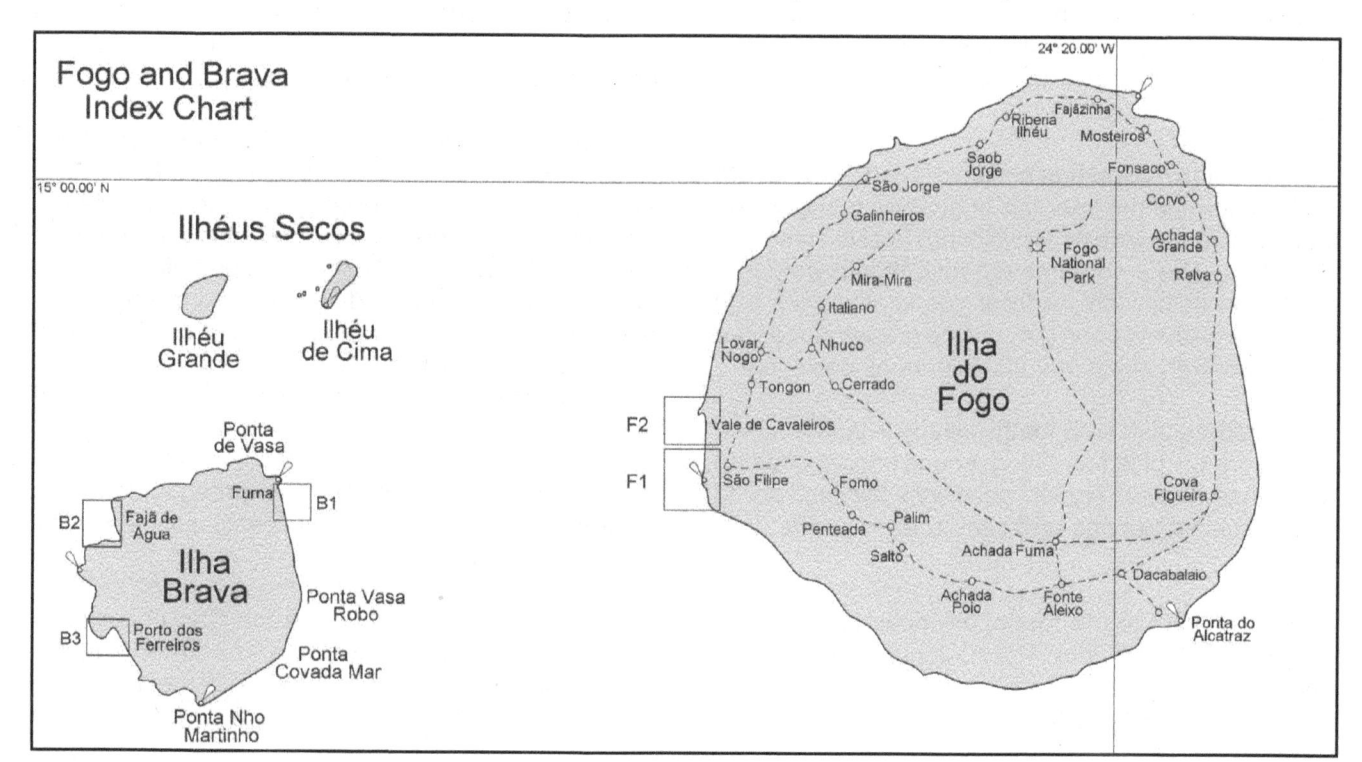

Brava. Arrange for someone there to keep an eye on the boat and take the daily ferry to Fogo. You can then spend a night in the volcano and, if you want to spoil yourself, a night or two in The Colonial B&B.

On my visit in 2009, my good friend Gerry Dom set me up. He arranged for his friend Domingo da Silva, who runs a bus service from São Filipe, the principal town, to Cha Das Caldeiras, the village in the volcano, to meet me at the airport. He then dropped me in town while he did his errands and filled his bus. We met about 1230 and he headed off to the village in the volcano, dropping off and picking up people and cargo en route.

The ride is, to say the least, exciting. Once in the village, he turned me over to his daughter who manages the little Sirio guest house and the next door Antares bar and restaurant. The accommodations were basic by any measure, but adequate, clean and comfortable.

If you go, take along a flashlight, as the electricity comes on at 1900 and goes off at 2300. Also bring a woolen hat, a woolen sweater or jumper, long trousers, and warm socks. Nobody spoke English, but we got along fine. I had a very simple but excellent dinner, drinks in the bar, and a breakfast of coffee, fruit, and a good omelette at 0600 to catch Domingo on his early bus trip back to town. The coffee at 0600 was a major victory. In 14 days in the Azores, and 17 days in the Cape Verdes, this was the only time I was able to have coffee before 0730.

I did a little exploration but did not find the vineyard (Gerry informed me later it is at an elevation of 3,000 feet on the north side of the volcano) but I did discover the winery. It is a very modern operation owned and run by an Italian firm. A local cooperative with 100 members cultivates and gathers the grapes, supplying the winery with about 100,000 kilograms each year.

The other cash crop for the village is pigeon peas. I found groups of ladies sitting around happily chatting while they shelled pigeon peas into big buckets to be transferred to bags and sent to town on the daily bus.

After a night in the rough, the next day I spoiled myself by signing into The Colonial B&B in São Felipe. This turned out to be the high point of my 5 trips through the Cape Verdes.

The Colonial was originally a private home, built sometime between 1880 and 1890, and recently refurbished into a very nice hotel. It has beautiful large rooms with 18-foot ceilings. Not all the nine rooms are en suite, but each has a private bathroom — it might be down the hallway. There is also a small swimming pool that reminded me of my Uncle Jack's house and pool in Bethesda, Maryland.

Uncle Jack bought the house during WWII when houses didn't have air conditioning. He and his wife, my Aunt Eleanor, were house hunting, and while she was inspecting the house, Jack would inspect the grounds. He decided to buy this house the minute he discovered it had a small swimming pool. He described the pool to his friends as his "three martini pool". He would arrive home hot and sweaty, dive in the pool, coast to the other end, climb out and have the martini that the maid had made for him. After finishing the martini, he would again dive in the pool and coast to the other end and have his second martini. When he finished that martini, he would dive into the pool again. He discovered that, after two martinis, his dive didn't give him enough momentum to coast to the other end of the pool without having to take a few strokes. So he would take a few strokes, climb out, have his third martini, and that would end the martini drinking and swimming for the day.

The pool at The Colonial is so small I think Uncle Jack could have *five* martinis before he could no longer coast to the other end of the pool.

I decided to splurge, and took the most expensive room in the house, with a huge double bed and a balcony. Sitting on the balcony, clothed in my pareu, a scotch on the table next to me to help me take my notes, looking at the town of São Filipe before me and the island of Brava in the distance, I felt the clock had been turned back 100 years. I expected, if I looked over to the balcony to my right, I might see Somerset Maugham sitting there with his notepad writing a short story.

I had an excellent dinner, a few green sandwiches (Heineken beers), and a good breakfast and the bill came to a total of €57.

In 2002, when I was touring the Cape Verdes by air and ferry, the young German I had met in Brava and become friendly with introduced me to a nice residencial where we both stayed. He also brought me to a rather cosmopolitan bar and restaurant looking westward toward Brava for the sunset. It was a lovely place to sit and watch for the green flash.

Fishing is a hard way to make a living. I saw a boat come in, and watched the interesting operation that followed. It approached the landing point under power, then hove-to. The crew then shipped two oars, about 18 feet long with long narrow blades, and ran the boat in to the beach on the back of a wave. About four fisherman who were standing by grabbed the bow of the boat and with the boat's crew ran her up the beach before the next wave arrived.

Shortly after landing, the crew came walking up the ramp. The first one was carrying a Spanish mackerel about four feet long and about eight other fish, each about a foot long. The next crew was carrying two 18-foot oars, the third one a gas can and a bag full of fishing gear, and the last crew member drew up the rear with an 8-horepower Honda over his shoulder. Most amazing, though, was their headgear. Three of them were wearing mortar boards, which you normally see only at university graduation ceremonies where the graduates wear the traditional cap and gown.

Resources

Domingo da Silva, bus service from São Filipe to Cha Das Caldeiras; +238 950-3631

Sirio guest house, Cha Das Caldeiras; +238 282-1528, chatour@chatourfogo.com, www.chatourfogo.com.

The Colonial B&B, San Felipe; +238 281-1900 or 281-3373, www.zebratravel.net.

São Filipe

Harbor chart F1
AP 14° 53.5' N; 24° 31.0' W

The anchorage off São Filipe is difficult in the extreme as you are anchoring on the back side of an almost vertical slope. This requires two anchors in very shoal water, or preferably dug in ashore, and a stern anchor to keep the boat from swinging ashore if the wind dies out at night.

It is one of those anchorages that requires some of the crew to be left on board at all times — if the boat drags off the shelf, the next stop is the Caribbean. Also, if the northwest groundswell were to come in, the boat would have to be moved.

The best anchorage, which also happens to be on the widest point of the shelf, is north of town where the fishing boats are pulled up on the beach.

A long ramp leads up into the town from where the fishing boats are pulled up. The only other way to reach the beach is by a set of steps at the south end of town. The steps are right behind a bar/restaurant at the lower end of the lower square in town.

São Filipe has a few rather un-super supermarkets, which supply the basic needs. Ample supplies of fresh fruit and vegetables are available on the roadside and in the main market.

There is an excellent Internet facility, with the wonderful cost of €2 per hour, and you do not get cut off. You use the Internet as long as you like then pay for the time used.

Kai Brosmann notes a couple of anchorages just south of the town which might be better protected from the northwest swell but provide no access to shore. My recommendation, if there's a groundswell, is to go to Furna on Brava.

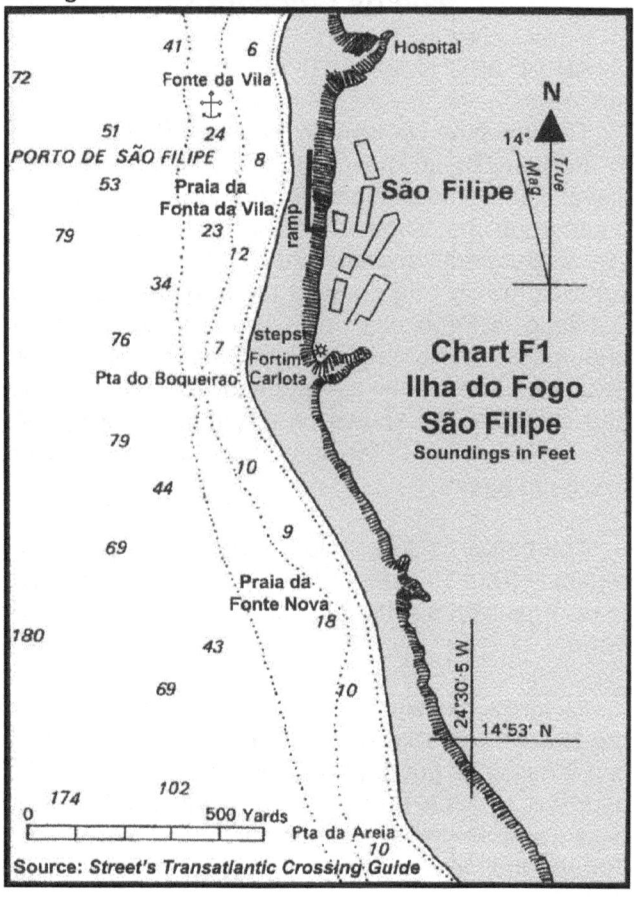

**Chart F1
Ilha do Fogo
São Filipe
Soundings in Feet**

Source: Street's Transatlantic Crossing Guide

Street's Guide to the Cape Verde Islands

São Felipe is well worth a visit for its orderly town square and restored small hotels.

Photo by Pitt Reitmaier

Vale de Cavaleiros
Harbor chart F2
AP 14° 55.0' N; 24° 31.0' W

The first time we were in the Cape Verde islands, in 1985, we did not know there was a harbor in Vale de Cavaleiros. We discovered it when I spotted an aerial photograph that showed the harbor on a postcard. We subsequently found a chart of the harbor, which consists mainly of a quay for the ferry that runs from Santiago to Fogo and on to Brava to lie alongside and unload. The original breakwater was largely destroyed in a northwest groundswell. It was rebuilt and extended, as shown on the Imray-Iolaire chart. As of November 2009, the breakwater was being extended again.

The harbor is subject to a surge to the point that regularly from December through April the ferry has to re-organize its schedule because it cannot stop at Fogo.

It might be possible for yachts to briefly lie alongside the dock when the ferry is not due in and the groundswell is not rolling in, but staying overnight is not on as the hydrofoil, which is 90 feet or more, and the converted fishing boat are there. At times, the passenger freighter that periodically calls by will also be alongside.

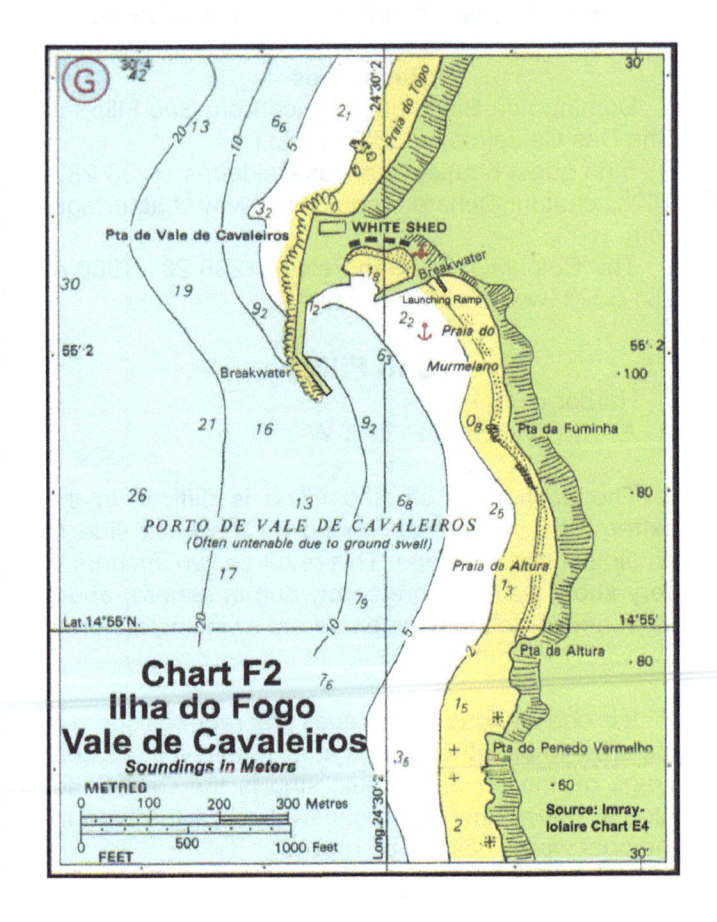

**Chart F2
Ilha do Fogo
Vale de Cavaleiros**
Soundings in Meters
Source: Imray-Iolaire Chart E4

130

It's possible to anchor behind the breakwater, but there's not much room. In December 2002, I noted two local boats anchored there on permanent moorings, which left little space for visiting yachts. There was possibly enough room for two more yachts.

In 2009, I visited the harbor and came to the conclusion that it is not a place to anchor a yacht as a sizeable fishing fleet has developed. Some boats were at anchor in the harbor and large number were hauled up ashore.

If you do anchor in or off the harbor, you'll have no problem getting a taxi. When the ferry arrives there are plenty of taxis on hand. At other times, just go to the head of the dock where there's a bar and restaurant that caters to the fishermen. Undoubtedly someone will have a cell phone and will be able to call a taxi for you or give you the number for you to call.

If there's no room at Vale de Cavaleiros, you'll have to go to São Filipe.

Ilha Brava
Imray-Iolaire E4
Harbor charts B1 – B3

Brava is not to be missed. Of all the islands I have visited in the Atlantic Basin — Azores, Madeiran Archipelago, Canaries, and Cape Verdes — I think Brava and Flores, in the Azores, run neck and neck as the most attractive islands a sailor can visit. Santo Antão is beautiful and a farmer's and walker's delight but a sailor's nightmare. Brava is a sailor's delight: It has two excellent anchorages and, in Nova Sintra, the nicest village in the whole Cape Verdes.

My friend Gerry Dom, who has lived and sailed in the Cape Verde islands since 1982, and who has also sailed extensively in the Caribbean, likens the island of Brava to the island of Saba in the Caribbean. Both are small islands with mountain peaks rising straight out of the sea. On both, the main town is up in the mountains rather than down on the coast, and both islands are famous for their seamen. The one big difference between Brava and Saba is, where Saba never had a harbor until quite recently, and even that is only an excuse for a harbor, Brava has an excellent natural harbor.

Saba provided seamen for the West Indian schooner traffic and for the worldwide deep-sea traffic in the days of sail. It was so much an island of seamen that Fritz Fenger, who sailed through the Caribbean in 1901 in an 18-foot rudderless canoe with bat-winged sails, pointed out in his book, *Cruise of the Yakaboo*, that on Saba in 1901 they had a small Naval College, where the men of Saba were taught celestial navigation. Right up until the middle 1960s, they were considered the top schooner skippers, as the Saba skippers were the only ones who knew celestial navigation.

Similarly, Brava has provided seamen to the world for centuries. As far back as the early 19th century, American whalers stopped at the wonderful harbor of Furna to pick up supplies and fill out their crews with sailors from Brava.

The *British Admiralty Pilot* and the old international edition of the *RCC Atlantic Islands Guide*, are wrong about Fajã. It's known locally as Fajã da Agua, rather than Porto da Fajã as shown on the chart. According to the topo map published by Attila Bertalan, the river at Fajã da Agua has water year round, so it's possible sailing ships called here for water, hence the entry in the *Pilot*. Admittedly, it is an anchorage, but it is a very secondary anchorage — so much so that, until the late 1970s, the small village there was not connected to the rest of the island by road. In the past, the only way to reach the rest of the island was to take the boat around the northwest corner of Brava to Furna, and from there take the cobblestone road that winds up the mountainside with ninety-nine switchbacks to Nova Sintra, the principal town.

The main anchorage in Fogo has always been Porto da Furna. From just looking at the chart, this seems unlikely, as it's wide open to the southeast, but, because of the shape of the harbor and the high cliffs that rise behind it, it's sheltered in all except southeast storms — i.e. the beginning of a hurricane. This makes it a pretty safe place to be in the months of December through March when yachts are most likely to visit. If your barometer starts plummeting, get out of Furna and go around to Fajã. Or better, just stay at sea during heavy weather in the Cape Verdes.

Despite Furna's small size, an old photograph of the harbor shows 14 boats moored there. Most are 80- to 90-foot schooners and the largest is a barkentine of about 150 feet. They are all nested tightly together.

Furna's harbor is small but provides one of the most secure anchorages in the Cape Verdes.

Progress is arriving on the island of Brava, largely because a number of emigrants who have made money in other countries have built vacation homes or have returned to Brava permanently and rebuilt the old family homesteads. Some emigrants spend two or three months a year on the island. One returnee is converting two large old manor houses so he can sell them or rent them out.

In Furna, the sun doesn't rise over the mountains until about 0900, and it sets behind the other mountain at about 1600, so it never gets hot. Because of the high hills, though, the wind is very shifty. Sailing the engineless *Iolaire* out of the anchorage at Furna not only was a test of seamanship and sail-handling, but it also put a few gray hairs in my beard!

Brava is a "must-stop" on any cruise to the Cape Verde Islands, as it is an ideal jump off spot for the Caribbean. Just an hour out of the harbor of Furna you are in the trade winds, and you don't have to contend with the wind shadow of Santo Antão, which is always a problem when leaving from Mindelo on São Vicente.

In the past, there was a problem in visiting Brava as you could not obtain exit clearance from the Cape Verdes at Brava; you could only do that in Mindelo or Praia. Officially, you should go back to Praia to obtain clearance. The solution was to tell them in Praia you are going to Fogo and Brava, then back to Praia to clear. Your papers would then be in order for Fogo and Brava.

However if you do leave Brava without clearance papers and sail on across the Atlantic and explain the problem to the customs and immigration officers when you arrive in Antigua, Martinique, St. Barths, or St. Martin, you should be able to talk your way out of trouble. You would definitely not want to make your landfall in the U.S. Virgin Islands as arriving there without a clearance from your last port would cause a major problem.

I am not sure how the authorities in Trinidad, Grenada, Guadeloupe, or St. Lucia will treat a boat arriving without clearance. In December 2007, when I explained the problem to customs and immigration in Antigua, they said it would not be a problem if you arrived in Antigua from the Cape Verdes without the proper clearance papers. This is just one more reason Antigua is the best place to make your landfall after crossing the Atlantic (see page 147 for landfalls in the Caribbean).

I hope I can say this problem no longer exists. In November 2009, the harbor police in Praia told me they would give boats onward clearance to Fogo and Brava and that they would not have to return to Praia to clear out of the Cape Verdes.

Brava has had close connections with the United States for a long time. From the early 19th century, whaling ships stopped at Brava to pick up crew on their way to the South American whaling grounds, but they didn't stop on the way home to New England. Over the years, a good many Cape Verdeans, many of them from Brava, wound up living in the U.S. Because of this growing population of Cape Verdeans, there existed in the early years of the 20th Century the Cape Verdean Packet Trade — schooners sailing from the Cape Verde Islands to New Bedford, Massachusetts, carrying passengers to and from the States. A large Cape Verdean colony in the New Bedford and Cape Cod area worked as fishermen and shipwrights and also was a source of cheap labor to harvest cranberries, a very important crop in the region.

Brava's main town, Nova Sintra, is up in the mountain peaks. It's connected to the port of Furna by a very nice road that climbs up to Nova Sintra by means of 99 switchbacks. I know the exact number because Gerry Dom decided it would be good exercise for the crew to walk the road, and, as we did so, we carefully counted our 99 switchbacks.

Nova Sintra has some un-super supermarkets, which supply fresh fruit and vegetables, and a few small residencials with bars that serve meals. It also has a couple of very nice churches, some schools, a small hospital, and a pleasant central square that's a wonderful spot to sit and have evening drinks. It's high enough to be cool, and it gets positively chilly as soon as the sun goes down, so when you go for a sundowner you should bring a sweater and woolen hat. A general rule in these islands is that for every 150-feet of altitude you loose one degree of Fahrenheit.

Nova Sintra may be a small town, but it is by far the most attractive town in the whole of the Cape Verdes. It's high enough to get rain, and there is plenty of water in Brava. Interestingly, they don't drill vertically to find water, they drill horizontally! The buildings are all well maintained, the main square is nicely planted, and one street is lined with trees, a complete change from other towns and villages in the Cape Verdes.

As I mention elsewhere, in my visit by air to the Cape Verde islands in December 2002, I stumbled across some satellite photographs. Studying them, I discovered there are a number of anchorages on the south coast of Brava. I did not even try to visit these anchorages by land as I was told it was a three hour walk to reach them.

Porto da Furna
Harbor chart B1
AP 14° 53.0' N; 24° 40.0' W

Note: The harbor chart on the Imray-Iolaire chart E4 (July 2007) does not agree with the main chart. The Longitude of the AP, taken from the main chart, would put you *inside* the harbor according to the inset. So, approach Furna by eyeball!

Looking at the harbor in Furna, one would think it would be absolutely hopeless as an anchorage as it faces right out into the northeast trades. However, the mountain rises so steeply from the harbor that it creates a back eddy, so there is virtually no wind in the harbor. It's easy to sail into but extremely difficult to sail out of, as we discovered on *Iolaire* in 1989. The wind shifts rapidly through 180 degrees.

When entering the harbor, keep Punta Badejo close aboard to starboard, drop your anchor 100 to 150 yards past Punta Badejo, then swing around so your stern is pointing north toward shore. Immediately run a couple of lines to shore, securing them either to ring bolts or to large boulders. Local people will realize quickly what is going on, and they are happy to help you secure your lines. When you depart, they will willingly throw your lines off for you after you have hauled your dinghy on deck — and, in wonderful contrast to the Eastern Caribbean, no one has his hand out for payment.

There is no danger of dragging here as you have dropped anchor into the center of a hole with 50 or more feet of water and it's pulling uphill against a 45-degree slope. So, even if your scope looks horrible, the anchor should hold.

You can tie off the dinghy on the steps on the eastern side of the harbor, but make sure you throw out a stern anchor. Everyone is very friendly and helpful, and there is no need to hire a boat boy— nor are there any boat boys around offering to "guard" your dinghy.

Street's Guide to the Cape Verde Islands

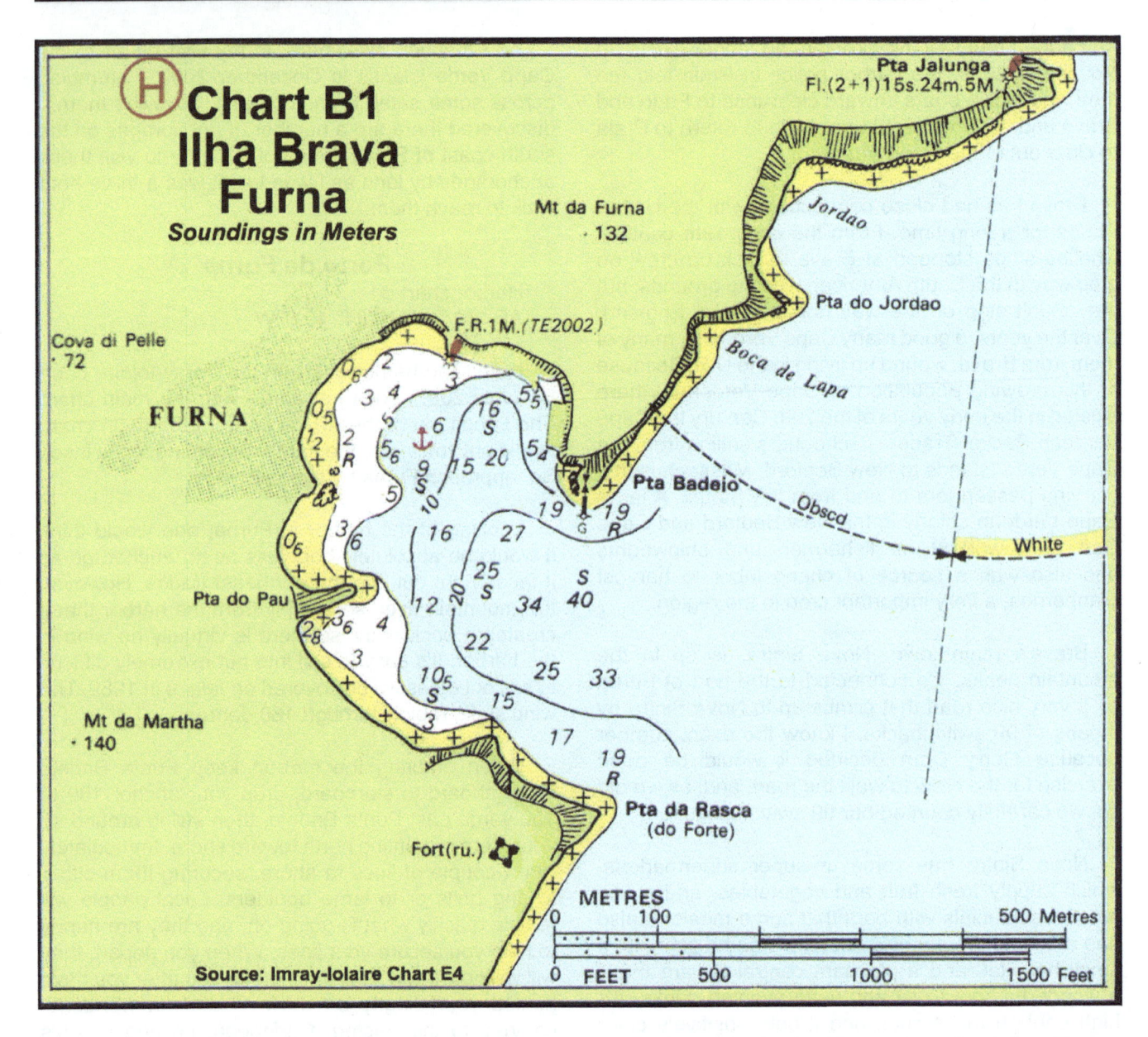

Chart B1 Ilha Brava Furna
Soundings in Meters

Source: Imray-Iolaire Chart E4

A nice dock has been built but it is strictly for the ferry, which comes only infrequently. One would think that, when no ferry is expected, this would be a good place for a yacht to lie alongside. However, our experience with *Sincerity* in 2005 showed us the dock master is unfriendly toward yachts, to say the least.

Sincerity arrived in Furna at 0700, shortly after sunrise, and moored alongside the dock. Having ascertained from bystanders that the ferry would not arrive until 1400, we figured we could do a quick run up to Nova Sintra and be back well before the ferry was due. The dock master soon arrived and in no uncertain terms insisted that we leave immediately.

Rather than anchor for such a short time Trygve jibbed around in the harbor mouth while most of the crew explored Furna and Nova Sintra. Let's hope that, in years to come, the dock master will become more friendly toward yachts.

There is a bakery in town and you can find some basic supplies.

Fresh water and diesel can only be had by jerrycanning. Ice is available early in the morning and in small quantities at the ice house, on the northwest corner of the harbor.

Fogo and Brava

Lobsters are available, just ask around. They keep the lobsters in cars in the harbor. Brava is so small and law abiding that the lobster cars are not even locked shut.

In Furna in 1989, you could buy lobster, still alive and kicking, for US$1.00 a pound — and they were happy to sell them at that price! Now, they are more expensive. Gerry claims you can get them for €14 euros a kilogram.

As of December 2005, while Furna had virtually no facilities for yachts, yachtsmen did have a friend there in Francisco Gonzalez, a Cape Verdean who returned to Furna after working in Norway for 40 years. His house is easy to spot as he flies the Norwegian flag. Needless to say, having worked in Norway for 40 years, he speaks a number of languages. He is most helpful to yachtsmen, and most especially Scandinavian yachtsmen.

In years gone by it was helpful to meet Juan Camilo, a typical product of Brava. He went to high school in New Jersey, joined the U.S. Navy, and served six years as a quartermaster. Upon discharge, he joined the Military Transport Service (MTS) and worked his way up from the deck gang to third mate, and then to second mate. When he quit, he had an unlimited U.S. chief mate's license. He took his money, returned to Brava, bought a warehouse, and set himself up in business — as a general merchant and owner of the Coconut Bar in Furna. He married a lovely 16-year-old girl from Fajã, and claims he did this because if he and his wife have an argument, she can't run home to her mother as she is on the other side of the mountain.

I was not able to make contact with Juan in 2005. He was living in Nova Sintra but was off the island on business.

Juan also told us that even though Brava seemed quite sleepy when we were there in November, the island is jumping in late June and in July and August, when the islanders who have gone off to make their fortunes all do their best to return to Brava for the summer — or as much of the summer as possible.

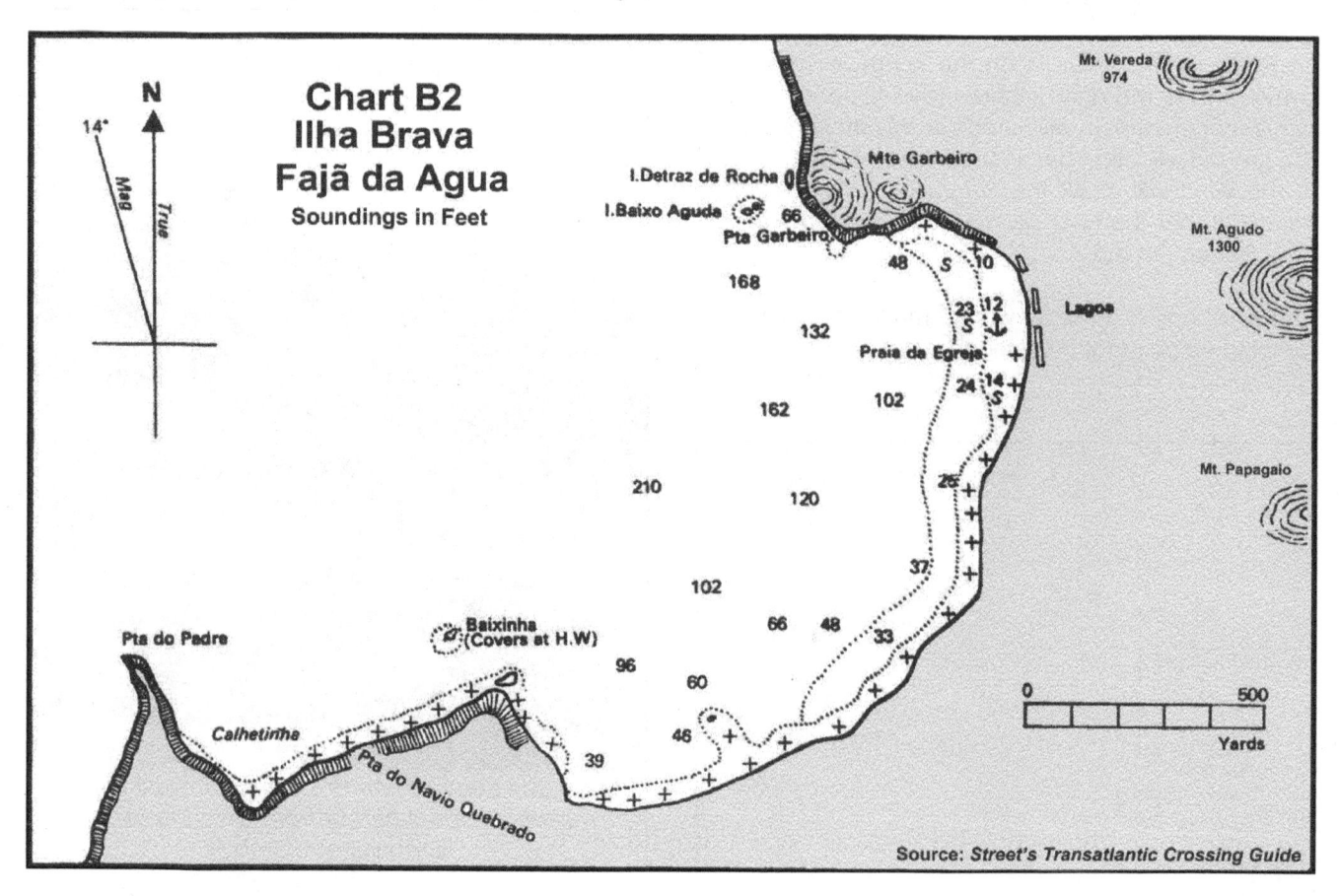

**Chart B2
Ilha Brava
Fajã da Agua**
Soundings in Feet

Source: *Street's Transatlantic Crossing Guide*

135

Fajã da Agua

Harbor chart B2
AP 14° 52.5' N; 24° 45.0' W
Note: here again the Longitude is questionable.

Fajã is the port and village on the west coast of Brava.

The anchorage is completely open, exposed to the groundswell from the west, and very steep-to. The village is smaller than that in Furna. The beach is shingle. Even at the best of times landing a dinghy is difficult, and often it's impossible.

As mentioned in Chapter 2, through various aid programs, Germany built an airport on the west side of Brava, just south of Fajã da Agua. It is not used.

There are a few small settlements inland but they, and Nova Sintra, are only accessible by four-wheel-drive vehicle.

Porto dos Ferreiros

Harbor chart B3
AP 14° 49.0' N; 24° 44.0' W

Porto de Ferreiros is on the southwest coast of Brava and is the only anchorage outside of Furna I can recommend. It will certainly be sheltered from the groundswell but, because of the high land around it, the wind will clock the compass. It is absolutely essential that the boat be moored bow and stern or on a Bahamian moor.

Porto dos Ferreiros would make an excellent jumping off point for crossing the Atlantic.

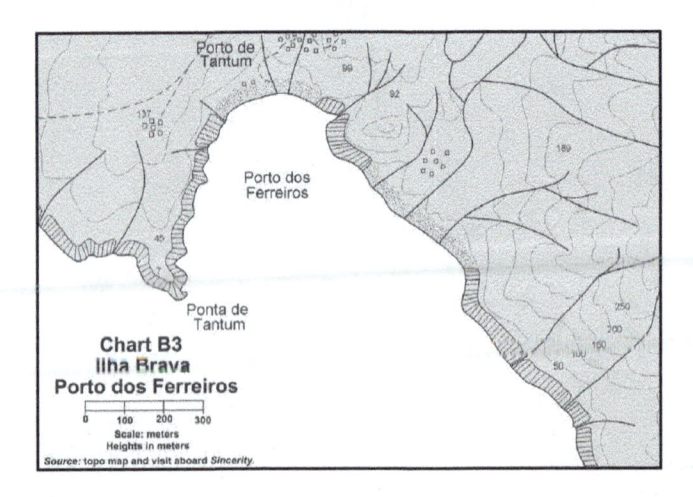

From looking at the topo map, it appeared that some of the bays on the south of Brava that are too small to show up on the Imray-Iolaire chart might be potential anchorages, so after we left Furna on *Sincerity*, we powered very close aboard along the island's south and southwest coasts. Along the way, we ascertained that Porto dos Ferreiros, on the extreme south west corner of Brava, was the only viable anchorage. It's well sheltered in all conditions except when the wind is from the south or southwest.

About 300 yards offshore, we found 30 feet of water. Again, not having an armed lead, we were not able to ascertain the bottom but felt it would be mixed sand and mud.

Ashore, we counted 24 fishing boats, all about 16 to 18 feet long and rowed with extremely long oars, with the oarlocks offset so the oarsman could row cross handed. They also had outboards. My guess is they rowed out to sea, fished, and used the outboard to get home. A building ashore was obviously used to store the fishermen's gear. Interestingly, in the valley on the eastern end of the harbor, we could

Porto dos Ferreiros on Brava's southwest corner makes a perfect harbor from which to set off across the Atlantic.

see an irrigation pipe and a veritable green garden of bananas and other crops.

Sincerity had a new Iridium satellite phone that was not working. Evidently it had to be activated. We discovered from the fishermen (they spoke only Portuguese but Ricky's Spanish got her by) that there was a rum shop on the hill that had a telephone. After a long climb up a narrow path, Ricky and Dan found the rum shop, found the phone, and, wonder of wonders, managed to make a phone call paid for in euros to Dan's ex-wife, who started the process to activate the phone. (Scandinavians seem to get along well with their ex-wives; Dan has two and still gets along with both of them.)

A pickup truck was parked outside the rum shop. Contrary to what I had heard, Porto dos Ferreiros *is* connected to Nova Sintra by a passable road.

When we were in Nova Sintra, a very attractive gal hopped in the aluguer carrying on her head in a large aluminum basin a rather large fish. She took it to Furna where we later saw her cutting it up and selling it. We discovered just how she got the fish to Nova Sintra later in the day.

It was evidently caught by the fishermen in Porto dos Ferreiros, carried up the 400-foot hill, then put in a pickup truck that followed the rough track, then the road to Nova Sintra where the good-looking gal bought it. By the time the fish was sold in Furna, it most definitely was not fresh out of the sea.

Ilhéus Secos ou do Rombo

This is a cluster of small islands to the north of Brava, about 5 miles from Furna. Again the *British Admiralty Pilot* and the *RCC Atlantic Islands Guide* (1980s edition), are wrong; there *is* an anchorage in these islands.

Gerry Dom tells me that at Ilhéu Grande, the westernmost island, you can anchor on the south side in the saddle between the hills in 4 or 5 fathoms of water over a sand bottom with good holding. He does not consider it an overnight anchorage, but it certainly is a good day anchorage in settled weather. From there, you can take your dinghy and explore the other islands and reefs, where there is excellent diving. The fishermen figure that a day's diving on these islands in settled conditions normally will produce more than a hundred pounds of lobster — which they keep in unlocked lobster cars in the harbor in Furna!

The easternmost island, Ilhéu de Cima, has a number of small coves and beaches, so a group can go over and everyone can scatter and have a private beach. There is good snorkeling in all the coves and a wonderful view from the light (which should be reliable, as it is a new, solar-powered untended light).

Weather conditions may not always permit anchoring off these islands. When we were in Furna, in 1989, it was blowing much too hard to explore the islands in *Iolaire* but Gerry Dom arranged for us to charter two small fishing boats. (He suggested two because if we took one and the engine quit, we would have a long, hard row home.) It took about an hour of a bouncy, exciting ride to get there. We spent about four hours exploring the islands, had an excellent time, and then had an exciting 40-minute downwind ride home. This is definitely a worthwhile side trip from Brava. It would definitely be possible in a good-sized RIB, but, since the next land to leeward is Barbados, take adequate safety precautions (see page 59).

Chapter 10
Setting up for a Trade Wind Passage

The Proper Downwind Rig

Everyone dreams about the perfect trade-wind passage — 15 to 18 kts of wind, light puff-ball clouds overhead, long swells rolling up from astern, perfect sailing day after day, and little necessity to do anything more than make minor adjustments to sheets and halyards to minimize chafe by changing the nip.

This is sometimes how it is but, other times, a few squalls will blow through with a reasonable 25 to possibly 30 knots. Some of the squalls might be massive gear-busting blasts packing up to 40 or more knots. In some years, the trades really honk and boats report a week or more of winds 25 to 30 knots and massive swells; in others, they die down to 10 to 12 knots for weeks at a time. On her 1989 passage from the Cape Verdes to Antigua, *Iolaire* had her spinnaker up for 10 days. Occasionally, the wind dies completely, as in 2005, when on *Sincerity* we powered for nine days.

For trade-wind sailing you must therefore be rigged for all eventualities.

The first and most essential piece of gear to put in place is a strong preventer on the main boom that can

A strop can be made by tying a length of line into a loop and seizing the ends.

be easily rigged and unrigged. The second thing to do is organize a way to sheet a headsail, via a block on a special bail, through the end of the main boom. Using the arrangement we developed on *Iolaire* almost 50 years ago, both the main boom preventer and the headsail sheet that leads through the end of the main boom can be set up at the same time.

Preventer

To set up an effective preventer, you need a strong bail on the end of the main boom, preferably angled forward at about 45 degrees.

If you don't have a suitable bail, you can use a loop of line to make a strop. Make the loop long

Setting Up for the Proper Downwind Rig

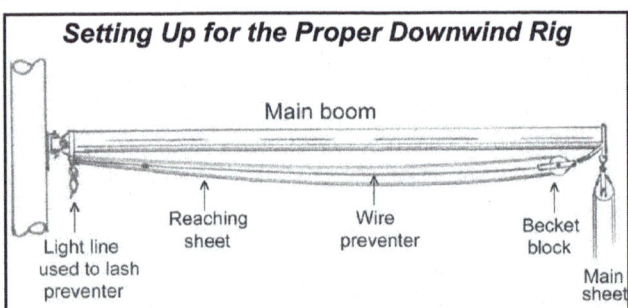

A becket block attached to the aft end of the main boom is used to lead the leeward headsail sheet and also as an anchoring point for a permanent preventer. When the headsail sheet is in use, one end is tied to the working sheet and the other led through a block at the rail and aft to a winch. The preventer is lashed to the boom near the gooseneck with a light line. In use, the preventer is clipped to a foreguy attached at the bow and the light line is used as a retrieval line.

Iolaire's reaching sheet clips onto the bail at the end of the boom.

Setting up for a Trade Wind Passage

enough that you can wrap it twice around the boom, tuck one end of the loop through the other, and work it tight. (The two wraps will ensure the strop doesn't slip along the boom.) To make the loop, take a piece of line of the appropriate length, tie the ends together with a sheet bend, and mouse the tails of the knot with electrical tape.

Secure a becket block to the bail (or to the strop). Secure a wire (or a length of high-tech line like Spectra or Dyneema) to the becket. This is the permanent part of the boom preventer. It should be about a foot shorter than the distance from the becket block to the gooseneck and have a thimble spliced into the gooseneck end of it. A lashing line tied into the thimble will allow you to snug the preventer up to the gooseneck and tight under the boom when it's not in use.

Lead two spinnaker-pole foreguys, one each side of the boat, through blocks at the stemhead or the end of the bowsprit. Clip the snap shackles to lifeline stanchions abreast of the mast and run the other ends aft to the cockpit.

To set up the preventer when you're sailing, all you have to do is untie the line under the boom from the gooseneck and clip the snap shackle of the leeward

Photo by Sean Thompson
If the boom has no bail or other secure attachment point, a rope strop will serve the same purpose.

foreguy into the thimble eye. Make the lashing line long enough that you can tie it loosely to the lifeline and use it as a retrieval line when it's time for a jibe.

Once the wind gets on the quarter and the boom is well eased, connect the preventer and set it up tight using a winch. If no winch is available, over ease the mainsheet, take up on the foreguy, then re-trim the main to make the foreguy tight. A jibe is now all but impossible.

Photo by Don Street
This photo, taken aboard Iolaire, shows the main boom preventer and the genoa sheeted via the boom.

Reaching Sheet

The becket block is there so you can permanently rig a reaching sheet with which to sheet a headsail via the end of the main boom. Lead the reaching sheet through the block and secure both ends to the gooseneck.

As soon as you are sailing with sheets eased, one end of the reaching sheet can be attached to the headsail and the other end led through a block on deck fairly close to the main rigging and thence aft to a cockpit winch. Leading the headsail sheet this way opens the slot between the main and the leech of the headsail. It allows the headsail to draw better while minimizing its backwind effect on the mainsail, thus allowing the main boom to be eased more.

Boom Vangs

A boom vang is essential on trade-wind passages. Pulling down on the foot of the sail, it takes out twist and allows the boom to be eased farther forward, thus reducing weather helm. It also keeps the sail from pressing heavily on the shrouds and spreaders, which is bad for the sail and for the spreaders.

Most cruising boats today are fitted with a centerline vang that attaches to the boom and to the base of the mast. Every year, boats arrive in the Eastern Caribbean from their Atlantic passages with failed boom vangs, failed attachments to the boom, or even with broken booms. This is because, although they are convenient to use, centerline vangs put the most load on the vang, boom, and fittings for the least mechanical advantage.

In 1951, the late Cutty Mason, in his interesting little book, *Ocean Racing*, pointed out that, to be the most effective, a boom vang should be rigged so it leads outboard from a strong fitting near the rail at an angle of 45 degrees (see diagram).

As long as the boat has adequately strong deck fittings, the vang can be easily rigged by wrapping a strop twice around the boom and through itself, working it tight, then attaching a tackle to the eye made by the strop's end. The tail of the tackle can be brought aft to the cockpit for adjusting.

This was a fairly standard arrangement on cruising boats before the centerline vang became popular and has the great advantage that it allows a dinghy to be stowed in the traditional place aft of the mast. The set-up works equally well as an emergency boom vang in

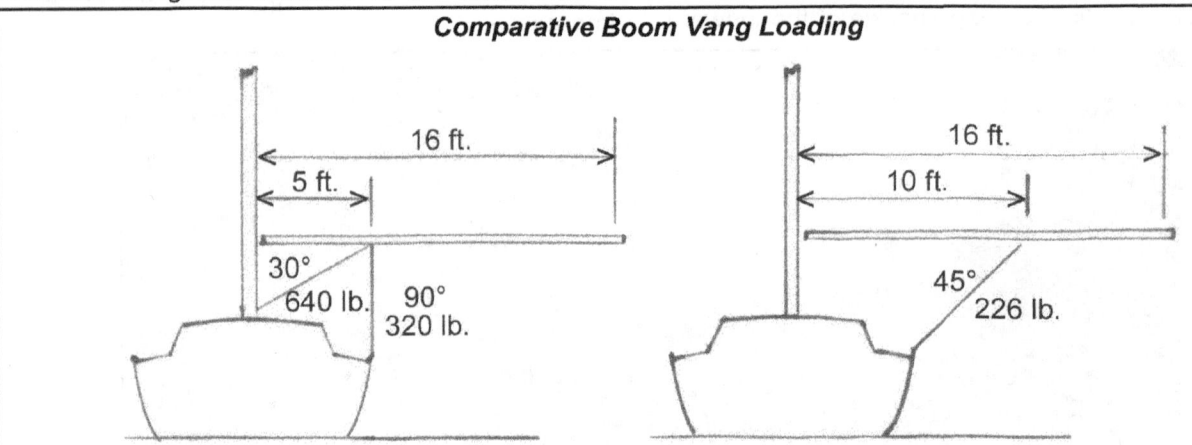

Comparative Boom Vang Loading

A vang attached to the rail and led to the boom at a 45-degree angle places considerably less load on the rail and the boom than a vang led vertically from rail to boom.

This simplified illustration representing a boat about 40 feet LOA shows that every 100 pounds of leech load at the end of the boom becomes a 226-pound load on the rail through a 45-degree vang. The same leech load would create 320 pounds via a vertical vang and 640 pounds through a centerline vang that makes an angle of 30 degrees with the boom.

The geometry and exact loads will vary from boat to boat, but the principle remains the same. Depending on the boat and the wind strength, the actual leech load might be less than or considerably more than 100 pounds.

Setting up for a Trade Wind Passage

the event the centerline vang or one of the fittings to which it's attached should fail.

Warren Brown used this system on his famous 63-foot cutter, *War Baby*, (ex *Tenacious* in which Ted Turner won the windy 1979 Fastnet Race), except that *War Baby* had a fixed attachment point on her aluminum boom from which a single-part line led via a block to a very powerful winch.

We have used this system on *Iolaire* with success for over 50 years. Proof that it works lies in the fact that, when racing, *Iolaire* always sails well above her rating on reaches, and the heavy weather helm she has without a vang rigged is completely eliminated when the vang is set up and the headsail sheeted through the block at the end of the main boom as described above.

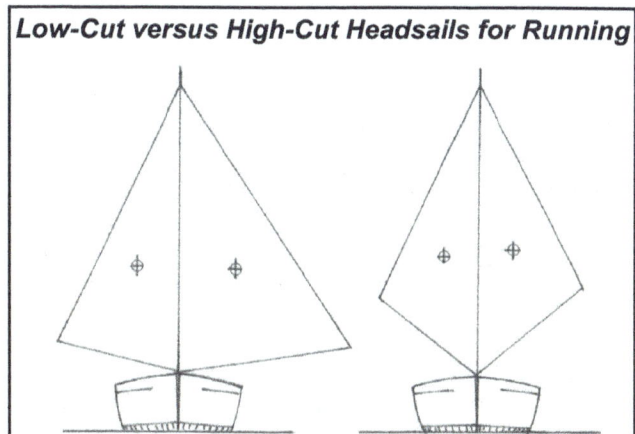

Low-Cut versus High-Cut Headsails for Running

For running downwind, low-cut genoas, with their low centers of effort, are less likely to induce rolling than high-cut jibs with their higher centers of effort.

This photo shows Iolaire's genoa sheeted to the end of the main boom.

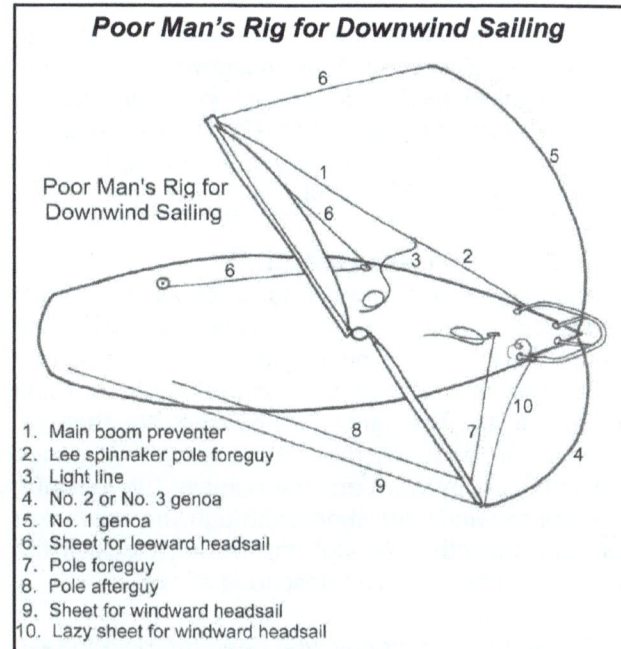

Photo by Don Street

Poor Man's Rig for Downwind Sailing

1. Main boom preventer
2. Lee spinnaker pole foreguy
3. Light line
4. No. 2 or No. 3 genoa
5. No. 1 genoa
6. Sheet for leeward headsail
7. Pole foreguy
8. Pole afterguy
9. Sheet for windward headsail
10. Lazy sheet for windward headsail

The light line (#3) is used as the retrieval line when disconnecting the preventer (#1) from its extension to the bow (#2), then for lashing the preventer to the gooseneck. For downwind sailing with two headsails the pole is set up with its own foreguy (#7) and afterguy (#8). When the wind is too far forward for the windward sail to set, its sheet (#9) is eased and the sail is allowed to lie inside the leeward sail where it's trimmed with #10. The pole stays in place.

141

> **Downwind Rig for Non-Transatlantic Sailing** 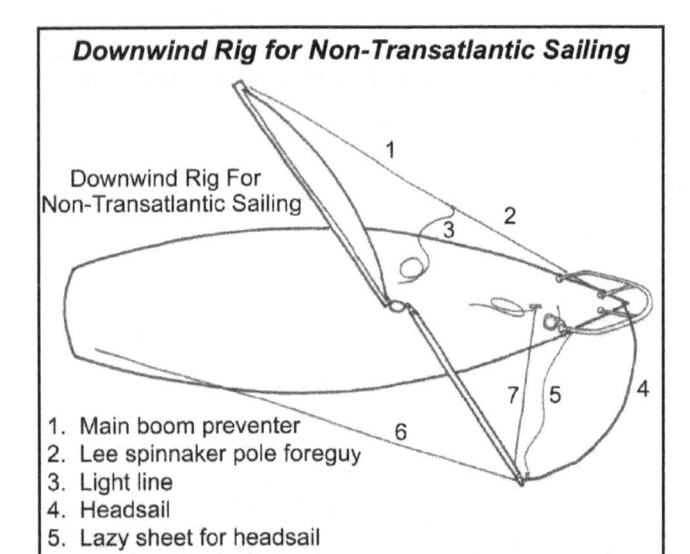
>
> 1. Main boom preventer
> 2. Lee spinnaker pole foreguy
> 3. Light line
> 4. Headsail
> 5. Lazy sheet for headsail
> 6. Working headsail sheet
> 7. Foreguy
>
> The working sheet (#6) is run through the end of the pole. If the wind is too far forward for the headsail to be poled to windward, this sheet is eased and the sail trimmed to leeward with the lazy sheet (#5). This rig is for normal downwind sailing en route to the Atlantic Islands, in the Atlantic Islands, and in the Caribbean. For the transatlantic run, rig the pole as per the poor man's rig (page 138).

Twin Headsails

The correct downwind rig for trade-wind sailing is two headsails set side by side. To minimize rolling, the center of effort of the headsails should be low. This makes two fairly low-cut genoas preferable to a pair of high-cut jibs. The flatter the headsails are sheeted, the less the boat will roll, so the number 2 genoa should be to windward and the number 1 to leeward. The sail to windward sheets through the spinnaker pole and the other through the becket block at the end of the main boom as described above.

To set this rig properly, you need the pole to take care of itself. Remember, you are not racing round the cans. Rig the spinnaker pole with its own foreguy, afterguy, and lift.

Before setting up the pole, lead the headsail sheet through the end of the pole. Raise the pole, square it, and secure it, then unfurl the headsail. It's now sheeted through the pole end.

If the headsail has to be reefed, leave the pole as is, ease the sheet, and roll up the sail.

When the wind goes light and it's time to set the spinnaker, roll up the headsails but don't touch the spinnaker pole guys or lift. Remove the headsail sheet from the clew of the headsail and attach it to the tack of the spinnaker. At the same time, attach to the tack of the spinnaker a retrieving line and lead it through a block near the stemhead or at the end of the bowsprit.

Once this is set up, unsnuff the spinnaker, two-block the spinnaker tack to the end of the pole using the old jib sheet, and trim the spinnaker.

When it's time to douse the spinnaker, swing the boat dead downwind to collapse it behind the mainsail (you don't have to worry about jibing as you have the main boom preventer rigged). Ease the sheet, take up on the retrieving line, and pull the snuffer down on the collapsed sail.

During all these operations the pole remains held in place by its foreguy, afterguy, and topping lift.

If you rig the pole in the normal round-the-cans fashion, when you try to carry out any of these operations, the pole will be sweeping around the foredeck trying to demolish the foredeck crew.

If you have headsail roller reefing and the headfoil has two slots, hoist both sails on the headfoil. If the two headsails are of different luff lengths, add a pendant to the shorter sail to make the luff lengths the same. When stowed, one sail is rolled up on top of the other. If it blows up in a squall, or if the trades are really honking and the two full genoas are too much, just ease the sheets slowly and roll up the sails one on top of the other until the desired amount of sail is still showing.

If the wind comes abeam, too far forward to fly the windward headsail, let the sail go to leeward and lie inside the leeward sail. To do this, come aback and, while leaving the pole in place, ease the windward sheet through the pole while taking up on the leeward sheet. You'll be sailing with one headsail on top of the other, but this works just fine. In fact, this system works so well that it was outlawed under the IOR after Ted Turner figured out that if he hoisted a low-cut genoa inside a high-cut reacher he could gain extra sail area without increasing his rating.

If the wind comes so far aft that the leeward headsail is blanketed by the main, drop the main and sail under the two headsails alone.

Hanked-on Sails

If you do not have roller-reefing headsails you can still rig a very good variation of the proper trade-wind rig with hanked on headsails.

Until 1987, when *Iolaire* was given Harken's first big roller-furling/roller-reefing headsail gear to test, she was rigged with roller-*furling* headsails. That is, they furled on their own wire luffs and were either all in or all out. But only the working sails were on furlers; the light-air and heavy-weather sails were hanked on.

To set up the proper trade-wind rig, we installed a jackstay for setting a second downwind sail. We replaced the spinnaker halyard block with a becket block and attached a wire to the becket. The wire was 6 inches shorter than the distance from the becket to the deck. When not in use as a jackstay, it was secured with a lashing line to a pad-eye alongside the upper shrouds.

To prepare for trade-wind sailing, we moved the jackstay to the bowsprit end and lashed it there. We hoisted the big hanked-on genoa on the headstay in the normal fashion and sheeted it to the end of the main boom, then hoisted the number 2 genoa on the jackstay and sheeted it through the end of the spinnaker pole as described above.

This rig worked fine for *Iolaire* on her 1975, and 1985 passages and for *Lone Star* on her 1984 passage.

As noted in Chapter 1, all those passages were fast.

Hanked on headsails can present a couple of problems when sailing downwind.

As the boat rolls back and forth, piston hanks, especially if they are old, tend to open up with the result that, after a while, you may find that the headsail is secured at the tack and head and nowhere else.

Also, it has been known for a piston hank to open and then lock closed over the other stay. If this happens, it's impossible to drop either sail. Both have to be dropped or partially dropped to clear the foul.

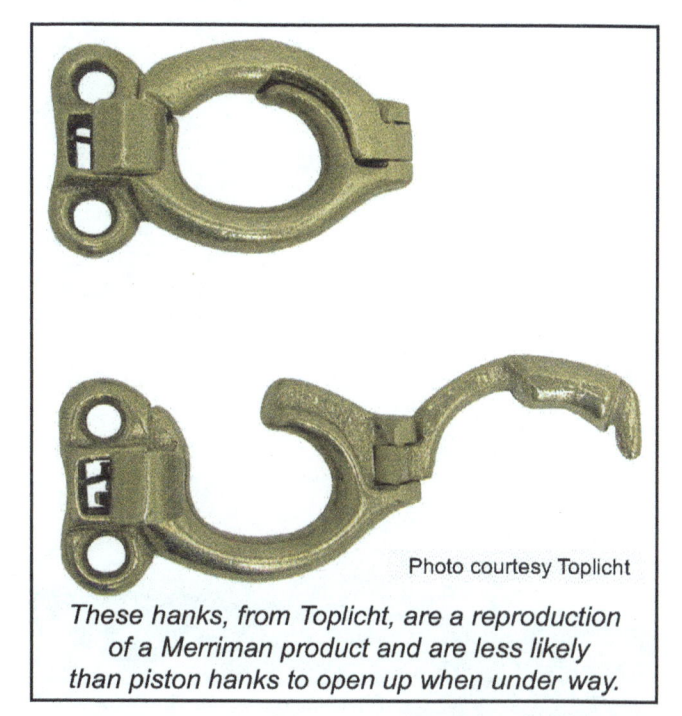

Photo courtesy Toplicht

These hanks, from Toplicht, are a reproduction of a Merriman product and are less likely than piston hanks to open up when under way.

To prevent the piston hanks on one stay from snapping over the other stay, set the hanks in opposite directions: On the headsail hoisted on the headstay, face the hanks to port; on the headsail on the jackstay face them to starboard. The hanks then cannot hook the two stays together.

Toplicht hanks open in the vertical plane. By fitting them to your sails you will eliminate the problem of hanks either inadvertently opening or hooking onto another stay or loose sheet.

We didn't install roller-furling/roller-reefing on *Iolaire* until Olaf Harken gave us the first big gear the Harken company made. He asked me to test it to see if it was indestructible. We tested it. That winter was a windy one and I put the bricks to it. It was indestructible!

The reason we did not install this kind of gear earlier was that broken and bent-up roller-reefing/roller furling gear was stacked up like cordwood in rigging lofts up and down the Eastern Caribbean.

Mizzen Staysails

Ketches and yawls come into their own downwind as they can set a mizzen staysail, which will not blanket the lee headsail whereas the mainsail will. A proper mizzen staysail that tacks down alongside the main rigging adds really useful sail area: On a yawl it

Lone Star storming along under twin running headsails, the leeward one sheeted to the end of the main boom.
Photo courtesy *Lone Star's* owners

Lone Star sailing dead downwind under headsails and no mainsail.
Photo courtesy *Lone Star's* owners

will be two thirds the size of the main and on a ketch it will be at least as large as the main.

When handled properly, a mizzen staysail is easy to set and douse. The sheet should be really long and have a stopper knot a foot forward of the bitter end. When preparing to set the mizzen staysail, attach the sheet to the clew but leave it slack while you hoist the sail. Take in on the sheet only after the halyard is two-blocked and secured.

When the time comes to douse the mizzen staysail, make sure the bitter end of the halyard is secured then blow the halyard but hold the sheet. The sail will rag off to leeward where it's easily muzzled. Once it's muzzled, you can ease the sheet.

This system works fine on boats to about 70 feet. On larger vessels, a temporary stay makes a difference in setting and dousing the sail. This stay can be a length of light 7 x 19 wire or Dyneema secured to the mizzen masthead and long enough to reach the deck at the main rigging, where it can be secured with a light lashing line. The mizzen staysail should have a few jib hanks attached to the luff.

Before hoisting the mizzen staysail, hank it to the temporary stay. You can then hoist and douse the sail as described above. Since it's secured to a temporary stay, one crew member can haul down on the luff once the halyard is blown.

When not in use, the stay can be stowed coiled on the mizzen mast around easily made fittings.

The late Wing Commander Bob Carson, RAF, installed this system on my recommendation on the 95-foot yawl, *Gitana IV*. He said it worked to perfection: Two crew could set or douse the mizzen staysail with no trouble.

Spinnaker Poles

A spinnaker pole 20 percent longer than the base of the fore triangle will allow you to set a 135-percent headsail really flat, minimizing the roll. This is where a telescoping pole earns its keep. Many companies make them but Forespar seems to have the best reputation. Whatever size the pole manufacturer recommends for your fore-triangle length, go one size larger. It's worth the expense as you shouldn't have to worry about an oversized pole bending and jamming.

If you can afford it, a carbon-fiber spinnaker pole is a very worthwhile investment. On a fore triangle of 18 feet with a hoist of 50 feet, a wooden pole will weigh about 45 pounds, an aluminum pole 35 pounds, and a carbon pole 18 pounds or less.

Sail Inventory

If you only have one headsail on your boat, you'll need to buy a second one. Remember you are cruising, not racing. Go to a company that specializes in secondhand sails (not too many companies in Europe do this but plenty in the States do) and purchase one of the approximate size that you want. Take it to a sailmaker and have him re-stitch the leech and the foot and 3 feet in from the leech on all the seams. You are using this sail downwind so a secondhand sail will do the job.

While we dream of consistent trade winds, all too often they are not, so carry a spinnaker or possibly two. Again, you are cruising, not racing. Leave the racing spinnaker in the sail locker. Buy one or two secondhand spinnakers.

If the wind goes light, set the spinnaker, but make an absolute rule that the spinnaker must be doused before any squall catches up with you. Make another rule that the spinnaker must be doused and the rig switched to the two headsails as soon as the boat's speed reaches the square root of the boat's waterline length plus 15 percent. Also, set the spinnaker with a light sheet, say about 3/8-inch *three-strand* Dacron. When the wind starts to blow up, the sheet will tend to unlay and become smaller, something even the dimmest on-deck crew will observe. If properly instructed, he will then call the skipper who can insist the spinnaker comes down before it blows.

A snuffer is essential gear when cruising with a spinnaker. When buying a snuffer, go with a nose cone one size larger than whatever size the sailmaker recommends. This will make it much easier to snuff the spinnaker. Snuffers do work as long as they are handled correctly. Before you try to snuff the sail, the boat must be headed dead downwind. You don't need to worry about jibing as you have a really good main boom preventer rigged. Leave the pole set up, take up on the retrieving line, and ease the tack of the sail (remember, you have the headsail sheet attached to it) so the spinnaker collapses behind the main, then pull down on the snuffer.

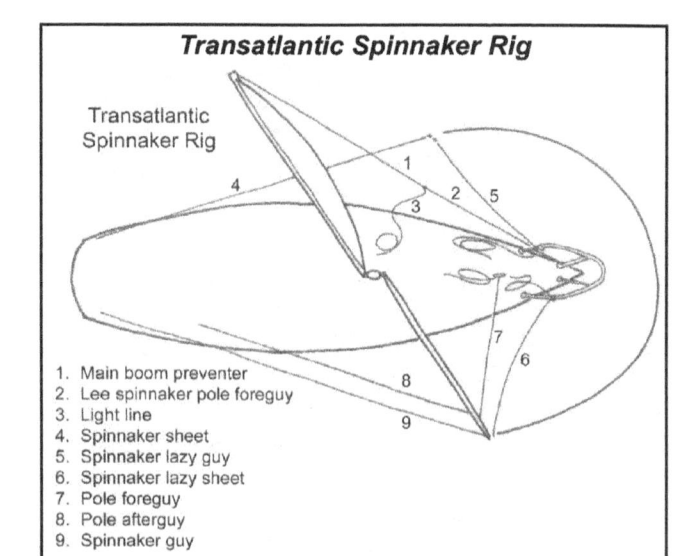

Transatlantic Spinnaker Rig

Transatlantic Spinnaker Rig

1. Main boom preventer
2. Lee spinnaker pole foreguy
3. Light line
4. Spinnaker sheet
5. Spinnaker lazy guy
6. Spinnaker lazy sheet
7. Pole foreguy
8. Pole afterguy
9. Spinnaker guy

For transatlantic sailing, when the boat is expected to be on starboard tack most of the time, the spinnaker pole can be set up more or less permanently with its own foreguy (#7) and afterguy (#8). The spinnaker sheet (#4) and lazy guy (#5) are tied to a single snapshackle. The spinnaker guy (#9) passes only through the jaw of the pole. It and the lazy sheet (#6) are tied to a single snapshackle. When it's time to drop the spinnaker, the pole stays in position. The spinnaker afterguy (#9) is eased and the sail retrieved using the lazy sheet.

If the snuffer line is rigged directly to the nose cone, a crew member can only pull down his or her own weight. If the resistance is greater than that, he will only lift himself off the deck. Two crew pulling down just get in each other's way. Lead the down line through a snatch block set at the forward end of the foretriangle, then one, two, or even more crew can heave on it and the snuffer will snuff. The foredeck crew on the J-Class yacht, *Shamrock V*, was having trouble with the snuffer until I suggested the haul-down line be led through a snatch block. Then *five* crew members tailed on the down line — and that was the end of the snuffer problem.

If you are unfortunate enough to end up with a spinnaker wrapped around the headstay, don't worry. Unwrapping it is dead simple. Just sail by the lee and it will unwind itself. Once it's unwound, head up slightly and all will be well. Since you have a main boom preventer rigged, there is little chance of jibing when sailing by the lee.

Asymmetric spinnakers are great. When using these sails, it's worthwhile installing a removable stub bowsprit as it allows you to sail deeper than when the sail is tacked down at the forward end of the fore triangle and makes jibing the sail much easier.

I've seen a system on some boats where they remove one of the bow rollers and fit a short bowsprit in its place. However it's done, it's important that the bowsprit is short enough that a crewmember can reach the end of it from *inside* the bow pulpit and does not have to climb outside the pulpit.

For the heavy- or moderate-displacement cruising boat, it's still essential to carry a spinnaker pole in case the wind goes dead aft.

Sailing the Angles Downwind

When sailing dead downwind, the apparent wind is dead aft. As soon as you head up to a reach, the apparent wind begins to move forward. The faster you sail, the farther forward the apparent wind goes and the faster you sail — up to a point.

Boats that sail really fast, either because they are very light or long or both, can sail 90-degree jibe angles and make money. For them — light displacement flyers or fairly light megayachts — tacking downwind with an asymmetric is a race winner, but a heavy-displacement cruising boat does not sail at a sufficiently greater speed when reaching to justify sailing at jibe angles of more than 20 degrees (i.e. 10 degrees above dead downwind). This was illustrated on *Sincerity's* 2005 transatlantic. She is an 88-foot ketch and sails very well but we had no pole, only a big asymmetric. To keep it full, we had to sail 90-degree jibe angles. We were doing 9 to 10 knots through the water but only 6 to 7 knots on the course to Antigua, as the diagram below shows.

I'm getting on in years so naturally I drew up a table the old-fashioned way by making a careful drawing and measuring off it using a ruler and dividers. I once gave it to a navigator who immediately discarded it. Later, Ben Bradley made the same calculation mathematically and found differences between his and my numbers only in the second decimal place.

With electronic navigation, it's very easy to find out what works best on your boat. Plug a waypoint into your GPS for your destination and watch your VMG toward it as you vary your course and adjust the sails accordingly.

The elapsed-time winner of the 2009 ARC was a Volvo 60 that set an asymmetric, sailed the angles, and completed the race in 11 days and 18 hours. Her sailing distance was 3,600 miles, which means she averaged 306 miles per day at an average speed of 12.75 knots. The second boat in, just 16 minutes later, was an 80-foot Wally. She sailed the same distance (it appears they might have been match racing!). Had she sailed a direct great-circle course, her sailing distance would have been about 2680 miles. To do

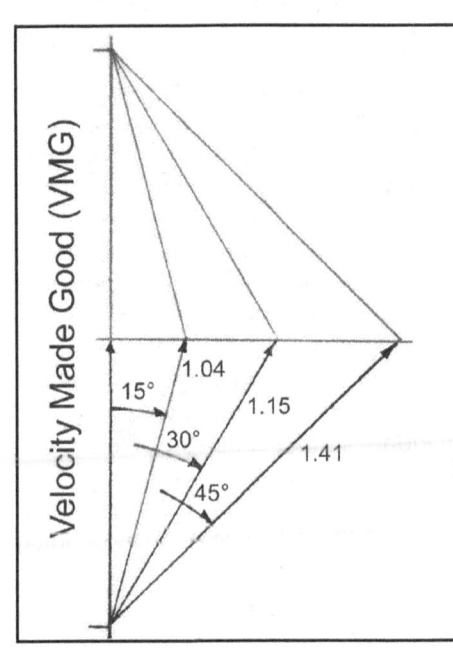

Velocity Made Good Downwind

This diagram shows the extra speed needed at various angles off course for the same VMG as along the direct course.

For example, if the boat can sail at 7 knots on a direct course, at 30 degrees off that course it would have to sail at 8.1 knots (7 x 1.15) to make the same VMG.

Tacking downwind can be beneficial in light winds when boat speed makes the apparent wind move forward significantly. In steady, brisk trade winds when a boat is making close to full speed, heading directly for the destination with all possible sails drawing results in the best velocity made good (VMG).

this distance in the same time, she would have had to average only 228 miles per day, or an average speed of 9.5 knots. Given her size, this would seem to have been easily achievable and would have required a lot less jibing, but it's possible she wasn't carrying a spinnaker pole and had no choice.

In the light of this, it's clear that, even if you are carrying an asymmetric, you should also carry a spinnaker pole so you can sail dead downwind if you need to.

Many boats have swept-back spreaders that restrict how far the main boom can be eased forward before the mainsail is plastered against the rigging. This almost forces such a boat to be sailed on reaches. In any event, before any long passage, the mainsail should be protected with chafe patches in areas where it contacts the spreaders, when reefed as well as when fully hoisted. Further protection can be had by padding the spreaders. Offcuts of indoor/outdoor carpet work very well for this.

Seeing Ahead

You are rigging the boat to sail the trade winds. Those trade winds will blow you to tropical islands with crystal clear water and harbors that are surrounded by coral reefs that in 10 yards will suddenly change the water depth from 30 or more feet to 2 feet.

Much more important than your GPS, chartplotter, or fathometer is the old-fashioned, good-old Eyeball Mark I navigational instrument that god, not an electronic specialist, gave you. When entering harbors or threading your way around reef-encumbered islands, a bow lookout is essential. He (or she) will be even more useful if standing on the bow pulpit. Better yet, install mast steps so you can send your spotter up to the speaders for a really good view.

Generating Electricity

You are rigged correctly, all is well, and you are enjoying a downwind passage. You will be needing electricity. The July 2008 issue of *Yachting World* reported the results of a survey of boats that took part in the 2007 ARC. Boats that used generators to produce electricity ran their generators an average of 4.9 hours per day, while those that used their engines ran them 3.2 hours per day on average. This unnecessary running of engines or generators to produce electricity not only introduces carbon dioxide and other nasty things into the global environment but, since you are going downwind, those exhaust fumes are coming aboard and blowing the length of the boat. Also, the noise of the engine is disturbing the blessed silence you enjoy when under sail. There are other ways to produce electricity.

Water-Driven Generators

You can generate all the electricity you need without turning on the engine if you install a taffrail water-driven generator.

The Aquair 100 taffrail generator (which Ampair developed from an application I invented and first installed on *Iolaire* in 1979) will produce 6 amps at 12 volts when sailing at 6 knots. That's 144 amp hours

Photo by Sean Thompson

Iolaire's trademark Ampair wind generator has been a fixture on her mizzenmast for over 40 years. With solid support from the towed generator, it kept Iolaire's crew in cold beer throughout all her last five transatlantic passages.

per day. At 7 knots it will generate 156 amp hours per day and the drag, as measured with a spring scale, is only 15 pounds.

As soon as you are under way, you toss over the stern a 12-inch diameter propeller on a 3-foot rod attached to 60 feet of ½-inch braided line and let her run.

To easily retrieve the propeller, you need a 14-inch plastic funnel split so you can slip it over the towline. It will slide down the line and muzzle the propeller so it stops spinning. The propeller and towline can then be hauled back aboard without the line becoming twisted. (This rig was invented in 1985 by Lou Lou Magras of Gustavia, St. Barths, who was also one of the founders of the St. Barths Bucket.)

At speeds higher than 8 knots, the propeller might jump or skip, so Aquair has developed a special propeller for bigger boats that might sail consistently at 8 knots or more. You can also lengthen the towline or add weight to it, both of which will help keep the prop in the water.

Wiring the Aquair is a simple matter of running two wires from the generator (which is slung from the stern pulpit) directly to the battery. If there's a chance of overcharging the batteries, just run the refrigerator longer than usual or turn on some lights.

On her last five transatlantic passages, the engineless *Iolaire* had cold beer all the way thanks to electricity provided by an old Ampair taffrail generator and an Ampair wind generator mounted on the *top* of the mizzen mast.

Output from the Aquair 100 flattens out at about 6 amps. If 144/156 ampere hours a day is insufficient for your needs, you can install a shaft-driven Electrodyne alternator that will produce more electricity than even the most electrically hungry boat can use.

Shaft generators have been around for 60 years. The 40-foot Block Island ketch, *Lang Syne*, sailed around the world in 1948/1949 with refrigeration and an electric autopilot, both of which used vast quantities of electricity. All the electricity used aboard was produced by a shaft generator.

Steve and Linda Dashew sailed around the world in the early 1970s on *Intermezzo*, a 55-foot aluminum cutter on which all electricity was produced by an Electrodyne low-rpm alternator driven by a 12-inch propeller.

At 6 knots, a correctly geared Electrodyne low-rpm alternator driven by an 18-inch propeller will produce somewhere between 40 and 60 amps at 12 volts. This is more than enough electricity for even the most power-hungry boats at a cost of $600 for the alternator plus installation. Allowing the prop to freewheel three or four hours would generate sufficient electricity for a day, after which the propeller shaft can be locked to minimize drag.

The ideal installation would be built around a controllable-pitch propeller. The pitch of the propeller could be adjusted to generate the desired amount of electricity when needed and at other times the propeller could be feathered to minimize drag. A controllable-pitch propeller is also more efficient for powering a boat as the pitch can be adjusted to suit the boat's speed and the sea conditions.

Why run noisy, smelly generators when you can generate electricity silently and without creating pollution?

Resources
Ampair/Aquair: www.Ampair.com
Electrodyne brushless alternators: 207 883 4121, www.electrodyne.com

Wind Generators

Wind generators are almost useless on trade-wind passages as, when sailing dead downwind or almost so, the apparent wind across the boat is not sufficient to produce useful amounts of electricity. All the same, do install a wind generator before taking off on your trade-wind passage as it will earn its keep once you reach the Caribbean.

Wind generators produce a useful amount of electricity when sailing between the islands in the Eastern Caribbean because, most of the time, the wind is abeam or forward of abeam. At anchor, whether or not the wind generator will produce enough electricity depends on the anchorage. In an exposed anchorage like the Tobago Cays or similar, or one on the windward side of small island like Carriacou, Mayreau, or Canouan, where the wind will not die out at night, it may produce all the electricity needed. However, when anchored in harbors on the large

Setting up for a Trade Wind Passage

islands where the wind dies out at night, the generator or main engine will have to be run to augment the amount produced by the wind generator.

The higher above the water, the greater is the wind velocity. To give the greatest benefit, a wind generator should be mounted high off the deck. On a ketch or a yawl, it should be on the top of the mizzen mast. Not only will it work at its best there but it won't interfere with the flying of a mizzen staysail.

Ampair makes a conversion kit that allows its taffrail generator to be driven by a windmill that can be hoisted in the rigging when at anchor.

From the first, I have been violently opposed to this rig as I feel it is an accident looking for someplace to happen, and I know of one bad accident. In my view, and many experienced sailors agree with me while others disagree, a wind generator should be permanently mounted at the head of the mizzenmast on a ketch or yawl or on a strong well-secured post on a sloop. It should certainly be mounted high enough that the tallest crew member coming out for his (or her) early morning stretch cannot get his fingernails trimmed by the spinning blades.

Properly handled, the Aquair does a fine job. Mr. and Mrs. Davies (parents of the famous female singlehander, Sam Davies), love their Aquair. Despite being on the high side of 60, they sail their 59-foot schooner. *Niñita*, without a crew all over the eastern Atlantic, including to the Azores, the Canaries, Madeira, the south coast of the UK, and Brittany. *Niñita*, a replica of the schooner, *Niña*, that won the 1928 transatlantic race to Spain and the 1928 Fastnet, is big enough they can hoist the windmill high in the rigging where it is effective in port. Under way, when driven by the water impeller, the Aquair produces 144 amp-hours a day at 6 knots, the same as running a generator for 3 hours. They are obviously very careful and competent seamen.

Before buying a wind generator it is vitally important to demand from the company selling it the names of three sailors who have bought its products. I say this as some of the very efficient wind generators are incredibly noisy whenever the wind gets over 20 knots.

One popular model, whenever a gust of 20 knots hits it, sounds like an outboard that has just kicked out of the water at full throttle. It was so noisy that smart skippers in the Caribbean, if they saw a boat with that type of wind generator, would anchor as far away from it as possible.

In contrast, the Ampair 100, which in various models has been on *Iolaire*'s mizzen masthead since 1975, is silent up to 40 knots and then emits a hum up to 60 or 70 knots, after which it becomes noisy but bearable.

The new Ampair 300 that has been on *Iolaire*'s mizzen masthead for two years is silent up to about 30 knots when it develops a gentle hum. It still makes a gentle hum at 40 knots and I hope I will not be around testing it in winds higher than that, but it can be electrically locked off when desired.

Solar panels are great on multihulls but monohulls don't have the deck area to spread out enough solar panels to produce really useful amounts of electricity.

Chapter 11
After the Atlantic Crossing

Landfalls in the Caribbean

When departing Cape Verde from Brava, the best landfall in the Caribbean is Antigua. The course to Antigua is a little north of west and the trades are usually a little north of east, thus you should be able to semi-permanently rig your spinnaker pole to starboard when you leave Brava and leave it there until Antigua comes abeam.

Antigua (Imray-Iolaire chart A27, and *Street's Guide, Anguilla to Dominica*) is the ideal landfall for boats sailing transatlantic. On the south coast, where you will make your landfall, are two excellent harbors, English Harbour and Falmouth Harbour, where you can choose between a number of berthing options. In Falmouth, you can go to the Catamaran Club, Falmouth Bay Marina, or the Antigua Yacht Club marina. In English Harbour you can tie alongside at Antigua Slipway or stern-to in Nelson's Dockyard. More important, in both harbors you will be able to anchor out if you don't want to use a marina.

Repair facilities in Antigua are second to none and better than you will find in European yachting centers as they are all concentrated in a very small area and readily accessible from where the boats are moored. St. Martin, where both Island Water World and Budget have their main stores, has a much better selection of marine supplies than does Antigua.

Until 2010, I considered the repair facilities in Antigua better than in St. Martin because of the haulout facilities available — a railway at Antigua Slipway and travel hoists at the Catamaran Club in Falmouth Harbour and at Jolly Harbour. Also, Stan Pearson, one of the organizers of the RORC Caribbean 600, runs one of the best rigging shops in the entire eastern Caribbean. When it comes to sail repair, especially big sails, Antigua Sails and A & F Sails, both in English Harbour are, in my mind, the best sail-repair and awning making facilities in the eastern Caribbean.

However, Bobby's Marina in Simpson Lagoon, St. Martin, has recently installed a 150-ton lift. It's within walking distance of the main offices of IWW, Budget, and FKG Marine Rigging and Fabrication (where Stan Pearson started his Caribbean career). FKG can handle rigging needs right up to megayachts and has an excellent metal and machine shop. St. Martin Marine, by the airport, has a 75-ton Sea Lift and is only a 10-minute dinghy ride away. Combine these facilities with the fact that it is much easier to import gear into St. Martin than into Antigua and it looks like St. Martin may replace Antigua as the best repair and refit location in the eastern Caribbean.

Bear in mind, though, that in St. Martin you have to negotiate the bridge and pay a fee to enter Simpson Lagoon. While anchored in Simpson Lagoon, you must pay a mooring fee if anchored out and dockage, of course, if in a marina.

Simpson Lagoon is an enclosed body of water, so it has no circulation and is foul to say the least. As my father said of the canals of Venice, "I don't know which is worse, to drown in the canal or be rescued from it."

I feel the same about Simpson Lagoon.

The charges to anchor in English Harbour or Falmouth are minimal and the harbors cleaner, so think about the situation, talk to people, keep your ears open at happy hour, and then make your decision.

In Antigua, diesel, gasoline, and water are readily available alongside in both English Harbour and Falmouth. Showers and laundry facilities are also on hand. Sam and Dave's Laundry Wash-and-Dry can not be beat. Years ago, I wrote in one of my guides that Sam and Dave's laundry was great. The clothes were washed and dried at a reasonable price but came back looking as though someone had tied knots in them. Evidently that story was shown to the gals at Sam and Dave's laundry. Now you send the dirty laundry to be washed and dried and it comes back so neatly folded that it looks as if it has all been ironed!

Boats bound for the southern end of the Caribbean often head for Barbados, which does not make a particularly good landfall. The best route is to pass north of the island and head south to Port St. Charles and clear in (see directions on the back of Imray-Iolaire chart B-2). Port St. Charles is a small marina built for a residential development and does not have space for visiting yachts except for a brief stay to check in. So it's south to Bridgetown, where there is no marina although they have been talking about building one for 40 years. You have to anchor out. Sometimes you will roll your guts out, and often you'll be kept awake until the early hours of the morning by music from the shore.

In Barbados, the infrastructure to support yachts is minimal.

From Barbados it is off to Tobago, where in winter the anchorages are rocky and rolly but a surfer's delight, or Grenada, with its dozens of superb harbors and coves and good infrastructure to support boats up to 70 feet. And there's Trinidad, which can haul even the largest megayachts if they are willing to use commercial shipyards. Owners of yachts of 70 feet and smaller have so many yards to choose from they cannot be listed. Spend four evenings at happy hour, then make your choice. If you have crossed in January, not too long after your arrival it will be time for Trinidad's internationally famous Carnival.

Of course, these are not the only choices for a Caribbean landfall. French sailors, hungry for baguettes and brie will head for Martinique or Guadeloupe. St. Lucia is also a popular first stop and is where the Atlantic Rally for Cruisers, which starts from Las Palmas, Gran Canaria, makes its finish. I heard recently from Ian Cowan (a longtime fixture in St. Lucia's marine infrastructure) that the marina in Rodney Bay is being brought up to date but without its character being destroyed.

Street's Guide to the Atlantic and Caribbean Basins, due out in 2012, will include a full description and analysis of all the landfalls in the Eastern Caribbean.

A Guide to Cruising Guides

I wrote my first guide, the Yachtsman's Guide to the Virgin Islands, in 1964. It was privately printed on a hand-powered mimeograph (Roneo to the British).

I followed this with my first hard-cover guide, the Cruising Guide to the Lesser Antilles, in 1966. This was the guide that opened the Caribbean to the cruising yachtsman and made bareboat chartering possible.

In 1974, I further updated and expanded this guide. In 1977, I expanded it again and divided the guide into three volumes: Puerto Rico, the Spanish, U.S. and British Virgin islands; Anguilla to Dominica; and Martinique to Trinidad.

In 1980, I added Street's Guide to Venezuela and the ABC Islands. Over the years, I expanded and updated the guides each time they came up for reprint.

Beginning in the late 1970s, new guides in English, Spanish, French, and German started popping up like mushrooms on a rotten log. I was often asked, "What does it feel like to be the most plagiarized yachting author in the world?" Patience Wales, for years the editor of *SAIL*, has said, "Other guide authors have just sailed in Street's and *Iolaire's* wake, avoiding the rocks and shoals that Street and *Iolaire* found."

Most of the guides were "flash in the pans" and died after one edition.

However, Chris Doyle's guides covering the Windward and Leewards and Venezuela as well as Simon and Nancy Scott's guide to the US and British Virgin Islands have stood the test of time.

More recently, Seaworthy Publications introduced a series of guides by Stephen J. Pavlidis that cover all the islands from the north coast of the Dominican Republic to Trinidad.

The cost of a guide in comparison to the cost of your Caribbean cruising is infinitesimal — about the price of a dinner ashore. I recommend you buy all the guides that are available for the area you intend to cruise. Study them all and cross reference them and you will be able to find quiet anchorages.

Chris Doyle's guides cover the Windwards, Leewards, and Trinidad and Tobago in three separate volumes. These are the standard books given to all bareboat charterers. They cover all the major anchorages well plus, since they are reissued every three years or so, they are pretty much up-to-date on marine-oriented facilities ashore as well as bars, restaurants, and hotels.

The Seaworthy guides by Stephen J. Pavlidis cover these islands in three volumes to become two volumes in 2011.

Street's guides cover this same area in two volumes.

Similarly, the guides to the U.S. and British Virgin Islands by Simon and Nancy Scott are written for the bareboaters and provide information of a similar nature to that in Doyle's guides. The Scotts also include some very interesting information on the flora, fauna, and fishes found in the Virgin Islands.

Street's Guide is the only one that covers the U.S., British, and Spanish Virgin Islands plus Puerto Rico in one volume. The Stephen J. Pavlidis Cruising Guide to Puerto Rico covers Puerto Rico, the Spanish Virgin Islands, and the northern coast of the Dominican Republic.

Imray's new guide is a translation of Jacques Patuelli's French guide. It gives a good overview of the entire island chain but, because it covers all the islands from Grenada to the Virgin Islands in one volume, it includes only the more popular anchorages.

In three volumes, Street's Guides cover all the islands in great detail, describing every possible anchorage in the Eastern Caribbean that is safe for a boat drawing 7 feet. They are also the only guides that give really good inter-island sailing directions and harbor piloting directions. They have not been updated since 2001, but rocks don't move by themselves. If they have been moved by dredging, or new breakwaters or marinas have been built, such changes will appear on the Imray-Iolaire charts. The combination of Street's Guides and Imray-Iolaire charts will provide the mariner with a wealth of up-to-date navigational information that is not found in the Scott, Doyle, or Pavlidis guides.

Be sure, though, to buy the Scott or Pavlidis guide to the Virgin Islands if you are cruising the Virgins and the relevant Doyle or Pavlidis guide if cruising the Windwards or Leewards, as these books will provide you with current information about marine facilities, hotels, restaurants, and other attractions and activities ashore.

Cross-check all the harbor information provided in the different books. Then circle in red all the harbors and coves mentioned in Street's guide that are not described in the other guides and you will be guaranteed an uncrowded anchorage. If there is another boat there, it probably has Street's Guide on board.

In the Caribbean, Street's Guides and Imray-Iolaire charts are stocked in the St. Martin, St. Lucia, and Grenada stores of Island Water World (www.islandwaterworld.com), in St. Barts at Sully Magras' LeShip (www.ship-sb.com), and in St. Lucia at Johnsons Marine Centre (www.johnsons-hardware.com) across the street from Rodney Bay Marina.

Cruising Guides to the Eastern Caribbean

Guides by Donald M. Street, Jr.
Street's Cruising Guide to the Eastern Caribbean: Puerto Rico, Spanish, U.S. & British Virgin Islands
Street's Cruising Guide to the Eastern Caribbean: Anguilla to Dominica
Street's Cruising Guide to the Eastern Caribbean: Martinique to Trinidad

Guides by Stephen J. Pavlidis
A Cruising Guide to Puerto Rico and the Spanish Virgin Islands
A Cruising Guide to the Virgin Islands including the British, U.S., and Spanish Virgin Islands
A Cruising Guide to the Leeward Islands
A Cruising Guide to the Windward Islands
A Cruising Guide to Trinidad & Tobago

Guide by Jacques Patuelli
Grenada to the Virgin Islands: A Cruising Guide to the Lesser Antilles

Guides by Nancy and Simon Scott
Cruising Guide to the Virgin Islands

Guides by Chris Doyle
Cruising Guide to the Leeward Islands
Sailors Guide to the Windward Islands
Cruising Guide to Trinidad and Tobago Plus Barbados and Guyana

Street's Guides are hard to find in the Caribbean. This is because they are print-on-demand from iUniverse.com, which only discounts to retailers 20 percent of the retail price. The marine stores in the Caribbean demand 40 percent discount. I have pointed out to all the marine suppliers that all they have to do to obtain their 40 percent mark up is to put a sticker over the iUniverse retail price and add $5 to it. I do not want to go into why they have not done so for fear of a lawsuit.

In the Caribbean, Street's Guides and Imray-Iolaire charts are stocked in the St. Martin, St. Lucia, and Grenada stores of Island Water World (www.islandwaterworld.com), in St. Barts at Sully Magras' LeShip (www.ship-sb.com), and in St. Lucia at Johnsons Marine Centre (www.johnsons-hardware.

com) across the street from Rodney Bay Marina. With IWW's new system, Street's Guides can be ordered online.

In the States, order Street's Guides from iUniverse or Bluewater Books & Charts (www.bluewaterweb.com).

In Europe, order from Imray (www.imray.com) or Kelvin Hughes (www.kelvinhughes.info). They can also be found sometimes in the major chandleries along the southwest coast of England and in most of the major chart agents in Europe.

The first foreign yacht to visit Venezuela was Iolaire in 1969. She subsequently visited the area every year for three to six weeks and the result was Street's Guide to Venezuela and the ABC Islands, which was first published in 1980 and updated and republished in 1990. I was in the midst of revising it in 1997 when I discovered the postal service had demolished three hours of tape that was updating the guide and, on the same day, heard that Cesar Chavez had survived the attempted coup.

I decided that god did not want me to revise the guide and, with Chavez in power, that few yachts would want to cruise Venezuelan waters.

Even though it has not been updated, Street's Guide to Venezuela will still be valid, as rocks do not move and few marinas have been built since 1990. It's now out of print, but can be found secondhand through the Internet.

Chris Doyle followed in Street's and *Iolaire's* wake. His Cruising Guide to Venezuela and Bonaire, last revised in 2007, has better coverage of the eastern end of Golfo de Cariaco than does Street's guide.

Off the Beaten Track in the Eastern Caribbean

All the time, I see articles and letters to editors in the yachting press on both sides of the Atlantic and in the Caribbean Compass in which sailors complain about crowded harbors in the Caribbean. They claim, too, that many anchorages are so full of mooring balls that there's no room left for anchoring.

That might be true for the popular anchorages, but sailors willing to get off the beaten track and forgo bars and restaurants can choose from probably 100 anchorages in the Eastern Caribbean where they will be completely alone or in the company of only one or two other boats. The crews of those other boats will not be a problem as they will be kindred souls also trying to get off the beaten track.

Starting at Tobago in the south and working north to Puerto Rico, all the anchorages mentioned in the following pages are well described in the various Street's guides or on the relevant Imray-Iolaire chart. Admittedly, entering almost all of them demands eyeball navigation with someone standing on *top* of the bow pulpit to con the helmsman in. A few anchorages require that someone stand or sit on the *lower spreaders*.

On modern yachts with internal halyards, climbing aloft is much more difficult than in the old days when all halyards were external. For this reason, on boats that will spend any time at all cruising in the tropics, a useful modification is to attach steps to the mast to enable a crew member to easily climb to the lower spreaders.

Tobago
Imray-Iolaire Chart B4

Tobago has a dozen uncrowded anchorages. They are described in *Street's Cruising Guide to the Eastern Caribbean: Martinique to Trinidad* (hereinafter abbreviated to SMT) pages 181 to 192. Admittedly those on the north coast should not be used in the winter months due to the prevalence of the northwest groundswell but, come summer, they are fine. If a hurricane approaches, head south to Trinidad or west to Golfo de Cariaco.

Doyle also describes these harbors. Read Street, Doyle, and the information on the back of Imray-Iolaire B4 and you will be up to speed on all the harbors in Tobago. The information on the back of the Imray-Iolaire chart is more up-to-date than Street's guide.

Grenada
Imray-Iolaire Chart B32

Grenada has dozens of uncrowded anchorages. On the southwest coast, Morne Rouge Bay (SMT pages 150-151) is wonderful. Boats drawing 6 feet or less can work their way well into the bay; deeper draft boats can drop their anchors on the edge of the shelf and back off.

The south coast has plenty of anchorages; it's always possible to find an uncrowded one. I recently discovered two new ones not mentioned in my guide.

They are anchorages where you are guaranteed to be alone as only one boat can fit in either of them at a time — first come first served.

As long as the wind is east or north of east, you'll find solitude in Petite Bacaye Bay, a half mile east of Westerhall Point.

Just east of this anchorage, to the west of Little Bacolet Point, is another one-boat anchorage. Work your way as far north as possible. There's plenty of water but it shoals suddenly.

These anchorages should only be used by experienced reef pilots who navigate by eyeball, use a hand-bearing compass, and judge the depth of the water by the color while cross checking against the fathometer.

If heading north up the east coast of Grenada (this is the easy way to go north — see the sailing directions on the back of Imray-Iolaire B32), Lascar Cove, Requin, and Le Petit Trou offer good anchorages (SMT page 161). You will find peace and quiet, no habitation, and no boats.

The anchorage at Grenville (SMT pages 162-165) is sheltered from the sea but not the wind and has crystal-clear water. It's not that hard to enter and is a wonderful base from which to make shoreside explorations of the northeast corner of Grenada. Visit one of the restored estate houses where you can enjoy a three-hour Grenadian estate lunch and an afternoon siesta.

When sailing out of Grenville, mind your Ps and Qs. It's probably advisable to motorsail but it is possible to sail out. Big *Iolaire* has done it with a non-working engine and the engineless *L'il Iolaire* has also sailed out of Grenville. The two shoal spots at the narrowest part of the channel, the outer end, are easy to spot as the sea humps up on them.

Sandy Island (SMT page 165) on the northeast corner of Grenada is another nice anchorage, off an uninhabited island seldom visited by yachts.

Enroute to Carriacou, in the summer months when it's not blowing hard, sometimes a daytime anchorage can be found in the lee of Les Tantes (SMT pages 138-139) where fishermen sometimes camp ashore.

Corn Store Bay, on the northwest corner of Isle de Ronde (SMT pages 137-138), is a good anchorage as long as the groundswell is not running.

The Grenadines

Imray-Iolaire Charts B31 and B311

When approaching Carriacou, instead of heading for crowded Tyrell Bay, head for the southeast corner of the island. In the summer, when it's not blowing too hard, try the anchorage behind One Tree Rock (SMT pages 136-137). There is room for one boat only and you'll find good diving on the reef to windward.

In the winter, when it's too windy to use One Tree Rock, you can find an anchorage to the east, west of White Island, and also northwest of Saline Island (SMT pages 135-136).

A short beat the next day brings you to Kendance Point and the entrance to Grand Bay (SMT pages 134-135) where you'll find five miles of sheltered water and good anchorages tight behind the reef.

In the late 1960s, Jim Squire would anchor his 55-foot schooner, *Te Hongi*, behind the reef and stay for a couple of days. He would take his charter party on diving trips and catch enough lobster to feed them lobster every night. Since the charter fee was figured with a cost of so many dollars per person per day for food, Jim was entertaining his charter party by taking them diving, feeding them well on lobster, and making money as he was not having to buy food.

Continue to sail north past St. Hilaire Point (boats drawing 7 feet or more should proceed dead slow or send the dinghy ahead to check the water depth) and anchor off Windward Side (SMT page 133) to admire local sloops and possibly a schooner under construction.

You can also anchor tight up behind Carib Island, which the late Hazen Richardson of Petit St. Vincent frequently used as a location for weddings for friends and resort guests.

If you go ashore at Windward Side, buy some "jack iron" rum. In my DVD, *Streetwise 1*, a one-hour video of a cruise through the Grenadines that includes some of Street's Useful Tips, I demonstrate how ice sinks in "jack iron" but floats in Mount Gay. I then drink some of the jack iron that's so strong ice cubes sink in it. Gary Jobson said it's the funniest scene ever presented in

After the Atlantic Crossing

a sailing video. (A list of Streetwise DVDs is available on the website www.street-iolaire.com, and they can be ordered via streetiolaire@hotmail.com.)

Sail on north and west to anchor behind Frigate Island, off Union Island (SMT page 121), a seldom used anchorage yet one of *Iolaire*'s favorites. We would sit, drink in hand, and admire the frigate birds soaring overhead. One will suddenly dive on another bird, to make it drop the fish it's carrying, then catch the dropped fish before it hits the water.

From Frigate Island, if the wind is south of east, head for Bloody Bay, which is a new discovery. It's not in the Street's Guide but directions are on the back of Imray-Iolaire Chart B31. It's a wonderful anchorage as long as the wind is south of east. If the wind is east or north of east forget about Bloody Bay.

On the windward side of Mayreau (SMT pages 116-117), you'll find a wonderful anchorage, just like the outer anchorage in the Tobago Cays but with no other boats.

The windward side of Canouan (SMT pages 104-106) is an excellent anchorage which, in years gone by, you would have had completely to yourself. Now, since The Moorings established a charter base in Canouan, you will sometimes have to share the anchorage with one or two Moorings catamarans, but the anchorage is big enough that you will never be crowded.

When you head north, try anchoring on the west side of Isle a Quatre (SMT page 96). If it's not blowing too hard, if you are a good eyeball navigator, and you can put a crew member on the *lower spreaders* (a crewmember standing on the bow pulpit will not be high enough), you will find another anchorage where you will be by yourself.

Do not try this unless light conditions are excellent and do not take any boat that draws more than 6 feet into this anchorage. You will have good diving within easy swimming distance of the boat, and if you hike up the hill to the abandoned house on the 400-foot-high ridge, you'll get a fantastic view of the surrounding area and of the cove on the south side of the island.

There is an anchorage on the lee side of Petit Nevis (SMT page 96). This is where the whales are butchered. You will be by yourself unless a whale has been caught. The beaches on Petit Nevis come and go according to the weather — sometimes there's nice white sand, at other times only a pebble beach.

If you are in Mustique and heading south, sail between Savan Island (STM pages 100-101) and the island to the southwest of it. This island has a hole through it that makes a great photo. Also, if it's not blowing hard, it's possible to anchor between the islands. You will probably need about three anchors out and possibly a line ashore. It can be done as the late Richard Scott-Hughes, one of the most colorful and skillful skippers that ever chartered in the islands, sometime anchored here with *Boekanier*, a 65-foot Alden-designed steel schooner built by de Vries Lentsch.

Out to windward of Bequia is Baliceaux (SMT pages 99-100), an uninhabited island visited by fishermen and occasionally by a yacht whose crew has tired of the crowded anchorage and launch traffic in Bequia's Admiralty Bay. This is a great jumping-off point for boats that want to sail up the windward side of St. Vincent and on to Vieux Fort, St. Lucia. As long as the wind is east or a little south of east, this is an excellent sail and avoids the problems on the lee side of St. Vincent with its lack of wind and ever-present boat boys, who are everything from in pains in the backside to petty thieves and to armed burglars. The west side of St. Vincent has been the Wild West for 50 years. It may change, but I doubt it.

Baliceaux is also an excellent landfall when sailing south from Vieux Fort or the Maria Islets off St Lucia's southeast coast.

Another easily reached quiet anchorage that provides refuge from Admiralty Bay is Anse Chemin (SMT pg 94). It's great as long as the wind is east or south of east. Tim and Pauline Carr of *Curlew* would use this anchorage when they tired of Admiralty Bay.

If you are in Anse Chemin and heading north to St. Lucia, sail up the windward side of St. Vincent for the reasons mentioned above.

St. Lucia
Imray-Iolaire Chart B1

Before taking the route north to windward of St. Vincent, check the section on tides on the back of the Imray-Iolaire chart. You can ascertain meridian passage of the moon from the table that shows up every month in the *Caribbean Compass* (courtesy of D.M. Street, Jr.). Head north across the Bequia Channel with the first of the weather-going tide, then stand north to Vieux Fort (SMT pages 63-64). It's about 40 miles from either Anse Chemin or Baliceaux. During the winter, it should be a close reach or a fetch. Come spring, when the wind tends to be south of east, it should be a good fast reach.

Once you've checked in at Vieux Fort, sail around the corner and anchor in Point Sable Bay (SMT pages 63-64). Tuck up really tight behind Maria Islet as in the main bay it tends to be rolly because the swell hooks around both sides of this small island.

Heading west, try Laborie, which I regard as the nicest village in St. Lucia (SMT pages 62-63). In years gone by, it was seldom visited by yachts so there were no moorings or boat boys. Now, unfortunately, there are moorings, but I am told that there is still space to anchor and the boat boys are not too pushy.

When heading south from St. Lucia after the ARC, everyone stops at the Pitons. From the Pitons head southeast to Laborie and on to Vieux Fort or Point Sable Bay. From either one of these anchorages it's a straight shot south to Baliceaux or Bequia. This is a glorious reach as the course is west of south, at about 200° magnetic.

Martinique
Imray-Iolaire Charts A30 and A 301

When heading north from St Lucia to Martinique, check in at Cul de Sac Marin (STM pages 31-33), then leave the crowded harbor of Marin and anchor off St. Anne (STM page 32-33) where you'll find plenty of room in crystal clear water. This is a good jumping-off spot for heading to the east coast of Martinique, a wonderful cruising ground where you will see few if any other cruising yachts. Those you will see are owned by local Martiniquais who keep their boats on the east coast.

In this area, Street's Guide (STM pages 34-35) is adequate, but if you really want to gunkhole, and especially if you have a shoal-draft boat, be sure to purchase the local guide by Philipe Lacheneze Huede and Jerome Nouel. Philipe is a "beke," which means he's directly descended from the first settlers of Martinique who arrived about 1640. He has sailed the east coast all his life. Jerome is a Frenchman who arrived in Martinique 30 years ago. He has cruised into every gunkhole in Martinique and has produced superb sketch charts.

There are so many anchorages that I will not try to list them. Many guides and sailing "experts" (x is the unknown quantity, the spert is a drip under pressure), bareboat managers who spend most of their time in the office, and sailors who have sailed the Caribbean for four or five years and know it all feel that the east coast of Martinique is too dangerous. *Iolaire* was the first foreign yacht to explore the east coast of Martinique, back in the early 1960s. The crew consisted of myself, my late wife, Marilyn, our daughter, Dory, aged 14 months, the Schipperke dog named Merde, and a semi-working engine.

People asked what we called the dog when in Martinique. Simple. Few people in Martinique in the late 1960s and early '70s spoke English, so we called Merde Shit when we were in Martinique. Schipperkes are very smart and Merde was bilingual and responded to commands in both English and French.

Schipperkes are wonderful boat dogs. They are smart and alert but have an awful reputation as continual barkers, but Merde would cease barking immediately upon being told to stop. Do not own a Schipperke unless you know how to train dogs. They are so smart they will train you.

In all my 50 plus years of sailing in the Caribbean and Europe, I have never heard of a boat that had a barking dog on board being boarded by a thief or burglar.

We have been back to the east coast of Martinique many times exploring, chartering, and just plain cruising. It's my wife, Trich's, favorite cruising area. She does not like early starts, or long sails ending just before sundown. Since the entrances to the harbors on the east coast of Martinique lie in an east-west axis, you cannot leave till the sun is high, at 1030 to 1100. You should be in the next anchorage before the sun is low in the west, so you should be in and anchoring by 1400 or 1500 by the latest. Thus, in the morning there is no rush to get under way; in the afternoon the anchor is down in time for a swim before the evening sundowner.

One important thing to remember on the east coast of Martinique is that, at the head of some of the harbors, the rise and fall of tide at springs can reach 3 feet. Check the depth and the state of the tide carefully before anchoring.

Dominica
Imray-Iolaire Chart A29

In Dominica there are few anchorages and none that are off the beaten track.

Îles des Saintes
Imray-Iolaire Chart A281

In the Saints (*Street's Guide to the Eastern Caribbean: Anguilla to Dominica*, hereinafter SAD, pages 156-157), everyone anchors off Terre d'en Haut, which has become a bit of France transferred to the Caribbean. Go to Terre d'en Bas. There you will find the Saints as they were 30 years ago. As long as the wind is east or north of east, the anchorage in Anse Fideling is good.

If it's not blowing hard, you can anchor on two anchors off the beach on the windward side of Terre d'en Bas. You have a lee shore behind you, but as long as it's not blowing hard and the wind is east or south of east, you are sheltered from the sea by Terre d'en Haut and Isle Cabrit 2 miles to windward. Because there is only 2 miles of fetch, a big sea cannot build up, only a rough chop.

Ashore, you will find a lot of good but unpretentious restaurants where they will not only not speak English but many will not even speak French. They only speak the local patois.

From the Saints, it's either an easy reach to the south coast of Grande Terre, the eastern half of Guadeloupe, or a beat to windward to Petite Terre, Marie Galante, and La Désirade.

Guadeloupe
Imray-Iolaire Charts A28 and A281

The south coast of Grande Terre (SAD pages 144-149) offers a number of uncrowded anchorages: Grand Baie, Gozier, Petite Havre, Anse Accul, St. Francois, and Passe Champagne.

Just southwest of the entrance to Pointe a Pitre is the seldom used anchorage of Sainte Marie, Bas Terre (SAD page 141), but do not try entering this harbor unless conditions are good, and I strongly recommend a crew member on the spreaders.

Petite Terre (SAD pages 151-152) is likely to be full of day trippers from about 1100 to 1500. Plan your arrival for about 1500 when they are leaving. You will have a wonderful anchorage all to yourself for the evening sundowner, early morning swim, and breakfast. You can then depart as the day trippers arrive.

Then sail on to Marie Galante (SAD pages 157-159) where you'll never be in a crowd as you can anchor anywhere along about 5 miles of shore under the lee of the island. You can always find a spot on the beautiful white sand beach that has no other boats or people.

From Marie Galante, head for La Désirade, (SAD pages 148-151) but first cross-check with Doyle's latest guide. Until recently, this island was never visited by yachts as the harbor was too shallow for anything but shoal-draft powerboats. Recently, a channel has been dug into the harbor, which is on the south side of the southwest corner of La Désirade. The channel is reportedly dredged to a depth of about 6 feet, and there's about 6 feet in most of the harbor and 7 feet alongside the fuel pier. If you run aground, Doyle points out it's soft mud. Remember that in June, July, and early August, the Caribbean is usually 18 inches lower than in winter. Thus the water depth between high water springs in winter and low water springs in June through early August can be as much as 3 feet.

If the wind is east or south of east, a sailor who really wants to get away from it all and have good bragging rights at the bar can stop at Port du Moule (SAD pages 138-139) on the north side of Grande Terre. Hans Hoff, captaining the 95-foot Rhodes motorsailer, *Fandango*, and Hank Strauss, in his 45-foot ketch, have both anchored in Port du Moule. Mind your Ps and Qs when entering, read the sailing directions carefully, and eyeball your way in. Once in and secured, go ashore and you will find restaurants serving excellent food and wine at reasonable prices. Here, they do not even know what a tourist is. The clientèle is strictly local Guadeloupeans.

From Marie Galante, Petite Terre, or La Désirade, once you've passed between La Désirade and Grande Terre, you'll have a glorious 58-mile reach to Antigua.

Antigua
Imray-Iolaire Charts A27 and A271

Check in at Falmouth Harbour or English Harbour, then, if you want to get away from it all, just a couple of miles east of English Harbour is the wonderful, secluded Indian Creek (SAD page 91). Watch out for the rock off the entrance. It has 6 feet of water over it and has nailed more than a few boats short tacking up the shore heading east from English Harbour or Falmouth Harbour.

From English Harbour or Falmouth Harbour to Green Island is a morning sail. It's not off the beaten track but it's seldom crowded and is a good jumping-off spot for some off-the-beaten-track anchorages.

If you are adventurous, you can try Indian Town Creek and Guana and Belfast bays (SAD pages 97-98), but only the good sailor who has a boat with a sound engine and who is willing to put a crew member on the *lower spreaders* should attempt them. Getting in these bays is relatively easy if you follow carefully the sailing directions in Street's Guide. Leaving by beating to windward through the narrow channel is impossible unless you have a small boat that goes to windward well and tacks readily.

David Simmonds (who built Antigua Slipway into the best yacht yard in the Eastern Caribbean), on his little sloop *Bacco*, and Graham Knight, in his small fiberglass sloop, have beaten to windward out of these two harbors. I have not entered these bays as I feel that, although beating to windward out of them on the engineless 46-foot yawl, *Iolaire*, might be possible, it would be too risky.

The directions for entering the harbor come from Jol Byerley, the late Desmond Nicholson, who would enter these harbors with the 88-foot steel schooner, *Freelance*, and the late Ken McKenzie, who entered them with the 72-foot ketch, *Ticonderoga*. David Simmonds and Graham Knight have also checked the sailing directions.

If the prospect of entering and leaving these harbors from seaward is too daunting, continue northeastward up the northeast coast of Antigua. In years gone by, this area (SAD pages 98-106) was considered by many to be the most dangerous coast in the Caribbean. This is because the northeast corner of Antigua is low and featureless and even the careful sailor would find himself in shoal water littered with coral heads. When off the northeast coast of Antigua, keep an eye on the fathometer and the color of the water and continually plot the GPS positions on the chart.

Sail north, then northwest, then west, avoiding the shoal water and detached coral heads. Finally, head south (SAD page 100) to enter North Sound via the northern entrance, not the northeastern entrance. In North Sound you'll find half a dozen anchorages. Pick one with no boat anchored in it and enjoy a calm but windswept and bugless anchorage. From North Sound you can explore both Guana and Belfast bays by dinghy via the channels between the islands and the shore.

If the government of Antigua would dredge two short channels to connect North Sound with Guana and Belfast bays, this fantastic cruising area with its dozens of anchorages in sheltered water would become easily accessible to cruising yachts.

Barbuda
Imray-Iolaire Chart A26

From North Sound, it's an easy 22-mile reach to Barbuda (SAD pages 114-119) where you'll find many anchorages and mile after mile of empty beaches. However, the approaches to many of the anchorages are littered with coral heads, like a minefield ready to catch the unwary mariner.

Doyle claims he has located every coral head around Barbuda. I say that is impossible.

I like to quote the story of the Maine pilot who was piloting a VLCC drawing 60 feet up Penobscot Reach, calmly puffing on his pipe and giving the helmsman courses and speeds but not checking the chart or taking bearings.

The captain of the tanker was getting more and more nervous. Finally, he said, "Pilot, do you know the location of every rock in Penobscot Bay?"

"Hell, no," the pilot calmly replied.

"If you do not know where every rock is in Penobscot Bay," the captain said, "how can you claim to be a pilot?"

The pilot took a few puffs on his pipe, then said, "I don't know where all the rocks are, but I know where they ain't," and went back to his pipe.

Stay on the ranges and transits on Imray-Iolaire Chart A26 and you will be safe. Off the ranges you are on your own. Only sail off the ranges if you are a good eyeball navigator and the light conditions are good.

Barbuda has mile after mile of white sand beaches, most of which are completely undeveloped. As of

2010, the situation is as follows: Working from east to west you have Cocoa point that does not like visiting yachtsmen (or women), K Club that has closed down, the hotel just west of the landing on the south coast now abandoned and overgrown, the restored Martello tower that is definitely worth a visit, a hotel on the southwestern tip of Barbuda, then nothing all the way north to Low Bay.

In 2009, new small very high-class hotel had been built at Low Bay with low-rise cottages, not a high-rise block. The management claimed that, by 2011, they would have their own helicopter with which they could pick up guests at the Antigua airport and have them in the hotel 20 minutes later.

In 2009, the drill was arrival by plane in Antigua, a night in an Antiguan hotel, an early morning catamaran trip to Barbuda, a bouncy 20-minute ride in a taxi to the dock in Codrington, then a fast ride in a launch to the hotel. By the time you arrived, you really did need a stiff welcoming drink.

Thanks, but I'll continue to visit Barbuda by boat — a nice 22-mile reach.

St. Kitts and Nevis
Imray-Iolaire Chart A25

Nevis is littered with mooring balls but the southwest coast of St. Kitts (SAD pages 64-66) has a number of anchorages that are never crowded: South Frigate, White House, Ballast, Shitten, Majors, and Banana/Cockleshell bays.

Developers have huge plans to develop a marina capable of servicing megayachts by dredging Salt Pond behind Ballast Bay and opening a channel to the sea. When construction will begin is a question, but 2011 is probably the last year cruising sailors will be able to enjoy the tranquil and uncroweded anchorage of Ballast Bay. The anchorages to the south will probably remain uncrowded for many years to come.

From May to early October, if it's not blowing hard, two anchorages on the east coast of St. Kitts, Sand Bank and Dieppe bays (SAD pages 66-68), are available to sailors who are good reef navigators and are willing to put a crewmember on the lower spreaders.

Statia
Imray-Iolaire Chart A25

Statia (SAD pages 59-61) is off the beaten track, but avoid the island at the time of spring tides. Sometimes, the flooding spring tide overcomes the normal westerly current. If this happens, the tide carries heavy bunker oil, which is frequently spilled when tankers are refueling or discharging fuel at the oil transfer depot, up to the anchorage. If this gets on your topsides it's all but impossible to remove.

Avoid Statia if the wind is south of east and if there is a northerly groundswell, which hooks around the south end of the island and creates a bad surge in the anchorage.

Everyone has heard the story of Lord Rodney capturing Statia, gathering plenty of loot, and cutting off the island as a transfer point for arms and ammunition for Washington's army in the Revolutionary War. Few know of the brilliant French operation where the island was recaptured with barely the loss of a man. Read it in SAD pages 59-60.

Anguilla, St. Martin, and St. Barths
Imray-Iolaire Charts A24, A 241, and A242

Finding an uncrowded anchorage in the Anguilla, St. Martin, and St. Barths area is pretty difficult. In Grande Case Bay, St. Martin (SAD pages 36-37) you will find other boats but the bay is so large that the anchorage is seldom crowded.

In Anguilla (SAD pages 9-24), be sure when checking in to ascertain where you are allowed to anchor. Rendezvous Bay (SAD page 18) on the south coast, if you are allowed to anchor there, is seldom crowded.

Shoal Bay, on the north coast, was to be developed into a major marina but, due to the worldwide recession, IGY Marinas, that was to have developed the area, has put it on the back burner until who knows when.

Under certain conditions, Prickly Pear Cays (SAD page 22) and Dog island (SAD page 24) make good anchorages *if you are allowed to anchor there*.

To really get off the beaten track, and as long as the northerly groundswell is not running, Scrub Island (SAD page 21) offers an interesting anchorage on its western side. I made the sketch chart that appears in SAD in an aircraft while flying around Anguilla with Jon Repke. I have never succeeded in exploring this anchorage with *Iolaire* or *L'il Iolaire* as, every time I tried to go there, conditions did not permit it.

I have secondhand information that one sailor of unknown skill reported the sketch chart is no good. Two other good sailors reported that the sketch chart is fine but should be backed up by eyeball navigation in good light. The small restaurant that once was on the eastern tip of Scrub is no more.

British Virgin Islands
Imray-Iolaire Chart A231 and A232

Street's Guide to Puerto Rico and the Spanish, U.S. and British Virgin Islands, is the only guide that covers the whole area in one volume. It's referred to from here forward as SPRVI.

When cruising the Virgin Islands, I recommend you not use Imray-Iolaire Chart A233. It is a combination of A231 and A232 with one chart printed on each side. Because it has charts on both sides, it does not have the tidal and piloting information that's printed on the backs of A231 and A232. Spend the extra money and obtain the information that's on the backs of the charts.

In the BVI, the first step in finding quiet anchorages is to obtain a copy from The Moorings or Sunsail of the special Imray-Iolaire A233 that shows the areas where bareboats are not permitted to anchor. In the areas barred to bareboats, you will find anchorages that are uncrowded and are not littered with mooring balls.

Money Bay and Windward Sound (PRVI page 191), on the south coast of Norman Island, are never crowded. The only firsthand information I have on Windward Sound is from the late Carleton Mitchell, who used this bay to hide from everyone when on his powerboat, *Sans Terre*.

There are numerous anchorages on the south coast of Peter Island: South, White, Whelk, and South Sprat bays, and Key Point (PRVI pages 192-193). In all these anchorages, you will be completely by yourself or in the company of one other boat at the most.

Ross Norgrove discovered Bluff Bay, on the south coast of Beef Island (PRVI page 182), in the mid 1960s and it became a favorite anchorage for his 60-foot schooner, *White Squall*, as well as for *Iolairo*, both of which boats draw 7½ feet. See the description of Bluff Bay in PRVI for an amusing story of rock piloting that involved pure luck and no skill.

On the south end of Guana Island there is a good anchorage for one boat behind Money Point. This is one of my late discoveries and is not in my guide, but directions for entering it are on the back of I-I A231 and A232. Take the dinghy ashore, climb across the rocks, and you will find a beautiful little sandy beach inaccessible except by the route you have taken— so a great place to bathe *au naturel*.

Eustatia Sound (PRVI pages 206-208), on the north coast of Virgin Gorda, has two bays, Deep Bay and Oil Nut Bay, where you will be completely alone. Also, unless it's blowing really hard, you can anchor close to leeward of the barrier reef, which breaks the swell but not the breeze. Thus it's a cool bug-free anchorage close enough to the reef you can snorkel from the boat — no need to mount an expedition by dinghy. Anchor bow and stern so that, if the wind dies out in the evening and the current changes, you are not swept onto the reef.

On the south coast of Virgin Gorda, South Sound (PRVI pages 207-208) provides an excellent anchorage that's sheltered from all directions. On the west coast, from mid-April on, when the danger of the northerly groundswell is largely gone, both Savanna and Mahoe bays (PRVI pages 201-202) provide uncrowded anchorages.

West of Anguilla Point (PRVI page 201), the western entrance to Gorda Sound makes an excellent anchorage, again from mid-April on when there is little danger from the northwest groundswell. Only use this anchorage from Monday to noontime on Friday as, over the weekend, the wakes from the continual stream of power boats in the passage between Mosquito Island and Anguilla Point make it uncomfortable to the point you can become seasick.

This anchorage became famous after Olaf Harken, when snorkeling, found a $100 bill sticking out of the sand. On a subsequent dive he found four twenties. The whole crew then frantically dove for an hour or so but found nothing more. Olaf decided to spend his new-found wealth on a dinner ashore for his crew, but it was a net loss as the dinner and drinks cost more than the $180.

The main anchorage in Anegada (PRVI pages 211-215) may be crowded but, if you draw 6 feet or less, go westward between the two stakes and anchor off the Soares complex, Neptunes Treasure. This is usually a calmer anchorage than the main anchorage plus the Soares family has some interesting stories to tell.

The anchorage behind Pomata Point, where there is a small hotel ashore, is never crowded. Also, come late spring, from mid-April on when the danger of a groundswell is negligible, there is an anchorage off the western end of Anegada where you're guaranteed to have a mile of so of completely deserted white sand beach.

The ultimate deserted anchorage in the BVI, and possibly in the whole Eastern Caribbean, is the cove on the lee side of Tobago Island (PRVI page 188), southwest of Jost Van Dyke. This tiny cove was a favorite spot of one of Jon Repke's mechanics, who would go hide there when he wanted time off. The only way Jon could find him was to get in his plane and search the normal anchorages. If he didn't find him in any of the normal anchorages, he would fly on to Little Tobago. If his mechanic was there and he really needed him. Jon would fly over the boat and flour-bomb it. The mechanic would then realize he was desperately needed.

U.S. Virgin Islands
Imray-Iolaire Chart A231

Despite what sailors and guide authors say, you can still find quiet uncrowded anchorages in the US Virgin Islands if you get off the beaten track.

Around St. John, just about all the anchorages within the area managed by the Parks Department will be crowded, and they are full of mooring balls that you are required to use.

However, on the north coast, there is an anchorage, Mary Creek, on the western side of Leinster Bay (PRVI pages 129-130), that's a favorite of Augie Hollen. Since it's on the western side of Leinster Bay, a cool breeze always blows into it. There's 6 feet of water over the bar at the entrance and 7 to 8 feet inside.

On the northeast coast of St. John, outside the National Park area, are two excellent anchorages for the experienced eyeball navigator. Newfound Bay and Haulover Bay (PRVI pages 130-131) are both suitable for only one boat, so if you get in and anchor you will be alone. On the southeast corner of St John is Salt Pond Bay (PRVI page 135). Again, it's out of the National Park area, has no mooring balls, and is seldom crowded.

St. Thomas and its offshore islands do provide some uncrowded anchorages. Buck Island (PRV page 117) does have day trippers but they leave by 1500 and don't arrive till after 1000, so the anchorage is deserted from evening to morning. What more can the sailor want? In the middle of the day, the sailor is sailing.

Lindbergh Bay (PRVI page 108) is slightly rocky and rolly. It's the old story here that, where there's a white sand beach it's not a good all-weather anchorage as it's the swell that puts the sand on the beach. The best feature of Lindbergh Bay is that the beach is within walking distance of the airport, or a short taxi ride from the airport to one of the hotels on the beach, so it's a good place to anchor if doing a crew change.

A warning: In periods of heavy weather, even with winds from the east, the swell hooks around Water Island and rolls into Lindbergh Bay. In 1958, the swell caused *Iolaire*'s anchor shackle to break and she ended up high and dry on the beach.

Brewers Bay (PRVI pages 108-109), north of the runway, is another deserted anchorage although the beach may be full of swimmers on weekends. This is a good anchorage in winter but, come late spring and summer, it's dubious as, with southeast winds, the sewage from the discharge pipe sometime finds its way into this bay.

The anchorage in the lee of Saba Island (PRVI page 117) is superb. Good diving can be had on rocks to the west, there's a nice beach ashore, and the wind sweeps across the sand spit between Turtle Dove Cay and Saba Island guaranteeing you a cool bug-free anchorage. On weekends, sailors from St. Thomas visit this anchorage, but it is deserted during the week. This anchorage makes a great jumping-off spot when heading west to the Spanish Virgins, or an excellent landfall if coming from the Spanish Virgins and heading for St. Thomas.

A number of anchorages on the western end and north coast of St. Thomas are not usable in the winter, when the groundswell is likely to come in and the wind can go into the northeast or north, but they bear investigating come late April or early May.

On the western end of St. Thomas, check out Mermaids Chair (PRVI page 110) or the anchorage in the bay on the southwest corner of West Cay.

Under power, go between West Cay and St. Thomas and investigate Sandy, Botany, Stumpy, Santa Maria, Hull, and Magens bays (PRVI pages 110-112), but in late spring and summer only. It's worthy of note that the Frenchtown fishermen keep their boats on the south side of St. Thomas in the winter but, come late April or early May, they move their boats to Hull Bay.

From the northern Virgins to St. Croix (PRVI pages 143-156, Imray-Iolaire A234) is a glorious sail — 38 miles on a close or beam reach depending on your jumping-off off point — and is well worth making. St. Croix bears investigating for a day in a rented car and the town of Christiansted warrants a good half day or perhaps a full day of exploration.

Then, sail off to Buck Island (PRVI pages 151-153). You'll see some day trippers from 1100 to 1500 but the island is yours morning, late afternoon, and night. The number of day-charter boats is strictly limited so the island is not overcrowded even during the day.

If you want to be completely alone, sail inside the barrier reef on the north side of St. Croix and work your way eastward from St. Croix Yacht Club into Knights Bay or Cotton Garden Bay. Here you will have a beautiful windswept anchorage but no sea, as the barrier reef breaks the entire swell, and you'll have no other boats.

There are anchorages inside the barrier reef on the north side of St Croix. The sailing is beautiful, but it's only for the good rock pilot with a good lookout on the bow or lower spreaders. Be sure when you are doing this you are consulting Steet's Guide (PRVI pages 151-153) and Imray-Iolaire Chart A234.

The only detailed charts of this area are the BA chart of St. Croix and Imray-Iolaire A234. Use the Imray-Iolaire chart as it is based on an unpublished 1985 NOAA survey plus explorations I have made in *Iolaire*'s dinghy and information supplied by experienced local sailors. The BA chart is based on a survey made by the U.S. Coast and Geodetic Survey in 1935. It has never been updated and has numerous errors.

Spanish Virgin Islands
Imray-Iolaire Chart A131

The Spanish Virgin Islands (PRVI pages 75-82), also known as the Passage Islands, lie between St. Thomas and Puerto Rico. They are a wonderful area to explore, and, ashore, they are like the British Virgins were in the late 1960s and early '70s. Space does not permit me to list all the anchorages in the Spanish Virgins but I'll describe a few of the best.

Bahia de Almodovar (PRVI pages 81-82) is fantastic, but only during the week as on the weekends the Puerto Rican Navy (power boats) invades this anchorage and parties all day and night.

Starting in late April, when the danger of northerly groundswells has diminished, the bay on the north side of Culebrita (PRVI page 82) offers fantastic and completely deserted white sand beaches. If you're looking for white sand beaches and a hotel ashore, try Flamingo Bay (PRVI page 81) on the north side of Culebra.

A close study of the chart and a check of Street's Guide will reveal almost a dozen anchorages in and around Culebra and its offshore islands.

On the eastern end of Vieques there are two anchorages, Bahia Icacos and Bahia Salina Del Sur (PRVI pages 88-89), that I feel are the best anchorages in the entire Eastern Caribbean. Use Imray-Iolaire A131 as this area was, from the early 1900s until about 2002, a U.S. Navy gunnery and bombing range. The only chart of the area was a DMA chart not available to the public, but I managed to obtain a photostat of it (ex submariners stick together) which enabled Imray to make the chart of this area.

After the navy moved out, these wonderful anchorages could be used 365 days a year. However, the Department of the Interior decided to find and blow up all of the unexploded ordnance. Since Vieques had been used as a gunnery and bombing range for over 100 years, this seems a bit of an impossibility, but a contractor is hard at it, piling up the unexploded ordnance then blowing it up with massive explosions that can be heard on the western end of Vieques. The contractor will not allow any yachts east of the old observation tower. How long this situation will last is anybody's guess. The U.S. Navy was kicked out because it was felt the prevailing easterly trades were carrying debris from the exploding ordnance and polluting the western end of the island. The navy is no longer exploding ordnance, but what about the explosions with which the unexploded ornance is destroyed? It looks to me like one step forward, two back.

To the west of these two anchorages one finds Bahia Jalova, Bahia Yoye, Ensenada Honda, Bahia de la Chiva, Puertos Ferro, Mosquito, Negro, and Real, and Ensenada Sun Bay (PRVI pages 82-87), all of which bear investigating.

Iolaire spent a little while "parked" near Puerto Real, an incident that reminded me of a story that Bill Robinson, who was for a long time the editor of Yachting, used to tell. It's about a yachtsman who, in the late 1950s, wanted to cruise the Bahamas for a month. His yacht, though, drew 7 feet, which he realized was a little deep for those waters, so he put word out that he wanted to hire the best pilot there was in all of the Bahamas.

A pilot who had been recommended to him came aboard, where the owner explained to him that his boat drew 7 feet, a lot more than the Bahamian sloops or schooners. To illustrate the point he pulled out his boathook, stood it on end, and put a piece of tape at the 7-foot mark.

"Ya, boss," the pilot said, "I see. No problem."

They cruised for almost a month. The pilot was fantastic and took them all sorts of places the owner figured there was not enough water. They didn't touch once.

But then, about a day or so before the end of the cruise, they were coming into a harbor that looked a little shoal to the skipper.

"Pilot," he said, "how is the water."

The owner heard the reply which he thought was, "Ten," so he put the engine in ahead and promptly ran up on the sandbank.

The boat wasn't damaged, but they had to run an anchor out astern and wait for high tide to lift them off.

The owner lit into the pilot: "Pilot, you have done a fantastic job for four weeks. How come you foul up on almost the last day? I asked how much water. You replied, 'ten' so, as we draw only 7 feet, I put her in ahead. And we ran aground!"

"Skip, I did not say ten," the pilot replied, "I said 'tin,' da water gettin' 'tin.'"

Alston, my Grenadian mate, knew this joke well.

We were exploring Puerto Rico and the Spanish Virgins in *Iolaire* and were approaching Esperanza, aiming between Cayo Real and Vieques.

The chart showed a shelf with 10 feet of water over it. Alston called out, "Skip, da water gettin' tin."

"No, Alston," I replied, "the chart shows 10 feet, it must be just very clear water."

"Skip, da water tin!"

"Crystal clear water," I replied, "Even if the chart is slightly off, we are heeled over. We will clear it."

As I said this, we slid to a halt.

We ran out an anchor ahead and took another line to the dock slightly off to port. Even when we put a lot of tension on both lines, nothing happened.

Finally, a friendly sport fisherman came along and took our spinnaker halyard, with which he hauled us down till the middle lifeline was in the water. Then, under a combination of the sails and tension on the lines ahead, we slid over the shoal into deeper water.

That happened over 25 years ago, yet, despite the fact that I have four times actually been in the NOAA office in Washington DC and have each time marked on the chart that there is only 6 feet of water where it shows 10, the chart still has not been corrected.

Over the years, *Iolaire* has been "parked" from one end of the Caribbean to the other.

"Parked" is not the same as aground. You are aground when you have hit something completely unexpectedly and the boat is in a dangerous situation. You are "parked" when you have been nudging your way into a calm anchorage and discover you do not have enough water. The boat is undamaged and is in no danger. The only damage caused is to the skipper's ego and reputation.

Puerto Rico
Imray-Iolaire Charts A11, A12, A13, A14, and A141

The eastern coast of Puerto Rico has only one uncrowded anchorage. It is to the west of Isla Pineros in Passe de Medio Mundo (PRVI pages 58-59). Otherwise, this coast has only crowded marinas to offer. But, on weekends, space can be found in the marinas as the Puerto Rican powerboats have departed to their favorite anchorages. Many sailors say the way to cruise Puerto Rican waters is to go to the anchorages during the week then, on Friday afternoon, go to a marina, stay until Sunday afternoon taking care of laundry, shopping, showers, refueling, and taking on water, then depart Sunday afternoon to the anchorages that will be empty by sundowner time.

The small cays to the east of Puerto Rico (PRVI pages 60-61) offer anchorages but only during the week because on weekends they are all crowded by the Puerto Rican powerboats.

The La Parguera area at the southwestern corner of Puerto Rico (PRVI pages 30-33) and the area to the eastward to Puerto Quijano provide so many choices of anchorages I cannot list them here. The main anchorage off La Parguera may be crowded but the offshore ones close behind a reef are always deserted.

The area is covered in detail by Imray-Iolaire A11, which was prepared from an unpublished Coast and Geodetic survey done in 1933.

It is possible to work your way eastward along the south coast without killing yourself beating to windward in heavy weather.

Depart your anchorage at first light and head eastward. By 1100 or 1200 the trades will have kicked in, but if you left early enough, you will be entering your next anchorage before they really start to blow hard. See the Sailing Directions in Street's Guide (PRVI pages 2-5).

There are good anchorages on the south coast but few deserted ones. The anchorage off the hotel east of Bahia de Guanica (PRVI pages 35-36) is never crowded.

Isla Caja de Muertos (PRVI pages 43-44) will be deserted during the week. Avoid the island over the weekend as this is where the sailors from Ponce come to throw fantastic parties. The sailors from Ponce can not fathom why the big "Nort Americanos" can't keep up with the little Puerto Ricans when it comes to drinking rum.

In Bahia de Jobos (PRVI pages 48-49), you can find quiet anchorages east of Salinas. Puerto Patillas (PRVI pages 50-51) is a good stopping place before the next leg to windward around the corner. It's not much of an anchorage, really just a harbor of refuge.

You can see from the descriptions of "off the beaten track" anchorages above that the contention of many yachting authors and sailors that all the anchorages in the Caribbean are crowded and filled with mooring balls does not hold water.

Street's Boast

In my 1979 *Cruising Guide to the Lesser Antilles*, I stated in print that, if anyone could come up with an anchorage safe for a boat drawing 7 feet that I had not described in my guide, I would buy the drinks. I have never had to pay off, but I almost had to once.

Hans Hoff, skippering *Fandango*, a 95-foot Rhodes motorsailer, claimed that he frequently used an anchorage in Anguilla with *Fandango* that I did not mention in the guide. We repaired to the Admiral's Inn (in English Harbour, Antigua) to discuss this unknown anchorage over a couple of beers.

This was before the British Admiralty re-surveyed Anguilla. Both the British and American charts showed a reef about a half mile offshore and shoal water inside the reef. Hans had discovered that the reef was a barrier reef with 20 feet of water inside it. The reef was shoal enough to break the worst of the sea and, if the wind was not blowing too hard, there was an anchorage inside the reef.

I had to admit Hans had me on this one so we had a couple of more beers. I then got up to pay the bill but Hans said, "Don, I make more money skippering *Fandango* than you make selling marine insurance, charts, and books and writing articles. If you will state in print that Hans Hoff of the 95-foot *Fandango* found an anchorage that Street did not know of, I'll buy us dinner and a bottle of wine."

Needless to say I quickly agreed. We had an excellent dinner and I have stated in print that Hans Hoff of *Fandango* discovered an anchorage I did not know of.

Appendices

Appendix 1: Contacts and Resources

Chapter 3: Infrastructure in the Cape Verde Islands
  Cape Verde Consulate in Boston: 535 Boylston Street, Boston MA 02116; 617-353-0014
  Cape Verde Embassy to the United States: 3415 Massachusetts Avenue, NW, Washington DC 20007; 202-965-6820
  Government of the Republic of Cape Verde: www.governo.cv
  Kai Brosmann, boatCV: www.boatcv.com
  Marina Mindelo: www.marinamindelo.com
  U.S. State Department, Cape Verde pages: www.state.gov/r/pa/ei/bgn/2835.htm
  U.S. Embassy to Cape Verde: Rua Abílio Macedo, 6, Praia; C.P.201; tel. (238) 260 8900; fax 2611 355; http://praia.usembassy.gov
  Cape Verde Airlines (TACV): www.flytacv.com
  Bela-Vista, reliable source for ferries and general Cape Verde activities: www.bela-vista.net

Chapter 4: The Mariner's Essentials
  Streetwise DVD - DVDs are available for $30 US from streetiolaire@hotmail.com. For a full list and description of the five Street DVDs, go to www.street-iolaire.com
  Tropical cyclone information - National Hurricane Center: www.nhc.noaa.gov
  Tropical cyclone historical data is online at www.nhc.noaa.gov/pastall.shtml.
  Tropical Cyclones of the North Atlantic Ocean, 1871 - 1998 is downloadable at www.aoml.noaa.gov/general/lib/lib1/nhclib/index.htm

Chapter 7: São Vicente and Santo Antão
  Marina Mindelo: +238 9972 322, +238 9915 878, mail@marinamindelo.com, www.marinamindelo.com
  Mar Tranquilidade: +238 2276 012, www.martranquilidade.com, info@martranquilidade.com

Chapter 8: Santiago and Maio
  Baia Verde (car rental): +238-266-1128 or 266-1407
  Hotel Marilú: +238 255-1198
  Hotel Sol Marina: +238 266-1219
  Kingfisher Resort: www.king-fisher.de

Chapter 9: Fogo and Brava
  Colonial B&B, San Felipe; +238 281-1900 or 281-3373, www.zebratravel.net.
  Domingo da Silva, bus service from São Filipe to Cha Das Caldeiras; +238 950-3631
  Sirio guest house, Cha Das Caldeiras; +238 282-1528, chatour@chatourfogo.com, www.chatourfogo.com.

Chapter 10: Setting up for a Trade-Wind Passage
  Ampair/Aquair: www.ampair.com
  Electrodyne brushless alternators: 207 883 4121, www.electrodyne.com

Appendix 2: Cape Verdean Words and Phrases

English	Portuguese	Crioulo
Good morning	Bomdia	Bom dia
See you tomorrow	Até amanhã	Ti manhan
See you soon	Até breve	Ti já
How are you	Como estás	Mo ki bu sta
Very well	Muito bem	Muto dretu
Thank you	Obrigado/a	Obrigado/a
Please	Por favor	Porfavor
Good afternoon	Boa Tarde	Boa tardi
Good evening	Boa Noite	Boa noti
Hello	Olá	Oi
Goodbye	Adeus	Tchau
See you later	Até logo	Ti logo
Anchorage	Ancoragem	Ancoragi
Bay	Baía	Baía
Beach	Praia de mar	Praia di mar
Boatyard	Estaleiro	Stalero
Boatbuilder	Construtor de barco	Construtor di barco
Bottle gas	Garrafa de Gaz	Garrafa gaz
Gas	Gaz	Gaz
Breakwater	Quebra-mar	Kebra mar
Buoy	Bóia	Bóia
Bus	Autocarro	Otocarro
Car hire	Aluguer de carro	Aluguer di carro
Chandlery	Drogaria	Drogaria
Cars	Carros	Carros
Customs	Alfândega	Alfândiga
Deep	Fundo	Fundo
Diesel	Gasoleo	Gasoleo
Draft	Calado	Caladu
Drydock	Doca seca	
Electricity	Eletrecidade	Eletricidadi
Engineer	Engenheiro	Enginhero
Harbor master	Capitão do porto	Capiton di porto
How much	Quanto	Kantu
Laundry	Lavandaria	Lavandaria
Length overall	Comprimento total	Cumprimento total
Mailing address	Endereço	Morada
Marina	Marina	Marina
Mechanic	Mecanico	Mecanico
Gasoline	Petroleo	Petrolio
Pontoon	Pontão / Ponte	Ponton / Ponti
Port (side)	Porto (lado)	Porto (lado)
Post office	Correios	Correio
Repairs	Reparações	Riparaçon
Sailing boat	Barco a vela	Barco di vela
Sailmaker	Fabricante de vela	Fabricanti di vela
Sand	Areia	Areia
Shops	Lojas	Lojas

English	Portuguese	Crioulo
Showers (washing)	Chuveiro (lavagem)	Chuvero (lavagi)
Starboard	Estibordo	Stibordo
Supermarket	Supermecado	Supermercado
Travellift	Elevador de viagem	Elivador di viaji
Water (drinking)	Água (para beber)	Agua (pa bebi)
Weather forecast	Previsão de tempo	Previson di tempo
Yacht club	Clube de regatas	Clubi di barcos

Appendix 3. Listing of Approach Points

Caution: Approach Points are NOT to be used for navigational purposes. The author and publisher take no responsibility for the misuse of the following waypoints.

Approach Point Description	Latitude	Longitude
Ilha do Sal		
Baia da Palmeira	16° 45.0' N	23° 01.0' W
Baia da Murdeira	16° 41.0' N	23° 00.0' W
Santa Maria	16° 35.0' N	22° 54.5' W
Baia de Pedra de Lume	16° 44.0' N	23° 53.0' W
Ilha da Boavista		
Porto de Sal-Rei	16° 10.5' N	23° 57.0' W
Ilha de São Nicolau		
Carrical	16° 32.3' N	24° 05.2' W
Baia Gombeza	16° 32.3' N	24° 05.2' W
Boca da Praia de Falcão	16° 35.3' N	24° 01.0' W
Baia da Chacina	16° 33.0' N	24° 07.7' W
Ponta do Ilhéu	16° 33.7' N	24° 08.0' W
Aquada da Garça	16° 34.3' N	24° 09.35' W
Ponta Posson	16° 34.9' N	24° 10.3' W
Porto da Lapa	16° 35.0' N	24° 13.7' W
Preguica	16° 35.0' N	24° 13.7' W
Bahia de Fidalgo	16° 28.4' N	24° 19.35' W
Tarrafal	16° 34.2' N	24° 22.3' W
Ponta do Galeão	16° 40.0' N	24° 26.0' W
Ilha de Santa Luzia		
Ilha de Santa Luzia	16° 44.0' N	24° 46.0' W
Ilha de São Vicente		
Porto Grande/Mindelo	16° 54.0' N	25° 01.0' W
Puerto de São Pedro	16° 49.0' N	25° 05.0' W
Bahia das Gatas	16° 53.0' N	24° 53.0' W
Ilha de Santo Antão		
Porto Novo	17° 00.0' N	25° 03.5' W
Tarrafal de Monte Trigo	16° 57.3' N	25° 19.5' W
Monte Trigo	17° 00.5' N	25° 20.5' W
Ponta do Sol	17° 13.0' N	25° 06.0' W
Porto do Paúl	17° 09.5' N	25° 00.0' W
Ilha de Santiago		
Tarrafal	15° 17.0' N	23° 46.5' W
Ribeira da Barca	15° 08.8' N	23° 46.7' W
Porto Rincão	15° 03.0' N	23° 47.0' W

Approach Point Description	Latitude	Longitude
Porto Mosquito	14° 56.5' N	23° 42.0' W
Porto Gouveia	14° 56.5' N	23° 42.0' W
Cidade Velha	14° 54.0' N	23° 36.5' W
Calheta de São Martinho	14° 53.7' N	23° 34.2' W
Porto da Praia	14° 53.7' N	23° 30.0' W
Baia de Angra	15° 18.0' N	23° 40.5' W
Porto Formoso	15° 16.0' N	23° 40.0' W
Mangue de Sete Ribeiras	15° 15.0' N	23° 37.5' W
Cove East of Ponta da Ribeira Brava	15° 15.0' N	23° 37.0' W
Veneza	15° 12.0' N	23° 35.0' W
Calheta de São Miguel	15° 12.0' N	23° 35.0' W
Porto Coqueiro	15° 10.0' N	23° 33.0' W
Ponta de Santa Cruz	15° 09.7' N	23° 32.0' W
Porto de Pedra Badejo	15° 08.4' N	23° 31.0' W
Ponta Pinha	15° 07.0' N	23° 29.0' W
Monte Negro	15° 06.0' N	23° 29.0' W
Ponta Porto	15° 04.3' N	23° 27.7' W
Ponta Salameia/Ponta Inglez	15° 03.0' N	23° 26.0' W
Praia de Moia Moia	15° 02.0' N	23° 25.8' W
Ponta Bomba	15° 00.5' N	23° 25.2' W
Porto Lobo	15° 00.0' N	23° 25.0' W
Ponta Leste and Porto de São Francisco	14° 58.2' N	23° 26.3' W
Portete Baixo	14° 57.3' N	23° 26.8' W

Ilha do Maio

Vila do Maio/Porto Inglez	15° 07.5' N	23° 14.0' W

Ilha do Fogo

São Filipe	14° 53.5' N	24° 31.0' W
Vale de Cavaleiros	14° 55.0' N	24° 31.0' W

Ilha Brava

Porto da Furna	14° 53.0' N	24° 40.0' W
Fajã da Agua	14° 52.5' N	24° 45.0' W
Porto dos Ferreiros	14° 49.0' N	24° 44.0' W

Index

A

Acha da Falcão 106–126
agriculture 22, 24, 27, 28, 72–75, 123
Aguas Belas 106, 107
Alvise Cadamosto 23
Amílcar Cabral 26-32, 106, 107
Ampair 15, 147-149, 165
Anchors 55, 56, 109
Antigua 18, 19, 21, 35, 36, 48, 87, 132, 138, 146, 150, 157-159, 164
Approach Point 116, 167, 168
Aquada da Garça 77, 167
ARC 19, 89, 146, 147, 156
Atlantic Rally for Cruisers 19, 89, 151
Azores 10, 15, 17-19, 27, 35, 73, 128, 131

B

Bahamian Moor 59
Bahia das Gatas 90, 167
Bahia de Fidalgo 79, 167
Bahia de Inferno 9, 110
Bahia de Pedra de Lume 62
Bahia debaixo da Rocha 79
Baia da Chacina 77, 167
Baia da Mordeira 50, 64
Baia de Angra 9, 116, 168
Baia de Chão Bom 105
Baia Gombeza 8, 43, 76, 167
Baixo João Valente 45, 52, 67, 71, 103
Baixo Vauban 43, 52, 70
Barbados 14, 15, 18, 23, 137, 150-152
Bermuda 15, 17, 36
Bertalan, Dr. Attila 46
boatCV 35, 36, 165
Boavista 8, 11, 22, 27, 32, 37-40, 43, 45, 52, 53, 62, 67, 68, 70-72, 75, 81, 90, 102, 103, 167
Boca da Praia de Falcão 8, 76, 167
Bowditch 49
Bratz, Trygve 13
Brava 9, 10, 13, 21, 22, 25, 27-29, 31, 38, 39, 42, 43, 45, 46, 50-52, 72, 73, 79, 111, 116, 117, 127-137, 150, 165, 168
British Admiralty Pilot 64, 131, 137
Brosmann, Kai 11, 12, 13, 17, 34, 36, 39, 46, 70, 79, 81, 84, 90, 94, 97, 98, 111, 123, 129, 165
buoyage 52

C

cable terminus 27
Calheta 9, 53, 111, 115, 118, 125, 126, 168
Calheta de São Martinho 9, 111, 115, 168
Calheta de São Miguel 9, 118, 168
Canal do São Vicente 85
Canaries 13, 15, 17-19, 21, 23, 25, 42, 50, 51, 61, 131
Canary Islands 18, 21, 22, 39, 42, 51, 54, 86, 116
Cape Verde Airlines 28, 39, 165
Caribbean Compass 114, 153, 155
Carrical 8, 31, 32, 43, 71, 74-76, 167
Cassard, Jacques 23, 99
Cha Das Caldeiras 128, 129, 165
Cidade Velha 9, 23, 25, 50, 99, 101, 111, 112, 115, 168
coal 25, 27, 36, 86
coaling station 25, 26, 87
Crioulo 13, 42, 166, 167
Cruising Guide to the Lesser Antilles 12, 14, 15, 152, 164
Cruising Guide to Venezuela 12
Cunliffe, Tom 14, 19
currency 42
customs 36, 112, 132

D

Diesel 70, 166
dinghy 36, 40, 42, 59-61, 64, 65, 68, 70, 76, 77, 79, 81, 84, 86-90, 94-96, 103, 104, 106, 111-113, 117, 119, 122, 123, 125, 126, 133, 136, 137, 140, 154, 158, 160, 162
Dom, Gerry 10-12, 31, 45, 46, 53, 67-69, 72, 99, 103-106, 113, 116, 120, 125, 128, 131, 133, 137
Dom, Indira 10, 11, 33, 47, 99, 107, 119
Drake, Sir Francis 23, 99
dry season 22, 47, 64
du Montrond, Duc 127

E

Eastern Caribbean 12, 15, 19, 25, 28, 42, 46, 48-50, 72, 87, 105, 133, 140, 143, 148, 151-153, 157, 158, 161, 162
Electrodyne 148, 165
Equatorial Current 48, 49
Ernestina 29
Espargos 64
expatriates 102

F

Fajã 9, 131, 135, 136, 168
Fajã da Agua 9, 131, 136, 168
ferry 10, 12, 39, 45, 91, 93, 95, 96, 98, 123, 128, 130, 131, 134
Figueral de Paúl 98
fishing boats 27, 29-32, 54, 66, 92, 95, 96, 98, 103, 106, 108, 111, 113, 117, 118, 120, 125, 129, 136, 137
Fogo 9, 13, 22, 25, 27, 31, 38-40, 42, 43, 45, 50-52, 111, 123, 127, 128, 130-133, 165, 168
Fort San Filipe 99, 115
fuel 19, 40, 41, 43, 60, 62, 64, 66, 71, 90, 111, 113, 116, 157, 159
Furna 9, 45, 50, 116, 129, 131-137, 168

G

Google Earth 46, 70, 73, 120
gopher 40, 89
GPS 15, 32, 46, 49, 50, 52-55, 64, 67, 73, 75, 84, 88, 93, 98, 146, 147, 158
Grand Canaria 19
Grenada 14, 15, 38, 48, 101, 132, 152-154
Grenadines 15, 57, 154
groundswell 39, 50, 51, 57, 62, 78, 91, 96-98, 103, 105, 106, 109, 110, 115, 125, 129, 130, 136, 153, 154, 159, 160, 161
Guinea-Bissau 11, 27

H

Hammick, Anne 106
harbor police 36, 64, 70, 86, 112-114, 133
harmattan 22, 52
Hurricane 50, 51, 55, 165
Hurricane Book 51
HWF&C 49

I

Ice 40, 134
Ilhas do Barlavento 22, 25, 50, 93, 102, 116
Ilhas do Sotavento 22, 23, 71, 102
Ilhéu dos Alcatrazes 9, 105, 110
Ilhéu dos Passaros 87, 88
Ilhéu Zinho 83
Ilhéus Secos ou do Rombo 137
Immigration 36, 37, 86
Imray-Iolaire E4 45, 62, 131

L

Lange, Donna 114
lead line 46, 54, 75, 79, 81, 116
Lone Star 17, 21, 143, 144

M

Madeira 13, 15, 17, 18, 21, 25, 27, 42, 50, 93
magnetic anomalies 52, 54, 71
magnetic variations 52, 62
Maio 9, 22, 27, 29, 31, 37, 38, 43, 45, 52, 70, 71, 99, 102, 123-126, 165, 168
Malhada 9, 122, 123
Mangue de Sete Ribeiras 9, 117, 168
Mar Tranquilidade 13, 50, 95, 96, 98, 165
Marina Mindelo 17, 34-36, 40, 42, 86, 90, 165
Martinique 15, 49, 132, 151-153, 156
meridian passage 48-50, 155
Meyer-Scheel, Lutz 12, 13, 34, 89
Mindelo 8, 12, 13, 17-19, 21, 23, 25-27, 30, 34-36, 39-43, 45, 49-52, 54, 71, 85-91, 93, 95, 98, 103, 104, 115, 116, 132, 165, 167
mizzen staysail 21, 143, 144, 149
Monte Negro 9, 120, 168
Monte Trigo 8, 31, 50, 94, 95, 97, 98, 167
Mosteiros 127

N

National Hurricane Center 51, 165
Nautical Almanac 14, 48, 49
New Bedford 29, 133
New England 15, 29, 133
NOAA 51, 165
notice to mariners 52
Nova Sintra 131, 133-137

P

Palmeira 8, 21, 30, 36, 43, 52, 54, 62-64, 167
piston hank 143
Ponta Bomba 122, 168
Ponta da Ribeira Brava 117, 168
Ponta de Bicuda 101
Ponta de Santa Cruz 9, 118, 119, 121, 168
Ponta do Atum 106, 109
Ponta do Galeão 8, 81, 167
Ponta do Ilhéu 77, 167
Ponta do Sol 8, 91-93, 98, 167
Ponta Inglez 9, 122, 168
Ponta Leste 123, 168
Ponta Malhada 122
Ponta Pinha 9, 120, 168

Index

Ponta Porto 9, 120, 168
Ponta Posson 8, 77, 167
Ponta Salameia 9, 122, 168
port captain 17, 64
Portete Baixo 9, 123, 168
Porto Coqueiro 9, 118, 168
Porto da Furna 131, 133, 168
Porto da Lapa 8, 78, 167
Porto de Pedra Badejo 9, 119, 168
Porto de São Francisco 123, 168
Porto do Mangue 117
Porto do Paúl 98, 167
Porto dos Ferreiros 9, 21, 31, 45, 50, 136, 137, 168
Porto Formoso 9, 117, 168
Porto Gouveia 9, 168
Porto Grande 8, 87, 167
Porto Inglez 9, 124, 168
Porto Lobo 123, 168
Porto Mosquito 9, 30, 31, 110, 115, 168
Porto Novo 8, 39, 50, 90-95, 97, 98, 167
Porto Rincão 9, 30-33, 50, 104, 106-108, 167
Portugal 22, 23, 25, 35, 99, 106
Praia 8-11, 13, 25, 32, 33, 36-41, 43, 45, 50-52, 54, 76, 86, 93, 99-102, 104, 105, 111-114, 116, 120, 122, 123, 132, 133, 165-168
Praia de Moia Moia 122, 168
Preguica 8, 50, 72-74, 76-9, 167
preventer 138, 139, 141, 142, 145
Prince Henry of Portugal 23
Puerto de São Pedro 90, 167

R

railway 35, 36, 112, 115
rainy season 22, 29, 57, 101, 110, 120, 124
RCC Atlantic Islands Guide 76, 131, 137
RCC guide 13, 98
reaching sheet 140
Reitmaier, Pitt 24, 26, 37, 46, 63, 73, 87, 92, 95, 107, 130, 132, 136
Republic of Cape Verde 11, 27, 37, 165
Ribeira Brava 25, 72, 73, 79, 117, 168
Ribeira da Barca 105-107, 167
Ribeira do Paúl 93
Ribeira Grande 23, 25, 91-93, 99
roller furling 143
roller reefing 142

S

Sahara 19, 22, 52
Sal 8, 10, 18, 22, 24, 25, 27, 30, 35-40, 42, 43, 50, 52, 54, 62-64, 66-72, 75, 86, 90, 102, 127, 167

Sal-Rei 8, 25, 39, 40, 43, 67-71, 90, 167
Sambala 101, 123
Santa Luzia 8, 22, 24, 43, 45, 49, 71, 72, 83-85, 167
Santa Maria 8, 18, 43, 64-66, 90, 113, 116, 162, 167
Santiago 9-11, 13, 18, 22, 23, 25-33, 36, 38-40, 42, 43, 45-47, 50-54, 67, 71, 86, 93, 99, 101, 102, 104-109, 111, 113, 116, 121, 123, 130, 165, 167
Santo Antão 8, 13, 21, 22, 25, 27-29, 31, 36, 37, 39, 45-50, 71, 86-88, 90, 91, 93-98, 131, 132, 165, 167
São Filipe 9, 45, 128, 129, 131, 165, 168
São Nicolau 8, 10, 13, 22, 25, 30-32, 37, 38, 41-43, 45, 46, 49, 50, 52, 71-73, 75, 79, 81, 84, 88, 167
São Vicente 8, 12, 13, 17, 18, 22, 24, 25, 29, 34, 36, 37, 39, 42, 43, 45, 49-51, 71, 85-88, 90, 93, 94, 97, 102, 103, 132, 165, 167
secondhand sails 145
Senegal 11, 22
shipyard 35, 39, 88, 89
Sincerity 10, 13, 17, 21, 30, 46, 49, 54, 62, 64, 72, 78, 79, 81, 82, 84, 87, 89, 99, 112-114, 134, 136-138, 146
slave trade 25, 70
snuffer 142, 145
spinnaker 19, 21, 138, 139, 142-147, 150, 163
spinnaker pole 19, 142-147, 150
St. Eustacia 25
surf 10, 31, 46, 52, 59, 60, 84, 94, 96, 106, 109, 125

T

TACV 28, 38, 39
taffrail generator 147, 148
Tarrafal 8, 9, 30, 31, 41, 43, 45, 50, 71-73, 76, 79, 81-83, 94, 95, 97, 98, 102-105, 116, 167
Tarrafal de Monte Trigo 8, 31, 50, 94-98, 167
tides 43, 47, 48, 50, 155, 159
Toplicht 143
Transatlantic Crossing Guide 10-12, 15, 35, 45, 49, 89
Transatlantic with Street DVD 19
transoceanic cables 87
tripping line 57
tropical storm 21, 51
twin headsails 21, 142

V

Vale de Cavaleiros 9, 130, 131, 168
vang 140
Veneza 9, 117, 168
Venezuela 12, 15, 93

Vernon Brenner 11
Vila da Ribeira Brava 72, 73, 79
Vila das Pombas 93, 98
Vila do Maio 9, 124, 126, 168
Virgin Islands 12, 15, 27, 38, 47, 48, 102, 116, 132, 151, 152, 160-162
visa 37

W

walking maps 10, 22, 27, 39, 46, 73
water-driven generators 147
waypoint 52, 54, 55, 81, 90, 146
weather 12, 18, 49, 51, 53, 58, 67, 70, 71, 76, 90, 95, 96, 104, 116, 119, 131, 137, 140, 141, 143, 155, 156, 161, 164
West Indies 18, 22, 31, 38, 48, 78, 103
wet season 22, 23, 47, 57, 64, 94
WGS 84 10, 46, 53, 55, 73, 98, 116
whaling 29
wind generator 15, 147-149
Windward Islands 22, 152
www.bela-vista.net 39, 165

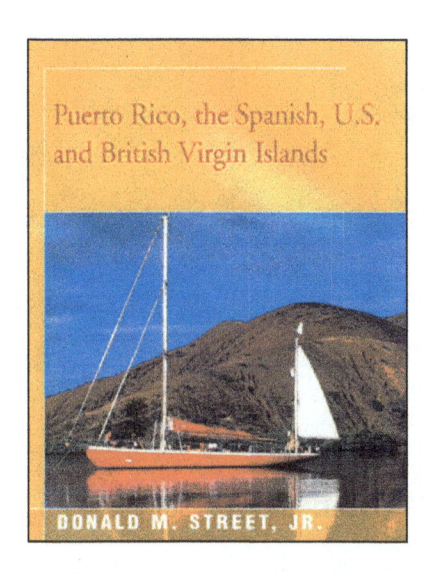

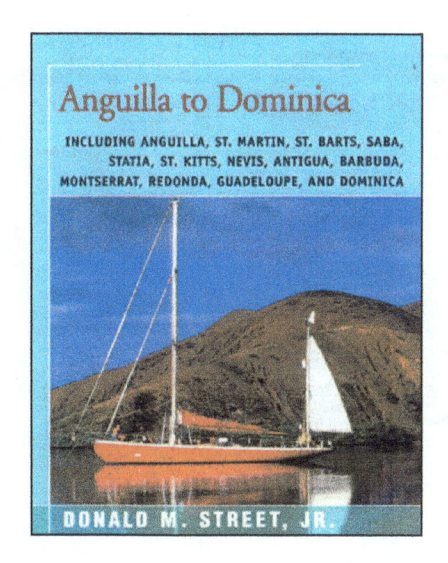

Street's Guides to the Eastern Caribbean

A guide with good sailing directions and harbor piloting directions is timeless, as Don Street found from personal experience. When Don arrived in the Caribbean in 1956, no cruising guides existed for the region. Shortly after Don bought *Iolaire* in 1957, his father found in Foyles bookstore in London a copy of the Norie & Wilson sailing directions to the West Indies, printed in 1867. Don used this as his guide until 1966 when he produced his own first hard-cover *Cruising Guide to the Lesser Antilles*, the book that opened up the Eastern Caribbean to the cruising yachtsman and made bareboat chartering possible in the region. This original guide, which contains a wealth of inter-island sailing and harbor piloting directions plus tidal information from the 1867 Norie & Wilson publication, is still available from iUniverse.com. It's a wonderful piece of nostalgia from the Caribbean in the late 1950s and early 1960s.

Over the years, Don rewrote and expanded this guide. The area from western Puerto Rico through the islands to Trinidad is now covered by three volumes: Puerto Rico, the Spanish, U.S., and British Virgin Islands; Anguilla to Dominica; Martinique to Trinidad. All three guides have been updated and were reprinted by iUniverse in 2001. A fourth guide covering Venezuela, its offshore islands, and the ABC islands is out of print (the second edition was published in 1990), but second-hand copies can be found on the Internet.

Street's guides cover all the anchorages in the eastern Caribbean. In the early 1980s, Don printed a challenge in his guides: He would buy drinks for anyone who could name a safe anchorage for boats drawing 7 feet that is not in his guides to the Eastern Caribbean. He has never had to buy the drinks. Street's guides are long on inter-island sailing and harbor-piloting directions. Rocks don't move, but any changes that affect navigation, such as dredging, harbor construction, or sandbars shifted by hurricanes, will appear on the Imray-Iolaire charts. Street's guides are out of date concerning the expanding marine infrastructure in the Eastern Caribbean, but this is not a problem because the Imray-Iolaire charts are updated with locations of facilities and their haulout capacities. Also, *All at Sea* annually publishes a free marine directory that lists basically every marine-oriented business in the Eastern Caribbean. Further, every island that has a decent marine infrastructure annually publishes a free marine directory of its resources. These free directories are much more up to date than any printed guide can possibly be.

The Scotts' guides to the Virgin Islands, and Doyle's guides to the Windward and Leewards are written for bareboat charterers. They are long on information on bars, restaurants, and the anchorages popular with bareboaters but ignore many superb anchorages and areas barred to bareboaters that Don describes with knowledge and affection. Many sailors who are familiar with the Caribbean will say, "Buy Street's guides and the relevant Scotts' or Doyle guides. In the Street's guides, circle in red the anchorages that are not mentioned in the other guides and you will have a quiet anchorage." A guide costs about the same as a dinner ashore for one. Buy Street's guides for the quiet anchorages and the piloting information, the relevant Doyle's or Scotts' guide for onshore activities, and the appropriate Imray-Iolaire charts. Then pick up the free marine directories for services and you will have all the information you need to enjoy a happy cruise . . .

Street's guides are available direct from iUniverse.com, in the UK from Imray and Kelvin Hughes, in the U.S. from Bluewater Books, and in the Caribbean at all Island Water World stores and Johnsons Marine Hardware in St. Lucia.

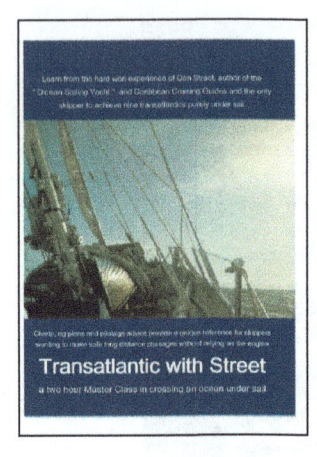

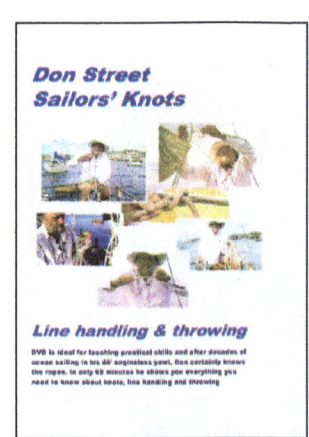

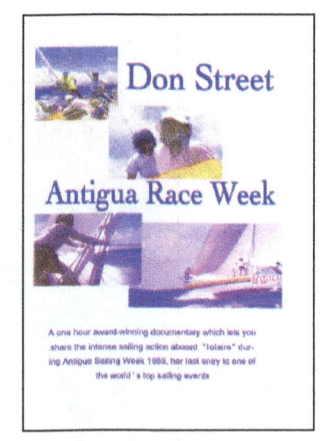

The Don Street DVD Collection
$29.95, €24.95, £19.95
www.street-iolaire.com

Herb McCormick on *Transatlantic with Street*
"Sailing legend Don Street's account of a Transatlantic voyage aboard his 46-foot, 22-ton, engineless yawl, *Iolaire*, is in turns an adventure tale, a cruising guide, and an extended lesson in seamanship, all told in Don's inimitable style. A surprise back-story is the transformation of London businessman Gavin Shaw from neophyte to passionate ocean sailor. It's like going to sea with Don — the only things missing are the cold Heinekens and the salt spray in your face."

Tom Cunliffe on *Transatlantic with Street*
"Shot in the mid 1980s, *Transatlantic with Street* reminds us that seafaring can be rough, tough, and wildly at odds with today's well-organized ARC crossings. The boat leaks, some hands defect, but on a remarkably fast trade-wind passage accompanied by whales we share the wonders of the deep as the crew navigates by sun and stars. The real magic, however, is the seamanlike wisdom of "Squeaky" himself, contrasted with the quiet, scholarly voice of his acolyte, Gavin Shaw. There's nobody quite like Street."

Streetwise
A favorite feature in *Sailing Quarterly* video magazine in the 1990s DVD 1 includes safety on deck, docking, getting off when aground, cruising with kids, plus a Grenadines cruise and a hilarious scene in which Don demonstrates the difference between Mount Gay and local Jack Iron rum.

DVD 2 includes Don's tried-and-tested recommendations on heavy weather, jibe prevention safety measures, and coastal navigation. We also join Don on a cruise in Venezuela's beautiful cruising grounds, in pre-Chavez days. Another cruise, along the southwest coast of Ireland, finishes memorably with a flourish of Irish dancing and singing at a traditional village festival in Glandore.

Sailors' Knots
In this 60-minute DVD Don Street indeed teaches several valuable sailors' knots, but he says the most important lesson, which every aspiring crew should study, is on handling and throwing docklines. "A crew skilled at handling lines can rescue a bad landing," Don says, "while a crew unable to properly throw a line can ruin a potentially good one."

Antigua Race Week
This award-winning film has terrific onboard action from Antigua Sailing Week, 1985. In this, her swan song in round-the-buoys racing, *Iolaire* went out in style, finishing a close third, only five points out of first place. *Caribbean Compass* says this DVD, which includes priceless footage of Don's son Mark, age 5, calling starboard on *Kialoa*, is the best record of the great regattas from the golden years of Caribbean yachting when racing was fun, not business.

Don Street's Enterprises

Don Street is at 81 the oldest and longest-serving yachting writer in the world who is still sailing, racing a 74-year-old wooden Dragon, writing cruising guides and articles and drinking Heineken beer.

Don's first article, Going South, apeared in the September 1964 Yachting. His first hard-cover guide, *A Cruising Guide to The Lesser Antilles*, has been in print since1966 and although the piloting information is still largely valid, today the stories in it invoke nostalgia for an era long gone.

Over the years, Don rewrote and expanded this guide into four volumes covering all the islands of the eastern Caribbean from the western end of Puerto Rico to Trinidad and westward along the Venezuelan coast and offshore islands to Aruba.

Imray-Iolaire Charts

After cruising, racing, chartering, charting, and writing guides to the eastern Caribbean for over two decades, Street had become very frustrated with NOAA and the BA as neither would correct their charts when he informed them of errors. In 1979, he made a deal with Imray, Laurie, Norie & Wilson, a British company with a history of preparing charts and pilot books that dates to 1680, to compile charts of the eastern Caribbean. It took 10 full years to pull it all together, but Imray-Iolaire charts now cover all the eastern Caribbean west to Aruba, all the Atlantic islands. Tying them all together is Imray-Iolaire Chart 100, a gnomic projection where a straight line is a great circle course. On its reverse, weather charts show average wind strength and direction and the frequency of gales and extreme wave heights for every month of the year.

Experienced sailors consider Imray-Iolaire charts to be the most accurate and up-todate charts in the world. Information for updates is obtained from BA, NOAA, and from the contacts Street has developed in his 55 years in the Caribbean. Corrections are available at www.imray.com.

All Maritime and Coastguard Agency (MCA) classed yachts are required by law to carry BA charts for the area they are cruising. Old-timers keep those charts in the bottom of the chart drawer and, for their day-to-day cruising in the Caribbean and Atlantic islands, keep the Imray-Iolaire charts on top of the chart table.

Replicas of the Imray-Iolaire charts from St. Thomas to Trinidad are available in electronic form on a memory stick. While they don't replace the paper charts, they do provide a convenient format for making and reviewing cruising plans.

Imray-Iolaire charts and memory sticks are available from all major chart agents in Europe, in limited quantities in Madeira and the Canary Islands, and throughout the Caribbean.

Imray-Iolaire charts are used in digital format by Garmin, Jepperson (C Map), Maptech, and Navionics.

Marine Insurance

Street has been in the marine insurance business for 49 years, 45 of them placing insurance at Lloyds of London through London brokers, and maintains his claim-settlement record cannot be matched.

When comparing quotes, Street says, the difference between which are very small in terms of the overall cost of running a boat, owners should consider the benefits of buying insurance through the broker who can give the best service and the widest coverage, and who has a proven record of prompt and fair settlement of claims. For more information, go to www.street-iolaire.com.

Design Consulting

Don Street is available for consultation on new construction of cruising sailboats, and on upgrades and alterations to existing cruising boats to make them faster, easier to handle, and more comfortable at sea and in port.

ampair®

Storm proof
Quiet & reliable

For nearly 40 years Ampair has been working in the renewable energy field.

Our high quality engineering facilities combined with our famous attention to detail is the reason why yachtsmen the world over have relied on Ampair products to provide them with power when it really matters.

Quote from Don Street: *"The engineless Iolaire has been five times across the Atlantic with cold beer all the way courtesy of Ampair wind and water generators that produced enough electricity to run two Adler Barbour air cooled refrigeration systems".*

t: +44 (0)1258 837 266
f: +44 (0)1258 837 496
w: www.ampair.com
e: sales@ampair.com

BONUS*
5% DISCOUNT
when you contact us and quote DON STREET

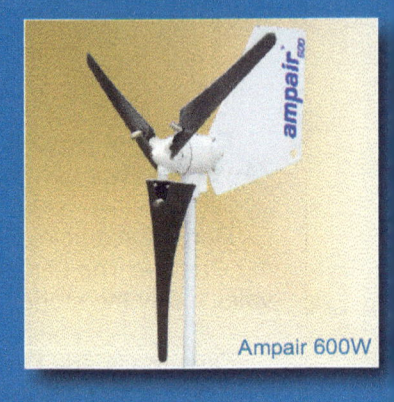

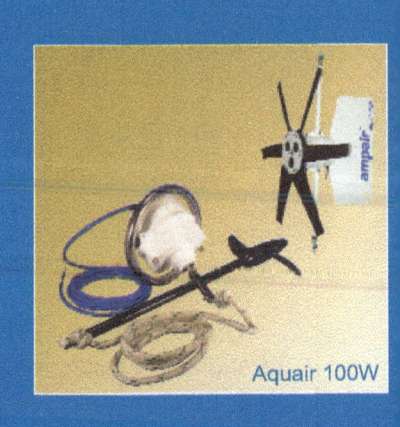

* Bonus Offer Terms & Conditions:
Offer valid until the end of 2012.
Offer not valid with any other offer.
Offer only available when purchasing directly from Ampair.

Ampair 600W

Ampair 300W

Ampair 100W

Aquair 100W

Ampair DSCVG2011